Microsoft®
Training &
Certification

MW01065697

Course 2277B: Implementing, Managing, and Maintaining a Microsoft® Windows® Server 2003 Network Infrastructure: Network Services

Released: 04/2003

Microsoft®

Course Number: 2277B
Part Number: X10-00831
Released: 04/2003

END-USER LICENSE AGREEMENT FOR MICROSOFT OFFICIAL CURRICULUM COURSEWARE –STUDENT EDITION

PLEASE READ THIS END-USER LICENSE AGREEMENT ("EULA") CAREFULLY. BY USING THE MATERIALS AND/OR USING OR INSTALLING THE SOFTWARE THAT ACCOMPANIES THIS EULA (COLLECTIVELY, THE "LICENSED CONTENT"), YOU AGREE TO THE TERMS OF THIS EULA. IF YOU DO NOT AGREE, DO NOT USE THE LICENSED CONTENT.

1.   **GENERAL.** This EULA is a legal agreement between you (either an individual or a single entity) and Microsoft Corporation ("Microsoft"). This EULA governs the Licensed Content, which includes computer software (including online and electronic documentation), training materials, and any other associated media and printed materials. This EULA applies to updates, supplements, add-on components, and Internet-based services components of the Licensed Content that Microsoft may provide or make available to you unless Microsoft provides other terms with the update, supplement, add-on component, or Internet-based services component. Microsoft reserves the right to discontinue any Internet-based services provided to you or made available to you through the use of the Licensed Content. This EULA also governs any product support services relating to the Licensed Content except as may be included in another agreement between you and Microsoft. An amendment or addendum to this EULA may accompany the Licensed Content.

2.   **GENERAL GRANT OF LICENSE.** Microsoft grants you the following rights, conditioned on your compliance with all the terms and conditions of this EULA. Microsoft grants you a limited, non-exclusive, royalty-free license to install and use the Licensed Content solely in conjunction with your participation as a student in an Authorized Training Session (as defined below). You may install and use one copy of the software on a single computer, device, workstation, terminal, or other digital electronic or analog device ("Device"). You may make a second copy of the software and install it on a portable Device for the exclusive use of the person who is the primary user of the first copy of the software. A license for the software may not be shared for use by multiple end users. An "Authorized Training Session" means a training session conducted at a Microsoft Certified Technical Education Center, an IT Academy, via a Microsoft Certified Partner, or such other entity as Microsoft may designate from time to time in writing, by a Microsoft Certified Trainer (for more information on these entities, please visit www.microsoft.com). WITHOUT LIMITING THE FOREGOING, COPYING OR REPRODUCTION OF THE LICENSED CONTENT TO ANY SERVER OR LOCATION FOR FURTHER REPRODUCTION OR REDISTRIBUTION IS EXPRESSLY PROHIBITED.

3.   **DESCRIPTION OF OTHER RIGHTS AND LICENSE LIMITATIONS**

3.1   *Use of Documentation and Printed Training Materials.*

3.1.1   The documents and related graphics included in the Licensed Content may include technical inaccuracies or typographical errors. Changes are periodically made to the content. Microsoft may make improvements and/or changes in any of the components of the Licensed Content at any time without notice. The names of companies, products, people, characters and/or data mentioned in the Licensed Content may be fictitious and are in no way intended to represent any real individual, company, product or event, unless otherwise noted.

3.1.2   Microsoft grants you the right to reproduce portions of documents (such as student workbooks, white papers, press releases, datasheets and FAQs) (the "Documents") provided with the Licensed Content. You may not print any book (either electronic or print version) in its entirety. If you choose to reproduce Documents, you agree that: (a) use of such printed Documents will be solely in conjunction with your personal training use; (b) the Documents will not republished or posted on any network computer or broadcast in any media; (c) any reproduction will include either the Document's original copyright notice or a copyright notice to Microsoft's benefit substantially in the format provided below; and (d) to comply with all terms and conditions of this EULA. In addition, no modifications may made to any Document.

Form of Notice:

© 2003. Reprinted with permission by Microsoft Corporation. All rights reserved.

Microsoft and Windows are either registered trademarks or trademarks of Microsoft Corporation in the US and/or other countries. Other product and company names mentioned herein may be the trademarks of their respective owners.

3.2   *Use of Media Elements.* The Licensed Content may include certain photographs, clip art, animations, sounds, music, and video clips (together "Media Elements"). You may not modify these Media Elements.

3.3   *Use of Sample Code.* In the event that the Licensed Content includes sample code in source or object format ("Sample Code"), Microsoft grants you a limited, non-exclusive, royalty-free license to use, copy and modify the Sample Code; if you elect to exercise the foregoing rights, you agree to comply with all other terms and conditions of this EULA, including without limitation Sections 3.4, 3.5, and 6.

3.4   *Permitted Modifications.* In the event that you exercise any rights provided under this EULA to create modifications of the Licensed Content, you agree that any such modifications: (a) will not be used for providing training where a fee is charged in public or private classes; (b) indemnify, hold harmless, and defend Microsoft from and against any claims or lawsuits, including attorneys' fees, which arise from or result from your use of any modified version of the Licensed Content; and (c) not to transfer or assign any rights to any modified version of the Licensed Content to any third party without the express written permission of Microsoft.

3.5 *Reproduction/Redistribution Licensed Content.* Except as expressly provided in this EULA, you may not reproduce or distribute the Licensed Content or any portion thereof (including any permitted modifications) to any third parties without the express written permission of Microsoft.

4. **RESERVATION OF RIGHTS AND OWNERSHIP.** Microsoft reserves all rights not expressly granted to you in this EULA. The Licensed Content is protected by copyright and other intellectual property laws and treaties. Microsoft or its suppliers own the title, copyright, and other intellectual property rights in the Licensed Content. You may not remove or obscure any copyright, trademark or patent notices that appear on the Licensed Content, or any components thereof, as delivered to you. **The Licensed Content is licensed, not sold.**

5. **LIMITATIONS ON REVERSE ENGINEERING, DECOMPILATION, AND DISASSEMBLY.** You may not reverse engineer, decompile, or disassemble the Software or Media Elements, except and only to the extent that such activity is expressly permitted by applicable law notwithstanding this limitation.

6. **LIMITATIONS ON SALE, RENTAL, ETC. AND CERTAIN ASSIGNMENTS.** You may not provide commercial hosting services with, sell, rent, lease, lend, sublicense, or assign copies of the Licensed Content, or any portion thereof (including any permitted modifications thereof) on a stand-alone basis or as part of any collection, product or service.

7. **CONSENT TO USE OF DATA.** You agree that Microsoft and its affiliates may collect and use technical information gathered as part of the product support services provided to you, if any, related to the Licensed Content. Microsoft may use this information solely to improve our products or to provide customized services or technologies to you and will not disclose this information in a form that personally identifies you.

8. **LINKS TO THIRD PARTY SITES.** You may link to third party sites through the use of the Licensed Content. The third party sites are not under the control of Microsoft, and Microsoft is not responsible for the contents of any third party sites, any links contained in third party sites, or any changes or updates to third party sites. Microsoft is not responsible for webcasting or any other form of transmission received from any third party sites. Microsoft is providing these links to third party sites to you only as a convenience, and the inclusion of any link does not imply an endorsement by Microsoft of the third party site.

9. **ADDITIONAL LICENSED CONTENT/SERVICES.** This EULA applies to updates, supplements, add-on components, or Internet-based services components, of the Licensed Content that Microsoft may provide to you or make available to you after the date you obtain your initial copy of the Licensed Content, unless we provide other terms along with the update, supplement, add-on component, or Internet-based services component. Microsoft reserves the right to discontinue any Internet-based services provided to you or made available to you through the use of the Licensed Content.

10. **U.S. GOVERNMENT LICENSE RIGHTS.** All software provided to the U.S. Government pursuant to solicitations issued on or after December 1, 1995 is provided with the commercial license rights and restrictions described elsewhere herein. All software provided to the U.S. Government pursuant to solicitations issued prior to December 1, 1995 is provided with "Restricted Rights" as provided for in FAR, 48 CFR 52.227-14 (JUNE 1987) or DFAR, 48 CFR 252.227-7013 (OCT 1988), as applicable.

11. **EXPORT RESTRICTIONS.** You acknowledge that the Licensed Content is subject to U.S. export jurisdiction. You agree to comply with all applicable international and national laws that apply to the Licensed Content, including the U.S. Export Administration Regulations, as well as end-user, end-use, and destination restrictions issued by U.S. and other governments. For additional information see <http://www.microsoft.com/exporting/>.

12. **TRANSFER.** The initial user of the Licensed Content may make a one-time permanent transfer of this EULA and Licensed Content to another end user, provided the initial user retains no copies of the Licensed Content. The transfer may not be an indirect transfer, such as a consignment. Prior to the transfer, the end user receiving the Licensed Content must agree to all the EULA terms.

13. **"NOT FOR RESALE" LICENSED CONTENT.** Licensed Content identified as "Not For Resale" or "NFR," may not be sold or otherwise transferred for value, or used for any purpose other than demonstration, test or evaluation.

14. **TERMINATION.** Without prejudice to any other rights, Microsoft may terminate this EULA if you fail to comply with the terms and conditions of this EULA. In such event, you must destroy all copies of the Licensed Content and all of its component parts.

15. <u>DISCLAIMER OF WARRANTIES.</u> **TO THE MAXIMUM EXTENT PERMITTED BY APPLICABLE LAW, MICROSOFT AND ITS SUPPLIERS PROVIDE THE LICENSED CONTENT AND SUPPORT SERVICES (IF ANY) *AS IS AND WITH ALL FAULTS*, AND MICROSOFT AND ITS SUPPLIERS HEREBY DISCLAIM ALL OTHER WARRANTIES AND CONDITIONS, WHETHER EXPRESS, IMPLIED OR STATUTORY, INCLUDING, BUT NOT LIMITED TO, ANY (IF ANY) IMPLIED WARRANTIES, DUTIES OR CONDITIONS OF MERCHANTABILITY, OF FITNESS FOR A PARTICULAR PURPOSE, OF RELIABILITY OR AVAILABILITY, OF ACCURACY OR COMPLETENESS OF RESPONSES, OF RESULTS, OF WORKMANLIKE EFFORT, OF LACK OF VIRUSES, AND OF LACK OF NEGLIGENCE, ALL WITH REGARD TO THE LICENSED CONTENT, AND THE PROVISION OF OR FAILURE TO PROVIDE SUPPORT OR OTHER SERVICES, INFORMATION, SOFTWARE, AND RELATED CONTENT THROUGH THE LICENSED CONTENT, OR OTHERWISE ARISING OUT OF THE USE OF THE LICENSED CONTENT. ALSO, THERE IS NO WARRANTY OR CONDITION OF TITLE, QUIET ENJOYMENT, QUIET POSSESSION, CORRESPONDENCE TO DESCRIPTION OR NON-INFRINGEMENT WITH REGARD TO THE LICENSED CONTENT. THE ENTIRE RISK AS TO THE QUALITY, OR ARISING OUT OF THE USE OR PERFORMANCE OF THE LICENSED CONTENT, AND ANY SUPPORT SERVICES, REMAINS WITH YOU.**

16. <u>EXCLUSION OF INCIDENTAL, CONSEQUENTIAL AND CERTAIN OTHER DAMAGES.</u> **TO THE MAXIMUM EXTENT PERMITTED BY APPLICABLE LAW, IN NO EVENT SHALL MICROSOFT OR ITS SUPPLIERS BE LIABLE FOR ANY SPECIAL, INCIDENTAL, PUNITIVE, INDIRECT, OR CONSEQUENTIAL DAMAGES WHATSOEVER (INCLUDING, BUT NOT**

LIMITED TO, DAMAGES FOR LOSS OF PROFITS OR CONFIDENTIAL OR OTHER INFORMATION, FOR BUSINESS INTERRUPTION, FOR PERSONAL INJURY, FOR LOSS OF PRIVACY, FOR FAILURE TO MEET ANY DUTY INCLUDING OF GOOD FAITH OR OF REASONABLE CARE, FOR NEGLIGENCE, AND FOR ANY OTHER PECUNIARY OR OTHER LOSS WHATSOEVER) ARISING OUT OF OR IN ANY WAY RELATED TO THE USE OF OR INABILITY TO USE THE LICENSED CONTENT, THE PROVISION OF OR FAILURE TO PROVIDE SUPPORT OR OTHER SERVICES, INFORMATION, SOFTWARE, AND RELATED CONTENT THROUGH THE LICENSED CONTENT, OR OTHERWISE ARISING OUT OF THE USE OF THE LICENSED CONTENT, OR OTHERWISE UNDER OR IN CONNECTION WITH ANY PROVISION OF THIS EULA, EVEN IN THE EVENT OF THE FAULT, TORT (INCLUDING NEGLIGENCE), MISREPRESENTATION, STRICT LIABILITY, BREACH OF CONTRACT OR BREACH OF WARRANTY OF MICROSOFT OR ANY SUPPLIER, AND EVEN IF MICROSOFT OR ANY SUPPLIER HAS BEEN ADVISED OF THE POSSIBILITY OF SUCH DAMAGES. BECAUSE SOME STATES/JURISDICTIONS DO NOT ALLOW THE EXCLUSION OR LIMITATION OF LIABILITY FOR CONSEQUENTIAL OR INCIDENTAL DAMAGES, THE ABOVE LIMITATION MAY NOT APPLY TO YOU.

17. **LIMITATION OF LIABILITY AND REMEDIES.** NOTWITHSTANDING ANY DAMAGES THAT YOU MIGHT INCUR FOR ANY REASON WHATSOEVER (INCLUDING, WITHOUT LIMITATION, ALL DAMAGES REFERENCED HEREIN AND ALL DIRECT OR GENERAL DAMAGES IN CONTRACT OR ANYTHING ELSE), THE ENTIRE LIABILITY OF MICROSOFT AND ANY OF ITS SUPPLIERS UNDER ANY PROVISION OF THIS EULA AND YOUR EXCLUSIVE REMEDY HEREUNDER SHALL BE LIMITED TO THE GREATER OF THE ACTUAL DAMAGES YOU INCUR IN REASONABLE RELIANCE ON THE LICENSED CONTENT UP TO THE AMOUNT ACTUALLY PAID BY YOU FOR THE LICENSED CONTENT OR US$5.00. THE FOREGOING LIMITATIONS, EXCLUSIONS AND DISCLAIMERS SHALL APPLY TO THE MAXIMUM EXTENT PERMITTED BY APPLICABLE LAW, EVEN IF ANY REMEDY FAILS ITS ESSENTIAL PURPOSE.

18. **APPLICABLE LAW.** If you acquired this Licensed Content in the United States, this EULA is governed by the laws of the State of Washington. If you acquired this Licensed Content in Canada, unless expressly prohibited by local law, this EULA is governed by the laws in force in the Province of Ontario, Canada; and, in respect of any dispute which may arise hereunder, you consent to the jurisdiction of the federal and provincial courts sitting in Toronto, Ontario. If you acquired this Licensed Content in the European Union, Iceland, Norway, or Switzerland, then local law applies. If you acquired this Licensed Content in any other country, then local law may apply.

19. **ENTIRE AGREEMENT; SEVERABILITY.** This EULA (including any addendum or amendment to this EULA which is included with the Licensed Content) are the entire agreement between you and Microsoft relating to the Licensed Content and the support services (if any) and they supersede all prior or contemporaneous oral or written communications, proposals and representations with respect to the Licensed Content or any other subject matter covered by this EULA. To the extent the terms of any Microsoft policies or programs for support services conflict with the terms of this EULA, the terms of this EULA shall control. If any provision of this EULA is held to be void, invalid, unenforceable or illegal, the other provisions shall continue in full force and effect.

Should you have any questions concerning this EULA, or if you desire to contact Microsoft for any reason, please use the address information enclosed in this Licensed Content to contact the Microsoft subsidiary serving your country or visit Microsoft on the World Wide Web at http://www.microsoft.com.

Si vous avez acquis votre Contenu Sous Licence Microsoft au CANADA :

DÉNI DE GARANTIES. Dans la mesure maximale permise par les lois applicables, le Contenu Sous Licence et les services de soutien technique (le cas échéant) sont fournis *TELS QUELS ET AVEC TOUS LES DÉFAUTS* par Microsoft et ses fournisseurs, lesquels par les présentes dénient toutes autres garanties et conditions expresses, implicites ou en vertu de la loi, notamment, mais sans limitation, (le cas échéant) les garanties, devoirs ou conditions implicites de qualité marchande, d'adaptation à une fin usage particulière, de fiabilité ou de disponibilité, d'exactitude ou d'exhaustivité des réponses, des résultats, des efforts déployés selon les règles de l'art, d'absence de virus et d'absence de négligence, le tout à l'égard du Contenu Sous Licence et de la prestation des services de soutien technique ou de l'omission de la 'une telle prestation des services de soutien technique ou à l'égard de la fourniture ou de l'omission de la fourniture de tous autres services, renseignements, Contenus Sous Licence, et contenu qui s'y rapporte grâce au Contenu Sous Licence ou provenant autrement de l'utilisation du Contenu Sous Licence. PAR AILLEURS, IL N'Y A AUCUNE GARANTIE OU CONDITION QUANT AU TITRE DE PROPRIÉTÉ, À LA JOUISSANCE OU LA POSSESSION PAISIBLE, À LA CONCORDANCE À UNE DESCRIPTION NI QUANT À UNE ABSENCE DE CONTREFAÇON CONCERNANT LE CONTENU SOUS LICENCE.

EXCLUSION DES DOMMAGES ACCESSOIRES, INDIRECTS ET DE CERTAINS AUTRES DOMMAGES. DANS LA MESURE MAXIMALE PERMISE PAR LES LOIS APPLICABLES, EN AUCUN CAS MICROSOFT OU SES FOURNISSEURS NE SERONT RESPONSABLES DES DOMMAGES SPÉCIAUX, CONSÉCUTIFS, ACCESSOIRES OU INDIRECTS DE QUELQUE NATURE QUE CE SOIT (NOTAMMENT, LES DOMMAGES À L'ÉGARD DU MANQUE À GAGNER OU DE LA DIVULGATION DE RENSEIGNEMENTS CONFIDENTIELS OU AUTRES, DE LA PERTE D'EXPLOITATION, DE BLESSURES CORPORELLES, DE LA VIOLATION DE LA VIE PRIVÉE, DE L'OMISSION DE REMPLIR TOUT DEVOIR, Y COMPRIS D'AGIR DE BONNE FOI OU D'EXERCER UN SOIN RAISONNABLE, DE LA NÉGLIGENCE ET DE TOUTE AUTRE PERTE PÉCUNIAIRE OU AUTRE PERTE

DE QUELQUE NATURE QUE CE SOIT) SE RAPPORTE DE QUELQUE MANIÈRE QUE CE SOIT À L'UTILISATION DU CONTENU SOUS LICENCE OU À L'INCAPACITÉ DE S'EN SERVIR, À LA PRESTATION OU À L'OMISSION DE LA 'UNE TELLE PRESTATION DE SERVICES DE SOUTIEN TECHNIQUE OU À LA FOURNITURE OU À L'OMISSION DE LA FOURNITURE DE TOUS AUTRES SERVICES, RENSEIGNEMENTS, CONTENUS SOUS LICENCE, ET CONTENU QUI S'Y RAPPORTE GRÂCE AU CONTENU SOUS LICENCE OU PROVENANT AUTREMENT DE L'UTILISATION DU CONTENU SOUS LICENCE OU AUTREMENT AUX TERMES DE TOUTE DISPOSITION DE LA U PRÉSENTE CONVENTION EULA OU RELATIVEMENT À UNE TELLE DISPOSITION, MÊME EN CAS DE FAUTE, DE DÉLIT CIVIL (Y COMPRIS LA NÉGLIGENCE), DE RESPONSABILITÉ STRICTE, DE VIOLATION DE CONTRAT OU DE VIOLATION DE GARANTIE DE MICROSOFT OU DE TOUT FOURNISSEUR ET MÊME SI MICROSOFT OU TOUT FOURNISSEUR A ÉTÉ AVISÉ DE LA POSSIBILITÉ DE TELS DOMMAGES.

LIMITATION DE RESPONSABILITÉ ET RECOURS.   MALGRÉ LES DOMMAGES QUE VOUS PUISSIEZ SUBIR POUR QUELQUE MOTIF QUE CE SOIT (NOTAMMENT, MAIS SANS LIMITATION, TOUS LES DOMMAGES SUSMENTIONNÉS ET TOUS LES DOMMAGES DIRECTS OU GÉNÉRAUX OU AUTRES), LA SEULE RESPONSABILITÉ 'OBLIGATION INTÉGRALE DE MICROSOFT ET DE L'UN OU L'AUTRE DE SES FOURNISSEURS AUX TERMES DE TOUTE DISPOSITION DEU LA PRÉSENTE CONVENTION EULA ET VOTRE RECOURS EXCLUSIF À L'ÉGARD DE TOUT CE QUI PRÉCÈDE SE LIMITE AU PLUS ÉLEVÉ ENTRE LES MONTANTS SUIVANTS : LE MONTANT QUE VOUS AVEZ RÉELLEMENT PAYÉ POUR LE CONTENU SOUS LICENCE OU 5,00 $US. LES LIMITES, EXCLUSIONS ET DÉNIS QUI PRÉCÈDENT (Y COMPRIS LES CLAUSES CI-DESSUS), S'APPLIQUENT DANS LA MESURE MAXIMALE PERMISE PAR LES LOIS APPLICABLES, MÊME SI TOUT RECOURS N'ATTEINT PAS SON BUT ESSENTIEL.

À moins que cela ne soit prohibé par le droit local applicable, la présente Convention est régie par les lois de la province d'Ontario, Canada. Vous consentez Chacune des parties à la présente reconnaît irrévocablement à la compétence des tribunaux fédéraux et provinciaux siégeant à Toronto, dans de la province d'Ontario et consent à instituer tout litige qui pourrait découler de la présente auprès des tribunaux situés dans le district judiciaire de York, province d'Ontario.

Au cas où vous auriez des questions concernant cette licence ou que vous désiriez vous mettre en rapport avec Microsoft pour quelque raison que ce soit, veuillez utiliser l'information contenue dans le Contenu Sous Licence pour contacter la filiale de succursale Microsoft desservant votre pays, dont l'adresse est fournie dans ce produit, ou visitez écrivez à : Microsoft sur le World Wide Web à http://www.microsoft.com

Contents

Appendix B: Implementation Plan Values

About This Course

This section provides you with a brief description of the course, audience, suggested prerequisites, and course objectives.

Description

This five-day instructor-led course provides students with the knowledge and skills to implement, manage, and maintain a Microsoft® Windows® Server 2003 network infrastructure. The course is intended for systems administrator and systems engineer candidates who are responsible for implementing, managing, and maintaining server networking technologies. These tasks include implementing routing; implementing, managing and maintaining Dynamic Host Configuration Protocol (DHCP), Domain Name System (DNS), and Windows Internet Name Service (WINS); securing Internet Protocol (IP) traffic with Internet Protocol security (IPSec) and certificates; implementing a network access infrastructure by configuring the connections for remote access clients; and managing and monitoring network access.

Audience

This is the fourth course in the Systems Administrator and Systems Engineer track for Windows Server 2003, and it is the final course in the Systems Administrator track.

This course is intended for individuals who are employed as or seeking employment as a systems administrator or systems engineer.

Student prerequisites

This course requires that students meet the following prerequisites:

- A+ Certification, or equivalent knowledge and skills.

- Network+ Certification, or equivalent knowledge and skills.

- Completed Course 2274, *Managing a Microsoft Windows Server 2003 Environment* or have equivalent knowledge and skills.

- Completed Course 2275, *Maintaining a Microsoft Windows Server 2003 Environment*, or have equivalent knowledge and skills.

- Completed Course 2276, *Implementing a Microsoft Windows Server 2003 Network Infrastructure: Network Hosts*, or have equivalent knowledge and skills.

Course objectives

After completing this course, the student will be able to:

- Configure routing by using the Routing and Remote Access.

- Allocate IP addressing by using Dynamic Host Configuration Protocol (DHCP).

- Manage and monitor DHCP.

- Resolve names.

- Resolve Host names by using Domain Name System (DNS).

- Manage and monitor DNS.

- Resolve NetBIOS names by using Windows Internet Service (WINS).

- Secure network traffic by using IPSec and certificates.

- Configure network access.

- Manage and monitor network access.

Student Materials Compact Disc Contents

The Student Materials compact disc contains the following files and folders:

- *Autorun.exe*. When the compact disc is inserted into the CD-ROM drive, or when you double-click the **Autorun.exe** file, this file opens the compact disc and allows you to browse the Student Materials compact disc.

- *Autorun.inf*. When the compact disc is inserted into the compact disc drive, this file opens Autorun.exe.

- *Default.htm*. This file opens the Student Materials Web page. It provides you with resources pertaining to this course, including additional reading, review and lab answers, lab files, multimedia presentations, and course-related Web sites.

- *Readme.txt*. This file explains how to install the software for viewing the Student Materials compact disc and its contents and how to open the Student Materials Web page.

- *Addread*. This folder contains additional reading pertaining to this course.

- *Appendix*. This folder contains appendix files for this course.

- *Flash*. This folder contains the installer for the Macromedia Flash 6.0 browser plug-in.

- *Fonts*. This folder contains fonts that may be required to view the Microsoft Word documents that are included with this course.

- *Labfiles*. This folder contains files that are used in the hands-on labs. These files may be used to prepare the student computers for the hands-on labs.

- *Media*. This folder contains files that are used in multimedia presentations for this course.

- *Mplayer*. This folder contains the setup file to install Microsoft Windows Media® Player.

- *Webfiles*. This folder contains the files that are required to view the course Web page. To open the Web page, open Windows Explorer, and in the root directory of the compact disc, double-click **Default.htm** or **Autorun.exe**.

- *Wordview*. This folder contains the Word Viewer that is used to view any Word document (.doc) files that are included on the compact disc.

Document Conventions

The following conventions are used in course materials to distinguish elements of the text.

Convention	Use
Bold	Represents commands, command options, and syntax that must be typed exactly as shown. It also indicates commands on menus and buttons, dialog box titles and options, and icon and menu names.
Italic	In syntax statements or descriptive text, indicates argument names or placeholders for variable information. Italic is also used for introducing new terms, for book titles, and for emphasis in the text.
Title Capitals	Indicate domain names, user names, computer names, directory names, and folder and file names, except when specifically referring to case-sensitive names. Unless otherwise indicated, you can use lowercase letters when you type a directory name or file name in a dialog box or at a command prompt.
ALL CAPITALS	Indicate the names of keys, key sequences, and key combinations—for example, ALT+SPACEBAR.
`monospace`	Represents code samples or examples of screen text.
[ ]	In syntax statements, enclose optional items. For example, [*filename*] in command syntax indicates that you can choose to type a file name with the command. Type only the information within the brackets, not the brackets themselves.
{ }	In syntax statements, enclose required items. Type only the information within the braces, not the braces themselves.
|	In syntax statements, separates an either/or choice.
▶	Indicates a procedure with sequential steps.
...	In syntax statements, specifies that the preceding item may be repeated.
. . .	Represents an omitted portion of a code sample.

Microsoft®
Training &
Certification

Introduction

Contents

Introduction

- Name
- Company affiliation
- Title/function
- Job responsibility
- Systems administration experience
- Microsoft Windows Server operating systems experience
- Expectations for the course

Course Materials

- Name card
- Student workbook
- Student Materials compact disc
- Course evaluation

The following materials are included with your kit:

- *Name card*. Write your name on both sides of the name card.

- *Student workbook*. The student workbook contains the material covered in class, in addition to the hands-on lab exercises.

- *Student Materials compact disc*. The Student Materials compact disc contains the Web page that provides you with links to resources pertaining to this course, including additional readings, review and lab answers, lab files, multimedia presentations, and course-related Web sites.

   Note   To open the Web page, insert the Student Materials compact disc into the CD-ROM drive, and then in the root directory of the compact disc, double-click **Autorun.exe** or **Default.htm**.

- *Assessments*. There are assessments for each lesson, located on the Student Materials compact disc. You can use them as pre-assessments to identify areas of difficulty, or you can use them as post-assessments to validate learning.

- *Course evaluation*. To provide feedback on the course, training facility, and instructor, you will have the opportunity to complete an online evaluation near the end of the course.

   To provide additional comments or feedback on the course, send e-mail to support@mscourseware.com. To inquire about the Microsoft® Certified Professional program, send e-mail to mcphelp@microsoft.com.

Additional Reading from Microsoft Press

Microsoft Windows Server 2003 books from Microsoft Press can help you do your job—from the planning and evaluation stages through deployment and ongoing support —with solid technical information to help you get the most out of the Windows Server 2003 key features and enhancements. The following titles supplement the skills taught in this course:

Title	ISBN
Understanding IPv6	0-7356-1245-5
Microsoft Windows Server 2003 Admin Pocket Consultant	0-7356-1354-0
Microsoft Windows Server 2003 TCP/IP Protocols and Services Technical Reference	0-7356-1291-9
Microsoft Windows Server 2003 Administrator's Companion	0-7356-1367-2
Deploying Virtual Private Networks with Microsoft Windows Server 2003 Technical Reference	0-7356-1576-4
Microsoft Windows Server 2003 Security Administrator's Companion	0-7356-1574-8

Prerequisites

* A+ Certification, or equivalent knowledge and skills
* Network+ Certification, or equivalent knowledge and skills
* Course 2274: *Managing a Microsoft Windows Server 2003 Environment,* or equivalent knowledge and skills
* Course 2275: *Maintaining a Microsoft Windows Server 2003 Environment,* or equivalent knowledge and skills
* Course 2276: *Implementing a Microsoft Windows Server 2003 Network Infrastructure: Network Hosts,* or equivalent knowledge and skills

This course requires that you meet the following prerequisites:

- A+ Certification, or equivalent knowledge and skills
- Network+ Certification, or equivalent knowledge and skills
- Course 2274, *Managing a Microsoft Windows® Server 2003 Environment,* or equivalent knowledge and skills
- Course 2275, *Maintaining a Microsoft Windows Server 2003 Environment,* or equivalent knowledge and skills
- Course 2276, *Implementing a Microsoft Windows Server 2003 Network Infrastructure: Network Hosts,* or equivalent knowledge and skills

Course Outline

- Module 1: Configuring Routing by Using Routing and Remote Access
- Module 2: Allocating IP Addressing by Using Dynamic Host Configuration Protocol (DHCP)
- Module 3: Managing and Monitoring Dynamic Host Configuration Protocol (DHCP)
- Module 4: Resolving Names
- Module 5: Resolving Host Names by Using Domain Name System (DNS)

Module 1, "Configuring Routing by Using Routing and Remote Access," provides you with the knowledge and skills to install and configure the Routing and Remote Access service, and configure packet filters.

Module 2, "Allocating IP Addressing by Using Dynamic Host Configuration Protocol (DHCP)," provides you with the knowledge and skills to add and authorize a DHCP Server service, configure a DHCP scope, configure a DHCP reservation, configure DHCP options, and configure a DHCP relay agent.

Module 3, "Managing and Monitoring Dynamic Host Configuration Protocol (DHCP)," provides you with the knowledge and skills to manage a DHCP database, monitor DHCP, and apply security guidelines for DHCP.

Module 4, "Resolving Names," provides you with the knowledge and skills to configure names on a client, configure host name resolution, and configure network basic input/output system (NetBIOS) name resolution.

Module 5, "Resolving Host Names by Using Domain Name System (DNS)," provides you with the knowledge and skills to install the DNS Server service, configure the properties for the DNS Server service, configure DNS zones, configure DNS zone transfers, configure DNS dynamic updates, configure a DNS client, and delegate authority for zones.

Course Outline *(continued)*

- Module 6: Managing and Monitoring Domain Name System (DNS)
- Module 7: Resolving NetBIOS Names by Using Windows Internet Name Service (WINS)
- Module 8: Securing Network Traffic by Using IPSec and Certificates
- Module 9: Configuring Network Access
- Module 10: Managing and Monitoring Network Access

Module 6, "Managing and Monitoring Domain Name System (DNS)," provides you with the knowledge and skills to configure the Time-to-Live (TTL) value, configure aging and scavenging, integrate DNS and Windows Internet Name Service (WINS), use the command-line utilities Nslookup, DNSCMD, and DNSLint, test the DNS server configuration, and monitor DNS server performance.

Module 7, "Resolving NetBIOS Names by Using Windows Internet Name Service (WINS)," provides you with the knowledge and skills to install and configure a WINS server, manage records in WINS, configure WINS replication, and manage the WINS database.

Module 8, "Securing Network Traffic by Using IPSec and Certificates," provides you with the knowledge and skills to implement Internet Protocol security (IPSec), implement IPSec with certificates, and monitor IPSec.

Module 9, "Configuring Network Access," provides the knowledge and skills to configure a virtual private network (VPN) connection, configure a dial-up connection, configure a wireless connection, control user access to a network, and centralize network access authentication and policy management by using Internet Authentication Service (IAS).

Module 10, "Managing and Monitoring Network Access," provides you with the knowledge and skills to manage the network access services, configure logging on a network access server, and collect and monitor network access data.

Appendices   Appendix A, "Differences Between the Microsoft Windows 2000 Server Family and the Microsoft Windows Server 2003 Family," explains the differences between the operating systems in the context of the tasks in each module. This appendix is provided for students who are familiar with Windows 2000 Server.

Refer to the values in Appendix B, "Implementation Plan Values", when completing the practices and labs.

Setup

- The classroom is configured as one Windows Server 2003 domain: nwtraders.msft

- London is a domain controller and the instructor computer

- Glasgow is a member server and is used as a remote computer for student labs

- The student computers are running Windows Server 2003, Enterprise Edition

Course files

There are files associated with the labs and practices in this course. The lab files are located in the C:\Moc\2277 folder on the student computers.

Classroom setup

The classroom configuration consists of one domain controller and multiple student computers. Each computer is running Windows Server 2003, Enterprise Edition.

The name of the domain is nwtraders.msft. It is named after Northwind Traders, a fictitious company that has offices worldwide. The names of the computers correspond with the names of the cities where the fictitious offices are located.

The domain controller, which is also the instructor's computer, is named London; the instructor also has a member server that is named Glasgow.

Microsoft Official Curriculum

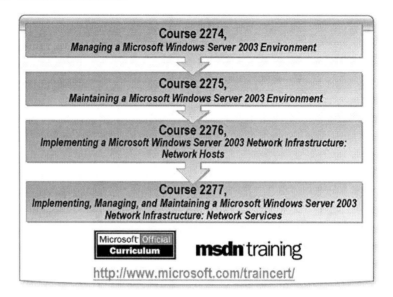

Introduction

Microsoft Training and Certification develops Microsoft Official Curriculum (MOC), including MSDN® Training, for computer professionals who design, develop, support, implement, or manage solutions by using Microsoft products and technologies. These courses provide comprehensive skills-based training in instructor-led and online formats.

Additional recommended courses

Each course relates in some way to another course. A related course may be a prerequisite, a follow-up course in a recommended series, or a course that offers additional training.

It is recommended that you take the following courses in this order:

- Course 2274, *Managing a Microsoft Windows Server 2003 Environment*
- Course 2275, *Maintaining a Microsoft Windows Server 2003 Environment*
- Course 2276, *Implementing a Microsoft Windows Server 2003 Network Infrastructure: Network Hosts*
- Course 2277, *Implementing, Managing, and Maintaining a Microsoft Windows Server 2003 Network Infrastructure: Network Services*
- Course 2278, *Planning and Maintaining a Microsoft Windows Server 2003 Network Infrastructure*
- Course 2279, *Planning, Implementing, and Maintaining a Microsoft Windows Server 2003 Active Directory® Infrastructure*

Other related courses may become available in the future, so for up-to-date information about recommended courses, visit the Training and Certification Web site.

Microsoft Training and Certification information

For more information, visit the Microsoft Training and Certification Web site at http://www.microsoft.com/traincert/.

Microsoft Certified Professional Program

Exam number and title	Core exam for the following track	Elective exam for the following track
70-291: *Implementing, Managing, and Maintaining a Microsoft Windows Server 2003 Network Infrastructure*	MCSA	n/a

Microsoft
C E R T I F I E D
Professional

http://www.microsoft.com/traincert/

Introduction

Microsoft Training and Certification offers a variety of certification credentials for developers and IT professionals. The Microsoft Certified Professional program is the leading certification program for validating your experience and skills, keeping you competitive in today's changing business environment.

Related certification exams

This course helps students to prepare for Exam 70-291: *Implementing, Managing, and Maintaining a Microsoft Windows Server 2003 Network Infrastructure*.

Exam 70-291 is a core exam for the Microsoft Certified Systems Administrator (MCSA) certification.

MCP certifications

The Microsoft Certified Professional program includes the following certifications.

- MCSA on Microsoft Windows Server 2003

  The Microsoft Certified Systems Administrator (MCSA) certification is designed for professionals who implement, manage, and troubleshoot existing network and system environments based on Microsoft Windows 2000 platforms, including the Windows Server 2003 family. Implementation responsibilities include installing and configuring parts of the systems. Management responsibilities include administering and supporting the systems.

- MCSE on Microsoft Windows Server 2003

  The Microsoft Certified Systems Engineer (MCSE) credential is the premier certification for professionals who analyze the business requirements and design and implement the infrastructure for business solutions based on the Microsoft Windows 2000 platform and Microsoft server software, including the Windows Server 2003 family. Implementation responsibilities include installing, configuring, and troubleshooting network systems.

- MCAD

  The Microsoft Certified Application Developer (MCAD) for Microsoft .NET credential is appropriate for professionals who use Microsoft technologies to develop and maintain department-level applications, components, Web or desktop clients, or back-end data services or work in teams developing enterprise applications. The credential covers job tasks ranging from developing to deploying and maintaining these solutions.

- MCSD

  The Microsoft Certified Solution Developer (MCSD) credential is the premier certification for professionals who design and develop leading-edge business solutions with Microsoft development tools, technologies, platforms, and the Microsoft Windows DNA architecture. The types of applications MCSDs can develop include desktop applications and multi-user, Web-based, N-tier, and transaction-based applications. The credential covers job tasks ranging from analyzing business requirements to maintaining solutions.

- MCDBA on Microsoft SQL Server™ 2000

  The Microsoft Certified Database Administrator (MCDBA) credential is the premier certification for professionals who implement and administer Microsoft SQL Server databases. The certification is appropriate for individuals who derive physical database designs, develop logical data models, create physical databases, create data services by using Transact-SQL, manage and maintain databases, configure and manage security, monitor and optimize databases, and install and configure SQL Server.

- MCP

  The Microsoft Certified Professional (MCP) credential is for individuals who have the skills to successfully implement a Microsoft product or technology as part of a business solution in an organization. Hands-on experience with the product is necessary to successfully achieve certification.

- MCT

  Microsoft Certified Trainers (MCTs) demonstrate the instructional and technical skills that qualify them to deliver Microsoft Official Curriculum through Microsoft Certified Technical Education Centers (Microsoft CTECs).

Certification requirements

The certification requirements differ for each certification category and are specific to the products and job functions addressed by the certification. To become a Microsoft Certified Professional, you must pass rigorous certification exams that provide a valid and reliable measure of technical proficiency and expertise.

For More Information   See the Microsoft Training and Certification Web site at http://www.microsoft.com/traincert/.

You can also send e-mail to mcphelp@microsoft.com if you have specific certification questions.

Acquiring the skills tested by an MCP exam

Microsoft Official Curriculum (MOC) and MSDN Training can help you develop the skills that you need to do your job. They also complement the experience that you gain while working with Microsoft products and technologies. However, no one-to-one correlation exists between MOC and MSDN Training courses and MCP exams. Microsoft does not expect or intend for the courses to be the sole preparation method for passing MCP exams. Practical product knowledge and experience is also necessary to pass the MCP exams.

To help prepare for the MCP exams, use the preparation guides that are available for each exam. Each Exam Preparation Guide contains exam-specific information, such as a list of the topics on which you will be tested. These guides are available on the Microsoft Training and Certification Web site at http://www.microsoft.com/traincert/.

Multimedia: Job Roles in Today's Information Systems Environment *(optional)*

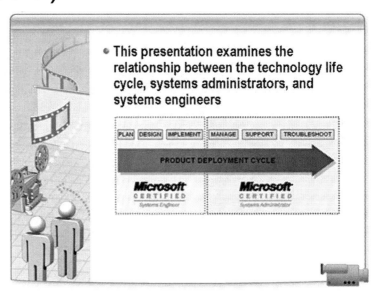

File location

To start the *Job Roles in Today's Information Systems Environment* presentation, open the Web page on the Student Materials compact disc, click **Multimedia**, and then click the title of the presentation.

Multimedia: Introduction to the Core Network Infrastructure

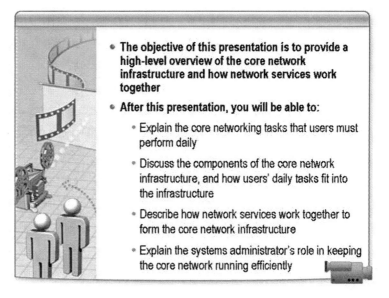

File location

To start the *Introduction to the Core Network Infrastructure* presentation, open the Web page on the Student Materials compact disc, click **Multimedia**, and then click the title of the presentation.

Objectives

At the end of this presentation, you will be able to:

- Explain the core networking tasks that users must perform daily.

- Discuss the components of the core network infrastructure and how users' daily tasks fit into the infrastructure.

- Describe how network services work together to form the core network infrastructure.

- Explain the systems administrator's role in keeping the core network running efficiently.

Key points

- The network infrastructure is made up of several network services, which work together to support the core network infrastructure.

- If one component fails, accessing resources can become difficult or impossible.

- As a systems administrator, it is your responsibility to ensure that the network services are operating correctly so that users can perform their daily networking tasks.

Facilities

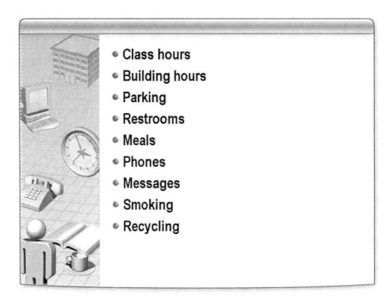

- Class hours
- Building hours
- Parking
- Restrooms
- Meals
- Phones
- Messages
- Smoking
- Recycling

Microsoft®
Training &
Certification

Module 1: Configuring Routing by Using Routing and Remote Access

Contents

Overview

- Multimedia: The Role of Routing in the Network Infrastructure
- Enabling and Configuring the Routing and Remote Access Service
- Configuring Packet Filters

Introduction

If you are a systems administrator, a thorough understanding of routers and how they function will help you effectively configure a routing solution for your network environment.

Important For more information about securing Routing and Remote Access, see the Windows Server 2003, Enterprise Edition Help documentation

Objectives

After completing this module, you will be able to:

- Describe the role of routing in the network infrastructure.
- Enable and configure the Routing and Remote Access service.
- Configure packet filters.

Multimedia: The Role of Routing in the Network Infrastructure

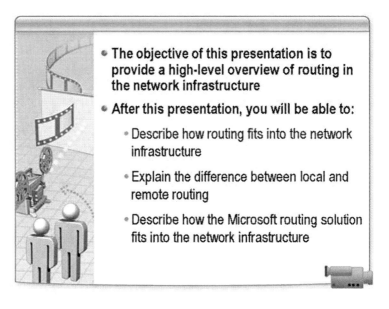

File location

To start the *Role of Routing in the Network Infrastructure* presentation, open the Web page on the Student Materials compact disc, click **Multimedia**, and then click the title of the presentation.

Objectives

At the end of this presentation, you will be able to:

- Describe how routing fits into the network infrastructure.

- Explain the difference between local and remote routing.

- Describe how the Microsoft® routing solution fits into the network infrastructure.

Key points

- Routing's role in the network infrastructure is to provide the primary means of joining two or more physically separated Internet Protocol (IP) subnets into a network.

- Connecting IP subnets allows the hosts on the connected subnets to communicate with each other, allowing users to gain access to resources.

- In an organization's routed environment, routers can connect many subnets.

- A routing table stores route paths to different subnets and calculates the most efficient route to forward a request to the appropriate subnet.

- Routing table information is shared between routers, both existing ones and new ones, by using routing protocols.

- Microsoft Windows® Server 2003 supports routing by using the Routing and Remote Access service.

Lesson: Enabling and Configuring the Routing and Remote Access Service

- What Are Routers?
- What Are Routing Interfaces?
- What Are Routing Protocols?
- What Are Routing Tables?
- Why Use the Windows Server 2003 Routing and Remote Access Service?
- How to Enable and Configure the Routing and Remote Access Service
- How to Add a Routing Protocol
- How to Add Routing Interface to a Routing Protocol

Introduction

By learning about the key components of routing, how they relate to each other, and how they function in a network, you can properly enable and configure a routing solution for your network.

This lesson presents the skills and knowledge that are required for you to enable and configure a software router.

Lesson objectives

After completing this lesson, you will be able to:

- Explain the function of a router.
- Explain what routing interfaces are.
- Explain what routing protocols are.
- Explain what a routing table is.
- Explain the purpose of the Windows Server 2003 Routing and Remote Access service.
- Enable and configure the Routing and Remote Access service.
- Add a routing protocol.
- Add a routing interface to a routing protocol.

What Are Routers?

Routers are an intermediate system at the network layer that is used to connect networks together based on a common network layer protocol

Router types	Example
Hardware router	A device that performs routing as a dedicated function
Software router	A router that is not dedicated to performing routing only, but performs routing as one of multiple processes running on the router computer

Main routing components include:

* Routing interface
* Routing protocol
* Routing table

Definition

Routers are an intermediate system at the network layer that is used to connect networks based on a common network layer protocol. Intermediate systems are network devices with the ability to forward packets between portions of a network. For example, in the Open Systems Interconnection (OSI) model:

- Hubs connect hosts at the physical layer.

- Switches connect hosts at the data-link layer.

- Routers connect hosts at the network layer.

Purpose of routers

Routers allow you to scale your network and to maintain bandwidth by segmenting network traffic. For example, an organization's test computers may be on one network segment while their production computers are on a separate network segment. A router connects these two separate segments.

Types of routers

The two types of routers that are used in a network environment are:

- *Hardware router.* A dedicated hardware device that runs specialized software for the exclusive purpose of routing.

- *Software router.* A router that is not dedicated to performing routing only, but which performs routing as one of multiple processes running on the router computer. Windows Server 2003 Routing and Remote Access is a service that performs routing as one of its multiple processes. When enabled as a network router, Windows Server 2003 supports both static and dynamic routing. In static routing, the administrator updates the routing table manually. In dynamic routing, the routing protocols update the routing table.

Main components of a routing solution

The three main components of a routing solution are:

- *Routing interface.* A physical or logical interface over which packets are forwarded.

- *Routing protocol.* A set of messages that routers use to share routing tables so that routers can determine the appropriate path by which data is forwarded.

- *Routing table.* A series of entries called *routes* that contain information about the location of the network IDs in the internetwork.

What Are Routing Interfaces?

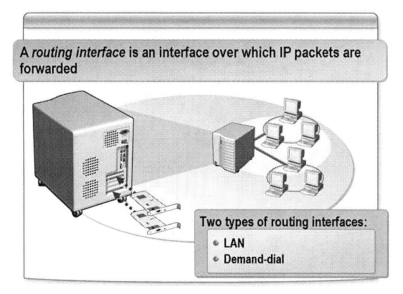

A *routing interface* is an interface over which IP packets are forwarded

Two types of routing interfaces:
- LAN
- Demand-dial

Definition

A *routing interface* is a physical or logical interface over which Internet Protocol (IP) packets are forwarded. The Windows Server 2003–based router uses a routing interface to forward IP packets.

Types of routing interfaces

- *Local area network (LAN) interfaces.* These interfaces usually represent an installed network adapter, although a wide area network (WAN) adapter can also be an interface. LAN interfaces typically do not require an authentication process to become active.

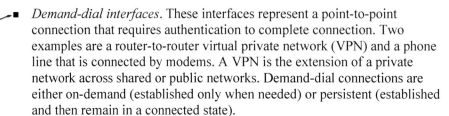

- *Demand-dial interfaces.* These interfaces represent a point-to-point connection that requires authentication to complete connection. Two examples are a router-to-router virtual private network (VPN) and a phone line that is connected by modems. A VPN is the extension of a private network across shared or public networks. Demand-dial connections are either on-demand (established only when needed) or persistent (established and then remain in a connected state).

Note For more information about demand-dial routing, refer to the resource kit for Microsoft Windows Server 2003, Enterprise Edition.

Example

A server running Windows Server 2003 Routing and Remote Access that is connected to both the local network and the Internet can route packets between a remote access client on the Internet and network resources on a corporate network. The router in this example is connected to the local area network through a LAN interface and to the Internet by a demand-dial interface.

What Are Routing Protocols?

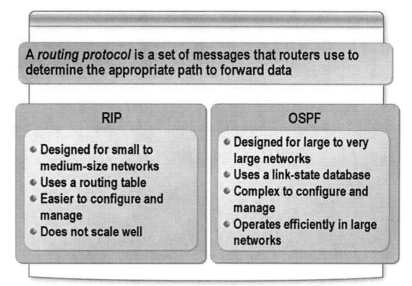

| Definition | A *routing protocol* is a set of messages that routers use to determine the appropriate path to forward data. Routing protocols automatically manage changes in the routing table that occur because of network changes. |

Definition

A *routing protocol* is a set of messages that routers use to determine the appropriate path to forward data. Routing protocols automatically manage changes in the routing table that occur because of network changes.

Example

A server running Windows Server 2003 Routing and Remote Access, that is not configured with a routing protocol, can only route between:

- Those networks to which the Routing and Remote Access server is physically connected.

- Those networks on which the Routing and Remote Access server has static routes configured (routes that an administrator entered manually).

However, when you add a routing protocol, this server can then communicate to all other routers in the network that are configured with the same routing protocol. The routing table of the Windows Server 2003 router is automatically updated with the routes of these other routers.

Note For more information about routing protocols, refer to the resource kit for Microsoft Windows Server 2003, Enterprise Edition.

Types of routing protocols

There are two types of routing protocols that Windows Server 2003 Routing and Remote Access supports:

- *Routing Information Protocol (RIP)*. Designed for exchanging routing information within a small to medium-size network.

- *Open Shortest Path First (OSPF)*. Designed for exchanging routing information within a large or very large network.

How RIP works

The RIP process prevents the management of the routing tables from becoming an administrative burden.

1. RIP dynamically builds routing tables by announcing the contents of its routing table to its configured interfaces.

2. Routers connected to those interfaces receive these announcements and use them to build the appropriate routing tables.

3. The routers that receive the announcements then compile their own routing table, which is then transmitted to other routers. This process continues in a manner that should provide each configured router with the routes from each of the other routers.

How OSPF works

Instead of exchanging routing table entries as RIP routers do, OSPF routers maintain a map of the network that is updated after any change in the network topology. This map is called the *link-state database*.

1. OSPF allows a router to calculate the shortest path for sending packets to each node.

2. The router sends information (called *link-state advertisements*) about the nodes to which it is linked to all other routers on the network. The router collects information from the other routers, which it uses for link-state information and to make calculations.

A comparison of RIP and OSPF

RIP is simple to configure and deploy. However, as networks grow larger the periodic announcements that each RIP router sends out can cause excessive traffic on the network. (RIP is typically used in networks with up to 50 servers.)

OSPF operates efficiently in large networks, because it computes the best route to use and because it requires fewer status messages. Unlike RIP, OSPF does not advertise all known routes to other routers, but only any changes that are made to its routes.

The disadvantage of OSPF is its complexity: It is harder to configure and requires more management time than RIP.

What Are Routing Tables?

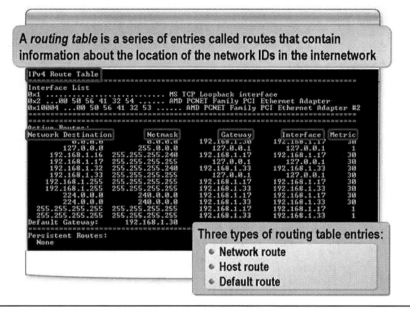

A *routing table* is a series of entries called routes that contain information about the location of the network IDs in the internetwork

Three types of routing table entries:
- Network route
- Host route
- Default route

Definition

A *routing table* is a series of entries called *routes* that contain information about the location of the network IDs in the internetwork.

Purpose of a routing table

The information in a routing table helps to determine the optimal route within an internetwork. The routing table is not exclusive to a router. Hosts (non-routers) may also have a routing table that they use to determine the optimal route.

Types of routing table entries

There are three types of routing table entries:

- *Network route.* A network route is a path to a specific network ID in the internetwork.

- *Host route.* A host route is a path to an internetwork address (network ID and node ID). Host routes are typically used to create custom routes to specific hosts to control or optimize network traffic.

- *Default route.* A default route is used when no other routes in the routing table are found. For example, if a router or host cannot find either a network route or a host route for the destination, the default route is used. The default route simplifies the configuration of hosts. Rather than configuring hosts with routes for all network IDs in the internetwork, a single default route is used to forward all packets with a destination network or internetwork address that was not found in the routing table.

Routing table structure

Each entry in the routing table consists of the following information fields:

- *Destination*. Specifies the network destination of the route. The destination can be an IP network address (where the host bits of the network address are set to 0), an IP address for a host route, or 0.0.0.0 for the default route.

- *Netmask*. Specifies the subnet mask that is associated with the network destination. The subnet mask can be the appropriate subnet mask for an IP network address, 255.255.255.255 for a host route, or 0.0.0.0 for the default route.

- *Gateway*. Specifies the forwarding or next-hop IP address over which the set of addresses that are defined by the network destination and subnet mask are reachable.

- *Interface*. Specifies the network interface number for the specified route. This is a port number or other type of logical identifier.

- *Metric*. Specifies an integer cost measurement of a route. Typically, the lowest metric is the preferred route. If multiple routes to a given destination network exist, the route with the lowest metric is used.

Note   You can type **route print** at a command prompt to display the entire contents of a routing table. To view other examples of **route** commands, see the Windows Server 2003 Help documentation.

Why Use Windows Server 2003 Routing and Remote Access Service?

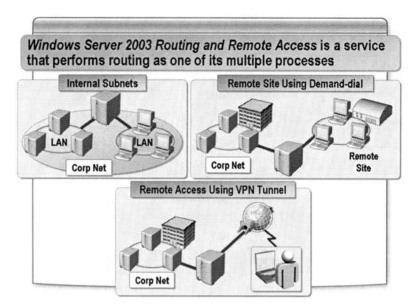

Purpose of Windows Server 2003 Routing and Remote Access service

Windows Server 2003 Routing and Remote Access is a service that performs routing as one of its multiple processes. You can use a server running Windows Server 2003 Routing and Remote Access to:

- Connect LAN segments (subnets) within a corporate network.

- Connect branch offices to corporate intranets and share resources as if all the computers are connected to the same LAN.

- Provide remote computers with access to corporate network resources.

As a systems administrator, you can use Routing and Remote Access to view and manage both router servers running Windows Server 2003 and remote access servers on your network.

The Routing and Remote Access service supports a wide variety of hardware platforms and network adapters. It is also extensible with application programming interfaces (APIs) that developers can use to create custom networking solutions.

How to Enable and Configure the Routing and Remote Access Service

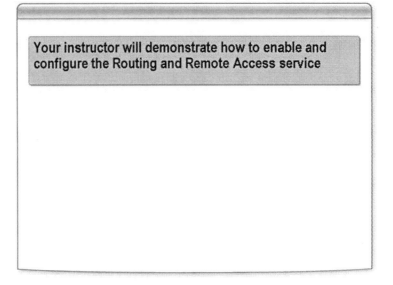

Your instructor will demonstrate how to enable and configure the Routing and Remote Access service

Introduction

In this procedure, you will use the Manage Your Server tool, a new Windows Server 2003 feature, to enable and configure the Routing and Remote Access service. The Manage Your Server tool is available in the Windows Server 2003 family on the **Start** menu.

Note   It is recommended that you log on by using an account that has non-administrative credentials, and that you use the **Run as** command to run the console with a user account that has appropriate administrative credentials to perform this task.

After you select **Add or remove a role**, the Configure Your Server Wizard appears and guides you through the appropriate steps for adding the new server role for routing.

After you select **Remote access / VPN server**, the Routing and Remote Access Server Setup Wizard appears and guides you through the final steps of setting up the Routing and Remote Access service.

Procedure for enabling and configuring the Routing and Remote Access service.

To enable and configure the Routing and Remote Access service:

1. Log on by using a non-administrative user account.

2. Click **Start**, and then click **Control Panel**.

3. In Control Panel, open **Administrative Tools**, right-click **Manage Your Server**, and then select **Run as**.

4. In the **Run As** dialog box, select **The following user**, enter a user account, with the appropriate password, that has the permissions to complete the task, and then click **OK**.

5. In the **Manage Your Server** tool, click **Add or remove a role**.

6. On the **Preliminary Steps** page, click **Next**.

7. On the **Server Role** page, select **Remote access / VPN server**, and then click **Next**.

Important The Remote access/VPN server role is the server role that you use to install and configure Windows Server 2003 routing and to provide remote access to your network.

---

8. On the **Summary of Selections** page, click **Next**.

9. On the **Welcome to the Routing and Remote Access Server Setup Wizard** page, click **Next**.

10. On the **Configuration** page, select **Custom configuration**, and then click **Next**.

11. On the **Custom Configuration** page, select the **LAN routing** option, and then click **Next**.

12. On the **Completing the Routing and Remote Access Server Setup Wizard** page, click **Finish**.

13. In the **Routing and Remote Access** warning dialog box, click **Yes** to start the service.

14. On the **This Server is Now a Remote Access/VPN Server** page, click **Finish**.

Note The **Manage Your Server** tool is also used to remove a server role, such as the Routing and Remote Access service.

Procedure for removing a server role

To remove a server role:

1. In the **Manage Your Server** tool, click **Add or remove a role**.

2. On the **Preliminary Steps** page, click **Next**.

3. On the **Server Role** page, select the server role that you wish to remove, and then click **Next**.

4. On the **Role Removal confirmation** page, select the **Remove the server role** option, and then click **Next**.

5. On the *Server Role* **removed** page, click **Finish**.

How to Add a Routing Protocol

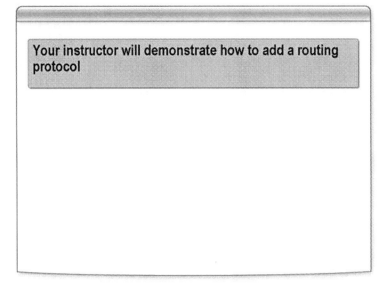

Introduction

After you enable and configure routing on a server, you can add a routing protocol to it. This enables the server to communicate with all other routers in your network that are configured with the same protocol.

The primary administration and management tool for configuring routing is the Routing and Remote Access console. It is available in the Administrative Tools folder in Control Panel. In this procedure, you will use the Routing and Remote Access console to add a routing protocol to your router server.

Note It is recommended that you log on by using an account that has non-administrative credentials and use the **Run as** command with a user account that has appropriate administrative credentials to perform this task.

Procedure

To add a routing protocol:

1. In the Routing and Remote Access console, expand the server, expand **IP Routing**, right-click **General**, and then click **New Routing Protocol**.

2. In the **New Routing Protocol** dialog box, select the appropriate routing protocol, and then click **OK**.

How to Add a Routing Interface to a Routing Protocol

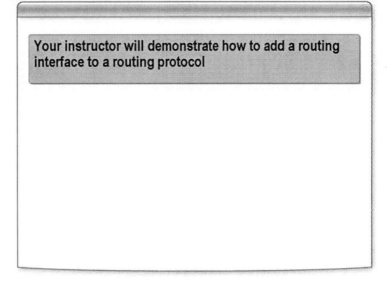

Your instructor will demonstrate how to add a routing interface to a routing protocol

Introduction

After you add a routing protocol to your router, you must add at least one interface to the protocol for it to function properly. However, you can also add multiple interfaces to a protocol. For example, if you want to communicate to a router on another subnet, you can add the interfaces for that subnet to the protocol that is configured on your router. This enables your router to communicate to the router on the new subnet.

Note It is recommended that you log on by using an account that has non-administrative credentials and use the **Run as** command with a user account that has appropriate administrative credentials to perform this task.

Procedure

To add a routing interface to a protocol:

1. In the Routing and Remote Access console, in the console tree, right-click the routing protocol to which you want to add an interface, and then click **New Interface**.

2. In the **New Interface** dialog box, select the appropriate interface, and then click **OK**.

3. If applicable, complete any configuration required for the interface.

Note To view installed and configured routing interfaces in the Routing and Remote Access console, click **Routing Interfaces** in the console tree.

Practice: Enabling and Configuring the Routing and Remote Access Service

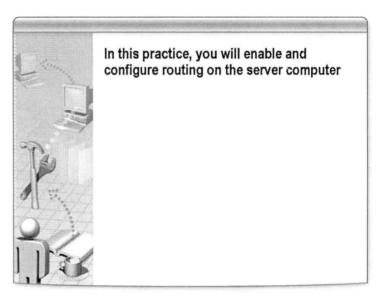

In this practice, you will enable and configure routing on the server computer

Objective

In this practice, you will enable and configure routing.

Instructions

To complete this practice, refer to the *Implementation Plan Values* document, located in the Appendix at the end of your student workbook.

You must be logged on with an account that has non-administrative credentials and use the **Run as** command with a user account that has appropriate administrative credentials to complete the task.

Scenario

The systems engineer has created a Lab department that is not connected to the corporate network. The Lab department will support computers for running tests on several applications prior to rolling them out to specific corporate desktops. Because the Lab department has several separate subnets and will not be connected to the corporate network, the systems engineer has designed the subnets in the Lab department to be connected to each other through routers.

You will enable and configure a server to run the Windows Server 2003 Routing and Remote Access service. You will verify routing at various times during configuration by using the **ping** command and documenting your results.

Practice

▶ **Disable the Classroom Network Connection**

■ Complete this task from the higher number student computer

1. Log on to the computer as *ComputerName***Admin** with the password of **P@ssw0rd** from the **nwtraders** domain.

2. In Network Connections, right-click **Classroom Network Connection**, and then click **Disable**.

3. Right-click **Partner Network Connection**, and then click **Properties**.

4. In the **Partner Network Connection Properties** dialog box, click **Internet Protocol (TCP/IP)**, and then click **Properties**.

5. Select **Use the following IP address**. In the **Default gateway** box, type the IP address of lower number student computers Partner Network Connection adapter, and then click **OK**.

6. Close the **Partner Network Connection Properties** dialog box.

7. Close the Network Connections window.

▶ **Verify routing to different computers**

● Complete this task from the higher number student computer

Action	Result
Use the **ping** command to attempt to connect to the IP address of the **Classroom Network Connection** of your partner's computer.	Successful
Use the **ping** command to attempt to connect to the IP address of the **Classroom Network Connection** of the **London** computer.	Unsuccessful
Use the **ping** command to attempt to connect to the IP address of the **Partner Network Connection** of the **Glasgow** computer.	Unsuccessful

▶ **Enable and configure routing on the server**

■ Complete this task from the lower number student computer

■ User account: *ComputerName***Admin**

■ Password: **P@ssw0rd**

■ Domain: **nwtraders**

► **Verify routing to different computers**

- Complete this task from the higher number student computer

Action	Result
Use the **ping** command to attempt to connect to the IP address of the **Classroom Network Connection** of your partner's computer.	Successful
Use the **ping** command to attempt to connect to the IP address of the **Classroom Network Connection** of the **London** computer.	Unsuccessful
Use the **ping** command to attempt to connect to the IP address of the **Partner Network Connection** of the **Glasgow** computer.	Unsuccessful

► **Add a routing protocol on the server**

- Complete this task from the lower number student computer

- Routing protocol: **RIP version 2**

► **Add two routing interfaces to the routing protocol on the server**

- Complete this task from the lower number student computer

- Routing protocol: **RIP version 2**

- Interface: **Classroom Network Connection**

- Interface: **Partner Network Connection**

► **Verify your configurations from the client**

- Complete this task from the higher number student computer

Action	Result
Use the **ping** command to attempt to connect to the IP address of the **Classroom Network Connection** of your partner's computer.	Successful
Use the **ping** command to attempt to connect to the IP address of the **Classroom Network Connection** of the **London** computer.	Successful
Use the **ping** command to attempt to connect to the IP address of the **Partner Network Connection** of the **Glasgow** computer.	Successful

Lesson: Configuring Packet Filters

* What Is Packet Filtering?
* How Packet Filters Are Applied
* How to Configure Packet Filters

Introduction

You can manage IP traffic to and from a host computer by using Transmission Control Protocol/Internet Protocol (TCP/IP) filtering. However, by configuring packet filtering on a router, you can control all IP traffic in a network that passes through that router.

Lesson objectives

After completing this lesson, you will be able to:

- Explain what packet filtering is.
- Describe how packet filters are applied.
- Configure packet filters.

What Is Packet Filtering?

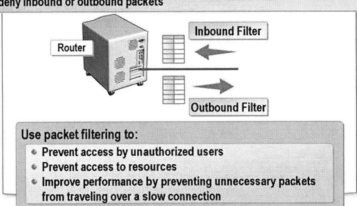

- *Packet filtering* specifies what type of traffic is allowed into and out of a router
- A *packet filter* is a TCP/IP configuration setting that is designed to allow or deny inbound or outbound packets

Router

Inbound Filter

Outbound Filter

Use packet filtering to:
- Prevent access by unauthorized users
- Prevent access to resources
- Improve performance by preventing unnecessary packets from traveling over a slow connection

---

Definition

Packet filtering prevents certain types of network packets from either being sent or received across a router.

A *packet filter* is a TCP/IP configuration setting that is designed to allow or deny inbound or outbound packets.

Filter configuration

Windows Server 2003 Routing and Remote Access supports IP packet filtering. By using Routing and Remote Access, you can specify packet filters per interface and then configure them to do one of the following:

- Pass through all traffic except packets that filters prohibit.

- Discard all traffic except packets that filters allow.

When configuring a packet filter, you first specify it as either an inbound filter or an outbound filter. You then select a filter action, either to accept all packets that the filter specifies or to drop all packets that the filter specifies.

Why use packet filtering?

You can use packet filtering to:

- Prevent access by unauthorized users.

- Prevent access to resources.

- Improve performance by preventing unnecessary packets from traveling over a slow connection.

Examples of using packet filters

For example, if you want to allow users on the Internet to connect to a Web server on your internal network through a Routing and Remote Access router, you can configure an inbound filter that allows only packets from TCP port 80 and the IP address of the Web server. No other packets would be accepted from the Internet.

If you want to restrict your internal network to allow access only to Web sites on the Internet that use port 80, you can create an outbound filter that only allows packets directed to TCP port 80. No other packets would be allowed past the Routing and Remote Access router.

How Packet Filters Are Applied

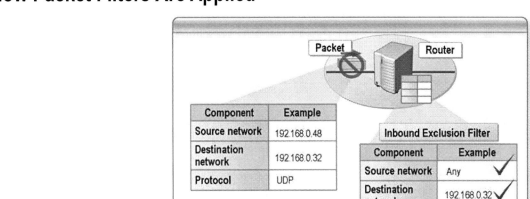

Introduction	You can set multiple parameters for an individual filter. You can also create a series of filters that indicate to the router the type of traffic that is allowed or disallowed on each configured interface. You can set these filters for both incoming and outgoing traffic.
When multiple parameters are applied to a particular filter	If multiple parameters are configured on a particular filter, then the parameters of the filter are compared through a logical AND when the filter is applied to the packet.
	For example, the fields in the packet must match all of the configured parameters of the filter. If the packet meets all of the parameters, then the filter's action to receive or drop is applied.
When multiple packet filters are configured	Because both the inbound and outbound filters can be defined for each interface, it is possible to create contradictory filters. When multiple filters are configured, the separate filters applied to the inbound or outbound packet are compared through a logical OR.
	For example, the input filter on one interface allows inbound traffic, but the outbound filter on the other interface does not allow the outbound traffic. The result is that the traffic is dropped and will not pass across the router. (If the packet matches at least one of the configured filters, it is received or dropped depending on the filter action setting.)

How packet filters are applied

Packet filters are applied by the following rules:

1. The inbound and outbound packets are checked against the packet filter on a router.

2. If the packet meets all of the first filter's parameters, then the filter action to receive or drop the packet is applied.

3. If the packet does not meet all of the first filter's parameters, then the packet is checked against the next packet filter on the router.

4. If none of the packet filters are applied and the router is configured with an exclusion filter, then the packet passes through the router. If the router is configured with an inclusion filter, then the packet is dropped and does not pass through the router.

How to Configure Packet Filters

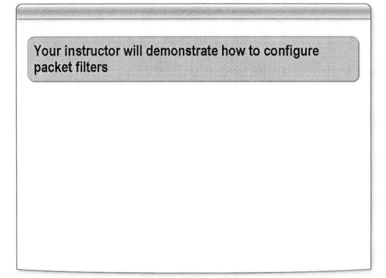

Introduction

To configure IP packet filtering in Windows Server 2003 Routing and Remote Access, you can create filters to allow or disallow certain types of traffic on a routing interface. If a packet does not meet a particular filter's requirements, it is discarded and not forwarded. Configuring a filter involves selecting an interface, specifying an input or output filter, and specifying a filter action.

> **Note** It is recommended that you log on by using an account that has non-administrative credentials and use the **Run as** command with a user account that has appropriate administrative credentials to perform this task.

Procedure

To configure packet filters:

1. In the Routing and Remote Access console, in the console tree, expand *ComputerName*, expand **IP Routing**, and then click **General**.

2. In the details pane, right-click the interface to which you want to add a filter, and then click **Properties**.

3. On the **General** tab, click either **Inbound Filters** or **Outbound Filters**, and then click **New**.

4. In the **Add IP Filter** dialog box, identify the source network by configuring the following settings:

    a. **IP address**. Type either the network ID of the source IP or a source IP address.

    b. **Subnet mask**. Type the subnet mask that corresponds to the source network ID, or type **255.255.255.255** for a source IP address.

5. In the **Add IP Filter** dialog box, identify the destination network by configuring the following settings:

   a. **IP address**. Type either the network ID of the destination IP or a destination IP address.

   b. **Subnet mask**. Type the subnet mask that corresponds to the destination network ID, or type **255.255.255.255** for a destination IP address.

Important The subnet mask bits for both the source and destination networks must encompass all of the bits that are being used in the **IP address** field. The IP address cannot be more specific than the subnet mask.

---

6. In the **Add IP Filter** dialog box, select the appropriate protocol:

   a. **TCP**. Select this option to specify a source TCP port and a destination TCP port.

   b. **TCP (established)**. Select this option to only include TCP packets that are part of a TCP connection that has been previously established.

   c. **UDP**. Select this option to specify a source UDP port and a destination UDP port.

Important When specifying the TCP and UDP protocols, you can provide one or both of the ports (source or destination) for either protocol. If you do not specify a port, the setting defaults to 0, meaning any port.

---

   d. **ICMP**. Select this option to specify ICMP code and an ICMP type.

Important You can specify either the protocol or the port, or both. If you do not specify a port, the setting defaults to 255, meaning any code or any type.

---

   e. **Any**. Select this option to make *any* IP protocol value applicable.

   f. **Other**. Select this option to specify any IP protocol.

Important You must specify the protocol by number. The file *%Systemroot%\System32\Drivers\Etc\Protocol* contains both a list of protocols that are compatible with the Windows Server 2003 family and the number for each protocol. You can enable Windows Server 2003 to recognize additional protocols by editing this file.

---

7. In the **Add IP Filter** dialog box, click **OK**.

8. In the **Filters** dialog box, select one of the following appropriate filter actions, and then click **OK**.

   a. **Receive all packets except those that meet the criteria below**

   b. **Drop all packets except those that meet the criteria below**

Important   After adding a filter, test your settings to make sure that the filters perform the action that you want and do not have any unintended side effects.

Note   To identify the ports that an application uses, see the documentation for that application. For a list of ports that Windows Server 2003 uses, see "Commonly Used Port Numbers," in **Additional Reading** on the Student Materials compact disc.

Practice: Configuring Packet Filters

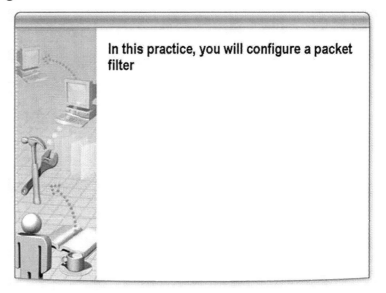

In this practice, you will configure a packet filter

Objective

In this practice, you will configure a packet filter.

Instructions

You must be logged on by using an account that has non-administrative credentials and use the **Run as** command by using a user account that has appropriate administrative credentials to complete the task.

Scenario

The systems engineer wants to connect the Lab department with a separate remote lab by using a router. To secure access to the remote lab, the systems engineer has designed IP packet filters for the router between the two labs.

You have installed and configured a server to run Windows Server 2003 Routing and Remote Access. Now you will configure a packet filter to secure access to the remote lab. You will also verify access to network resources both before and after configuring the packet filters.

Practice

▶ **Verify access to network resources**

- Complete this task from the higher number student computer

Action	Result
Use the **ping** command to attempt to connect to the IP address of the **Partner Network Connection** of the **Glasgow** computer.	Successful

▶ **Configure an inbound filter**

- Complete this task from the lower number student computer

- General interface: **Partner Network Connection**

- Filter type: **Inbound Filter**

- Destination network IP address: **192.168.100.2**

- Destination network subnet mask: **255.255.255.255**

- Protocol: **ICMP**

- Filter action: **Receive all packets except those that meet the criteria below**

▶ **Verify access to network resources on the client computer**

- Complete this task from the higher number student computer

Action	Result
Use the **ping** command to attempt to connect to the IP address of the **Partner Network Connection** of the **Glasgow** computer.	Unsuccessful

Lab A: Configuring Routing by Using Routing and Remote Access

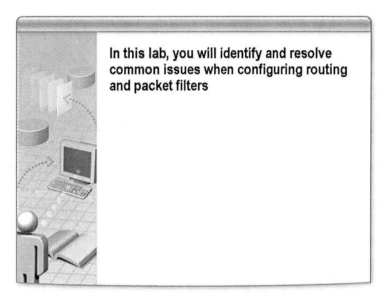

In this lab, you will identify and resolve common issues when configuring routing and packet filters

Objective

In this lab, you will be able to identify and resolve common issues when configuring routing and packet filters.

Estimated time to complete this lab: 30 minutes

Exercise 1
Identifying and Resolving Common Issues When Configuring Routing and Packet Filters

In this exercise, you will identify and resolve common issues when configuring routing and packet filters.

Instructions

To complete this lab, refer to the *Implementation Plan Values* document, located in the Appendix at the end of your student workbook.

You must be logged on by using an account that has non-administrative credentials and use the Run as command with a user account that has appropriate administrative credentials to complete the tasks. When completing the lab, assume that you will log on by using a non-administrative account (example: ComputerNameUser), unless the Specific Instructions in the lab state otherwise.

Scenario

Your test-lab users are experiencing problems with routing in their subnet. They are also having difficulty accessing the staging lab which exists in another subnet. You will use the **ping** command to identify the cause of the routing issues. You will then take the necessary corrective actions to restore routing. After performing the corrective actions, you will use the **ping** command again to validate connectivity both within and between the test and staging subnets.

Important At the end of the lab, the instructor must complete the following steps:

- Remove the Remote access/VPN server role from the London computer.

- Remove the default gateway value for the Partner Network Connection on the Glasgow computer.

- Enable the Classroom Network Connection on the Glasgow computer.

Tasks	Specific instructions
Perform the following task only on the computer with the higher student number.	
1. Verify routing to different computers by using the **ping** command.	■ Use the **ping** command to connect to the IP address of: <ul><li>The Classroom Network Connection of the London computer. The result should be successful.</li><li>The Partner Network Connection of the Glasgow computer. The result should be unsuccessful.</li><li>The Classroom Network Connection of your partner's computer. The result should be successful.</li></ul>
Perform the following task only on the computer with the lower student number. Use the **Run as** command to open a command prompt with administrative rights on the local computer to run the script.	
2. Re-create the routing issues that were experienced in the test lab by running the following script: **C:\Moc\2277\Labfiles\ Lab01\Routing.vbs**.	■ Close the Routing and Remote Access console, and then run the following script at a command prompt: **C:\Moc\2277\Labfiles\Lab01\Routing.vbs**.
Perform the following tasks only on the computer with the higher student number.	
3. Verify changes to routing to different computers by using the **ping** command.	■ Use the **ping** command to connect to the IP address of: <ul><li>The Classroom Network Connection of the London computer. The result should be unsuccessful.</li><li>The Partner Network Connection of the Glasgow computer. The result should be successful.</li><li>The Classroom Network Connection of your partner's computer. The result should be successful.</li></ul>
4. Verify that the default gateway IP address is correct.	■ If the default gateway value for the computer with the higher student number is incorrect, then perform the corrective action. (Refer to the *Implementation Plan Values* document.)

Tasks	Specific instructions
✋ Perform the following task only on the computer with the lower student number.	
5. Identify routing configuration issues and correctly configure routing and packet filters.	a. If both of the interfaces on the router are not already added to the RIP protocol, then add the **Partner Network Connection** interface and the **Classroom Network Connection** interface appropriately to the RIP protocol.
	b. If the **Partner Network Connection** interface is not configured with the correct packet filter, then remove any incorrect packet filters and use the following variables to add the correct packet filter:
	• General interface: **Partner Network Connection**
	• Filter type: **Inbound Filter**
	• Destination network IP address: **192.168.100.2**
	• Destination network subnet mask: **255.255.255.255**
	• Protocol: **ICMP**
	• Filter action: **Receive all packets except those that meet the criteria below**
✋ Perform the following task only on the computer with the higher student number.	
6. Verify routing connectivity by using the **ping** command.	▪ Use the **ping** command to connect to the IP address of:
	• The Classroom Network Connection of the London computer. The result should be successful.
	• The Partner Network Connection of the Glasgow computer. The result should be unsuccessful.
	• The Classroom Network Connection of your partner's computer. The result should be successful.
✋ Perform the following task only on the computer with the lower student number.	
7. Remove all packet filters and then remove Routing and Remote Access.	a. On the Partner Network Connection, delete any Inbound Filters.
	b. Remove Routing and Remote Access.
✋ Perform the following task only on the computer with the higher student number.	
8. Remove the default gateway IP address from the Partner Network Connection, and enable the Classroom Network Connection.	a. Log on to the computer as ComputerNameAdmin with the password of P@ssw0rd from the nwtraders domain.
	b. From Control Panel, open Network Connections.
	c. Right-click Partner Network Connection, and then click Properties.
	d. In the Partner Network Connection Properties dialog box, click Internet Protocol (TCP/IP), and then click Properties.
	e. In the Default gateway box, remove the IP address of your partner's Partner Network Connection adapter, and then click OK.
	f. Close the Partner Network Connection Properties dialog box.
	g. In Network Connections, right-click Classroom Network Connection and then click Enable.
	h. Close the Network Connections window.

Microsoft®
Training &
Certification

Module 2: Allocating IP Addressing by Using Dynamic Host Configuration Protocol (DHCP)

Contents

Overview

- Multimedia: The Role of DHCP in the Network Infrastructure
- Adding and Authorizing a DHCP Server Service
- Configuring a DHCP Scope
- Configuring a DHCP Reservation
- Configuring DHCP Options
- Configuring a DHCP Relay Agent

Introduction

A thorough understanding of Dynamic Host Configuration Protocol (DHCP) and how it functions will help you, as a systems administrator, effectively allocate Internet Protocol (IP) addressing in your network environment.

Objectives

After completing this module, you will be able to:

- Describe the role of DHCP in the network infrastructure.

- Add and authorize a DHCP Server service.

- Configure a DHCP scope.

- Configure DHCP options.

- Configure a DHCP reservation.

- Configure a DHCP relay agent.

Multimedia: The Role of DHCP in the Network Infrastructure

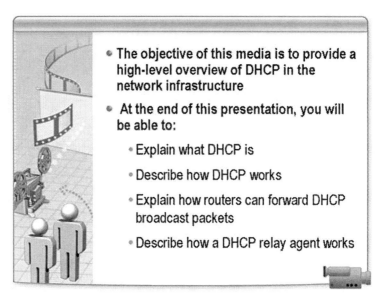

File location

To start the *The Role of DHCP in the Network Infrastructure* presentation, open the Web page on the Student Materials compact disc, click **Multimedia**, and then click the title of the presentation.

Objectives

At the end of this presentation, you will be able to:

- Explain what DHCP is.
- Describe how DHCP works.
- Explain how routers can forward DHCP broadcast packets.
- Describe how a DHCP relay agent works.

Key points

- All Transmission Control Protocol/Internet Protocol (TCP/IP) hosts, such as client computers or network devices, require TCP/IP address and configuration data; and you can use DHCP to assign automatically the TCP/IP configuration data to each TCP/IP host.

- TCP/IP configuration data can include: TCP/IP address, subnet mask, and additional IP data, such as router information and information on other types of servers.

- Systems administrators can either manually configure and maintain IP configuration for clients or use DHCP to dynamically assign, configure, and maintain the TCP/IP configuration data for each host.

- Because DHCP centrally manages address allocation, it both helps to prevent address conflicts and reduces administrative effort.

- You can configure routers to allow DHCP packets to be forwarded to remote subnets.

- You can use a relay agent to relay DHCP packets between clients and servers on separate subnets.

Lesson: Adding and Authorizing a DHCP Server Service

- Why Use DHCP?
- How DHCP Allocates IP Addresses
- How the DHCP Lease Generation Process Works
- How the DHCP Lease Renewal Process Works
- How to Add a DHCP Server Service
- How a DHCP Server Service Is Authorized
- How to Authorize a DHCP Server Service

Introduction

By learning about DHCP processes and how DHCP works, you can properly add a server role to a server and authorize the DHCP Server service for your network.

Lesson objectives

After completing this lesson, you will be able to:

- Explain the purpose of DHCP.
- Describe how DHCP allocates IP addresses.
- Describe how the DHCP lease generation process works.
- Describe how the DCHP lease renewal process works.
- Add the DHCP Server service.
- Describe how a DHCP Server service is authorized.
- Authorize the DHCP Server service.

Why Use DHCP?

DHCP reduces the complexity and amount of administrative work by using automatic TCP/IP configuration

Manual TCP/IP Configuration

- IP addresses are entered manually on each client computer
- Possibility of entering incorrect or invalid IP address
- Incorrect configuration can lead to communication and network issues
- Administrative overload on networks where computers are frequently moved

Automatic TCP/IP Configuration

- IP addresses are supplied automatically to client computers
- Ensures that clients always use correct configuration information
- Client configuration is updated automatically to reflect changes in network structure
- Eliminates a common source of network problems

Definition

Dynamic Host Configuration Protocol (DHCP) is an IP standard for simplifying management of host IP configuration. The DHCP standard allows you to use DHCP servers to manage dynamic allocation of IP addresses and other IP-related configuration data for DHCP-enabled clients on your network.

Why use DHCP?

For TCP/IP-based networks, DHCP reduces the complexity and amount of administrative work involved in reconfiguring computers.

To understand why DHCP is useful for configuring TCP/IP on client computers, it is helpful to compare manual TCP/IP configuration with automatic configuration, which uses DHCP.

Manual TCP/IP configuration

When you configure the IP configuration data for each host by manually typing information, such as the IP address, subnet mask, or default gateway, it can lead to typographical errors. These errors can cause communication problems or problems associated with duplicate IP addresses. Moreover, there is an administrative overhead on networks where computers are frequently moved from one subnet to another. In addition, when you need to change one IP value for several clients, you have to update each client's IP configuration.

Automatic TCP/IP configuration

When you configure the DHCP server to support DHCP clients, the DHCP server automatically supplies the configuration information to DHCP clients. It also ensures that network clients use correct configuration information. Furthermore, if you need to make a change to several clients' IP configuration data, you can make the change once on the DHCP server, and DCHP then automatically updates client configuration information to reflect the change.

Example

For example: you need to configure 100 computers with IP configuration information. Without DHCP, you would need to manually configure each of the 100 computers individually. In addition, you would have to keep track of what IP configuration information is on what client. If you have to make a change to the IP configuration of the clients, you would have to manually reconfigure the IP address configuration data on each computer.

With DHCP, you would add a single DHCP server role that would support all 100 network clients. When you needed to make a change to the IP configuration, you would have to make the change only once on the DHCP Server service, and then require each TCP/IP host to renew their DHCP client configuration.

How DHCP Allocates IP Addresses

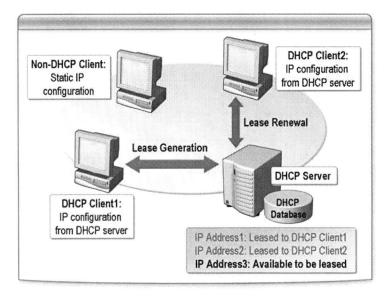

Introduction	DHCP allows you to manage IP address allocation from a central location. You can configure a DHCP server to allocate IP addresses either for a single subnet or for multiple subnets. The DHCP server can assign client IP address configuration data to clients automatically.
Definition	A *lease* is the length of time for which a DHCP client can use a dynamically assigned IP address configuration. Before the lease time expires, the client must either renew the lease or obtain a new lease from DHCP.
How DHCP allocates IP addresses	DHCP manages the assignment and release of the IP address configuration data by leasing the IP address configuration to the client. The DHCP lease states how long the client can use the IP configuration data before returning it to the DHCP server and then renewing the data. The process of assigning IP address configuration data is known as the *DHCP lease generation process*. The process of renewing the IP address configuration data is known as the *DHCP lease renewal process*.

The first time a DHCP client is added to the network, that client requests IP address configuration data from a DHCP server. When the DHCP server receives the client request, the server selects an IP address from a range of addresses that the administrator has defined in its scope. The DHCP server offers this IP address configuration data to the DHCP client.

If the client accepts the offer, the DHCP server leases the IP address to the client for a specified period of time. The client then uses the IP address configuration data to access the network.

How the DHCP Lease Generation Process Works

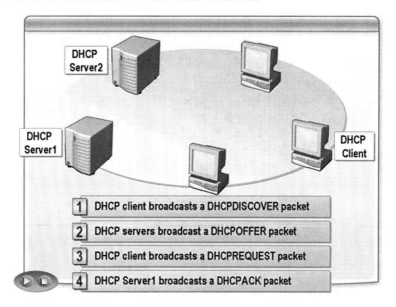

1	DHCP client broadcasts a DHCPDISCOVER packet
2	DHCP servers broadcast a DHCPOFFER packet
3	DHCP client broadcasts a DHCPREQUEST packet
4	DHCP Server1 broadcasts a DHCPACK packet

Introduction

DHCP uses a four-step process to lease IP addressing information to DCHP clients. The four steps are named after the DHCP packet types.

1. DHCP discover
2. DHCP offer
3. DHCP request
4. DHCP acknowledgement or DHCP negative acknowledgement

Definition

The *DHCP lease generation process* is the process by which the DHCP client receives IP addressing configuration data from the DHCP server.

The DHCP client broadcasts a DHCPDISCOVER packet

The DHCP client broadcasts a DHCPDISCOVER packet to locate a DHCP server. A DHCPDISCOVER packet is a message that DHCP clients send the first time that they attempt to log onto the network and request IP address information from a DHCP server.

There are two ways that the lease generation process can begin. The first occurs when a client computer either starts up or initializes TCP/IP for the first time. The second occurs when a client attempts to renew its lease and is denied. (For example, a client can be denied a renewal when you move it to another subnet.)

The DHCP server broadcasts a DHCPOFFER packet

Know

The DHCP server broadcasts a DHCPOFFER packet to the client. A DHCPOFFER packet is a message that DHCP servers use to offer the lease of an IP address to a DHCP client when it starts on the network.

Each responding DHCP server reserves the offered IP address in order not offer it to another DHCP client before the requesting client's acceptance.

If the client does not receive an offer after four requests, it uses an IP address in the reserved range from 169.254.0.1 to 169.254.255.254. The use of one of these auto-configured IP addresses ensures that clients located on a subnet with an unavailable DHCP server are able to communicate with each other. The DHCP client continues to attempt to find an available DHCP server every five minutes. When a DHCP server becomes available, clients receive valid IP addresses, allowing those clients to communicate with hosts both on and off their subnet.

The DHCP client broadcasts a DHCPREQUEST packet

The DHCP client broadcasts a DHCPREQUEST packet. A DHCPREQUEST packet is a message that a client sends to the DHCP server to request or renew the lease of the client's IP address.

The DHCP client responds to the first DHCPOFFER packet that it receives by broadcasting a DHCPREQUEST packet to accept the offer. The DHCPREQUEST packet includes the identification of the server whose offer the client accepted. All other DHCP servers then retract their offers and retain their IP addresses for other IP lease requests.

The DHCP server broadcasts a DHCPACK packet

The DHCP server broadcasts a DHCPACK packet to the client. A DHCPACK packet is a message that the DHCP server sends to a client to acknowledge and complete a client's request for leased configuration. This message contains a valid lease for the IP address and other IP configuration data.

When the DHCP client receives the acknowledgment, TCP/IP initializes by using the IP configuration data that the DHCP server provides. The client also binds the TCP/IP protocol to the network services and network adapter, permitting the client to communicate on the network.

The DHCP server sends a DHCP negative acknowledgement (DHCPNAK packet) if the IP address that was offered is no longer valid or is now in use by another computer. The client must then begin the lease process again.

Important   A DHCP server and a DHCP client communicate by using User Datagram Protocol (UDP) ports 67 and 68. Some switches do not properly forward DHCP broadcasts by default. For DHCP to function correctly, you may need to configure these switches to forward broadcasts over these ports.

How the DHCP Lease Renewal Process Works

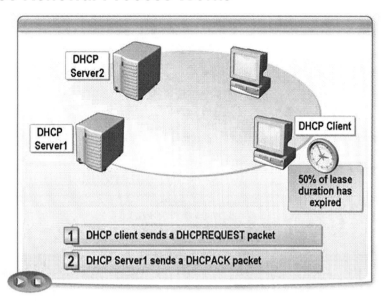

Definitions

8 days

The *DHCP lease renewal process* is the process by which the DHCP client renews or updates its IP address configuration data with the DHCP server.

Purpose of the DHCP lease renewal process

The DHCP client renews its IP configuration data prior to the expiration of the lease time. If the lease period expires and the DHCP client has not yet renewed its IP configuration data, then the DHCP client loses the IP configuration data and begins the DHCP lease generation process again.

Lease period

The lease renewal process is the result of the lease period value. The lease period value ensures that DHCP maintains the IP address information and that clients regularly update or renew their IP address configuration data. Having DHCP maintain this information means that you can manage IP addressing from the DHCP server.

The client must renew its IP configuration data before the lease period expires. At specific intervals, a DHCP client attempts to renew its lease to ensure that it has up-to-date configuration information.

At any time during the lease period, the DHCP client can send a DHCPRELEASE packet to the DHCP server to release the IP address configuration data and to cancel any remaining lease.

Automatic lease renewal process

A DHCP client automatically attempts to renew its lease as soon as 50 percent of the lease duration has expired. The DHCP client will also attempt to renew its IP address lease each time that the computer restarts. To attempt a lease renewal, the DHCP client sends a DHCPREQUEST packet directly to the DHCP server from which the client obtained the lease.

If the DHCP server is available, it renews the lease and sends the client a DHCPACK packet with the new lease duration and any updated configuration parameters. The client updates its configuration when it receives the acknowledgment. If the DHCP server is unavailable, the client continues to use its current configuration parameters.

If the DHCP client fails to renew its lease the first time, then the DHCP client broadcasts a DHCPDISCOVER packet to update its address lease when 87.5 percent of the current lease duration expires. At this stage, the DHCP client accepts a lease that any DHCP server has issued.

Note   If a client requests an invalid or duplicate address for the network, a DHCP server can respond with a DHCP denial message (DHCPNAK packet). This forces the client to release its IP address and obtain a new, valid address.

If the DHCP client restarts on a network where no DHCP server responds to the DHCPREQUEST packet, the DHCP client will attempt to connect to the configured default gateway. If the attempt to connect to the default gateway fails, the client will cease using the leased address.

If a DHCP server responds with a DHCPOFFER packet to update the client's current lease, the client can renew its lease based on the server that offered the message and continue operation.

If the lease expires, the client must immediately discontinue its use of the current IP address. The DHCP client then begins the DHCP lease discovery process in an attempt to lease a new IP address. If the DHCP client fails to receive an address, the client will assign itself an address by using automatic IP address assignment in the 169.254.0.0 range.

Manual lease renewal

You can renew an IP lease manually if you need to update DHCP configuration information immediately. (For example: if you want DHCP clients to obtain immediately the address of a newly installed router from a DHCP server, renew the lease from the client to update its information.)

How to Add a DHCP Server Service

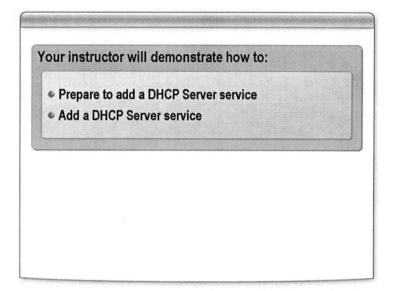

Introduction

To add a DHCP server, you must install the DHCP service on a computer running Microsoft® Windows® Server 2003.

Note It is recommended that you log on with an account that has non-administrative credentials and use the **Run as** command with a user account that has appropriate administrative credentials to perform this task.

Guidelines for preparing to add a DHCP Server service

Before adding a DHCP Server service:

- Verify that the IP address configuration on the server is correct.
- Verify that the user account has the correct permissions.

Procedure

To add a DHCP Server service:

1. Log on by using a non-administrative user account.
2. Click **Start**, and then click **Control Panel**.
3. In Control Panel, open **Administrative Tools**, and right-click **Manage Your Server**, and then select **Run as**.
4. In the **Run As** dialog box, select **The following user**, type a user account and password that have the appropriate permissions to complete the task, and then click **OK**.
5. In the Manage Your Server window, click **Add or remove a role**.
6. On the **Preliminary Steps** page, click **Next**.
7. In the Configure Your Server Wizard, select **DHCP server**, and then click **Next**.

8. On the **Summary of Selections** page, click **Next**.

9. In the New Scope Wizard, click **Cancel** to discontinue creating a scope at this time.

Note   To learn how to configure a scope, see the Configuring a DHCP Scope lesson, in this module.

---

10. In the Configure Your Server Wizard, click **Finish**.

How a DHCP Server Service Is Authorized

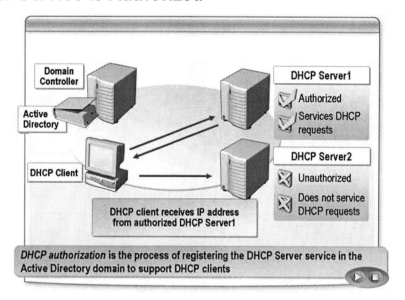

DHCP authorization is the process of registering the DHCP Server service in the Active Directory domain to support DHCP clients

---

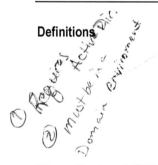

Definitions

① Requires Active Dir.
② must be in a Domain environment

DHCP authorization is the process of registering the DHCP Server service in the domain for Active Directory® directory service for the purpose of supporting DHCP clients. DHCP authorization is only for DHCP servers running Windows Server 2003 and Windows 2000 in an Active Directory domain.

An *authorized DHCP server* is a DHCP server that has been authorized in Active Directory to support DHCP clients.

Why authorize a DHCP server?

Authorizing a DHCP server provides you with the ability to control the addition of DHCP servers to the domain.

Authorization must occur before a DHCP server can issue leases to DHCP clients. Requiring authorization of the DHCP servers prevents unauthorized DHCP servers from offering potentially invalid IP addresses to clients.

If you are configuring a DHCP server, authorization must occur as part of an Active Directory domain. If you do not authorize the DHCP server in the Active Directory domain, the DHCP service will fail to start properly, and then the DHCP server will not be able to support requests from DHCP clients.

A DHCP server controls IP addressing configuration data that is sent to DHCP clients in a given network environment. If a DHCP server is improperly configured, then the clients that receive incorrect IP address configuration data from this DHCP server will also be also incorrect.

Why an authorized DHCP server requires Active Directory

Active Directory is required to authorize a DHCP server. With Active Directory, unauthorized DHCP servers will not be able to support DHCP clients. The DHCP Server service, on a server that is a member of Active Directory, checks with the Active Directory domain controller to verify that the DHCP server is registered in Active Directory. If the DHCP server is not registered, then the DHCP Server service does not start, and therefore the DHCP server cannot support DHCP clients.

Example

When the member server named DHCP Server1 starts, it checks with the domain controller to obtain a list of authorized DHCP servers in the domain. If DHCP Server1 finds its own IP address on the list, the service starts and can support DHCP clients.

When the member server named DHCP Server2 checks the list, it does not find its own IP address on the list of authorized DHCP servers for the domain. Consequently, the DHCP Server service does not start and it cannot support DHCP clients.

Stand-alone DHCP server

Under certain circumstances, a DHCP server running Windows 2000 or Windows Server 2003 initializes even if it is not authorized. If a DHCP server running Windows Server 2003 or Windows 2000 is installed as a stand-alone server that is not a member of Active Directory, and if it is located on a subnet where DHCPINFORM will not be transmitted to other authorized DHCP servers, then the DHCP Server service will start and provide leases to the clients on the subnet. A stand-alone server running Windows 2000 or Windows Server 2003 will broadcast DHCPINFORM packets. If there is no response to the DHCPINFORM packet, then the DHCP Server service will initialize and begin servicing clients. If an authorized DHCP server hears the DHCPINFORM packet and responds with a DHCPACK, then the DHCP Server service will stop. The stand-alone DCHP server will continue functioning if it receives a DHCPACK from another DHCP server that is not a member of the Active Directory.

How to Authorize a DHCP Server Service

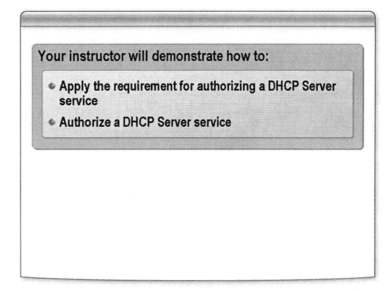

Your instructor will demonstrate how to:

- Apply the requirement for authorizing a DHCP Server service
- Authorize a DHCP Server service

Introduction

To authorize a DHCP Server service, a member of the Enterprise Administrators group adds the DHCP server to a list of DHCP servers, which can service DHCP clients, in the domain. The authorization process only works with servers running Windows Server 2003 and Windows 2000 in a domain. Authorization is not possible if DHCP servers are running earlier versions of Microsoft Windows NT® or other DHCP server software.

Note It is recommended that you be logged on with an account that has non-administrative credentials and use the **Run as** command with a user account that has appropriate administrative credentials to perform the task.

Requirement for authorizing a DHCP Server service

To authorize the DHCP Server service, the DHCP server must be authorized in an Active Directory domain environment. To authorize the DHCP server in Active Directory, you must authorize the DHCP server by using a user account that has appropriate permissions. By default, members of the Domain Administrators group can authorize DHCP servers.

Procedure

To authorize a DHCP Server service:

Note The task of authorizing the DHCP Server service typically occurs after the DHCP server has been both installed and configured. However, for learning purposes, this module teaches how to authorize a DHCP server prior to configuring the DHCP server so that the student will be able to complete the remaining practices.

1. Open the DHCP console.

2. In the console tree, select the server.

3. On the **Action** menu, click **Authorize**.

4. To verify that the DHCP server is authorized: in the console tree, press F5 to refresh the view, and verify that the DHCP server now displays with a green up arrow.

Practice: Adding and Authorizing a DHCP Server Service

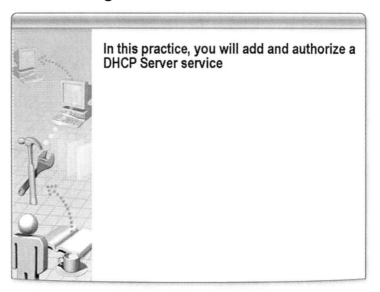

In this practice, you will add and authorize a DHCP Server service

Objectives

In this practice, you will add and authorize a DHCP Server service.

Instructions

To complete this practice, refer to the *Implementation Plan Values* document, located in the Appendix at the end of your student workbook.

You must be logged on with an account that has non-administrative credentials and use the **Run as** command with a user account that has appropriate administrative credentials to complete the task.

Scenario

The systems engineer has approved a new subnet for the Lab department. This new subnet will support computers for running tests on several applications prior to installing the applications on selected corporate desktops. The systems engineer has approved the installation of a new DHCP server to provide addressing to the new subnet. The systems engineer has sent an e-mail confirming that you have authorization privileges.

Practice

▶ **Add the DHCP server**

■ Complete this task from both student computers.

■ User account: *ComputerName***Admin**

■ Password: **P@ssw0rd**

■ Domain: **nwtraders**

■ Note: Do not configure a scope at this time.

Note   To practice configuring a scope, see the Configuring a DHCP Scope lesson in this module.

▶ **Authorize the DHCP Server service**

- Complete this task from both student computers.

- User account: *ComputerName***Admin**

- Password: **P@ssw0rd**

- Domain: **nwtraders**

- Why did **Authorize** not display on the **Action** menu?

  _____

  _____

- User account: **DHCPAdmin**

- Password: **P@ssw0rd**

- Domain: **nwtraders**

- Close the DHCP console.

Lesson: Configuring a DHCP Scope

- What Are DHCP Scopes?
- How to Configure a DHCP Scope

Introduction

By learning about what scopes are and how they work, you can properly configure a DHCP scope for your network.

Lesson objectives

After completing this lesson, you will be able to:

- Explain what DHCP scopes are.
- Configure a DHCP scope.

What Are DHCP Scopes?

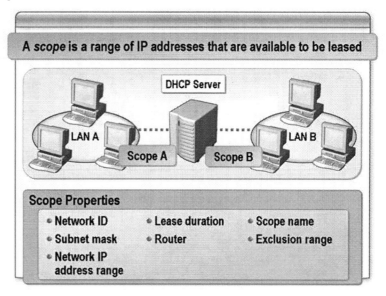

Definition	A *scope* is a range of valid IP addresses that are available for lease or assignment to client computers on a particular subnet. You configure a scope on the DHCP server to determine the pool of IP addresses that the server can assign to DHCP clients.
Why use DHCP scopes?	Scopes determine which IP addresses are allocated to the clients. You must define and activate a scope before DHCP clients can use the DHCP server for dynamic TCP/IP configuration. You can configure as many scopes on a DHCP server as needed for your network environment.
Scope properties	A scope has the following properties.

Scope property	Description
Network ID	The Network ID for the range of IP addresses
Subnet mask	The subnet mask for the Network ID
Network IP address range	The range of IP addresses that are available to clients
Lease duration	The period of time that the DHCP server holds a leased IP address for a client before removing the lease
Router	A DHCP option that allows DHCP clients to access remote networks
Scope name	An alphanumeric identifier for administrative purposes
Exclusion range	The range of IP addresses in the scope that are excluded from being leased

Cannot be edited

Each subnet can have a single DHCP scope that has a single continuous range of IP addresses. Specific addresses or groups of addresses can be excluded from the range that the DHCP scope specifies. Normally, only one scope can be assigned to a subnet. If more than one scope is required on a subnet, the scopes must first be created, and then combined into a superscope.

Note For information about superscopes and multicast scopes, refer to the Windows Server 2003 Help documentation.

To provide fault-tolerance, more than one DHCP server may be configured to provide IP address leases for a particular subnet. A scope is configured on each DHCP server for the specified subnet. It is important in this configuration to make sure that the address pool is divided between the two scopes. An IP address lease should never appear in more than one scope, or it would be possible that two different DHCP servers would attempt to lease the same IP address.

Example

If you have two physical subnets (as illustrated in the slide), you may create two separate scopes for the two separate subnets on one DHCP server. You would create separate scopes because the subnets have different IP addressing schemes and different option needs.

The following table provides an example of the scope properties and values for one of these subnets. This solution for subnets includes a physical network that serves 12 lab computers. The lab computers will be rebuilt every two days.

Scope property	Scope values
Network ID	192.168.0.32
Subnet mask	255.255.255.240 /28
Network IP address range	192.168.0.33 to 192.168.0.46
Lease duration	2 days
Router	192.168.0.33
Scope name	Test Lab Scope
Exclusion range	192.168.0. 33 (for the router)

How to Configure a DHCP Scope

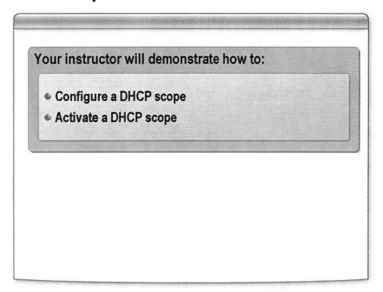

Introduction

After adding the DHCP server role, the next task is to configure a DHCP scope. You can either configure a DHCP scope while you are adding the DHCP server role, or at a later time after you added the role.

Note   It is recommended that you log on with an account that has non-administrative credentials and use the **Run as** command with a user account that has appropriate administrative credentials to perform this task.

Procedure for configuring DHCP scopes

To configure a DHCP scope:

1. Open the DHCP console.

2. In the console tree, click the applicable DHCP server.

3. On the **Action** menu, click **New Scope**.

4. In the **New Scope Wizard**, click **Next**.

5. On the **Scope Name** page, configure the **Name** and **Description**.

6. On the **IP Address Range** page, configure the **Start IP address, End IP address**, and **Subnet mask**.

7. On the **Add Exclusions** page, configure the **Start IP address** and **End IP address** if applicable. If there is only one IP address exclusion, configure only that IP address as the Start IP address.

8. On the **Lease Duration** page, configure the **Days, Hours**, and **Minutes**.

Tip   The default lease duration is 8 days.

9. On the **Configure DHCP Options** page, select **No, I will configure these options later**.

Note   For the purpose of instruction, you are not configuring the router, the domain name and DNS server, and the WINS server options at this time.

---

10. On the **Completing the New Scope Wizard** page, click **Finish**.

Note   Notice that the **Completing the New Scope Wizard** page instructs you to configure options and to activate the scope to complete the process.

Procedure for activating a DHCP scope

To activate a DHCP scope:

■   In the console tree, right-click the applicable scope, and then click **Activate**.

Important   Activate the scope only *after* configuring the scope and any applicable options.

Practice: Configuring a DHCP Scope

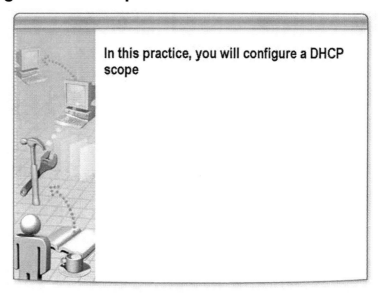

In this practice, you will configure a DHCP scope

Objectives

In this practice, you will configure a DHCP scope.

Instructions

To complete this practice, refer to the *Implementation Plan Values* document, located in the Appendix at the end of your student workbook.

You must be logged on with an account that has non-administrative credentials and use the **Run as** command with a user account that has appropriate administrative credentials to complete the task.

Scenario

75 additional computers are being added to the Lab department. The systems engineer has designed a new DHCP scope to provide IP address allocation for the additional computers. You will configure the DHCP server with this new scope to support the new computers in the lab.

Practice

▶ **Configure a DHCP scope**

- Complete this task from both student computers.

- Scope name: *ComputerName* **Scope** (where *ComputerName* is the name of your partner's computer)

- Start IP address: the IP address of your partner's Partner Network Connection

- End IP address: the IP address of your partner's Partner Network Connection

- Subnet Length: **24**

- Lease duration: **1 hour**

- Options: **None**

Note   For the purpose of instruction, you are using only one IP address in the scope for your partner. You are not configuring the router, the domain name and DNS server, and the WINS server options at this time.

- Activate the DHCP scope.

▶ **Obtain a DHCP leased IP address**

- Complete this task from: the higher number student computer.

- User account: *ComputerName***Admin**

- Password: **P@ssw0rd**

- Domain: **nwtraders**

▶ **Configure the Partner Network Connection TCP/IP configuration to obtain an IP address automatically.**

- Use the **ipconfig /renew** command to obtain an IP address from the DHCP server.

- Using the **ipconfig /all** command, verify that the DHCP server IP address for the Partner Network Connection is the IP address of the DHCP server's Partner Network Connection.

▶ **Verify the DHCP leased IP address**

- Complete this task from: the lower number student computer.

- In the DHCP console, click **Address Leases** in the console tree, and then verify that *ComputerName* displays (where *ComputerName* is the name of your partner's computer).

Lesson: Configuring a DHCP Reservation

* What Is a DHCP Reservation?
* How to Configure a DHCP Reservation

Introduction

By learning about DHCP reservations and how they work, you can properly configure a DHCP reservation for your network.

Lesson objectives

After completing this lesson, you will be able to:

- Explain what a DHCP reservation is.
- Configure a DHCP reservation.

What Is a DHCP Reservation?

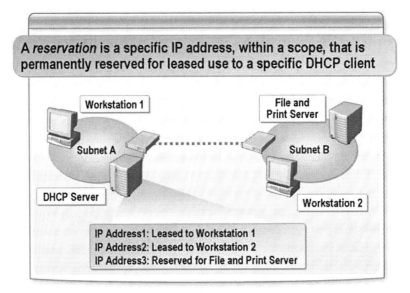

Definition	A *reservation* is a permanent IP address assignment. It is a specific IP address, within a scope, that is permanently reserved for leased use to a specific DHCP client.
Why use a DHCP reservation?	You can use reservations for DHCP-enabled devices that need to have the same IP address on your network, such as file and print servers or other application servers.
Characteristics	A reservation consists of the following information.

Element	Description
Reservation name	Name that the administrator assigns
IP address	IP address from the scope for the client
MAC address	Client's media access control (MAC) address (entered without hyphens)
Description	Description that the administrator assigns
Supported type	DHCP reservation, Boot Protocol (BOOTP) reservation, or both

Lease period for a reservation	Reservations use the same lease period value as the scope. Therefore, the client that uses the reservation goes through the same lease renewal process as the other clients in the scope, except that the IP address that was reserved for the client is leased to the client.
Example	Referring to the example in the slide, a reservation is made for the server that has the role of File and Print server.
	The IP address assigned for the File and Print server will remain assigned to that server until the network administrator removes the reservation.

How to Configure a DHCP Reservation

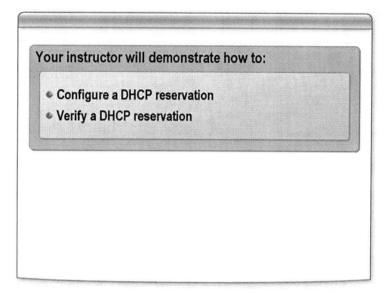

Introduction

You can configure a DHCP reservation when you need to reserve a permanent IP address assignment. You then verify that the reservation is active.

Note It is recommended that you log on with an account that has non-administrative credentials and use the **Run as** command with a user account that has appropriate administrative credentials to perform this task.

Procedure for configuring a DHCP reservation

To configure a DHCP reservation:

1. Open the DHCP console.

2. In the console tree, click **Reservations**.

3. On the **Action** menu, click **New Reservation**.

4. In the **New Reservation** dialog box, provide the values for the following fields:

   a. Reservation name

   b. IP address

   c. MAC address (without hyphens)

   d. Description

5. Under **Supported types**, select one of the following options:

   a. Both

   b. DHCP only

   c. BOOTP only

6. In the **New Reservations** dialog box, click **Add**, and then click **Close**.

Procedure for verifying the DHCP reservation

To verify the DHCP reservation:

1. On the client computer, at a command prompt, using the **ipconfig /release** command, release the client's IP address.

2. On the server computer, in the DHCP console, under **Address Leases**, verify that the reservation displays as inactive.

3. On the client computer, at a command prompt, using the **ipconfig /renew** command, renew the client's IP address.

4. On the server computer, in the DHCP console, under **Address Leases**, verify that the reservation displays as active.

Practice: Configuring a DHCP Reservation

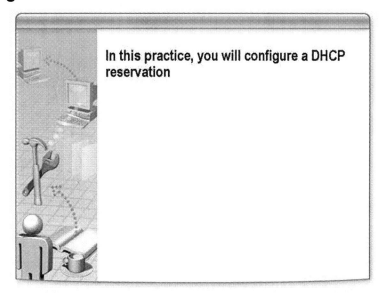

Objectives

In this practice, you will configure a DHCP reservation.

Instructions

To complete this practice, refer to the *Implementation Plan Values* document, located in the Appendix at the end of your student workbook.

You must be logged on with an account that has non-administrative credentials and use the **Run as** command with a user account that has appropriate administrative credentials to complete the task.

Scenario

The Lab department has just received a new File and Print server for testing. The systems engineer asked that this server be configured with a reservation. You will configure this DHCP reservation from the scope that was already created on the DHCP server.

Practice

▶ **Configure a DHCP reservation**

- Complete this task from both student computers.

- Reservation name: *ComputerName* (where *ComputerName* is the name of your partner's computer)

- IP address: the IP address of your partner's Partner Network Connection

- MAC address: the MAC address of your partner's Partner Network Connection

- Description: **Client Reservation**

- Supported types: **DHCP only**

► **Obtain the DHCP lease reservation**

■ Complete this task from the higher number student computer.

1. Use the **ipconfig /renew** command to obtain an IP address from the DHCP server.

2. Using the **ipconfig /all** command, verify that the DHCP server IP address for the Partner Network Connection is the IP address of the DHCP server's Partner Network Connection.

► **Verify the DHCP reservation**

■ Complete this task from the lower number student computer.

■ In the DHCP console, under **Address Leases**, verify that the reservation displays as active.

► **Delete the DHCP reservation**

■ Complete this task from the lower number student computer.

■ In the DHCP console, under **Address Leases**, delete the client reservation.

► **Obtain a DHCP leased IP address**

■ Complete this task from the higher number student computer.

1. Use the **ipconfig /release** command to release the IP address from the DHCP server.

2. Use the **ipconfig /renew** command to renew the IP address from the DHCP server.

3. Using the **ipconfig /all** command, verify that the DHCP server IP address for the Partner Network Connection is the IP address of the DHCP server's Partner Network Connection.

Lesson: Configuring DHCP Options

* What Are DHCP Options?
* How DHCP Server, Scope, and Reserved Client Options Are Applied
* How DHCP Class-level Options Are Applied
* How to Configure DHCP Options

Introduction

By learning about how DHCP options work, you can properly configure DHCP options for your network.

Lesson objectives

After completing this lesson, you will be able to:

■ Explain what DHCP options are.

■ Describe how DHCP server, scope, and reserved client options are applied.

■ Describe how DHCP class-level options are applied.

■ Configure DHCP options.

What Are DHCP Options?

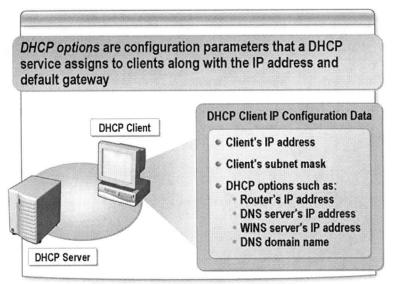

DHCP options are configuration parameters that a DHCP service assigns to clients along with the IP address and default gateway

DHCP Client

DHCP Server

DHCP Client IP Configuration Data

- Client's IP address
- Client's subnet mask
- DHCP options such as:
  - Router's IP address
  - DNS server's IP address
  - WINS server's IP address
  - DNS domain name

Definition

DHCP options are configuration parameters that a DHCP service assigns to clients when it assigns the IP address and default gateway.

Why use DHCP options?

An option allows increased functionality on the network. The lease generation process provides the DHCP client with an IP address and a subnet mask. DHCP options allow you to configure additional IP configuration data for your DHCP clients.

Common DHCP options

The following table describes the common options that you can configure.

Option	Description
Router (Default Gateway)	The addresses of any default gateway or router. This router is commonly referred to as the default gateway.
Domain name	A DNS domain name defines the domain to which a client computer belongs. The client computer can use this information to update a DNS server so that other computers can locate the client.
DNS and WINS servers	The addresses of any DNS and WINS servers for clients to use for network communication.

How DHCP Server, Scope, and Reserved Client Options Are Applied

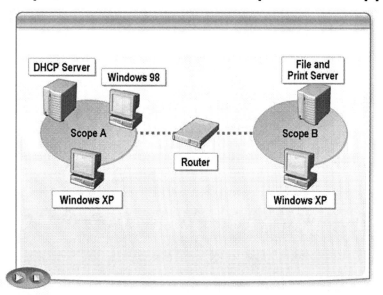

Why use levels of DHCP options?

DHCP applies options to client computers in a specific order:

1. Server level
2. Scope level
3. Class level
4. Reserved client level

As a result, you can define DHCP-assigned options with varying levels of authority so that certain options take precedence over other options.

How DHCP options are applied

How options are applied relates directly to where they are configured. The following table describes the levels of DHCP options and their precedence.

DHCP option	Precedence
Server-level option	A server-level option is assigned to all DHCP clients of the DHCP server.
Scope-level option	A scope-level option is assigned to all clients of a scope.
Class-level option	A class-level option is assigned to all clients that identify themselves as members of a class.
Reserved client-level option	A reservation-level option is assigned to one DHCP client.

For example, the server option makes the largest impact (by affecting all clients that the DHCP server supports), while the reserved client-level option makes the least amount of impact (by affecting only one client that the DHCP server supports).

If you create a reservation for a specific computer, you can assign a reserved client-level option that will then apply only to that reservation. By using reservations and reserved client-level options, you can map specific options to specific computers.

Example

Referring to the first example in the slide, the DHCP server-level option has been applied to both Scope A and Scope B, in addition to the DHCP server, Scope B's File and Print server, and all clients.

In the second example, the DHCP scope-level option has been applied to Scope B, in addition to Scope B's File and Print server and the Windows XP client.

In the third example, the DHCP reserved client-level option has been applied only to the File and Print server.

Additional examples

The following three examples each use a server, scope, or reserved client-level option.

- By using an option at the *server level*, you can configure all clients to use the same DNS server or WINS server. For example, you may have only one DNS server or WINS server for a large number of client computers and want to configure the option only once. If you configure a server-level option, all scopes and reservations inherit this option. As a result, you can configure servers once for multiple uses.

- By using an option at the *scope level*, you can define a unique router address for each scope, when each subnet requires a unique scope. For example, it is common to create one scope per physical subnet. If you create one scope per physical subnet, then each subnet will have at least one unique router value.

- By using an option at the *reserved client level*, you can configure a specified DHCP client to use a specific router to access resources outside the client's subnet You might want to create a reserved client-level option of a dedicated router for a computer that always needs to test access across the router.

How DHCP Class-level Options Are Applied

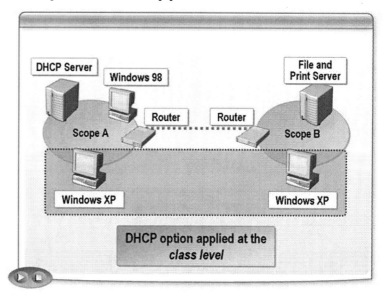

How DHCP class-level options are applied	Class options are added on to the server, scope, or reserved client-level option. Their settings are applied to a subset of DHCP clients that match the class ID.

Why use class-level options?

Class-level options are most often used either to override or to augment standard DHCP option values that are set at either the server, scope, or reserved client level.

Types of class-level options

Class-level options apply to any DHCP client that identifies itself as a member of the class. You can use vendor- and user-class options to provide unique configurations to specific types of client computers.

- *Vendor-class* is an administrative feature that allows DHCP clients to be identified and leased according to their vendor and hardware configuration types.

- *User-class* is an administrative feature that allows DHCP clients to be grouped logically according to a shared or common identifier.

Vendor classes

Vendor-class options identify the vendor type of a DHCP client's operating system and its configuration, and provide unique options that are only applicable to the specified vendor class. You can configure vendor class options to manage DHCP options that are specific to the vendor type and are assigned to clients of that vendor type. Vendor options are not used to configure standard TCP/IP options, but rather to configure options specific to the vendor type.

You can also define additional vendor identifiers on the DHCP server if they are provided in the vendor's DHCP client software. Before you configure additional vendor-class options, you must determine which identifier, if any, a specific vendor uses; you can do this by contacting the vendor of the client operating system or network software. The administrator cannot add vendor identifiers on the DHCP client; vendor identifiers are written into the TCP/IP protocol program code.

Examples of vendor classes

The three default vendor identifiers in a DHCP server running Windows Server 2003 are:

- Microsoft Windows 2000 Options
- Microsoft Windows 98 Options
- Microsoft Options

For example, one of the vendor class options that is supported by Windows 2000 and later is Microsoft Disable NetBIOS Option which disables network basic input/output system (NetBIOS) over TCP/IP. Enabling this option would disable network basic input/output system (NetBIOS) over TCP/IP for all Windows 2000 or later clients on the scope or server on which the option is defined.

User classes

User-class options provide a property that assists a DHCP server in identifying a DHCP client that belongs to a specified group. You assign user class options to a client based on an identifier, and the client sends this identifier to the DHCP server to identify itself.

You configure user class options to manage DHCP options that you want to assign to clients that require a common configuration.

Examples of user classes

A user-class option could be configured to identify a group of computers (such as kiosks, notebooks, or the computers in a computer lab). For example: you can configure user-class options to provide a shorter lease time for notebooks that are dial-in clients, to return the addresses to the IP address lease pool more quickly.

There are two default user-class identifiers that are configured on DHCP clients running Windows Server2003.

- Default Routing and Remote Access Class
- Default BOOTP Client Class

These classes cannot be deleted or modified.

Note For more information about configuring class-based options, see the Windows Server 2003 resource kit.

How to Configure DHCP Options

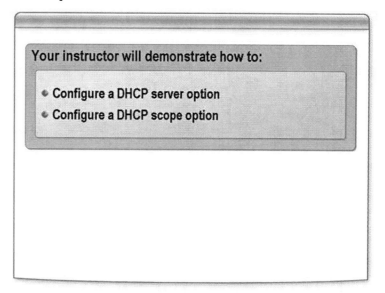

Your instructor will demonstrate how to:

- Configure a DHCP server option
- Configure a DHCP scope option

Introduction

After configuring a DHCP scope, the next task is to configure DHCP options. You can either configure DHCP options while you are configuring a DHCP scope, or at a later time after configuring a DHCP scope.

Note It is recommended that you log on with an account that has non-administrative credentials and use the **Run as** command with a user account that has appropriate administrative credentials to perform this task.

Procedure for configuring DHCP server options

To configure a DHCP server option:

1. Open the DHCP console.

2. In the console tree, under the server name, click **Server Options**.

3. On the **Action** menu, click **Configure Options**.

4. In the **Server Options** dialog box, in the list of **Available Options**, select the option that you want to configure.

5. Under **Data entry**, complete the information that is required to configure this option.

6. In the **Server Options** dialog box, click **OK**.

Procedure for configuring DHCP scope options

To configure a DHCP scope option:

1. Open the DHCP console, and, under the appropriate scope, click **Scope Options**.

2. On the **Action** menu, click **Configure Options**.

3. In the **Scope Options** dialog box, in the list of **Available Options**, select the option that you want to configure.

4. Under **Data entry**, complete the information that is required to configure this option.

5. In the **Scope Options** dialog box, click **OK**.

Practice: Configuring DHCP Options

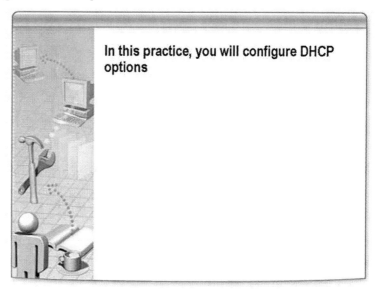

Objectives

In this practice, you will configure DHCP options.

Instructions

To complete this practice, refer to the *Implementation Plan Values* document, located in the Appendix at the end of your student workbook.

You must be logged on with an account that has non-administrative credentials and use the **Run as** command with a user account that has appropriate administrative credentials to complete the task.

Scenario

The Lab department has just received a new DNS server for testing. The systems engineer has asked that any new scopes that are configured on the DHCP server for the Lab department use this new DNS server as the DNS option. In addition, the Lab scope needs to reflect the addition of two new WINS servers that were added to the Lab department. You will configure these options on the DHCP server.

Practice

▶ **Configure DHCP options at the scope level**

- Complete this task from both student computers.

- Option level: **Scope**

- Option: **003 Router**

- Option IP address: the IP address of your Partner Network Connection

▶ **Obtain the DHCP scope option**

- Complete this task from the higher number student computer.

1. Use the **ipconfig /renew** command to obtain an IP address from the DHCP server.

2. Using the **ipconfig /all** command, verify that the default gateway IP address for the Partner Network Connection is the IP address of the DHCP server's Partner Network Connection.

Lesson: Configuring a DHCP Relay Agent

* What Is a DHCP Relay Agent?
* How a DHCP Relay Agent Works
* How a DHCP Relay Agent Uses Hop Count
* How a DHCP Relay Agent Uses Boot Threshold
* How to Configure a DHCP Relay Agent

Introduction

By learning about the DHCP relay agent and how it works, you can properly configure a DHCP relay agent for your network.

Note In most cases, routers support DHCP/BOOTP relay. Alternatively, if a router cannot function as a DHCP/BOOTP relay agent, a DHCP relay agent may be the solution.

Lesson objectives

After completing this lesson, you will be able to:

■ Explain what a DHCP relay agent is.

■ Describe how a DHCP relay agent works.

■ Describe how a DHCP relay agent uses hop count.

■ Describe how a DHCP relay agent uses boot threshold.

■ Configure a DHCP relay agent.

What Is a DHCP Relay Agent?

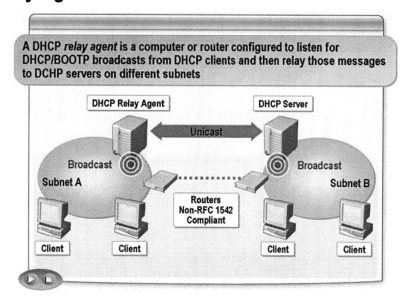

A DHCP *relay agent* is a computer or router configured to listen for DHCP/BOOTP broadcasts from DHCP clients and then relay those messages to DCHP servers on different subnets

Definition

A DHCP *relay agent* is a computer or router that is configured to listen for DHCP/BOOTP broadcasts from DHCP clients and then relay those messages to DCHP servers on different subnets. DHCP/BOOTP relay agents are part of the DHCP and BOOTP standards, and they function according to the Request for Comments (RFCs) standard documents that describe protocol design and related behavior.

An *RFC 1542–compliant router* is a router that supports the forwarding of DHCP broadcast traffic.

Why use a DHCP relay agent?

■   DHCP clients utilize broadcasts to secure a lease from a DHCP server. Routers normally do not pass broadcasts unless specifically configured to do so. Consequently, without additional configuration, DHCP servers can only provide IP addresses to clients located on the local subnet. Many organizations find it more efficient to centralize the servers that provide the DCHP Server service. To do so, they must configure the network so that DHCP broadcasts will be passed from the client to the DCHP server. This can be done in one of two ways: by configuring the routers that connect the subnets to forward DHCP broadcasts, or by configuring them to implement DCHP relay agents. Windows Server 2003 supports the Routing and Remote Access service that is configured to function as a DHCP relay agent.

DHCP strategies in a routed network

To understand why you would use a Microsoft DHCP relay agent, it is important to identify three strategies that can be implemented in a routed network.

- Include at least one DHCP server on each subnet.

  This method requires at least one DHCP server on each subnet to directly respond to DHCP client requests. However, this configuration potentially requires more administrative and equipment overhead because of the need to locate a DHCP server on each individual subnet rather than providing DHCP server services from a centralized location to multiple subnets. In addition, to provide fault tolerance, this solution would require two servers configured on each subnet as DHCP servers. Placing two DHCP servers on each subnet is often not practical.

- Configure an RFC 1542–compliant router to forward DHCP messages between subnets.

  An RFC 1542–compliant router is a router that can be configured to selectively forward DHCP broadcasts to another subnet. Although this option is preferable to using DHCP servers on each subnet, it can complicate router configuration and cause unnecessary broadcast traffic to be forwarded to other subnets.

- Configure a Microsoft DHCP relay agent on each subnet to forward DHCP messages to one or more particular DHCP servers on another subnet.

  Configuring a Microsoft DHCP relay agent on each subnet has several advantages over the other options. It limits broadcasts to the subnet in which they originate; and by adding DHCP relay agents to multiple subnets, a single DHCP server can provide IP addresses to multiple subnets more efficiently than when using RFC 1542–compliant routers. You can also configure a Microsoft DHCP relay agent to delay its response to a client request by a few seconds, in effect creating primary and secondary DHCP responders.

DHCP relay agents vs. dual DHCP servers

To provide fault tolerance, you should have at least two responders to DHCP client requests on every subnet. If you have only one subnet, then ideally you would have two DHCP servers servicing it.

However, if you have two or more subnets, you can utilize DHCP relay agents to provide fault tolerance and to keep management overhead at a minimum. In this case, you should dedicate a DHCP server to each subnet, and create non-overlapping scopes for both subnets on both servers. You should then deploy a DHCP relay agent on each subnet that is configured to forward requests, with a slight delay, to the DHCP server in another subnet.

This configuration will allow you to designate one DHCP server as the primary responder to DHCP requests, and to provide a backup route to another server if needed.

Example

Referring to the example in the slide (in which the client and server are separated by a router that does not forward DHCP broadcast traffic), you can use the DHCP relay agent to support the lease generation process between the DHCP client and the DHCP server.

How a DHCP Relay Agent Works

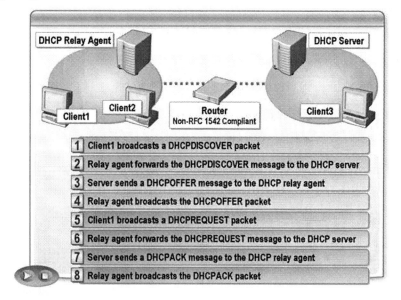

1	Client1 broadcasts a DHCPDISCOVER packet
2	Relay agent forwards the DHCPDISCOVER message to the DHCP server
3	Server sends a DHCPOFFER message to the DHCP relay agent
4	Relay agent broadcasts the DHCPOFFER packet
5	Client1 broadcasts a DHCPREQUEST packet
6	Relay agent forwards the DHCPREQUEST message to the DHCP server
7	Server sends a DHCPACK message to the DHCP relay agent
8	Relay agent broadcasts the DHCPACK packet

Introduction

The DHCP lease generation process relies on broadcasts. If the DHCP server and DHCP client are separated by a router that does not forward DHCP broadcasts, then the DHCP lease generation process will fail and the DHCP client will not receive an IP address lease from the DHCP server.

The DHCP relay agent supports the lease generation process between the DHCP client and the DHCP server when they are separated by a router. This enables the DHCP client to receive an IP address from the DHCP server.

How a DHCP relay agent works

The following steps describe how a DHCP relay agent works:

1. The DHCP client broadcasts a DHCPDISCOVER packet.

2. The DHCP relay agent on the client's subnet forwards the DHCPDISCOVER message to the DHCP server by using unicast.

3. The DHCP server uses unicast to send a DHCPOFFER message to the DHCP relay agent.

4. The DHCP relay agent broadcasts the DHCPOFFER packet to the DHCP client's subnet.

5. The DHCP client broadcasts a DHCPREQUEST packet.

6. The DHCP relay agent on the client's subnet forwards the DHCPREQUEST message to the DHCP server by using unicast.

7. The DHCP server uses unicast to send a DHCPACK message to the DHCP relay agent.

8. The DHCP relay agent broadcasts the DHCPACK to the DHCP client's subnet.

How a DHCP Relay Agent Uses Hop Count

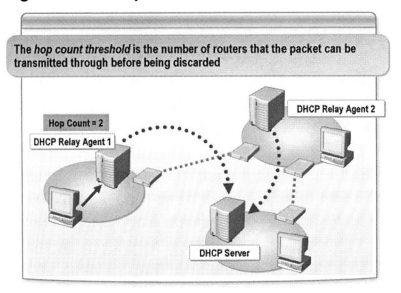

Definition The *hop count threshold* is the number of routers that the packet can be transmitted through before being discarded.

Why use hop count?   The DHCP relay agent uses the hop count value to determine the maximum number of routers a DHCP broadcast can travel across to get to the DHCP server before being discarded. You use hop count to reflect the number of routers between the DHCP client and the farthest DHCP server. If the path to the DHCP server is greater than the hop count number, then the DHCP packet will not reach the DHCP server.

How a DHCP relay agent uses hop count   The DHCP relay agent sends the DHCP client traffic (DHCPDISCOVER and DHCPREQUEST packets) to the DHCP server or to servers that the administrator has configured on the DHCP relay agent. The DHCP relay agent uses the hop count to let the packet know how many routers it can cross before it expires.

Each time a packet passes through a router, the hop count is incremented by one. If the incremented hop count number exceeds the maximum hop count, then the packet is dropped. The maximum hop count is 16.

If you configure the DHCP relay agent with only one DHCP server IP address to forward broadcasts to, then the hop count would equal the number of routers between the DHCP relay agent and the DHCP server. However, if you configure the DHCP relay agent with multiple DHCP server IP addresses, then the hop count must equal the maximum number of routers required to reach the most distant DHCP server.

Example   For example, the slide illustrates four routers between DHCP Relay Agent 1 and the DHCP server. However, there are only two routers between DHCP Relay Agent 2 and the DHCP server. Therefore, the hop count has been set at 4.

How a DHCP Relay Agent Uses Boot Threshold

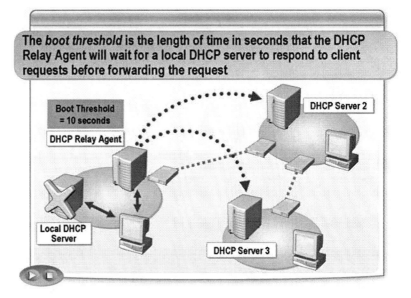

Definition

The *boot threshold* is the length of time in seconds that the DHCP relay agent will wait before sending the DHCPDISCOVER packet to the DHCP server.

Why use boot threshold?

You can configure the DHCP relay agent to provide fault tolerance by forwarding DHCP traffic to a remote DHCP server if a local DHCP server is not responding. In this scenario, you can configure the boot threshold to delay the forwarding of DHCP traffic from the DHCP relay agent to the remote DHCP server. Because the client will always respond to the first DHCPOFFER packet it receives, the local DHCP server will normally respond to the DHCP client before the remote DHCP server responds to the DHCP client. If for any reason the local DHCP server is down, the DHCP relay agent will wait the number of seconds defined in the boot threshold and then forward the packet to the configured DHCP server.

How a DHCP relay agent uses boot threshold

The boot threshold is the time that the relay agent waits before forwarding the DHCP traffic to its DHCP servers. If a DHCP server located on the same subnet as the DHCP relay agent is handling traffic, then the DHCP clients will receive their IP addressing configuration data before the DHCP relay agent forwards the DHCP packet to another DHCP server. When the DHCP relay agent finally forwards the DHCP traffic, then the DHCPOFFER packet that is returned to the DHCP client is discarded because the DHCP client has already obtained its DHCP IP configuration data.

If the DHCP client has not received IP configuration data, then the DHCPOFFER packet that is returned to the DHCP client from the remote DHCP server is used obtain the DHCP IP configuration data.

Example

For example, you can configure the DHCP relay agent to wait ten seconds before it forwards the DHCPDISCOVER packet to the specified remote DHCP servers.

This ten second lag allows time for the local DHCP server to respond to the DHCP client.

How to Configure a DHCP Relay Agent

Your instructor will demonstrate how to:

- Apply guidelines for setting the hop count and boot threshold
- Add a DHCP Relay Agent
- Configure a DHCP Relay Agent with the IP address of the DHCP server
- Enable the DHCP Relay Agent on a router interface

Introduction

To forward DHCP messages between subnets, you can configure a DHCP relay agent. While configuring a DHCP relay agent, you can also set the hop count and boot threshold.

Note It is recommended that you log on with an account that has non-administrative credentials and use the **Run as** command with a user account that has appropriate administrative credentials to perform this task.

Guidelines for setting the hop count and boot threshold

Guidelines for setting the hop count and boot threshold include the following:

- Setting the hop count number too high can result in excess network traffic when relay agents are incorrectly configured.

- If you have a DHCP server on the local subnet, the boot threshold number should be high enough so that the local DHCP server responds to client broadcasts before the DHCP relay agent forwards client requests. Then the DHCP relay agent will only contact a remote DHCP server if the local DHCP server is not available. This mechanism provides for fault tolerance, because a correctly configured DHCP relay agent on a network segment that has a DHCP server only contacts a DHCP server on a remote network when the local DHCP server does not respond. If you notice that the DHCP relay agent forwards client requests even though there is a DHCP server on the local network, increase the boot threshold.

Procedure for adding a DHCP relay agent

To add a DHCP relay agent:

1. Open the Routing and Remote Access console.

2. Right-click the server, and then click **Configure and Enable Routing and Remote Access**.

2. On the **Welcome to the Routing and Remote Access Server Setup Wizard** page, click **Next**.

3. On the **Configuration** page, select **Custom configuration**, and then click **Next**.

4. On the **Custom Configuration** page, select **LAN routing**, and then click **Next**.

5. On the **Completing the Routing and Remote Access Server Setup Wizard** page, click **Finish**.

6. In the **Routing and Remote Access** warning dialog box, click **Yes** to start the service.

7. On the **This Server is Now a Remote Access/VPN Server** page, click **Finish**.

8. In the console tree, expand the server, expand **IP Routing**, and then select **General**.

9. Right-click **General**, and then click **New Routing Protocol**.

10. In the **New Routing Protocol** dialog box, click **DHCP Relay Agent**, and then click **OK**.

Procedure for configuring a DHCP relay agent with the IP address of the DHCP server

To configure a DHCP relay agent with the IP address of a DHCP server:

1. Open the Routing and Remote Access console.

2. In the console tree, select **DHCP Relay Agent**.

3. Right-click **DHCP Relay Agent**, and then click **Properties**.

4. On the **General** tab, in the **Server address** field, type the IP address of the DHCP server that you wish to forward DHCP requests to, click **Add**, and then click **OK**.

Procedure for enabling the DHCP relay agent on a router interface

To enable the DHCP relay agent on a router interface:

1. Open the Routing and Remote Access console.

2. In the console tree, select **DHCP Relay Agent**.

3. Right-click **DHCP Relay Agent**, and then click **New Interface**.

4. Select the interface on which you want to enable the DHCP relay agent, and then click **OK**.

5. In the **DHCP Relay Properties** dialog box, on the **General** tab, verify that the **Relay DHCP packets** check box is selected.

6. Configure the **Hop-count threshold** and **Boot threshold (seconds)** if appropriate, and then click **OK**.

Practice: Configuring the DHCP Relay Agent

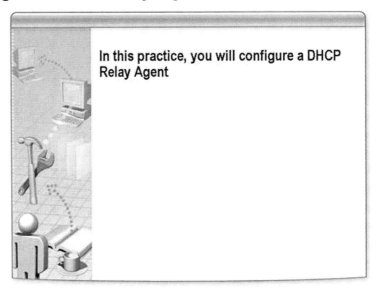

Objectives

In this practice, you will configure a DHCP relay agent.

Instructions

To complete this practice, refer to the *Implementation Plan Values* document, located in the Appendix at the end of your student workbook.

You must be logged on with an account that has non-administrative credentials and use the **Run as** command with a user account that has appropriate administrative credentials to complete the task.

Important   The instructor must configure LAN Routing on London by using the RIP protocol, configured with both the Partner Network Connection interface and the Classroom Network Connection interface, prior to students beginning this practice. At the end of this practice, the Instructor must remove Routing and Remote Access from London.

Scenario

The systems engineer has created a separate subnet in the Lab department that includes a new DHCP server. To test the new DHCP server, he has configured a DHCP scope to handle IP addressing for all Lab department computers. The systems engineer has instructed you to deactivate your scope on your DHCP server, and to configure your DHCP server as a DHCP relay agent for the new DHCP server.

Practice

▶ **Install and configure LAN routing**

- Complete this task from the lower number student computer.
- User account: *ComputerName***Admin** (where *ComputerName* is the name of your computer)
- Password: **P@ssw0rd**
- Domain: **nwtraders**
- Routing protocol: **RIP version 2**
- Interface: **Classroom Network Connection**
- Interface: **Partner Network Connection**

▶ **Add the DHCP relay agent**

- Complete this task from the lower number student computer.

▶ **Configure the DHCP relay agent with the IP address of a DHCP server**

- Complete this task from the lower number student computer.
- DHCP server IP address: **192.168.***x***.200** (where *x* is your classroom number)

▶ **Enable the DHCP relay agent on a router interface**

- Complete this task from the lower number student computer.
- Interface: Partner Network Connection
- Hop-count threshold: 2
- Boot threshold (seconds): 5

▶ **Deactivate the DHCP scope**

- Complete this task from the lower number student computer.
- Deactivate the DHCP scope.

▶ **Verify the DHCP relay agent**

- Complete this task from the higher number student computer.

1. Using the **ipconfig /all** command, verify that the IP address of the DHCP server displays as the IP address of your partner's Partner Network Connection.

2. Why is the DHCP server your partner's server computer?

_____

_____

3. Use the **ipconfig /renew** command to renew the IP address.

4. Using the **ipconfig /all** command to verify that the IP address of the DHCP server displays as **192.168.x.200** (where *x* is your classroom number).

5. Why is the DHCP server the London server?

_____

_____

▶ **Activate the DHCP scope**

▪ Complete this task from the lower number student computer.

▪ Activate the DHCP scope.

▶ **Verify the DHCP lease from your partner's DHCP server**

▪ Complete this task from the higher student computer.

1. Using the **ipconfig /release** command, release the IP address.

2. Using the **ipconfig /renew** command, renew the IP address.

3. Using the **ipconfig /all** command, verify that the IP address of the DHCP server displays as the IP address of your partner's Partner Network Connection.

4. Why is the DHCP server your partners' server?

_____

_____

▶ **Remove Routing and Remote Access**

▪ Complete this task from the lower number student computer.

▪ From the Routing and Remote Access console, remove Routing and Remote Access by using the following account information.

- User account: *ComputerName***Admin**

- Password: **P@ssw0rd**

- Domain: **nwtraders**

Lab A: Identifying and Resolving Common Issues When Allocating IP Addressing by Using DHCP

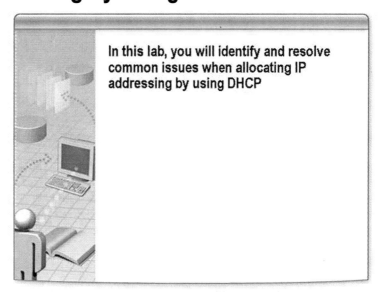

In this lab, you will identify and resolve common issues when allocating IP addressing by using DHCP

Objectives

In this lab, you will identify and resolve common issues when allocating IP addressing by using DHCP.

Estimated time to complete this lab: 30 minutes

Exercise 1
Identifying and Resolving Common Issues When Allocating IP Addressing by Using DHCP

In this exercise, you will identify and resolve common issues when allocating IP addressing by using DHCP.

Instructions

To complete this lab, refer to the *Implementation Plan Values* document, located in the Appendix at the end of your student workbook.

You must be logged on with an account that has non-administrative credentials and use the **Run as** command with a user account that has appropriate administrative credentials to complete the tasks. When completing the lab, assume that you will log on with a non-administrative account (example: *ComputerName*User), unless the Specific Instructions in the lab state otherwise.

Scenario

During the testing of your DHCP server in the lab, you identify several configuration issues with the DHCP server and corresponding effects on DHCP clients.

You have set up a lab for new DHCP administrators to experience these DHCP configuration issues and the corresponding corrective actions.

In this lab, you will first verify that DHCP is properly functioning, by running tests from the client and from other server. You will execute a script that will reconfigure the DHCP server to reflect configuration issues. You will run the tests again, to verify that the DHCP server has configuration issues. You will then locate and identify the DHCP server configuration errors, and implement corrective actions. Finally, you will verify that the DHCP server is functioning properly, by running the test again from both the server and the client.

The correct configuration data for this lab is located in the *Implementation Plan Values* document in the Appendix at the end of your student workbook.

Tasks	Specific instructions
✋ Perform the following task only on the computer with the higher student number.	
1. Verify your DHCP lease information.	a. Use the **ipconfig /all** command to verify the following IP configuration data that was leased from the DHCP server. • IP address: The IP address of your Partner Network Connection • Default gateway: The IP address of your partner's Partner Network Connection • DHCP sever: The IP address of your partner's Partner Network Connection • Lease Period: **1 hour**
✋ Perform the following task only on the computer with the lower student number. Use the **Run as** command to start a command prompt with administrative rights on the local computer to run the script.	
2. Change the DHCP server configuration to simulate configuration issues by running a script.	▪ Close the DHCP console and at a command prompt, type **C:\MOC\2277\labfiles\lab02\DHCP.vbs**
✋ Perform the following task only on the computer with the higher student number.	
3. Verify the effects of the DHCP server configuration issues on the client by running tests.	▪ Use the **ipconfig /release**, the **ipconfig /renew**, and the **ipconfig /all** commands to verify that the client computer is not receiving the DHCP IP configuration data.
✋ Perform the following task only on the computer with the lower student number.	
4. Determine the reason why the DHCP server is not allocating IP address configuration data, and then implement corrective actions.	a. Determine whether the DHCP scope is deactivated. b. Activate the DHCP scope.
✋ Perform the following task only on the computer with the higher student number.	
5. Verify that the DHCP client receives the incorrect router value from the DHCP server.	a. Use the **ipconfig /release**, the **ipconfig /renew**, and the **ipconfig /all** commands on the client to verify that the IP address of the router option is incorrect. b. The correct router value is the IP address of your partner's Partner Network Connection.
✋ Perform the following task only on the computer with the lower student number.	
6. Determine the reason why the DHCP server is not allocating the correct IP address configuration data for the router option, and then implement corrective actions.	a. Determine whether the scope router option is configured with the incorrect value. b. Configure the router scope option with the correct value. The correct value for the DHCP scope option Router is the IP address of your partner's Partner Network Connection.

	Perform the following task only on the computer with the higher student number.	
7.	Verify that the DHCP client receives the correct IP configuration data from the DHCP server.	a. Use the **ipconfig /release**, the **ipconfig /renew**, and the **ipconfig /all** commands to verify that the DHCP client has received the correct value for the DHCP router option. b. The correct value for the DHCP scope option Router is the IP address of your partner's Partner Network Connection.
	Perform the following task only on the computer with the higher student number.	
8.	Verify that the DHCP client receives the correct IP configuration data for the lease period from the DHCP server.	a. Use the **ipconfig /all** command to verify that the DHCP client has received the incorrect value for the DHCP lease duration. b. The correct lease duration value is 1 hour.
	Perform the following task only on the computer with the lower student number.	
9.	Determine the reason why the DHCP server is not allocating the correct IP address configuration data for the lease period, and then implement corrective actions.	a. Determine whether the DHCP scope is configured with the incorrect lease duration value. b. Configure the DHCP lease duration value to **1 hour**.
	Perform the following task only on the computer with the higher student number.	
10.	Verify that the DHCP client receives the correct lease period value from the DHCP server.	▪ Use the **ipconfig /release**, the **ipconfig /renew**, and the **ipconfig /all** commands to verify that the DHCP client has received the correct value for the DHCP lease duration. • The correct DHCP lease period is 1 hour.
	Perform the following task only on the computer with the higher student number.	
11.	Verify that the DHCP client receives the correct lease duration value from the DHCP server.	a. Use the **ipconfig /all** command to verify the following IP configuration data, which was leased from the DHCP server. • IP address: The IP address of your Partner Network Connection • Default gateway: The IP address of your partner's Partner Network Connection • DHCP sever: The IP address of your partner's Partner Network Connection • Lease Period: **1 hour**

Microsoft®
Training &
Certification

Module 3: Managing and Monitoring Dynamic Host Configuration Protocol (DHCP)

Contents

Overview

- Managing a DHCP Database
- Monitoring DHCP
- Applying Security Guidelines for DHCP

Introduction

Installing and configuring the Dynamic Host Configuration Protocol (DHCP) service is only part of a network solution. The DHCP service must be managed to reflect changing client Internet Protocol (IP) addressing needs. It is also important for an administrator to monitor DHCP server performance, because the DHCP environment is dynamic. Furthermore, security guidelines must be applied for DHCP.

Objectives

After completing this module, you will be able to:

- Manage a DHCP database.
- Monitor DHCP.
- Apply security guidelines for DHCP.
- Manage DHCP.

Lesson: Managing a DHCP Database

* Overview of Managing DHCP
* What Is a DHCP Database?
* How a DHCP Database Is Backed Up and Restored
* How To Back Up and Restore a DHCP Database
* How a DHCP Database Is Reconciled
* How To Reconcile a DHCP Database

Introduction

It is important to protect your DHCP database, manage the growth of your DHCP database, and ensure DHCP database consistency. This can be accomplished by backing up, restoring, and reconciling the DHCP database.

Lesson objectives

After completing this lesson, you will be able to:

* Explain the purpose of managing DHCP.
* Explain what a DHCP database is.
* Describe how a DHCP database is backed up and restored.
* Back up and restore a database.
* Describe how a DHCP database is reconciled.
* Reconcile a DHCP database.
* Manage a DHCP database.

Overview of Managing DHCP

The DHCP service needs to be managed to reflect changes in the network and the DHCP server

Scenarios for managing DHCP:

- Managing DHCP database growth
- Protecting the DHCP database
- Ensuring DHCP database consistency
- Adding clients
- Adding new network service servers
- Adding new subnets

Why manage a service?

After a service is installed, consideration must be given to the steps that are required to manage and maintain the service so that it continues to provide the services that clients require over time. When you configure a network service, you are solving a network issue at a given point in time. Because the network environment can change, you need to monitor the service and, potentially, to modify the solution to keep it current.

Why manage the DHCP service?

You need to manage the DHCP service to reflect changing client IP addressing needs. Client IP addressing needs can change if new clients, new subnets, or new servers are added to or subtracted from the network.

You also need to manage the DHCP service to respond to changing DHCP server conditions, and to protect the DHCP database from failure.

Scenarios for managing DHCP

The following table lists common scenarios in which an administrator would manage DHCP. Also listed are the corresponding tasks and tools for managing DHCP.

Scenarios	Tasks	Tools for managing DHCP
Managing DHCP database growth	Compact the DHCP database	Jetpack.exe
Protecting the DHCP database	Back up and restore the DHCP database	DHCP console
Ensuring DHCP database consistency	Reconcile DHCP scopes	DHCP console
Adding clients	Configure or modify scopes	DHCP console
Adding new network service servers	Configure or modify options	DHCP console
Adding new subnets	Configure the DHCP relay agent	DHCP console

Note This module only covers how to manage a DHCP database. Because the procedural steps for *managing* scopes, options, and DHCP relay agents are similar to the procedural steps for *configuring* scopes, options, and DHCP relay agents, you can refer to Module 2, "Allocating IP Addressing by Using Dynamic Host Configuration Protocol (DHCP)" in Course 2277, *Implementing, Managing, and Maintaining a Microsoft® Windows® Server 2003 Network Infrastructure: Network Services*.

What Is a DHCP Database?

The *DHCP database* is a dynamic database that is updated when DHCP clients are assigned or as they release their TCP/IP address leases

- The DHCP database contains DHCP configuration data, such as information about scopes, reservations, options, and leases
- Windows Server 2003 stores the DHCP database in the directory %*Systemroot*%\System32\Dhcp
- The DHCP database files include:

  - DHCP.mdb
  - Tmp.edb
  - J50.log and J50*.log

  - Res*.log
  - J50.chk

Definition

The *DHCP database* is a dynamic database that is updated when DHCP clients are assigned or as they release their Transmission Control Protocol/Internet Protocol (TCP/IP) address leases.

Purpose of a DHCP database

The DHCP database contains the DHCP configuration data (such as information about scopes, reservations, options, leases, etc.). The DHCP service will not start without the database.

Where a DHCP database is stored

Windows Server 2003 stores the DHCP database in the directory %*systemroot*%\System32\Dhcp. By default, the database is automatically backed up to the Backup\New directory, which is located in the database directory.

DHCP files

The DHCP database is made up the following files, which are stored in the \%*Systemroot%*\System32\Dhcp directory.

File	Description
DHCP.mdb	The database file for the DHCP service. The file contains two tables: the IP-address-Owner-ID mapping table and the name-to-IP address mapping table.
Tmp.edb	A temporary file that the DHCP database uses as a swap file during database index maintenance operations.
J50.log and J50*.log	Logs of all transactions that are made with the database. DHCP uses these logs to recover data, if necessary.
Res*.log	Reserved log files that are used to record the existing transactions if the system runs out of disk space.
J50.chk	A checkpoint file.

Caution   Do not tamper with or remove any of these files. The DHCP service will not load without these files, so if you make any changes to them you risk failure of your DHCP server.

How a DHCP Database Is Backed Up and Restored

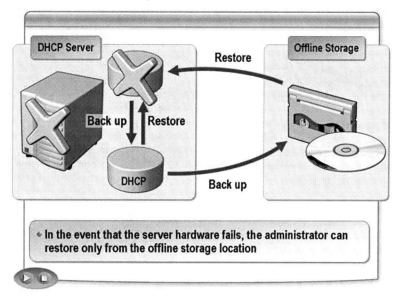

- In the event that the server hardware fails, the administrator can restore only from the offline storage location

Why back up and restore a DHCP database?

To provide fault tolerance in the case of a failure, it is important to back up the DHCP database. This will enable you to restore the database from the backup copy if the hardware fails.

How a DHCP database is automatically backed up

By default, the DHCP service automatically backs up the DHCP database and related registry entries to a backup directory on the local drive every 60 minutes. By default, automatic backups are stored in the \%*Systemroot%*\System32\Dhcp\Backup\New directory. The administrator can change the backup location.

How a DHCP database is manually backed up

The administrator can then copy the backed up DHCP files to an offline storage location (such as a tape or a disk).

You can also back up the DHCP database manually. By default, manual backups are stored in the \%*systemroot%*\System32\Dhcp\Backup\New directory. The administrator can change the backup location.

How a DHCP database is restored

When the DHCP service starts, if the original DHCP database is unable to load, then the DHCP service automatically restores to a backup directory on the local drive.

In the event that the DHCP database fails, the administrator can choose either to restore from the backup directory on the local drive or to restore from the offline backup location.

In the event that the server hardware fails and the local backup is unavailable, the administrator can only restore from the offline backup location.

How to Back Up and Restore a DHCP Database

> **Your instructor will demonstrate how to:**
>
> - Apply guidelines when backing up and restoring a DHCP database
> - Configure a DHCP database backup path
> - Manually back up a DHCP database to the backup directory on a local drive
> - Manually restore a DHCP database from the backup directory on a local drive

Introduction

If you cannot repair the database by using Jetpack.exe, you can restore the database from the backup directory on the local drive. If restoring the DHCP database from the backup directory on the local drive is unsuccessful, you must restore the DHCP database from an offline storage location.

Even though you can both *automatically* and *manually* back up and restore a DHCP database to and from a backup directory on the local drive, you can only *manually* back up and restore a DHCP database to and from an offline storage location.

Note   It is recommended that you log on with an account that has non-administrative credentials and use the **Run as** command with a user account that has appropriate administrative credentials to perform this task.

Guidelines

When backing up and restoring a DHCP database, apply the following guidelines.

- Manually back up the DHCP database to a location other than *%Systemroot%*\System32\Dhcp\Backup\Jet\New, which is the default location for the automatic backup. If you store a manually created copy of the DHCP database in the same location as the copy that was created automatically, the DHCP service will not function properly.

- Maintain a copy of the backed up DHCP database offline (for example, on a tape or a disk). Because the DHCP service automatically backs up a copy of the DHCP database to a location on the local drive, you lose both the original DHCP database and the backup DHCP database if the hardware fails.

Procedure for configuring a DHCP database backup path

To configure a DHCP database backup path:

1. In the DHCP console, in the console tree, select the appropriate DHCP server.

2. On the **Action** menu, click **Properties**.

3. On the **Advanced** tab, in the **Backup path** field, type the appropriate backup path and then click **OK**.

Procedure for manually backing up a DHCP database to the backup directory on a local drive

To manually back up a DHCP database to the backup directory on a local drive:

1. In the DHCP console, in the console tree, select the appropriate DHCP server.

2. On the **Action** menu, click **Backup**.

3. In the **Browse For Folder** dialog box, select the appropriate folder to back up to, and then click **OK**.

Procedure for manually restoring a DHCP database from the backup directory on a local drive

To manually restore a DHCP database from the backup directory on a local drive:

1. In the DHCP console, in the console tree, select the appropriate DHCP server.

2. On the **Action** menu, click **Restore**.

3. In the **Browse For Folder** dialog box, select the folder where the backup resides and then click **OK**.

4. In the **DHCP** dialog box, click **Yes** to stop and then restart the service.

5. If the status of the service doesn't update, refresh the DHCP console.

Note   For more information about how to manually back up and restore a DHCP database to and from an offline storage location, refer to Course 2275, *Maintaining a Microsoft Windows Server 2003 Environment*.

How a DHCP Database Is Reconciled

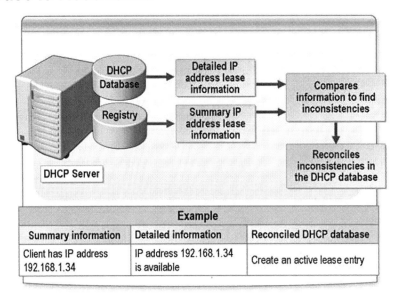

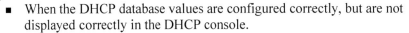

Example		
Summary information	Detailed information	Reconciled DHCP database
Client has IP address 192.168.1.34	IP address 192.168.1.34 is available	Create an active lease entry

Definition

Reconciling is the process of verifying DHCP database values against DHCP registry values.

When to reconcile a DHCP database

It is recommended that you reconcile your DHCP database:

- When the DHCP database values are configured correctly, but are not displayed correctly in the DHCP console.

- After you have restored a DHCP database, but the restored DHCP database does not have the most recent values.

For example: your existing database is deleted, and you must restore an older version of the database. If you start DHCP and open the console, you will notice that the scope and options display, but the active leases do not. Reconciling populates the client lease information from the registry to the DHCP database.

How a DHCP database is reconciled

When you reconcile a server or a scope, the DHCP service uses both the summary information in the registry and the detailed information in the DHCP database to reconstruct the most current view of the DHCP service.

For example: after a DHCP database is restored, an active lease is not displaying in the DHCP console The process of reconciliation will verify the summary information for that address lease in the registry with the detailed information in the DHCP database. The summary information shows that a client has the IP address, but the detailed information shows that the IP address is available. After the information between the registry and the database is compared, the DHCP database is updated with this active lease information. The active lease will then display in the DHCP console.

How to Reconcile a DHCP Database

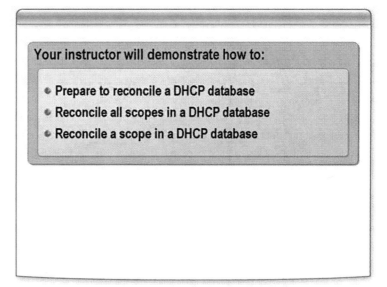

Your instructor will demonstrate how to:

• Prepare to reconcile a DHCP database
• Reconcile all scopes in a DHCP database
• Reconcile a scope in a DHCP database

Introduction

You can choose to reconcile all scopes on the server by selecting the DHCP server, or you can reconcile one scope by selecting the appropriate scope.

Note It is recommended that you log on with an account that has non-administrative credentials and use the **Run as** command with a user account that has appropriate administrative credentials to perform this task.

Preparing to reconcile

Before using the Reconcile feature to fully recover client information for a DHCP scope from the registry, the server computer needs to meet the following criteria.

■ All DHCP server registry keys must either be restored, or exist and remain intact from previous service operations on the server computer.

■ A new version of the DHCP server database file must be generated in the %*Systemroot*%\System32\Dhcp folder on the server computer.

When the registry and database meet the previous criteria, you can restart the DHCP service. At this point, upon opening the DHCP console, you might notice that scope information is present, but that there are no active leases displayed. To regain your active leases for each scope, you use the Reconcile feature to recover each scope.

Procedure for reconciling all scopes in a DHCP database

To reconcile all scopes in a DHCP database:

1. In the DHCP console, in the console tree, select the DHCP server.

2. On the **Action** menu, click **Reconcile All Scopes**.

3. In the **Reconcile All Scopes** dialog box, click **Verify**.

4. In the **DHCP** dialog box, click **OK**.

Procedure for reconciling a scope in a DHCP database

To reconcile a scope in a DHCP database:

1. In the DHCP console, select the appropriate scope in the console tree.

Note   You can choose to reconcile one scope by selecting the appropriate scope, or reconcile all scopes on the server by selecting the DHCP server.

2. On the **Action** menu, click **Reconcile**.
3. In the **Reconcile** dialog box, click **Verify**.
4. In the **DHCP** dialog box, click **OK**.

After reconciling

After using the Reconcile feature, when viewing properties for individual clients that are shown in the list of active leases, you might notice that client information is displayed incorrectly. This information is corrected and updated in DHCP Manager as scope clients renew their leases.

Practice: Managing a DHCP Database

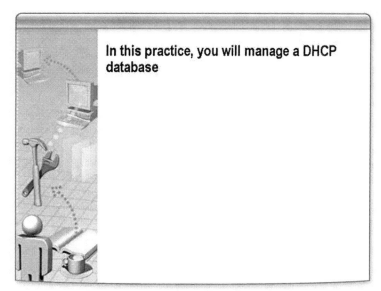

In this practice, you will manage a DHCP database

Objective

In this practice, you will manage a DHCP database.

Instructions

You must be logged on with an account that has non-administrative credentials and use the **Run as** command with a user account that has appropriate administrative credentials to complete the task.

Scenario

The systems engineer has decided to run some tests against the DHCP server hardware in the Lab department. You need to manually back up the DHCP database. After the test has been run on the DHCP server, you will reconcile the server to ensure that the DHCP server database is correct.

Practice

▶ **Configure the DHCP database backup path**

- Complete this task from both student computers.

- Backup path: **C:\Moc\2277\Labfiles\Lab03**

▶ **Manually back up a DHCP database to the backup directory on a local drive**

- Complete this task from both student computers.

- Backup path: **C:\Moc\2277\Labfiles\Lab03\Manual Backup**

▶ **Manually restore a DHCP database from the backup directory on a local drive**

- Complete this task from both student computers.

- Restore path: **C:\Moc\2277\Labfiles\Lab03\Manual Backup**

▶ **Reconcile all scopes in a DHCP database**

- Complete this task from both student computers.

- Reconcile all scopes.

Lesson: Monitoring DHCP

- Overview of Monitoring DHCP
- Multimedia: Creating a Performance Baseline *(Optional)*
- What Are DHCP Statistics?
- How to View DHCP Statistics
- What Is a DHCP Audit Log File?
- How DHCP Audit Logging Works
- How to Monitor DHCP Server Performance by Using the DHCP Audit Log
- Guidelines for Monitoring DHCP Server Performance
- Common Performance Counters for Monitoring DHCP Server Performance
- Guidelines for Creating Alerts for a DHCP Server

Introduction

You can monitor DHCP by using the:

- DHCP console for DHCP statistics.
- DHCP audit log and Event Viewer for DHCP events.
- Performance console for DHCP performance data.

Note For more information about using the Event Viewer to monitor DHCP events, please refer to Course 2274, *Managing a Microsoft Windows Server 2003 Environment*.

Lesson objectives

After completing this lesson, you will be able to:

- Explain the purpose of monitoring DHCP.
- Explain what DHCP statistics are.
- View DHCP statistics.
- Explain what a DHCP audit log file is.
- Describe how DHCP audit logging works.
- Monitor DHCP server performance by using the DHCP audit log.
- Apply guidelines for monitoring DHCP server performance.
- Apply guidelines for common performance counters when monitoring DHCP server performance.
- Apply guidelines for creating alerts for a DHCP server.
- Monitor DHCP.

Overview of Monitoring DHCP

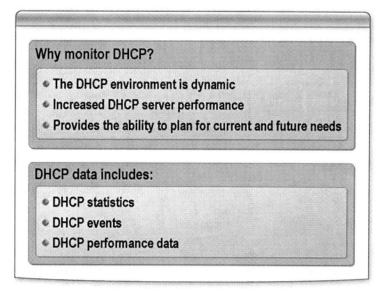

Why monitor DHCP?

- The DHCP environment is dynamic
- Increased DHCP server performance
- Provides the ability to plan for current and future needs

DHCP data includes:

- DHCP statistics
- DHCP events
- DHCP performance data

Introduction

Monitoring the DHCP service requires you to collect and view data about the DHCP service. You need to monitor both the DHCP clients and the DHCP server. This module focuses on monitoring the DHCP server.

Why monitor DHCP?

The DHCP environment is dynamic. Client needs are always changing as clients are added or removed, new options are configured, organizational needs change, and scopes are added to handle additional clients. Consequently, it is important to verify that the DHCP server is performing within expected norms on the network as the network changes.

Because of the importance of DHCP servers to the networking infrastructure, it is important to establish performance baselines that you can use when you are assessing server performance. These baselines are also valuable in the planning of changes and additions to the network.

Primary subsystems and the DHCP server

Although it is important to monitor DHCP functions, it is just as important to understand that many servers that host the DHCP Server service also host other applications and network services. Consequently, when assessing performance, you should review the interaction of all services that run on the DHCP server and their respective utilization of system resources.

The DHCP service uses memory, processor, disk, and network subsystems. Although all of these subsystems are important for the DHCP service to perform optimally, you can obtain the greatest benefit by monitoring the performance of network subsystems.

Where can you find DHCP data?

You can find DHCP data in DHCP statistics, DHCP events, and DHCP performance data.

DHCP data	Description	Examples	Tools for monitoring DHCP
DHCP statistics	Represent statistics collected at either the server level or the scope level since the DHCP service was started.	■ DHCP service start and stop times ■ Number of IP addresses available in a scope ■ Number of leases in use in a scope ■ Number of clients in use	■ DHCP console
DHCP events	Any significant occurrence either in the system or in an application that requires users to be notified or an entry to be added to a log.	■ When the service was stopped or started, and by whom ■ DHCP service errors ■ DHCP service authorizations	■ DHCP audit log ■ Event Viewer
DHCP performance data	The DHCP service includes a set of performance counters that the administrator can use to monitor various types of server activity.	■ Number of leases renewed for a period of time ■ Number of DHCPACK or DHCPNACK packets for a period of time ■ Amount of disk space that the DHCP database uses ■ Number of IP address conflicts	■ Performance console

Note For more information about monitoring server performance by using the Event Viewer, refer to Course 2274, *Managing a Microsoft Windows Server 2003 Environment*

Multimedia: *(Optional)* Creating a Performance Baseline

- **The objective of this presentation is to provide high-level steps for creating a performance baseline**
- **After this presentation, you will be able to:**
  - Explain the purpose of a performance baseline
  - Explain that a performance baseline is the level of system performance that you find acceptable
  - Explain that server performance is critical to efficient network operations

File location

To view the *Creating a Performance Baseline* presentation, open the Web page on the Student Materials compact disc, click **Multimedia**, and then click the title of the presentation.

Objectives

After completing this presentation you will be able to:

- Explain the purpose of a performance baseline.
- Explain that a performance baseline is the level of system performance that you find acceptable.
- Explain that server performance is critical to efficient network operations.

Key points

- You should take samples of counter values every 30 to 45 minutes for a week, during peak, low, and normal operations.
- The general steps for creating a baseline are:
  - Identify resources
  - Capture data
  - Store data
- The four major system resources for performance baselines are:
  - Memory
  - Processor
  - Physical disk
  - Network
- A performance object is the data that a system component or resource generates. Each performance object provides counters, which represent data about specific aspects of system performance.

What Are DHCP Statistics?

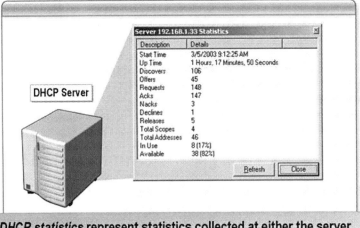

Server 192.168.1.33 Statistics

Description	Details
Start Time	3/5/2003 9:12:25 AM
Up Time	1 Hours, 17 Minutes, 50 Seconds
Discovers	106
Offers	45
Requests	148
Acks	147
Nacks	3
Declines	1
Releases	5
Total Scopes	4
Total Addresses	46
In Use	8 (17%)
Available	38 (82%)

DHCP Server

Refresh   Close

DHCP statistics represent statistics collected at either the server level or scope level since the DHCP service was last started

---

Definition

DHCP statistics represent statistics that are collected at either the server level or the scope level since the DHCP service was last started.

Purpose of DHCP statistics

Statistics provide a real-time view that you can use to check the status of your DHCP server or scopes. These statistics can be provided either for a particular scope or at the server level; the latter shows the aggregate of all the scopes that the server manages

DHCP server and scope statistics

Using the DHCP console, you can view the DHCP statistics, for both a server and a scope, as listed in the following table.

DHCP statistics	Description	Server statistics	Scope statistics
Start Time	When the DHCP service was started	X	
Up Time	Period of time the DHCP service has been active	X	
Discovers	Number of client DHCPDISCOVERs received	X	
Offers	Number of client DHCPOFFERs sent	X	
Requests	Number of client DHCPREQUESTs received	X	
Acks	Number of client DHCPACKs sent	X	
Nacks	Number of client DHCPNACKs sent	X	
Declines	Number of client DHCPDECLINEs received	X	
Releases	Number of client DHCPRELEASEs received	X	
Total Scopes	Total number of scopes on the DHCP server	X	
Total Addresses	Total number of IP addresses configured for clients	X	X
In Use	Number of IP addresses currently leased	X	X
Available	Number of IP addresses available for lease	X	X

How to View DHCP Statistics

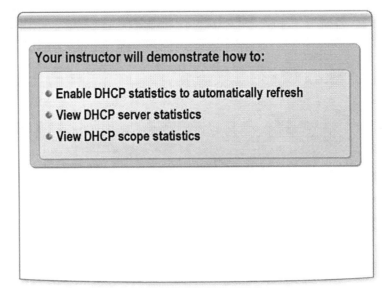

Introduction

You can view DHCP statistics for both a server and a scope. For greater ease in viewing DHCP statistics, you can enable DHCP server statistics to refresh automatically, which also enables the DHCP scope statistics to refresh automatically.

Note It is recommended that you log on with an account that has non-administrative credentials and use the **Run as** command with a user account that has appropriate administrative credentials to perform this task.

Procedure for enabling DHCP statistics to automatically refresh

To enable DHCP statistics to automatically refresh:

1. In the DHCP console, in the console tree, select the appropriate DHCP server.

2. On the **Action** menu, click **Properties**.

3. On the **General** tab, select **Automatically update statistics every**, configure the **Hours** and **Minutes** fields appropriately, and then click **OK**.

Procedure for viewing DHCP server statistics

To view DHCP server statistics:

1. In the DHCP console, in the console tree, select the appropriate DHCP server.

2. On the **Action** menu, click **Display Statistics**.

Procedure for viewing DHCP scope statistics

To view DHCP scope statistics:

1. In the DHCP console, in the console tree, select the appropriate DHCP scope.

2. On the **Action** menu, click **Display Statistics**.

What Is a DHCP Audit Log File?

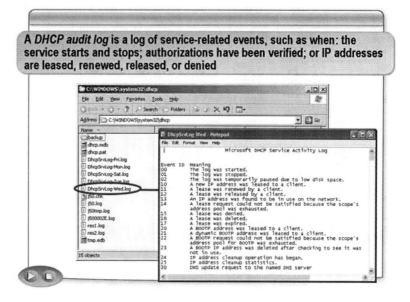

Definition

A *DHCP audit log file* is a log of service-related events, such as when:

- The service starts and stops.
- Authorizations have been verified.
- IP addresses are leased, renewed, released, or denied.

Purpose of a DHCP audit log

A DHCP audit log gives the administrator a day-to-day collection of DHCP events. DHCP audit logs provide you with the information that you may need for monitoring your DHCP server.

You can use DHCP audit logs to view activity for one specified day, or collect the log files to analyze DHCP server activity over longer periods of time.

DHCP audit log file

The log files are comma-delimited text files that contain log entries representing a single line of text. A DHCP audit log file includes the following fields.

Fields	Description
ID	A DHCP server event ID code
Date	The date on which this entry was logged on the DHCP server
Time	The time at which this entry was logged on the DHCP server
Description	A description of this DHCP server event
IP Address	The IP address of the DHCP client
Host Name	The host name of the DHCP client
MAC Address	The media access control address that the network adapter hardware of the client uses

Examples of common event ID codes

DHCP server audit log files use reserved event ID codes to provide information about the type of server event or activity logged. The following table describes a sample of common event ID codes in more detail.

Event ID	Description
00	The log was started.
01	The log was stopped.
02	The log was temporarily paused due to low disk space.
10	A new IP address was leased to a client.
11	A client renews a lease.
12	A client releases a lease.
13	An IP address was found in use on the network.
14	A lease request could not be satisfied because the address pool of the scope was exhausted.
15	A lease was denied.
20	A BOOTP (Boot Protocol) address was leased to a client.

How DHCP Audit Logging Works

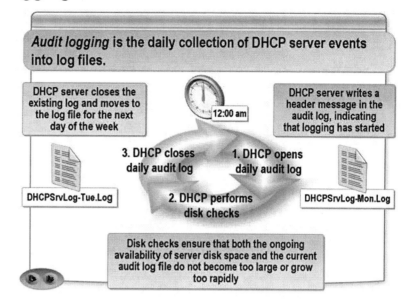

Definition	*Audit logging* is the daily collection of DHCP server events into log files.
Why use DHCP audit logging?	Logging DHCP server data allows you to gather information about DHCP Server service operations on the network. You can view a single day's log file for information, or you can collect log files on a separate server for analysis of DHCP server data over a longer period of time. This information can be helpful when you are deciding whether you need to add more DHCP servers.
How DHCP audit logging works	The following process describes how audit logging starts, performs, and ends during a 24-hour day.

1. Whenever a DHCP server starts, or whenever a new day begins (when the local time on the computer is 12:00 A.M.), the server writes a header message in the audit log file, indicating that logging has started. Then, depending on whether the audit log file is a new or an existing file, the following actions occur:

    - If the file already existed without modification for more than a day, it is overwritten.

    - If the file already existed, but was modified within the previous 24 hours, the file is not overwritten. Instead, new logging activity is appended to the end of the existing file. This would be the case if either the system or the DHCP Server service was restarted.

2. After audit logging starts, the DHCP server performs disk checks at regular intervals, both to ensure the ongoing availability of server disk space and to ensure that the current audit log file does not become too large and that log-file growth is not occurring too rapidly. The DHCP server performs a full disk check whenever either of the following conditions occurs:

    - A set number of server events are logged. By default, the set number of server events is 50.

    - When the server computer reaches 12:00 A.M. on its locally set clock.

Each time a disk check is completed, the server determines whether disk space is filled. The disk is considered full if either of the following conditions is true:

- Disk space on the server computer is lower than the required minimum amount for DHCP audit logging. By default, if the amount of free disk space remaining on the server disk reaches less than 20 megabytes, audit logging is halted.

- The current audit log file is larger than one-seventh (1/7) of the maximum allotted space or size for the combined total of all audit logs currently stored on the server. The default setting is configured in the registry at 70 MB, which means that if the current audit log is more than 10 MB, then logging will cease.

In either case, if the disk is full, the DHCP server closes the current file and ignores further requests to log audit events either until 12:00 A.M. or until disk status is improved and the disk is no longer full.

Even if audit logged events are ignored because of a disk full condition, the DHCP server continues checking the disk every 50 events (or at the currently set interval) to determine whether disk conditions have improved. If subsequent disk checks determine that the required amount of server disk space is available, the DHCP server reopens the current log file and resumes logging.

3. At 12:00 A.M. local time on the server computer, the DHCP server closes the existing log and moves to the log file for the next day of the week. For example, if the day of the week changes at 12:00 A.M. from Wednesday to Thursday, the log file named DhcpSrvLog-Wed is closed, and the file named DhcpSrvLog-Thu is opened and used for logging events.

Important   If you want to keep the audit log information for a period greater than a week, then you need to remove logged files from the directory before the following week's audit log overwrites it.

How to Monitor DHCP Server Performance by Using the DHCP Audit Log

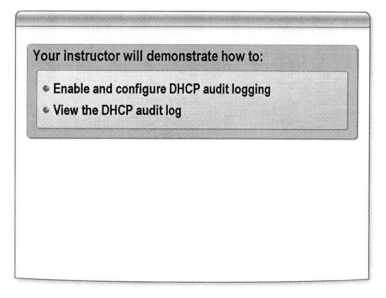

Introduction

DHCP audit logging is enabled by default. You can configure where the log files will be stored. Since DHCP audit logging is enabled by default, as soon as DHCP is installed and configured, you can view the DHCP audit logs to view the information that you need to monitor your DHCP server.

Note It is recommended that you log on with an account that has non-administrative credentials and use the **Run as** command with a user account that has appropriate administrative credentials to perform this task.

Procedure for enabling and configuring DHCP audit logging

To enable and configure DHCP audit logging:

1. In the DHCP console, in the console tree, select the appropriate DHCP server.

2. On the **Action** menu, click **Properties**.

3. On the **General** tab, verify that the **Enable DHCP audit logging** option is selected.

4. On the **Advanced** tab, in the **Audit log file path** field, type the appropriate Audit log file path, and then click **OK**.

5. In the **DHCP** dialog box, click **Yes** to stop and then restart the service.

Procedure for viewing a DHCP audit log

To view a DHCP audit log:

- Using Windows Explorer, go to the directory where you are storing the audit log file, and double-click the appropriate log file.

Note By default, the DHCP service stores audit logs in the %*Systemroot*%\System32\Dhcp folder. An audit log file contains the Event IDs and Event ID meanings in the file. Audit logs are named DhcpSrvLog-*day*.log where *day* is the three-letter abbreviation for the day of the week. For example, the audit log for Wednesday would be DhcpSrvLog-Wed.log.

Guidelines for Monitoring DHCP Server Performance

> • Create a baseline of performance data on the DHCP server
>
> • Check the standard counters for server performance, such as processor utilization, paging, disk performance, and network utilization
>
> • Review DHCP server counters to look for significant drops or increases that indicate a change in DHCP traffic

Purpose of monitoring the performance of a DHCP server

One of the primary goals of performance monitoring of the DHCP server is to diagnose problems before they impair the clients' ability to get a DHCP lease. For example, if the DHCP implementation is not functioning correctly, then client leases may not renew, which results in the clients' failure to function on the network.

Guidelines for monitoring the performance of a DHCP server

Consider the following guidelines when monitoring the performance of a DHCP server:

- Create a baseline of performance data on the DHCP server.

  You can compare the baseline with counters that can indicate if the server hosting DHCP is overloaded, or if the network is failing to send DHCP requests to the server.

- Check the standard counters for server performance (such as processor utilization, paging, disk performance, and network utilization).

  Because DHCP is often installed on a server that also hosts other services or applications, it is important to understand the total application and service load on the server, and how the load on the server might affect the operation of the DHCP Server service.

- Review DHCP server counters (such as acks/per second) to look for significant drops or increases that indicate a change in DHCP traffic.

  A sudden increase in activity could result from the addition of new DHCP clients, or it could reflect a change to a shorter DCHP lease. A sudden decrease in activity could indicate a lengthening of the DHCP lease, a failure of the network to transmit DHCP requests, or a failure of the DHCP server to process the requests.

Common Performance Counters for Monitoring DHCP Server Performance

Performance counters	What to look for after a baseline is established
Packets received/second	Monitor for sudden increases or decreases which could reflect problems on the network
Requests/second	Monitor for sudden increases or decreases which could reflect problems on the network
Active queue length	Monitor for increases both sudden and gradual which could reflect increased load or decreased server capacity
Duplicates dropped/second	Monitor for any activity which could indicate that more than one request is being transmitted on behalf of clients

Performance console

There is an administrative utility, called the Performance console, which you can use to monitor DHCP server performance. When you open the Performance console, the console tree has two nodes. The first node is System Monitor, and the second node is Performance Logs and Alerts.

System Monitor is where you can add performance objects and counters to any one of three graphical views: graph, histogram, and report. You can also view logged data. If you add a counter that has more than one instance, then you have the option to select the instance.

Definitions

In System Monitor, a *performance object* is a logical collection of counters that is associated with a resource or service that can be monitored.

In System Monitor, a *performance counter* is a data item that is associated with a performance object. For each counter selected, System Monitor presents a value corresponding to a particular aspect of the performance that is defined for the performance object.

In System Monitor, a *performance object instance* is a term used to distinguish between multiple performance objects of the same type on a computer.

Common performance counters

The following table provides a sampling of common performance counters, along with explanations of what the data might mean and the data's implications. (The performance object is the DHCP server.)

Performance counters	What data is collected	What the data means	What to look for after a baseline is established
Packets received/second	The number of message packets that the DHCP server receives per second.	A large number indicates heavy DHCP-related message traffic to the server.	Monitor for sudden increases or decreases, which could reflect problems on the network.
Requests/second	The number of DHCP request messages that the DHCP server receives per second from clients.	A sudden or unusual increase in this number indicates a large number of clients trying to renew their leases with the DHCP server. This might indicate that scope lease durations are too short.	Monitor for sudden increases or decreases, which could reflect problems on the network.
Active queue length	The current length of the internal message queue of the DHCP server. This number equals the number of unprocessed messages that the server receives.	A large number might indicate that the DHCP server cannot keep up with the load of requests being presented.	Monitor for increases both sudden and gradual, which could reflect increased load or decreased server capacity.
Duplicates dropped/second	The number of duplicated packets that the DHCP server drops per second.	This number can be affected by multiple DHCP relay agents or network interfaces that are forwarding the same packet to the server. A large number indicates that the server is not responding fast enough, or that the relay agent's boot threshold time is not set high enough.	Monitor this counter for any activity which could indicate that more than one request is being transmitted on behalf of clients.

Guidelines for Creating Alerts for a DHCP Server

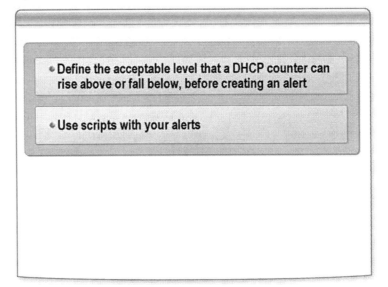

* Define the acceptable level that a DHCP counter can rise above or fall below, before creating an alert

* Use scripts with your alerts

Definition

An *alert* is a feature that detects when a predefined counter value either rises above or falls below a specified setting. The specified setting on the counter is called the *alert threshold*.

Why create alerts for a DHCP server?

The counters that are available for the DHCP server performance object are also available for creating alerts. If you know the acceptable level that a counter can rise above or fall below before an issue occurs, then you can create an alert to both notify you and run a program or script.

Guidelines for creating alerts for a DHCP server

The following guidelines are recommended when you are creating alerts for a DHCP server:

- Define the acceptable level that a DHCP counter can rise above or fall below, before creating an alert.

    - This can be done by logging the DHCP counter for a period of time to create a baseline. Using this baseline, you can then ascertain the normal operating range for a given DHCP counter, and then create alerts to notify you when the activity for this DHCP counter is outside of the normal operating range.

- Use scripts with your alerts.

    - Use DHCP Netshell commands in a script to respond to the alert.

Example of applying guidelines

You have been monitoring DHCP server activity by using System Monitor. You have been viewing the following counter:

- *Discover/sec.* The number of DHCP discover messages (DHCPDISCOVERs) received per second by the server.

  Clients send these messages when they log on to the network and obtain a new address lease. A sudden or unusual decrease in the number of DHCP requests per second could indicate that a router or DHCP relay agent has stopped forwarding DHCP packets, and that therefore clients' leases will soon expire. Having an alert to notify you of this condition will allow you to be proactive and to diagnose the problem before the IP address leases start to expire.

Practice: Monitoring DHCP

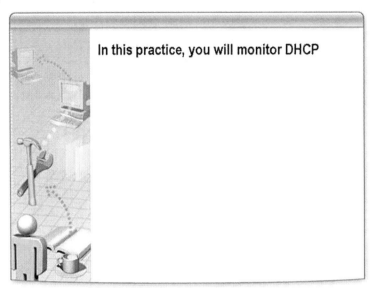

In this practice, you will monitor DHCP

Objective

In this practice, you will monitor DHCP server performance by using the Performance console. You will have an opportunity to perform real-time monitoring of a DHCP server and create an alert.

Instructions

To complete this practice, refer to the *Implementation Plan Values* document, located in the Appendix at the end of your student workbook.

You must be logged on with an account that has non-administrative credentials and use the **Run as** command with a user account that has appropriate administrative credentials to complete the task.

Scenario

A large group of computers were removed from the Lab department. Some of the remaining client computers are experiencing IP addressing conflicts, and some are unsuccessful at leasing an IP address from the DHCP server.

The systems engineer has designed a DHCP server audit logging strategy. You will enable and configure DHCP server audit logging, and then view the audit logs for DHCP client lease errors.

Practice: Enabling and configuring DHCP audit logging

▶ **Enable and configure DHCP audit logging**

- Complete this task from both student computers.

- Audit log file path: **C:\Moc\2277\Labfiles\Lab03\Audit**

▶ **Renew the IP address lease from the DHCP client**

- Complete this task from the higher number student computer.

- On the DHCP client computer, at a command prompt, use the **ipconfig** command to release and then renew the IP address.

▶ View a DHCP audit log

- Complete this task from the lower number student computer.

- Go to C:\Moc\2277\Labfiles\Lab03\Audit.

- Answer the following question by viewing today's log file.

    - What is the time stamp on the last assigned lease? _____

Scenario

New client computers have been added to the Lab department. The systems engineer wants you to compare the number of IP addresses currently leased as displayed on the Lab department's DHCP server, with the number of IP addresses currently leased as outlined in the Implementation Plan. You will view the DHCP server statistics to verify the number of IP addresses that are currently leased.

Practice: Enabling DHCP statistics to automatically refresh

▶ Enable DHCP statistics to automatically refresh

- Complete this task from the lower number student computer

- Configure the statistics to automatically update every 1 minute.

▶ View DHCP server statistics

- Complete this task from the lower number student computer

- Answer the following questions by viewing the statistics:

    - How long has the DHCP server been running? _____

    - Total addresses in use? _____

    - Total addresses available? _____

Scenario

You have been receiving calls from the Help Desk administrators because some DHCP clients have not been receiving IP addresses. You collect DHCP data for analysis. You create a log of DHCP data by using the Performance console, the DHCP server object, and counters.

Practice: Configuring System Monitor to collect real-time data for a DHCP server

▶ **Configure System Monitor to collect real-time data for a DHCP server**

- Complete this task from: both student computers

1. Open the Performance console.

2. Delete any counters in the default System Monitor view.

3. Add the following counters from the **DHCP Server** Performance object to the System Monitor view.

    - **Acks/sec**
    - **Discovers/sec**
    - **Offers/sec**
    - **Packets Received/sec**
    - **Releases/sec**

4. In the **System Monitor Properties** dialog box, on the **Graph** tab, under **Vertical scale**, in the **Maximum** field, type **5** and then click **OK**.

Important Do not close the Performance console until you have created both a chart and an alert, and then saved the Performance console.

▶ **Create an alert**

- Complete this task from: both student computers

1. In the Performance console, under **Performance Logs and Alerts**, select **Alerts**.

2. On the **Action** menu, click **New Alert Settings**.

3. In the **New Alert Settings** dialog box, type **DHCP Renew Alert** and then click **OK**.

4. In the **DHCP Renew Alert** dialog box, on the **General** tab, in the **comment** field, type **Alert when DHCP client renews IP lease** and then click **Add**.

5. In the **Add Counters** dialog box, in the **Performance object** field, select **DHCP Server**, add the counter **Acks/sec**, and then click **Close**.

6. In the **DHCP Renew Alert** dialog box, on the **General** tab, in the **Limit** field, type **1**

7. In the **DHCP Renew Alert** dialog box, on the **General** tab, in the **Interval** field, type **1**

8. In the **Run As** field, type *ComputerName***Admin** and then click **Set Password**.

9. In the **Set Password** dialog box, in the **Password** and **Confirm password** fields, type **P@ssw0rd** and then click **OK**.

10. On the **Action** tab, select **Send a network message to**, and then type *ComputerName***User**

11. On the **Schedule** tab, under **Start scan**, verify that **Manually (using the shortcut menu)** is selected, and then click **OK**.

12. Save the **Performance** console as DHCP, and then save it to the **All Users** folder on your desktop.

13. Minimize **the Performance** console. You will use it in the lab.

▶ **Configure the Messenger service to start**

■ Complete this task from: both student computers

1. In the Services administrative tool, configure the **Messenger** service to start automatically.

2. In the Services administrative tool, start **Messenger** service.

Lesson: Applying Security Guidelines for DHCP

- Guidelines for Restricting an Unauthorized User from Obtaining a Lease
- Guidelines for Restricting an Unauthorized, non-Microsoft DHCP Server from Leasing IP Addresses
- Guidelines for Restricting Who Can Administer the DHCP Service
- Guidelines for Securing the DHCP Database

Introduction

It is important to follow best practices for security when using DHCP servers on your network. This lesson covers known security issues for DHCP and related protocols.

Lesson objectives

After completing this lesson, you will be able to:

- Apply guidelines for restricting an unauthorized user from obtaining a lease.
- Apply guidelines for restricting an unauthorized, non-Microsoft DHCP server from leasing IP addresses to DHCP clients.
- Apply guidelines for restricting who can administer the DHCP service.
- Apply guidelines for securing the DHCP database.

Guidelines for Restricting an Unauthorized User from Obtaining a Lease

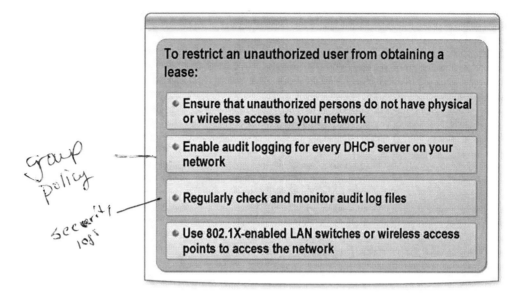

To restrict an unauthorized user from obtaining a lease:

- Ensure that unauthorized persons do not have physical or wireless access to your network
- Enable audit logging for every DHCP server on your network
- Regularly check and monitor audit log files
- Use 802.1X-enabled LAN switches or wireless access points to access the network

Purpose

When a user connects to the network, the user is not required to provide credentials to obtain a lease. Therefore, an unauthenticated user can obtain a lease for any DHCP client whenever a DHCP server is available to provide a lease.

Malicious users with physical access to the DHCP-enabled network can instigate a denial-of-service attack on DHCP servers by requesting many leases from the server, thereby depleting the number of leases that are available to other DHCP clients.

Guidelines

Guidelines for restricting an unauthorized user from obtaining a lease are as follows.

- Ensure that unauthorized persons do not have physical or wireless access to your network.

- Enable audit logging for every DHCP server on your network.

- Regularly check audit log files, and monitor them when the DHCP server receives an unusually high number of lease requests from clients.

- Use 802.1X-enabled local area network (LAN) switches or wireless access points to access the network

    - When clients running Microsoft Windows XP use 802.1X-enabled LAN switches or wireless access points to access the network, authentication occurs before the DHCP server assigns a lease, thereby providing greater security for DHCP.

Denial-of-service attacks against the DNS server through the DHCP server

When the DHCP server is configured to act as a Domain Name System (DNS) proxy server for DHCP clients and to perform DNS dynamic updates, it is possible for a malicious user to perform a denial-of-service attack against both the DHCP server and the DNS server by flooding the DHCP server with requests for leases.

Note For more information about how to identify a denial-of-service attack, see the Windows Server 2003 Help documentation.

Guidelines for restricting an unauthorized user from obtaining a lease through the DHCP server are as follows.

- Ensure that unauthorized persons do not have physical or wireless access to your network.
- Use the DHCP audit logs, located by default at %*Systemroot*%\System32\Dhcp, to monitor DNS dynamic updates by the DHCP server. The IP address of the DHCP client is included in the DHCP audit log, providing the ability to locate the source of the denial-of-service attack.

Note For more information, see "Analyzing Server Log Files and Audit Logging" in the Windows Server 2003 Help documentation.

Guidelines for Restricting Unauthorized, Non-Microsoft DHCP Servers from Leasing IP Addresses

To restrict an unauthorized, non-Microsoft DHCP server from leasing IP addresses:

* Ensure that unauthorized persons do not have physical or wireless access to your network

* **Microsoft DHCP Server**
  * Only DHCP servers running Windows 2000 or Windows Server 2003 can be authorized in Active Directory
* **Unauthorized, non-Microsoft DHCP Server**
  * Non-Microsoft DHCP server software does not include the authorization feature that is included in Windows 2000 and Windows Server 2003

Microsoft DHCP server

Only DHCP servers running Windows 2000 or Windows Server 2003 can be authorized in the Active Directory® directory service. If a DHCP server running Windows 2000 or Windows Server 2003 discovers that it is not authorized in Active Directory, the DHCP server stops servicing DHCP clients. Because of this authorization feature, if a malicious or incompetent user installs an unauthorized DHCP server running Windows 2000 or Windows Server 2003 on the organization network, the server cannot assign incorrect or conflicting leases, configure DHCP clients with inaccurate options, or disrupt network services.

Unauthorized, non-Microsoft DHCP server

Non-Microsoft DHCP server software does not include the authorization feature that is included in DHCP for Windows 2000 and Windows Server 2003. Because DHCP clients broadcast DHCPDISCOVER messages to the nearest DHCP server, if a malicious user installs a non-Microsoft DHCP server on the organization network, nearby DHCP clients will receive incorrect leases that might conflict with the IP addresses assigned to other DHCP clients on the network. In addition, the non-Microsoft DHCP server can configure DHCP clients that obtain a lease from it with option information that is inaccurate. This might reroute network traffic, causing the network to function improperly.

Guideline

To restrict unauthorized, non-Microsoft DHCP servers from leasing IP addresses, ensure that unauthorized persons do not have physical or wireless access to your network.

Guidelines for Restricting Who Can Administer the DHCP Service

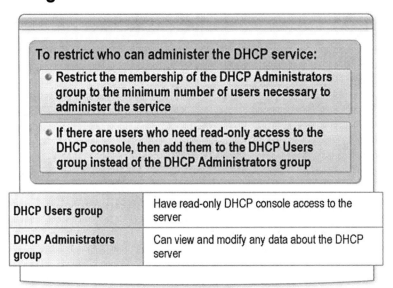

To restrict who can administer the DHCP service:

- Restrict the membership of the DHCP Administrators group to the minimum number of users necessary to administer the service

- If there are users who need read-only access to the DHCP console, then add them to the DHCP Users group instead of the DHCP Administrators group

DHCP Users group	Have read-only DHCP console access to the server
DHCP Administrators group	Can view and modify any data about the DHCP server

Introduction

You must be a member of the Administrators group or the DHCP Administrators group to administer DHCP servers by using the DHCP console or the Netsh commands for DHCP. In addition, by default, only members of the Enterprise Admins group can authorize or unauthorize a DHCP server in Active Directory. Members of the Enterprise Admins group can also delegate the right to authorize DHCP servers to other security principals.

When you install the DHCP Server service on a member server or a stand-alone server, two local groups are created: DHCP Users and DHCP Administrators. When you install the DHCP Server service on a domain controller, the two groups are created as domain local groups. The groups created do not have any members, nor are they members of any other group; and for them to be of value, you must populate them.

DHCP Users

Members of the DHCP Users group have read-only access to the DHCP console on the server, which allows DHCP Users to view, but not to modify, server data, including DHCP server configuration, registry keys, DHCP log files, and the DHCP database. DHCP Users cannot create scopes, modify option values, create reservations or exclusion ranges, or modify the DHCP server configuration in any other way.

DHCP Administrators

Members of the DHCP Administrators group can view and modify any information in the DHCP service. DHCP Administrators can create and delete scopes, add reservations, change option values, create superscopes, or perform any other activity that is needed to administer the DHCP server, including exporting or importing the DHCP server configuration and database. DHCP administrators perform these tasks by using either the Netsh commands for DHCP or the DHCP console. For more information, see "DHCP Tools" in the Windows Server 2003 Help documentation.

Members of the DHCP Administrators group do not have unlimited administrative rights. For example, if a DHCP server is also configured as a DNS server, a member of the DHCP Administrators group can view and modify the DHCP configuration, but cannot modify DNS server configuration on the same computer.

Because members of the DHCP Administrators local group have rights on the local computer only, DHCP Administrators cannot authorize or unauthorize DHCP servers in Active Directory. Only members of the Enterprise Admins group or those they delegate can perform this task. If you want to authorize or unauthorize a DHCP server in a child domain, you must have enterprise administrator credentials for the parent domain. For more information about authorizing DHCP servers in Active Directory, see "Authorizing DHCP Servers" in the Windows Server 2003 Help documentation.

Administering DHCP servers in a domain

You can use groups to administer DHCP servers in a domain. When you add a user or group to a DHCP Users or DHCP Administrators group on a DHCP server, the rights of the DHCP group member do not apply to all of the DHCP servers in the domain. The rights apply only to the DHCP service on the local computer. To assign rights to a user or group that apply to all of the DHCP servers in the domain, you can add the user or group to the DHCP Administrators group on each DHCP server in the domain.

Note For more information about delegating administration, see "To Delegate Ability to Authorize DHCP Servers to a Non-Enterprise Administrator" in the Windows Server 2003 Help documentation.

Guidelines

Guidelines for restricting who can administer the DHCP service are as follows.

- Restrict the membership of the DHCP Administrators group to the minimum number of users necessary to administer the DHCP service on that computer.

- If there are users who need read-only access to the DHCP console, then add them to the DHCP Users group instead of to the DHCP Administrators group.

Note For more information, see "DHCP Groups" in the Windows Server 2003 Help documentation.

Guidelines for Securing the DHCP Database

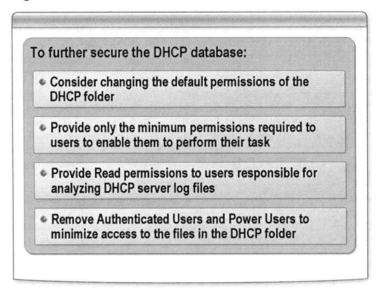

To further secure the DHCP database:

- Consider changing the default permissions of the DHCP folder

- Provide only the minimum permissions required to users to enable them to perform their task

- Provide Read permissions to users responsible for analyzing DHCP server log files

- Remove Authenticated Users and Power Users to minimize access to the files in the DHCP folder

Purpose

The default permissions for the DHCP folder are intended to restrict access to the database files and audit files to authorized users only. Change these default permissions as necessary to provide file access to individuals who will be performing administrative tasks (such as analyzing and backing up the DHCP server log files).

Note For more information about analyzing the DHCP server logs, see "Managing DHCP Servers" in the Windows Server 2003 Help documentation.

Default permissions

The default permissions for \%*Systemroot*%\System32\Dhcp are as follows:

- Administrators: Full Control
- Creator/Owner: Full Control
- Power Users: Read & Execute
- Authenticated Users: Read & Execute
- System: Full Control

Note If DHCP Server service is installed on a domain controller, then the Power Users local group is replaced with the Server Operators global group.

Guidelines

To further secure the DHCP database, apply the following guidelines.

- Consider changing the default permissions of the DHCP folder.

- Provide only the minimum, required permissions to users to enable them to perform their tasks.

- Provide Read permissions to users who are responsible for analyzing DHCP server log files.

- Remove Authenticated Users and Power Users to minimize access to the files in the DHCP folder.

Important Do not change the permissions for the System or Administrators groups. Changing these permissions from the default permissions may cause the DHCP server to malfunction and prevent administrators from performing DHCP maintenance, such as backing up the database.

Lab A: Managing and Monitoring DHCP

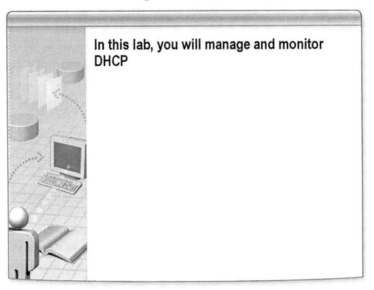

In this lab, you will manage and monitor DHCP

Objectives

Estimated time to complete this lab: 15 minutes

In this lab, you will manage and monitor DHCP.

Exercise 1
Managing and Monitoring DHCP

In this exercise, you will manage and monitor DHCP.

Instructions

To complete the lab, refer to the Implementation Plan Values document, located in the Appendix at the end of your student workbook.

You must be logged on with an account that has non-administrative credentials and use the **Run as** command with a user account that has appropriate administrative credentials to complete the tasks. When completing the lab, assume that you will log on with a non-administrative account (example: *ComputerName*User), unless the Specific Instructions in the lab state otherwise.

Scenario

There seems to be an increase in TCP/IP traffic on the network. You will use the Performance console that you created earlier to verify that the increase is due to DHCP TCP/IP traffic. You will run a script to generate IP traffic, and then use the Performance console and alert that you created to verify the DHCP settings.

Tasks	Specific instructions
✋ Perform the following tasks only on the computer with the lower student number.	
1. Manually start DHCP Renew Alert.	▪ Switch to the System Monitor, and, in the Performance console, select **Alerts**, and then manually start DHCP Renew Alert.
2. Select **System Monitor view**.	▪ In the Performance console, select System Monitor view.
✋ Perform the following task only on the computer with the higher student number.	
3. Use the **ipconfig** command to generate DHCP traffic by releasing and renewing the client computer's IP address.	▪ On the client computer, at a command prompt, use the **ipconfig** command to release and renew the client's IP address three times.
✋ Perform the following task only on the computer with the lower student number.	
4. Verify that the DHCP Alert message displays on the server where you are logged on.	a. On the server computer, record the text in the **Performance alert** dialog box. b. Performance Alert text:_____ c. Close the **Performance alert** dialog box. d. Stop DHCP Renew Alert.
✋ Perform the following task only on the computer with the lower student number.	

Tasks	Specific instructions
5. View the captured DHCP counter data in System Monitor, and record the information.	a. On the server computer, in the Performance console, stop the System Monitor chart.
	b. Record the values for the counters that you find in the System Monitor chart.
	• Acks/sec _____
	• Discovers/sec _____
	• Offers/sec _____
	• Packets Received/sec _____
	• Releases/sec _____
✋	Perform the following task only on the computer with the lower student number.
6. Close the Performance console.	▪ On the server computer, close the Performance console.
✋	Perform the following task only on the computer with the higher student number.
7. Configure the Partner Network Connection to use the IP address of your Partner Network Connection.	▪ Configure the Partner Network Connection TCP/IP configuration to use the following IP address information:
	• IP address: the IP address of your Partner Network Connection
	• Subnet mask: **255.255.255.0**

Microsoft®
Training &
Certification

Module 4: Resolving Names

Contents

Overview

- **Multimedia: Introduction to the Name Resolution Process**
- **Viewing Names on a Client**
- **Configuring Host Name Resolution**
- **Configuring NetBIOS Name Resolution**

Introduction

Microsoft® Windows® Server 2003, Standard Edition uses name resolution to translate numerical Internet Protocol (IP) addresses, which are necessary for Transmission Control Protocol/Internet Protocol (TCP/IP) communications, to computer names that are easier for users to remember and use than 32-bit IP addresses. With name resolution, you can assign computer names to the IP addresses of the source and destination hosts, and then use the computer names to contact the hosts.

There are two types of names to resolve:

- Host names
- Network basic input/output system (NetBIOS) names

Objectives

After completing this module, you will be able to:

- Describe the name resolution process.
- View names on a client.
- Configure host name resolution.
- Configure NetBIOS name resolution.
- Resolve names.

Multimedia: Introduction to the Name Resolution Process

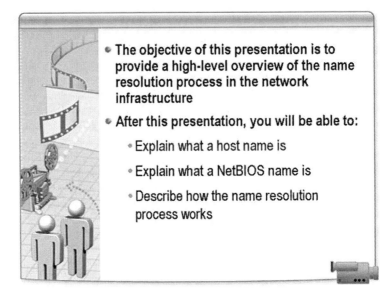

File location

To start the *Introduction to the Name Resolution Process* presentation, open the Web page on the Student Materials compact disc, click **Multimedia**, and then click the title of the presentation.

Objectives

At the end of this presentation, you will be able to:

- Explain what a host name is.

- Explain what a NetBIOS name is.

- Describe how the name resolution process works.

Key points

- Part of a successful communication process in a TCP/IP network is name resolution.

- There are two types of names that are used in a TCP/IP network: host names and NetBIOS names.

- Host names and NetBIOS names are display names that users employ to access resources. However, computers use IP addresses to connect to each other. Therefore, display names must be resolved to IP addresses for users to access resources on the network.

Lesson: Viewing Names on a Client

* How Names Are Mapped to IP Addresses
* What Are Host Names?
* What Are NetBIOS Names?
* How to View Names On a Client

Introduction

A name is an identifier of your computer on the network. Each computer typically has two names: an alphanumeric name, and a numerical IP address. As a systems administrator, you will need to know how to view both of these names for a computer, and also how to change them to reflect the needs of your network.

Lesson objectives

After completing this lesson, you will be able to:

* Describe how names are mapped to IP addresses.
* Explain what host names are.
* Explain what NetBIOS names are.
* View names on a client.

How Names Are Mapped to IP Addresses

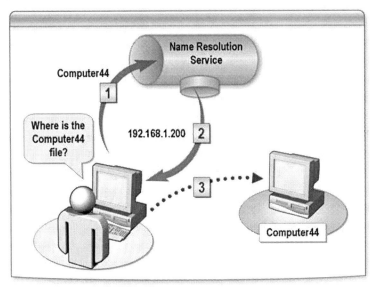

Definitions

Name resolution is the process of having software automatically translate between alphanumeric names (such as Server1 or Computer44) and numerical IP addresses (such as 192.168.1.200 or 10.0.0.1). IP addresses are more difficult for users to work with than names, but they are necessary for TCP/IP communications.

A *name resolution service* is a service that Windows Internet Name Service (WINS) and Domain Name System (DNS) provide. The name resolution service allows *display* (or alphanumeric) names to be resolved to an address. Name resolution services also allow TCP/IP hosts to query for specific types of network resources or services, such as a domain controller or a Simple Mail Transfer Protocol (SMTP) messaging server, and receive in return the name and IP address of the computers that provide that resource or service.

Process

For people to connect computers to resources, there must be a method that matches names to IP addresses. A user can then request a resource by using the name Server1, and the computer can determine that the name Server1 is associated with the IP address 192.168.1.200. The computer can then connect to the resource, Server1, by using the IP address 192.168.1.200.

The process of name resolution is similar to using a telephone book. You want to call your friend on the phone. You look for your friend's name in the telephone book to find their telephone number. The telephone book provides you with the telephone number associated with your friend's name. You can then use the number to telephone your friend.

Characteristics of name resolution

Important characteristics of name resolution are as follows.

- People use alphanumeric names because they are easier to remember.

- Computers require IP addresses to communicate via TCP/IP.

- A host name may map to more than one IP address for a particular name. For example, three separate servers may host a replica of the same Web site and be accessed with the same name.

- Name resolution is the process of returning one or more IP addresses for a given name.

- There are two types of names in networking: host and NetBIOS.

- There is more than one method of resolving host names, and more than one method of resolving NetBIOS names. These methods have evolved over time to meet various needs.

- The applications and services that are used to enter the names determine what type of name has been entered. The configuration of the operating system determines how the name resolution process resolves the name. For example: The user enters a name in an application or service. The application or service is designed to query either a host name or a NetBIOS name. After the query is presented to the operating system, it begins the process of attempting to resolve the name based on the name's configuration.

What Are Host Names?

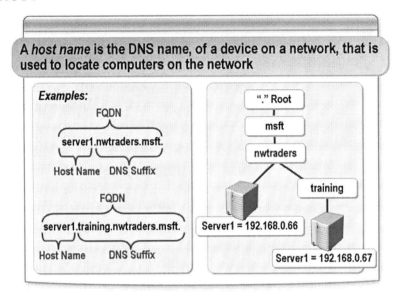

A *host name* is the DNS name, of a device on a network, that is used to locate computers on the network

Examples:

FQDN

server1.nwtraders.msft.

Host Name   DNS Suffix

FQDN

server1.training.nwtraders.msft.

Host Name   DNS Suffix

"." Root

msft

nwtraders

training

Server1 = 192.168.0.66

Server1 = 192.168.0.67

Definitions

A *name* is the identifier of your computer on the network.

A *host name* is the DNS name of a device on a network.

A *fully qualified domain name (FQDN)* is a DNS domain name that has been stated unambiguously to indicate with absolute certainty its location in the domain namespace tree.

Purpose of host names

Host names are used to locate computers on the network. For the computer to contact another computer by using a host name, the host name must either appear in the Hosts file or be known by a DNS server. For most computers running Windows Server 2003 or Windows XP, the host name and the NetBIOS name are the same.

Host names are created based on the standard naming convention that is used on the Internet. Host names provide the capability for name resolution on the Internet. A host name is part of an FQDN, which uses a hierarchical structure. Host names are typically part of the DNS namespace that allows you to access resources in a DNS structure.

Host name and suffix

Host names are part of the DNS namespace; they allow a client to locate resources worldwide through the global DNS namespace.

A host name can exist as a single-part name, or it can be used with the suffix to create the identifier for a resource on a TCP/IP network. The host name and suffix are known together as the fully qualified domain name.

In a fully qualified domain name, such as Server1.training.nwtraders.msft, the host name portion of the FQDN is Server1. Training.nwtraders.msft is known as the *suffix*. Together, the host name (Server1) and the suffix (training.nwtraders.msft) reference a single, specific resource on a TCP/IP network. The suffix is essential to the host name, because it allows two identical host names to exist on the network without conflict. Server1.training.nwtraders.msft can exist on the same network with Server1.nwtraders.msft. The suffix is used to differentiate between the two names.

Note For more information about DNS, refer to Module 5, "Resolving Host Names by Using Domain Name System (DNS)," and Module 6, "Managing and Monitoring Domain Name System (DNS)" in Course 2277, *Implementing, Managing, and Maintaining a Microsoft Windows Server 2003 Network Infrastructure: Network Services*.

When the administrator installs the operating system, the computer identifier and DNS suffix are combined to create the host name. The host name and suffix can be modified on most computers if needed.

Important Because so many networking elements rely on the DNS namespace, it is important to follow an implementation plan when creating host names and suffixes.

Characteristics of a host name

Host names are used in virtually all TCP/IP environments. The following list provides a description of a host name:

- A host name is an alias that an administrator assigns to a computer to identify a TCP/IP host.

- Although in Windows Server 2003 and Windows XP the host name will default to the same name as the NetBIOS name, the host name does not need to match the NetBIOS computer name.

- The host name can be any 255-character string.

- A single host name can be assigned to a host. Name resolution methods, such as the Hosts file or DNS, can have multiple host names which will map to the IP address of the same host. For example, the host Server1.nwtraders.msft could have entries in DNS for both Server1.nwtraders.msft and www.nwtraders.msft. Either name will resolve to the IP address of Server1.nwtraders.msft.

- It is possible for one host name to resolve to more than one IP address. For example, three identical Web servers are all identified in DNS with the name www.nwtraders.msft. When a client attempts to connect to www.nwtraders.msft through a Web browser, three IP addresses are returned from the DNS query.

- A host name simplifies the way that a user references other TCP/IP hosts. Host names are easier to remember than IP addresses.

- A host name can be used in place of an IP address when using the Ping utility or other TCP/IP utilities.

- To be of value for name resolution, a host name and its corresponding IP address must be configured either in a database on a DNS server or in a Hosts file.

- The Hostname utility displays the host name that is assigned to your system. By default, the host name is the same as the computer name of your Windows-based computer.

Examples

The following table shows examples of FQDNs, host names, and DNS suffixes.

Referring to the slide, notice that there is a trailing period (.) at the end of an FQDN. This trailing period (.) represents the Root location in the tree, and is neither required nor often used in practice.

Fully Qualified Domain Name (FQDN)

Host name	DNS suffix
server1	training.nwtraders.msft
server1	nwtraders.msft
www	microsoft.com
computer44	nwtraders.msft

What Are NetBIOS Names?

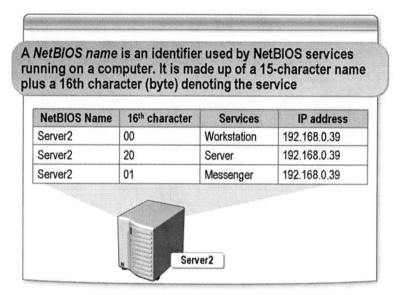

A *NetBIOS name* is an identifier used by NetBIOS services running on a computer. It is made up of a 15-character name plus a 16th character (byte) denoting the service

NetBIOS Name	16ᵗʰ character	Services	IP address
Server2	00	Workstation	192.168.0.39
Server2	20	Server	192.168.0.39
Server2	01	Messenger	192.168.0.39

Server2

Definition

A *NetBIOS name* is an identifier that is used by NetBIOS services running on a computer. It is made up of a 15-character name plus a 16th character (byte) denoting the service.

Purpose of NetBIOS names

NetBIOS names are used to identify resources in a NetBIOS network. NetBIOS names do not provide the capability for name resolution on the Internet because NetBIOS names are single-part names and do not have any hierarchical structure.

NetBIOS names are flat, which means that there are no suffixes added to the NetBIOS name and that there is no way to differentiate two computers that have the same NetBIOS name. This means that each NetBIOS name in any one network must be unique. For example, Server2 is the NetBIOS name of a resource in a NetBIOS network. Consequently if any other computer on the same network has the name Server2, an error will result.

Characteristics of NetBIOS names

Characteristics of NetBIOS names are as follows:

- NetBIOS names are used to support services that require NetBIOS. Windows Server 2003, Windows 2000, and Microsoft Windows XP use DNS names for most functions, but a NetBIOS name resolution method must exist on any network with computers that are running earlier versions of Windows, or for applications that still depend on NetBIOS names.

- A NetBIOS name is an alias that is assigned to a computer by an administrator to identify a NetBIOS service running on a TCP/IP host.

- The NetBIOS name does not have to match the host name.

- NetBIOS names are 15 characters or less in length, compared to 255 or fewer characters for DNS host names. The host name and the NetBIOS name on a computer running Windows Server 2003 are generated together. If the host name is more than 15 characters, the NetBIOS name is the first 15 characters of the host name.

- NetBIOS names must be unique on their networks.

- When you start your computer, various services (such as the server service or the workstation service) registers a unique NetBIOS name that is based on the computer name. The registered name is the 15-character NetBIOS name, plus a sixteenth character (byte) that uniquely identifies the server service. (Each character is one byte rendered in ASCII text, but the sixteenth character is normally rendered in hexadecimal notation rather than in ASCII text, so it is often referred to as the sixteenth byte rather than the sixteenth character.)

- NetBIOS names are also registered for groups of computers that provide network services. For example, if london.nwtraders.msft is a domain controller, it will register the NetBIOS name, London, and will also register names that identify its roles as a domain controller in the nwtraders domain at the same time. This allows clients to search for all NetBIOS hosts that provide domain controller services in the nwtraders domain without the client knowing the actual names of the domain controllers.

- A NetBIOS name simplifies the way that a user references other TCP/IP hosts. NetBIOS names are easier to remember than IP addresses.

- A NetBIOS name can be resolved if the name and IP address are stored either in a database on a WINS server or in an LmHosts file. A broadcast can also resolve a NetBIOS name.

- The Nbstat utility displays the NetBIOS names that NetBIOS services use on your computer.

The NetBIOS name is created while the operating system is being installed. When the computer name is created, the install automatically creates both a host name and a NetBIOS name that are based on the entered computer name.

Examples

For example, Server2 is the NetBIOS name of the computer in the diagram. The computer is running several NetBIOS services, including workstation, server, and messenger. Each of the services is associated with the same NetBIOS name (Server2).

How to View Names on a Client

> **Your instructor will demonstrate how to:**
>
> - View host names and DNS suffixes by using the Ipconfig utility
> - View host names by using System Properties
> - View NetBIOS names by using the Nbtstat command
> - View your computer's NetBIOS name by using System Properties
> - Rename a computer

Introduction

Configuring names on a client includes viewing host names, viewing NetBIOS names, renaming a computer, and changing the DNS suffix of your computer.

Note   It is recommended that you log on with an account that has non-administrative credentials and use the **Run as** command with a user account that has appropriate administrative credentials to perform this task.

Procedures for viewing host names

To view your host name and DNS suffix by using the Ipconfig utility:

1. On the **Start** menu, point to **All Programs**, point to **Accessories**, and then right-click **Command Prompt**.
2. At the command prompt, type **ipconfig /all** and then press ENTER.
3. View the values for the **Host name** and the **Primary DNS Suffix** fields.

To view your host name by using the Hostname utility:

- At the command prompt, type **hostname** and then press ENTER.

To view your computer's host name by using System Properties:

1. Log on as an account with appropriate permissions.
2. In Control Panel, open **System**.
3. On the **Computer Name** tab, click **Change**.

The host name displays in the **Computer name** field. Notice that the full computer name displays under the **Computer name** field.

Procedure for viewing NetBIOS names

To view the NetBIOS names by using the **Nbtstat** command:

- At the command prompt, type **Nbtstat -n** and then press ENTER.

NetBIOS names that are registered to NetBIOS services will display.

- At the command prompt, type **Nbtstat –A** *IPAddress* (Where *IPAddress* is the IP address of the remote server), and then press ENTER.

NetBIOS names that are registered to NetBIOS services of the identified server will display.

Note   You must be logged on as either an administrator or a member of the Administrators group to complete this procedure. If your computer is connected to a network, network policy settings may also prevent you from completing this procedure.

To view your computer's NetBIOS name by using System Properties:

1. In the **System Properties** dialog box, on the **Computer name** tab, click **Change**.
2. In the **Computer Name Changes** dialog box, click **More**.
3. View the NetBIOS name in the **NetBIOS computer name** field.

Procedure for renaming a computer

To rename a computer:

Note   You must be logged on as either an administrator or a member of the Administrators group to complete this procedure. If your computer is connected to a network, network policy settings may also prevent you from completing this procedure.

---

1. In the **System Properties** dialog box, on the **Computer name** tab, click **Change**.
2. On the **Computer Name** tab, click **Change**.
3. Under **Computer name**, type a new name for the computer, and then click **OK**.

Note   If the computer is a member of a domain, you will be prompted to provide a user name and user password to rename the computer in the domain.

Practice: Viewing Names on a Client

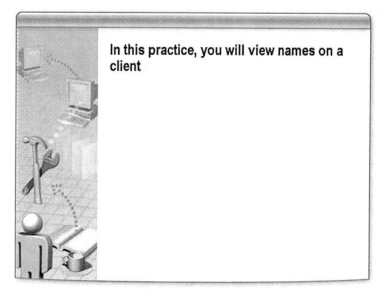

In this practice, you will view names on a client

Objective

In this practice, you will view names on a client.

Scenario

You are moving client computers to the lab for testing. The client computers are running Microsoft Windows XP Professional, and they were configured originally for the corporate network. Due to the Lab department's computer name schema, you need to configure the client computers with new names, and then to verify that the correct host and NetBIOS names have been configured.

Instructions

You must be logged on as either an administrator or a member of the Administrators group to complete parts of this procedure. Log on as *ServerName*Admin for the entire practice. When you have completed the practice, log on as *ServerName*User.

Practice

▶ **View Host name and Primary DNS Suffix by using the ipconfig command**

- Complete this task from: both student computers

- What is the Host Name? _____

- What is the Primary DNS Suffix?_____

▶ **View the NetBIOS name of your server by using the nbtstat command**

- Complete this task from: both student computers

- What is the NetBIOS name of your computer?

  _____

▶ **View the NetBIOS name of your partner's computer by using their IP address and the nbtstat command**

- Complete this task from: both student computers

- What is the NetBIOS name of your partner's computer?

  _____

Lesson: Configuring Host Name Resolution

* The Host Name Resolution Process
* Client Resolver Cache
* How to View and Flush the Client Resolver Cache
* Hosts File
* How to Preload the Client Resolver Cache by Using a Hosts File

Introduction

Windows 2000 and later Microsoft operating systems depend primarily on host name resolution for resolving the names of computers to IP addresses. Host name resolution can resolve a name by using the client resolver cache, DNS servers, and the Hosts file.

Note This lesson describes how you can use the client resolver cache and the Hosts file to resolve host names to IP addresses. Module 5, "Resolving Host Names by Using Domain Name System (DNS)" in Course 2277, *Implementing, Managing, and Maintaining a Microsoft Windows Server 2003 Network Infrastructure: Network Services* covers how you can use a DNS server to resolve host names to IP addresses.

Lesson objectives

After completing this lesson, you will be able to:

■ Describe the host name resolution process.

■ Explain what a client resolver cache is.

■ View and flush the client resolver cache.

■ Explain what a Hosts file is.

■ Preload the client resolver cache by using a Hosts file.

■ Configure host name resolution.

The Host Name Resolution Process

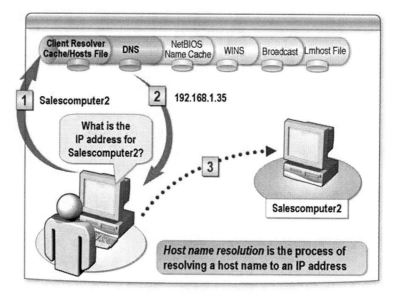

Definition

Host Name resolution is the process of resolving a host name to an IP address.

Host name resolution process

The host name resolution process is functions as follows:

1. The process begins when an application or service that is being used passes the host name to the DNS client service.

2. The DNS client service then searches the client resolver cache for the host name-to-IP address mapping. All entries into the Hosts file are preloaded into the client resolver cache.

3. If the DNS client service does not locate a mapping in the client resolver cache, then the DNS client service forwards a host name query to a DNS server.

4. If the configured host name resolution methods fail, then the configured NetBIOS name resolution methods are employed to attempt to resolve the name. This only occurs if the Host name is 15 characters or less.

5. When the host name is found, then the corresponding IP address is returned to the application.

Methods of host name resolution

The Microsoft implementation of TCP/IP uses the DNS client service to resolve host names to IP addresses by using the following methods.

Standard methods of resolution	Description
DNS client resolver cache	A cached storage location on the local computer where the DNS client service stores resolved host-to-IP address mappings.
DNS server	A server that maintains a database of IP address/computer name (host name) mappings.
Hosts file	A local text file in the same format as the 4.3 Berkeley Software Distribution (BSD) UNIX\Etc\Hosts file. This file matches host names to IP addresses. This file is typically used to resolve host names for TCP/IP utilities.

Client Resolver Cache

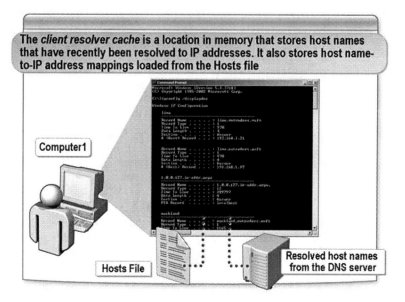

Definitions

The *client resolver cache* is a location in memory that stores host names that have recently been resolved to IP addresses. It is also a location that stores host name-to-IP address mappings that are loaded from the Hosts file.

Negative cache entries are host names entered into the cache that were queried but could not be resolved.

Purpose of client resolver cache

The client resolver cache is the first place that the DNS client looks for host name-to-IP address mappings. The client resolver cache resolves IP addresses quicker than the other host name resolution methods, such as the DNS server and the Hosts file. In addition, the client resolver cache does not create network traffic.

Purpose of negative cache entries

Negative cache entries are created automatically when a host name query fails to resolve the IP address for a particular name. By default, the failed name is cached for five minutes, so that if the same failed name is queried again, then the client does not query the DNS server but instead resolves the host name query from the cache.

Information sources for the client resolver cache

The local client resolver cache can include name information that is obtained from two possible sources.

- Hosts file

  If a Hosts file is configured locally, then any host name-to-address mappings from that file are preloaded into the cache.

- Any resolved names

  Resource records obtained in answered responses from previous DNS queries are added to the cache and kept for a period of time based on the Time To Live (TTL).

Client resolver cache   The client resolver cache maintains resolved host name information, including the record name, TTL, and IP address.

Mappings for host names to IP addresses only remain in the DNS resolver cache for a limited time. This means that if you need to resolve a host name, you can find the mapping in the client resolver cache. For example, if your applications are constantly resolving the same host names, then the client resolver cache could quickly resolve the host name.

However, the mapping for a host name to an IP address is maintained for a period of time known as the *Time To Live*. Whether or not the name is accessed before the time period expires, the mapping is removed. This helps keep the cache from growing too large and from maintaining mappings that may change and become invalid.

The resolver of the host name provides the Time-To-Live value for a resolved host name-to-IP address mapping. For example, if the DNS server resolves a mapping, then the DNS server provides the Time-To-Live value.

Example   In the screen shot, you can see the results of the **ipconfig /displaydns** command. This screen shot shows the resource records that are cached.

How to View and Flush the Client Resolver Cache

> **Your instructor will demonstrate how to:**
>
> - Display a client resolver cache by using the Ipconfig command
> - Flush a client resolver cache by using the Ipconfig command

Introduction

Flushing is purging or releasing any client resolver cache entries. This ensures that incorrect mappings are flushed from the client resolver cache.

Note It is recommended that you log on with an account that has non-administrative credentials and use the **Run as** command with a user account that has appropriate administrative credentials to perform this task.

Procedure for displaying a client resolver cache

To display a client resolver cache by using the **ipconfig** command:

- At the command prompt, type **ipconfig /displaydns**

The ipconfig /flushdns command

The **ipconfig /flushdns** command provides you with a means to flush and reset the contents of the DNS client resolver cache. During DNS troubleshooting, if necessary, you can use this procedure to discard negative cache entries from the cache, along with any other dynamically added entries.

Although the **ipconfig** command is provided for earlier versions of Windows, the **/flushdns** option is only available for use at computers running Windows 2000, Windows XP, or Windows Server 2003. The DNS Client service must also be started.

Procedure for flushing a client resolver cache

To flush a client resolver cache by using the **ipconfig** command:

- In the command prompt, type **ipconfig /flushdns**

Hosts File

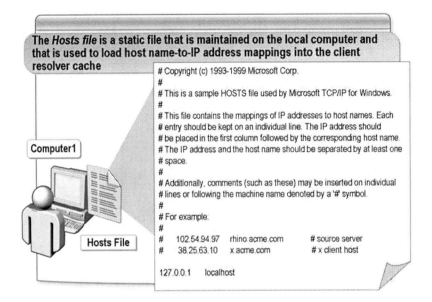

The *Hosts file* is a static file that is maintained on the local computer and that is used to load host name-to-IP address mappings into the client resolver cache

```
# Copyright (c) 1993-1999 Microsoft Corp.
#
# This is a sample HOSTS file used by Microsoft TCP/IP for Windows.
#
# This file contains the mappings of IP addresses to host names. Each
# entry should be kept on an individual line. The IP address should
# be placed in the first column followed by the corresponding host name.
# The IP address and the host name should be separated by at least one
# space.
#
# Additionally, comments (such as these) may be inserted on individual
# lines or following the machine name denoted by a '#' symbol.
#
# For example:
#
#     102.54.94.97    rhino.acme.com        # source server
#     38.25.63.10     x.acme.com            # x client host

127.0.0.1       localhost
```

Computer1

Hosts File

Definition

The *Hosts file* is a static file that is maintained on the local computer and that is used to load host name-to-IP address mappings into the client resolver cache.

Purpose of a Hosts file

You can use the Hosts file to preload permanent host name-to-IP address mappings into the client resolver cache. This decreases the response time for queries and reduces network traffic.

Hosts file

Characteristics of a Hosts file include the following:

- A single entry in the Hosts file consists of an IP address corresponding to one or more host names. The host name in the hosts file can be a single-part name such as Server1, or an FQDN such as server1.nwtraders.msft.

- A Hosts file must reside on each computer. The client resolver cache searches locally for the Hosts file.

- The Hosts file is found in the *%Systemroot%*\System32\Drivers\Etc\ folder and is named Hosts.

- When you create a host name-to-IP address mapping in the Hosts file and then save the Hosts file, the mapping is loaded into the client resolver cache.

- The host name mapping entry, from the host file, does not contain a Time-To-Live period. The host name mapping will remain in the client resolver cache until it is removed from the Hosts file.

- The Hosts file provides compatibility with the UNIX Hosts file.

Example

The illustration shows you the contents of a Hosts file. This sample Hosts file can be found in the *%Systemroot%*\System32\Drivers\Etc\ folder, and is named Hosts. If you were to make entries to this Hosts file and the save it, those entries would be immediately loaded into your DNS client resolver cache.

How to Preload a Client Resolver Cache by Using a Hosts File

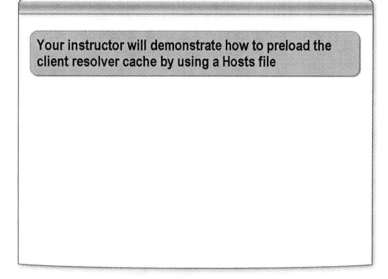

Introduction

You can use the Hosts file to preload permanent host name-to-IP address mappings into the client resolver cache.

Guideline

You must rename the file from Hosts.txt to Hosts. The DNS client service will search for a file named Hosts, rather than a file named Hosts.txt.

Note   It is recommended that you log on with an account that has non-administrative credentials and use the **Run as** command with a user account that has appropriate administrative credentials to perform this task.

Procedure

To preload a client resolver cache by using a Hosts file:

1. On the client computer, open the **Run** dialog box.

2. In the **Run** dialog box, type the following command:
   notepad *%systemroot%***system32\drivers\etc\Hosts**
   The Hosts file opens for editing in Notepad.

3. In the Hosts file, add additional host name-to-address mappings on separate lines to be preloaded into the client resolver cache. Remember to follow the format of the example in the Hosts file.

4. On the **File** menu, click **Save As**.

5. In the **Save As** dialog box, in the **Save as type** field, select **All Files,** and then click **hosts**.

6. In the **Save As warning** dialog box, click **Yes** to overwrite hosts.

- It is very important that you save the file as Hosts and not as Hosts.txt.

7. Exit Notepad.

As an option, you can verify that your changes have been updated in the client resolver cache by viewing its contents by using the **ipconfig /displaydns** command. If you do not see the mappings that you entered into the Hosts file displayed, then verify that you saved the Hosts file correctly. If the Hosts file has a .txt extension (the icon will be a **Notepad** icon), then the file will not preload mappings into the cache.

Note To edit the Hosts file from a command prompt, first open the command prompt with **Run as** by using a user account that has the appropriate Administrative rights. Then, in the command prompt, type **Notepad %systemroot%\system32\drivers\etc\hosts**

Practice: Configuring Host Name Resolution

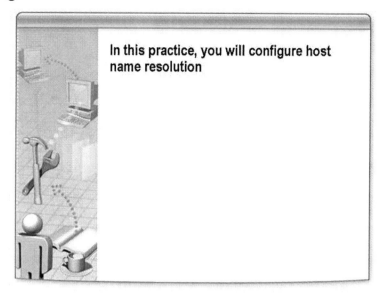

In this practice, you will configure host name resolution

Objective

In this practice, you will configure host name resolution.

Instructions

To complete this practice, refer to the *Implementation Plan Values* document, located in the Appendix at the end of your student workbook.

You must be logged on with an account that has non-administrative credentials and use the **Run as** command with a user account that has appropriate administrative credentials to complete the task.

Scenario

While the systems engineer was reviewing network traffic logs in the lab test, she noticed that there was a large amount of DNS traffic in the Lab department. This traffic is generated from queries for the IP address of the test Web server. The systems engineer has asked you to reduce the DNS query traffic for this host name. You will use the Hosts file on each computer to configure an entry that will be preloaded into the client resolver cache.

Practice

▶ **Flush the client resolver cache**

Complete this procedure from both student computers.

- Flush the client resolver cache by using the **ipconfig /flushdns** command.

▶ **Preload the client resolver cache**

Complete this procedure from both student computers.

- Open a command prompt by using **Run as**.
- Username: *ComputerName***Admin**
- Password: **P@ssw0rd**
- Add the following entry to the Hosts file (where *x* is the classroom number).

IP address	Host name
192.168.*x*.100	Glasgow

- Save the Hosts file.

▶ **Verify that the entry that you added now displays in the client resolver cache**

- Complete this procedure from: both student computers
- Verify that the entry that you added now displays in the client resolver cache by using the **ipconfig /displaydns** command.

Lesson: Configuring NetBIOS Name Resolution

- NetBIOS Name Resolution Process
- NetBIOS Name Cache
- How to View and Release the NetBIOS Name Cache
- Broadcasts
- Lmhosts File
- How to Preload a NetBIOS Name Cache by Using an Lmhosts File

Introduction

You can use the NetBIOS name cache, WINS server, broadcast, or Lmhosts file to resolve NetBIOS names to IP addresses.

Note This lesson describes how you can use the NetBIOS cache, broadcast, and Lmhosts file to resolve host name-to-IP address mappings. For more information about how to use a WINS server to resolve host name-to-IP address mappings, see Module 7, "Resolving NetBIOS Names by Using Windows Internet Name Service (WINS)" in Course 2277 *Implementing, Managing, and Maintaining a Microsoft Windows Server 2003 Network Infrastructure: Network Services*.

Lesson objectives

After completing this lesson, you will be able to:

- Describe the NetBIOS name resolution process.
- Explain what the NetBIOS name cache is.
- View and release the NetBIOS name cache.
- Explain what broadcasts are.
- Explain what an Lmhosts file is.
- Preload the NetBIOS name cache by using an Lmhosts file.
- Configure NetBIOS name resolution.

NetBIOS Name Resolution Process

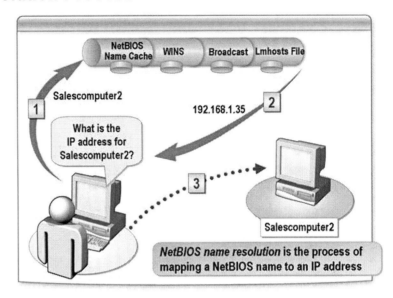

Definition	*NetBIOS name resolution* is the process of mapping a NetBIOS name to an IP address.
NetBIOS name resolution process	The NetBIOS name resolution process is configurable. The default order, in which the client is configured to query a WINS server and to use Lmhosts lookup, is as follows.

1. When an application needs to resolve a NetBIOS name to an IP address, the application searches in the NetBIOS cache for a mapping.

2. If the NetBIOS cache does not resolve the NetBIOS name to an IP address, then the WINS server is queried.

3. If the WINS server does not resolve the NetBIOS name to an IP address, then a NetBIOS name query is sent to the local network as a broadcast.

4. If the broadcast does not resolve the NetBIOS name to an IP address, then the local Lmhosts file is searched.

5. When the NetBIOS name is found, then the corresponding IP address is returned to the application.

Methods of NetBIOS name resolution

The Microsoft implementation of TCP/IP uses the NetBIOS redirector service to resolve host names to IP addresses by using the following methods. The NetBIOS redirector is the service that takes a NetBIOS query from an application or service and manages the NetBIOS resolution process.

Standard methods of resolution	Description
NetBIOS name cache	A cache storage location for resolved NetBIOS names to IP addresses. The local cache contains the NetBIOS names that the local computer has recently resolved.
NetBIOS name server	A NetBIOS name server can also be a WINS server that maintains a database of NetBIOS names.
Local broadcast	The NetBIOS name query is broadcast onto the local network.

NetBIOS Name Cache

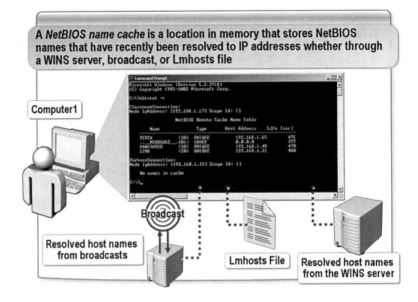

A *NetBIOS name cache* is a location in memory that stores NetBIOS names that have recently been resolved to IP addresses whether through a WINS server, broadcast, or Lmhosts file

Computer1

Broadcast

Resolved host names
from broadcasts

Lmhosts File

Resolved host names
from the WINS server

Definition

A *NetBIOS name cache* is a location in memory that stores NetBIOS names that have recently been resolved to IP addresses, whether through a WINS server, broadcast, or Lmhosts file. It is also a location that stores host name-to-IP address mappings that are preloaded from the Lmhosts file.

Purpose of a NetBIOS name cache

The NetBIOS name cache is the first place that the NetBIOS redirector searches for an IP address to map to a NetBIOS name. NetBIOS name cache resolves IP addresses more quickly than a WINS server, broadcast, or Lmhosts file, and it does not create network traffic.

In addition, the NetBIOS name cache can be preloaded with often-used NetBIOS name-to-IP address mappings by using the Lmhosts file.

NetBIOS name cache

The NetBIOS name cache contains the NetBIOS names that the local computer has recently resolved and also the name resolution results. Name resolution is performed more quickly, because the cached results are accessed for name resolution. However, name resolution data is limited to recently resolved names.

When a user initiates a NetBIOS name query by using an application or service, such as **net use**, the NetBIOS name resolution process begins. The NetBIOS name cache is checked for the NetBIOS name/IP address mapping of the destination host. The NetBIOS name cache contains the most recently resolved NetBIOS names. If the NetBIOS name is not found in the cache, the client running Windows attempts to determine the IP address of the destination host by using other methods.

Note For a command, such as **net use** and other commands that call the Server Message Block (SMB) protocol, Windows 2000 and later can employ either direct hosting over SMB or the traditional NetBIOS over TCP/IP. If both the direct-hosted and NetBIOS over TCP/IP are enabled, then both methods are tried at the same time, and the first to respond is used. NetBIOS over TCP/IP will attempt to use NetBIOS name resolution. Direct hosting will use host name resolution.

After a NetBIOS name is resolved to an IP address, a mapping entry is made in the NetBIOS name cache and is given a refresh interval (or TTL) of 10 minutes. If the name in the NetBIOS cache is accessed within the TTL, then the TTL is reset to 10 minutes. If the TTL is reached without the name being accessed, then the mapping is removed from the NetBIOS name cache. When you view the NetBIOS name cache, the TTL displays as life in seconds.

NetBIOS names can be one of two types: *Unique* or *Group*. A *Unique* NetBIOS name refers to a NetBIOS service hosted on an individual computer. A *Group* NetBIOS name refers to a NetBIOS service hosted on a group of computers.

Example

The following table illustrates examples of NetBIOS name-to-IP address mappings stored in a NetBIOS name cache. Notice that the:

- *Name* includes the 16th character that identifies the service registering the NetBIOS name.

- NetBIOS names are Unique.

- *Life* shows the number of seconds remaining before the NetBIOS name is removed.

Name	Type	Host address	Life (seconds)
Server3 <20>	UNIQUE	192.168.1.156	515
Computer9 <20>	UNIQUE	192.168.1.101	430

How to View and Release the NetBIOS Name Cache

Your instructor will demonstrate how to:

- View the contents of the local computer's NetBIOS name cache
- Release the NetBIOS name cache and reload the #PRE-tagged entries in the local Lmhosts file
- Display and view the NetBIOS name table of the local computer

Introduction

Releasing the NetBIOS name cache removes all dynamic NetBIOS name-to-IP address mappings that are stored in the NetBIOS name cache. This is helpful when you must remove incorrect mappings.

Note It is recommended that you log on with an account that has non-administrative credentials and use the **Run as** command with a user account that has appropriate administrative credentials to perform this task.

Nbtstat utility

The tool used to view the NetBIOS name cache is the nbtstat utility. The Nbtstat utility displays both protocol statistics and current TCP/IP connections by using NetBIOS over TCP/IP (NBT).

When Nbtstat is used without parameters, it displays Help for using the command.

Procedure for viewing the NetBIOS name cache

To view the contents of the local computer's NetBIOS name cache:

- In the command prompt, type **nbtstat –c**

Procedure for releasing the NetBIOS name cache

To release the NetBIOS name cache and reload the #PRE-tagged entries in the local Lmhosts file:

- In the command prompt, type **nbtstat –R**

Procedure for viewing the NetBIOS name table of the local computer

To display and view the NetBIOS name table of the local computer:

- In the command prompt, type **nbtstat -n**

Broadcasts

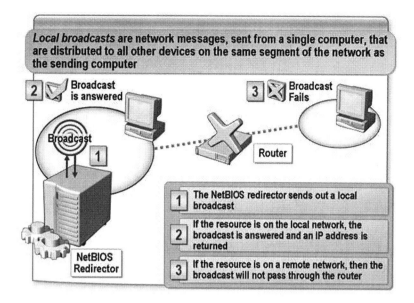

	Definition
Definition	*Local broadcasts* are network messages, sent from a single computer, that are distributed to all other devices on the same segment of the network as the sending computer.
Purpose of broadcasts	If the NetBIOS name is not resolved by the NetBIOS cache or by the WINS server, then the NetBIOS redirector sends a NetBIOS broadcast. Unlike an Lmhosts file, the administrator does not need to configure a NetBIOS broadcast
Broadcast	A NetBIOS client can issue on the local network a broadcast for the IP address of the destination NetBIOS name. The host that owns the NetBIOS name replies with its IP address, and the host that initiated the broadcast can then connect to the host that owns the NetBIOS name.

Note   You can reduce broadcast traffic by using a WINS server rather than local broadcasts to resolve NetBIOS name resolution. In addition, routers are not normally configured to forward NetBIOS broadcasts, which limit NetBIOS name resolution to a single network.

Example

The NetBIOS redirector sends out a local broadcast. If the resource is on the local network, then the broadcast is answered and an IP address is returned. If the resource is on a remote network, then the broadcast will not pass through a router. Therefore, the query will fail and an IP address will not be returned.

Lmhosts File

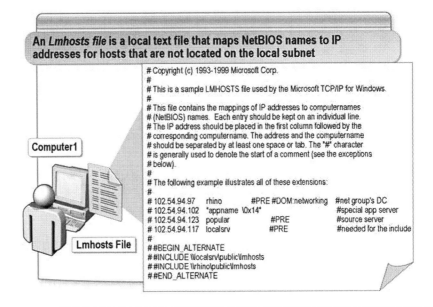

An *Lmhosts file* is a local text file that maps NetBIOS names to IP addresses for hosts that are not located on the local subnet

```
# Copyright (c) 1993-1999 Microsoft Corp.
#
# This is a sample LMHOSTS file used by the Microsoft TCP/IP for Windows.
#
# This file contains the mappings of IP addresses to computernames
# (NetBIOS) names.  Each entry should be kept on an individual line.
# The IP address should be placed in the first column followed by the
# corresponding computername. The address and the computername
# should be separated by at least one space or tab. The "#" character
# is generally used to denote the start of a comment (see the exceptions
# below).
#
# The following example illustrates all of these extensions:
#
# 102.54.94.97    rhino          #PRE #DOM:networking  #net group's DC
# 102.54.94.102   "appname \0x14"                      #special app server
# 102.54.94.123   popular        #PRE                  #source server
# 102.54.94.117   localsrv       #PRE                  #needed for the include
#
##BEGIN_ALTERNATE
##INCLUDE \\localsrv\public\lmhosts
##INCLUDE \\rhino\public\lmhosts
##END_ALTERNATE
```

Definition

An *Lmhosts file* is a local text file that maps NetBIOS names (commonly used for computer names) to IP addresses for hosts that are not located on the local subnet.

Purpose of the Lmhosts file

The Lmhosts file is a static file on the local computer that can aid in the resolving of a NetBIOS name. You can add NetBIOS-to-IP address mappings to the file to support NetBIOS name resolution. You can also preload into the NetBIOS name cache any mappings that you choose.

Lmhosts file

The Lmhosts file can be configured to be read by Microsoft clients after a broadcast has been sent attempting to resolve a NetBIOS name on the same subnet as the resolving computer. Only if the broadcast does not return an IP address will the Lmhosts file be read. The Lmhosts file is a static ASCII text file that is used to resolve the NetBIOS names of remote NetBIOS-based computers. The Lmhosts file has the following characteristics:

- A single entry consists of one NetBIOS name and its corresponding IP address. The entry must match the NetBIOS name of the target computers or an alias will fail.

- An Lmhosts file must reside on each computer.

- The default directory location of the Lmhosts file is in the *%Systemroot%*\System32\Drivers\Etc\ folder and has the extension of .sam. The .sam extension must be removed for the file to be read.

- Those entries in the Lmhosts file with the #PRE keyword will be preloaded into the NetBIOS name cache. The NetBIOS name mappings with the #PRE keyword will remain in the NetBIOS cache until the mappings with the #PRE keyword are removed from the Lmhosts file.

Predefined keywords

An Lmhosts file contains predefined keywords that enable you to manage the mappings in the Lmhosts file. Each of the predefined keywords is prefixed with a hash symbol (#). The following table lists the possible Lmhosts keywords.

Predefined keyword	Description
#PRE	Defines which entries must be initially preloaded as permanent entries in the name cache. Preloaded entries reduce network broadcasts, because names are resolved from the cache rather than by broadcast or by searching the Lmhosts file. Entries with a **#PRE** tag are loaded either automatically at initialization or manually by typing **nbtstat –R** at a command prompt.
#DOM:[*domain_name*]	Facilitates domain activity, such as logon validation over a router, account synchronization, and browsing.
#BEGIN_ALTERNATE **#END_ALTERNATE**	Defines a redundant list of alternate locations for Lmhosts files. The recommended way to include remote files is by using a universal naming convention (UNC) path, to ensure access to the file. The UNC names, with a proper IP address to NetBIOS name translation, must exist in the Lmhosts file
#INCLUDE	Loads and searches NetBIOS entries in a separate file from the default Lmhosts file. Typically, a #INCLUDE file is a centrally located and shared Lmhosts file.

Note The NetBIOS name cache and file are always read sequentially. Add the most frequently accessed computers to the top of the list. Add the entries tagged with **#PRE** near the bottom, because they will not be accessed again after TCP/IP initializes. For more information about the Lmhosts file, read the instructions in the Lmhosts file or see the Windows Server 2003 Help documentation.

Example

The illustration is shows you the contents of an Lmhosts file. This sample Lmhosts file can be found in the *%Systemroot%*\System32\Drivers\Etc\ folder and is named Lmhosts.

How to Preload NetBIOS Name Cache by Using an Lmhosts File

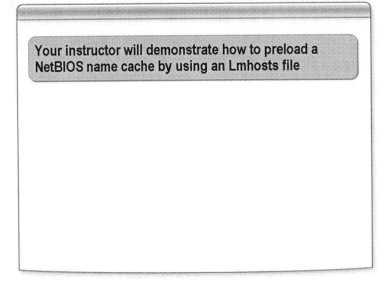

Introduction

You can use the Lmhosts file to preload NetBIOS name-to-IP address mappings into the NetBIOS name cache.

Guideline

You must rename the file from Lmhosts.sam to Lmhosts. The NetBIOS redirector will search for a file named Lmhosts, rather than a file named Lmhosts.sam.

Note It is recommended that you log on with an account that has non-administrative credentials and use the **Run as** command with a user account that has appropriate administrative credentials to perform this task.

To edit the Lmhosts.sam file from a command prompt, first open the command prompt with **Run as** by using a user account that has the appropriate administrative rights. Then, in the command prompt, type
notepad %systemroot%\system32\drivers\etc\lmhosts.sam

Remember to save the file without the .sam extension as Lmhosts.

Procedure

To preload the NetBIOS name cache by using an Lmhosts file:

1. In the **Run** dialog box, type the following command:
   notepad *%systemroot%***system32\drivers\etc\lmhosts.sam**

2. The Lmhosts.sam file opens for editing in Notepad.

3. In the Lmhosts file, add additional NetBIOS name-to-address mappings on separate lines. Remember to follow the format of the example in the Lmhosts file.

4. At the end of the NetBIOS name-to-IP address mapping entry, type the **#PRE** keyword to load the entry into the NetBIOS name cache.

5. On the **File** menu, click **Save As**.

6. In the **Save As** dialog box, in the **Save as type** field, select **All Files,** and then, in the **File name** field, type "**lmhosts**" (Remember to type the quotation marks. Using the quotation marks allows you to save the file without an extension.)

   - It is very important that you save the file as Lmhosts and not as Lmhosts.txt.

7. Exit Notepad.

8. In Windows Explorer, in the **Folder Options** dialog box, on the **View** tab, select **Hide extensions for known file types**.

Practice: Configuring NetBIOS Name Resolution

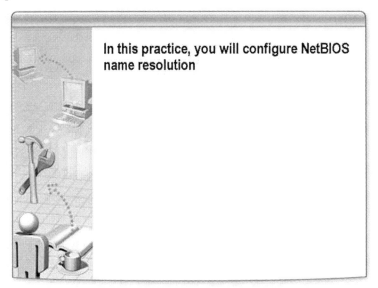

In this practice, you will configure NetBIOS name resolution

Objective

In this practice, you will configure NetBIOS name resolution.

Instructions

To complete this practice, refer to the *Implementation Plan Values* document, located in the Appendix at the end of your student workbook.

You must be logged on with an account that has non-administrative credentials and use the **Run as** command with a user account that has appropriate administrative credentials to complete the task.

Scenario

The Lab department is renovating its facilities, during which time the WINS servers will be offline for a period of time. To support NetBIOS name resolution, the correct entries in the Lmhosts file need to be configured for each lab computer. You will add the NetBIOS name-to-IP address mappings to the Lmhosts file to support NetBIOS name resolution while the WINS servers are offline.

Practice

▶ **View the NetBIOS name cache**

Complete this procedure from both student computers.

• Verify that the NetBIOS name cache does not contain an entry for the Glasgow computer.

▶ Preload a NetBIOS name cache by using an Lmhosts file

Complete this procedure from both student computers.

- Open a command prompt by using **Run as**.
- Username: *ComputerName***Admin** (where *ComputerName* is the name of your computer)
- Password: **P@ssw0rd**
- Edit the file by using the following command in the command prompt: **Notepad C:\windows\system32\drivers\etc\lmhosts.sam**
- Add the following entry to the Lmhosts file (where *x* is the classroom number).

IP address	Host name	Predefined keyword
192.168.*x*.100	Glasgow	#PRE

- Save the Lmhosts file without the .sam extension.

▶ Release the NetBIOS name cache and reload from the Lmhosts file

Complete this procedure from both student computers.

- Open a command prompt by using **Run as**.
- Username: *ComputerName***Admin**
- Password: **P@ssw0rd**

▶ View the NetBIOS name cache

Complete this procedure from both student computers.

- Verify that the NetBIOS name cache contains an entry for the Glasgow computer.

Lab A: Resolving Names

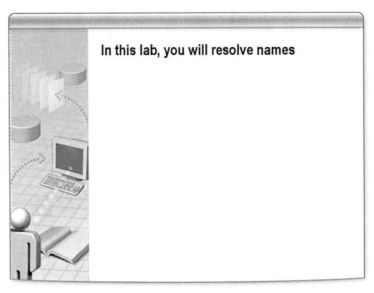

Objectives

In this lab, you will resolve names.

Estimated time to complete this lab: 15 minutes

Exercise 1
Resolving Names

In this exercise, you will resolve names.

Instruction

Complete this exercise from the server computer.

To complete the lab, refer to the *Implementation Plan Values* document, located in the Appendix at the end of your student workbook.

You must be logged on with an account that has non-administrative credentials and use the **Run as** command with a user account that has appropriate administrative credentials to complete the tasks. When completing the lab, assume that you will log on with a non-administrative account (example: *ComputerName*User), unless the Specific Instructions in the lab state otherwise.

Scenario

The Lab department is undergoing a renovation, during which time the DNS and WINS servers will be offline for a period of time. To support both host name resolution and NetBIOS name resolution, the correct entries in the Hosts file and LmHosts file need to be configured for each lab computer. You will add the correct entries to the Hosts file and the LmHosts file to support name resolution during the absence of the DNS and WINS servers.

Tasks	Specific instructions
Perform the following steps from both student computers.	
1. Verify that you can connect to Glasgow's NetBIOS name by using the **ping** command.	▪ Use the **ping** command.
2. Verify that you can view shares on Glasgow.	▪ Use the **Net View** command.
3. Modify the host name and NetBIOS name resolution files.	▪ At the command prompt, type **C:\moc\2277\labfiles\lab04\names.vbs**
4. Verify that you cannot connect to Glasgow.	▪ Use the **ping** command.
5. Verify that you cannot view the shares on Glasgow.	▪ Use **Net View** command.
6. Verify that the incorrect entry for Glasgow is in the Lmhosts file, and then correct the entry.	▪ IP address: **192.168.*x*.100** ▪ Computer name: **Glasgow** ▪ Lmhosts file switch: **#PRE**

Tasks	Specific instructions
7. Verify that the incorrect entry for Glasgow is in the NetBIOS name cache.	■ The NetBIOS name cache should contain an incorrect entry for Glasgow.
8. Reload the NetBIOS name cache, and then verify that the correct entry for Glasgow is in the NetBIOS name cache.	■ IP address: 192.168.*x*.100 ■ Computer name: Glasgow
9. Verify that the incorrect entry for Glasgow is in the client resolver cache.	■ The client resolver cache should contain an incorrect entry for Glasgow.
10. Verify that the incorrect entry for Glasgow is in the Hosts file, and then correct the entry.	■ IP address: 192.168.*x*.100 ■ Computer name: Glasgow
11. Verify that the correct entry for Glasgow is in the client resolver cache.	■ IP address: 192.168.*x*.100 ■ Computer name: Glasgow
12. Verify that you can connect to Glasgow by using the **ping** command.	■ Use the **ping** command.
13. Verify that you can view the share on Glasgow.	■ Use **Net View** command.
14. Move the Hosts and Lmhosts files to C:\Moc\2277\Labfiles\ Lab04, and then flush the DNS resolver name cache and reload the NetBIOS name cache (to prepare for the next module).	■ Move the Host and Lmhosts files to C:\Moc\2277\Labfiles\Lab04. ■ Flush the DNS resolver name cache. ■ Reload the NetBIOS name cache.

Microsoft®
Training &
Certification

Module 5: Resolving Host Names by Using Domain Name System (DNS)

Contents

Overview

- Multimedia: The Role of DNS in the Network Infrastructure
- Installing the DNS Server Service
- Configuring the Properties for the DNS Server Service
- Configuring DNS Zones
- Configuring DNS Zone Transfers
- Configuring DNS Dynamic Updates
- Configuring a DNS Client
- Delegating Authority for Zones

Introduction

A network solution needs to include Domain Name System (DNS) to connect the components of the network infrastructure. An important factor in connecting components is the resolution of the host names to Internet Protocol (IP) addresses. In this module, you will learn how to resolve host names by using DNS.

Objectives

After completing this module, you will be able to:

- Describe the role of DNS in the network infrastructure.
- Install the DNS Server service.
- Configure the properties for the DNS Server service.
- Configure a DNS zone.
- Configure DNS zone transfers.
- Configure dynamic updates.
- Configure a DNS client.
- Delegate authority for zones.

Multimedia: The Role of DNS in the Network Infrastructure

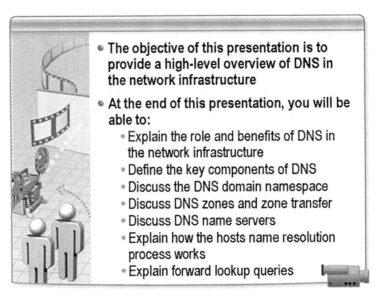

File location

To start the *Role of DNS in the Network Infrastructure* presentation, open the Web page on the Student Materials compact disc, click **Multimedia**, and then click the title of the presentation.

Objectives

At the end of this presentation, you will be able to:

- Explain the role and benefits of DNS in the network infrastructure.

- Define the key components of DNS.

- Discuss the DNS domain namespace.

- Discuss DNS zones and zone transfer.

- Discuss DNS name servers.

- Explain how the hosts name resolution process works.

- Explain forward lookup queries.

Key points

- DNS is a distributed database system that can serve as the foundation for name resolution in an Internet Protocol (IP) network.

- DNS is used by most internetworking software (such as electronic mail programs and Web browsers) to locate servers and to *resolve*, or map, a user-friendly name of a computer to its IP address.

- The domain namespace provides the structure of a DNS distributed database.

- Domains can be organized into zones, which are discrete and contiguous areas of the domain namespace.

- The name-to-IP address data for all computers located in a zone is stored in a zone database file on a DNS name server.

Lesson: Installing the DNS Server Service

- Overview of Domain Name System
- What Is a Domain Namespace?
- Standards for DNS Naming
- How to Install the DNS Server Service

Introduction

The first step in being able to resolve host names is to install the DNS Server service.

Lesson objectives

After completing this lesson, you will be able to:

- Explain the purpose and basics of DNS.
- Explain what a domain namespace is.
- Explain the standards for DNS naming.
- Install the DNS Server service.

Overview of Domain Name System

> *Domain Name System (DNS)* is a hierarchical, distributed database that contains mappings of DNS domain names to various types of data, such as IP addresses
>
> * DNS is the foundation of the Internet naming scheme and the foundation of an organization's naming scheme
> * DNS supports accessing resources by using alphanumeric names
> * InterNIC is responsible for delegating administrative responsibility for portions of the domain namespace and for registering domain names
> * DNS was designed to solve issues that arose when there was an increase in the:
>   * Number of hosts on the Internet
>   * Traffic generated by the update process
>   * Size of the Hosts file

Introduction

DNS is a name resolution service. DNS resolves human readable addresses (such as www.microsoft.com) into IP addresses (such as 192.168.0.1).

Definition

Domain Name System (DNS) is a hierarchical, distributed database that contains mappings of DNS host names to IP addresses. DNS enables the location of computers and services by using alphanumeric names, which are easy to remember. DNS also enables the discovery of network services, such as e-mail servers and domain controllers in the Active Directory® directory service.

Purpose of DNS

DNS is the foundation of the Internet naming scheme, and it is also the foundation of an organization's Active Directory domain-naming scheme. DNS supports accessing resources by using alphanumeric names. Without DNS, you would have to locate the IP addresses of resources to access those resources. Because resource IP addresses can change, it would be difficult to maintain an accurate list of which IP addresses match which resources. DNS allows users to focus on alphanumeric names, which remain relatively constant in an organization, rather than on IP addresses.

With DNS, the host names reside in a database that can be distributed among multiple servers, decreasing the load on any one server and providing the ability to administer this naming system on a per-partition basis. DNS supports hierarchical names and allows registration of various data types in addition to the host name-to-IP address mapping that is used in the Hosts files. Because the DNS database is distributed, its size is unlimited and performance does not degrade much when more servers are added.

InterNIC

The conceptual naming system on which DNS is based is a hierarchical and logical tree structure called the domain namespace. The Internet Network Information Center (InterNIC) manages the root, or the highest level of the domain namespace.

InterNIC is responsible for delegating administrative responsibility for portions of the domain namespace, and also for registering domain names. Domain names are managed through the use of a distributed database system of name information stored on name servers, which are located throughout the network. Each name server has database files that contain recorded information for a selected region within the domain tree hierarchy.

Note For more information about InterNIC, go to http://www.internic.net.

History of DNS

DNS began in the early days of the Internet, when the Internet was a small network that the United States Department of Defense established for research purposes. The host names of the computers in this network were managed by the use of a single Hosts file that was located on a centrally administered server. Each site that needed to resolve host names on the network downloaded this single file.

As the number of hosts on the Internet grew, the traffic that was generated by the update process increased—in addition to the size of the Hosts file. There was an increasing need for a new system that would offer features such as scalability, decentralized administration, and support for various data types.

DNS was introduced in 1984 and became this new system.

What Is a Domain Namespace?

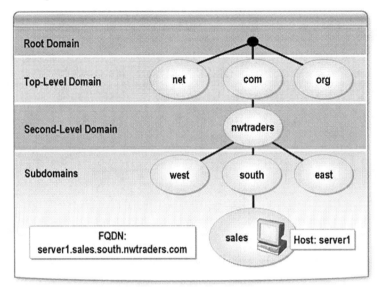

Introduction	A DNS namespace includes the root domain, top-level domains, second-level domains, and (possibly) subdomains. Together, the DNS namespace and the host name are the fully qualified domain name (FQDN).
Purpose of a domain name space	The DNS namespace allows display names of resources to be organized in a logical structure that is easy for users to understand. Because of the hierarchical structure of the DNS namespace, organizing and locating resources is greatly simplified.
Domain namespace	The *domain namespace* is a hierarchical naming tree that DNS uses to identify and locate a given host in a given domain relative to the root of the tree.
	The names in the DNS database establish a logical tree structure called the domain namespace. The domain name identifies a domain's position in the name tree relative to its parent domain. For the purposes of using and administering a DNS service, the domain namespace refers to any domain name tree structure in its entirety, from the top-level root of the tree to the bottom-level branches of the tree. The tree must fit the accepted conventions for representing DNS naming. The principal convention is simply this: for each domain level, a period (.) is used to separate each subdomain descendent from its parent-level domain.
Domain	A *domain*, in DNS, is any tree or subtree within the overall domain namespace. Although the names for DNS domains are used to name Active Directory domains, they are not the same as and should not be confused with Active Directory domains.
Root domain	This is the root node of the DNS tree. It is unnamed (null). It is sometimes represented in DNS names by a trailing period (.) to designate that the name is at the root or highest level of the domain hierarchy.

Top-level domain

This is the trailing (rightmost) portion of a domain name. Usually a top-level domain is stated as a two or three-character name code that identifies either organizational or geographical status for the domain name. In the example www.microsoft.com., the top-level domain name is the ".com" portion of the domain name, which indicates that this name has been registered to a business organization for commercial use.

Note An internal corporate namespace, such as an Active Directory forest, does not have to end in a valid top-level domain. You can use the domain corp.example.local, or another namespace that is not recognized on the Internet, for internal purposes.

Second-level domain

A second-level domain name is a unique name of varying length that InterNIC formally registers to an individual or organization that connects to the Internet. In the example of www.microsoft.com, the second-level name is the ".microsoft" portion of the domain name, which InterNIC registers and assigns to the Microsoft Corporation.

Subdomain

In addition to a second-level name that is registered with InterNIC, a large organization can choose to further subdivide its registered domain name by adding further subdivisions or departments that are each represented by a separate name portion. Examples of subdomain names are as follows.

- .sales.microsoft.com.

- .finance.microsoft.com.

- .corp.example.local.

Fully qualified domain name

A *fully qualified domain name (FQDN)* is a DNS domain name that has been stated unambiguously for the purpose of indicating with absolute certainty its location in the domain namespace tree.

Example

The illustration in the slide shows the DNS namespace for a company that is Internet-connected.

The root domain and first-tier domains .net, .com, and .org represent the Internet namespace, that portion of the namespace under the administrative control of the Internet governing body.

The second-tier domain nwtraders, and its subdomains west, south, east, and the subdomain sales, all represent the private namespace, under administrative control of the company, Northwind Traders.

The FQDN for the host server1, server1.sales.south.nwtraders.com., tells you exactly where this host resides in the namespace relative to the root of the namespace.

Standards for DNS Naming

The following characters are valid for DNS names:

* A-Z
* a-z
* 0-9
* Hyphen (-)

The underscore (_) is a reserved character

Purpose of DNS naming standards

DNS naming standards are designed to allow for consistency between any implementations of DNS. DNS naming standards are the global rules, so that no matter who implements DNS, their implementation can interoperate with other DNS implementations. Because of DNS naming standards, organizations that implement a DNS namespace can also use the same namespace on the Internet.

DNS naming standards

DNS naming standards allow a limited subset of the ASCII character set for DNS. Request for Comments (RFC) 1123 specifies the following characters as valid for DNS names.

- A-Z
- a-z
- 0-9
- Hyphen (-)

    All characters that are invalid are replaced by hyphens. For example, if you use an underscore in the computer name, then it will be replaced by a hyphen.

Although DNS servers running Microsoft® Windows® 2000 and later include support for extended ASCII and Unicode characters, it is strongly recommended that DNS names be limited to the characters specified in RFC 1123.

The underscore (_) character is reserved for special purposes in SRV records. For more information, see RFC 2782

How to Install the DNS Server Service

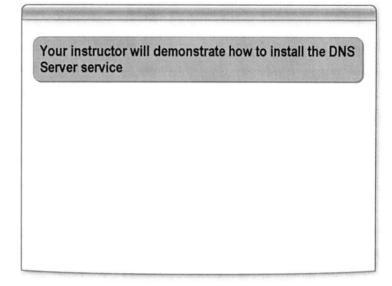

Your instructor will demonstrate how to install the DNS Server service

Introduction

The first step in creating a DNS solution for resolving host names is to install the DNS Server service.

Note It is recommended that you log on with an account that has non-administrative credentials and use the **Run as** command with a user account that has appropriate administrative credentials to perform this task.

Guideline

You need to have administrative rights to install the DNS Server service.

Procedure for installing the DNS Server service

To install a DNS server:

Note For instructional purposes, this procedure only covers installing a DNS Server service. To learn about and practice configuring the DNS server, see the Configuring the Properties for the DNS Server Service lesson, in this module.

1. Log on with a non-administrative user account.
2. Click **Start,** and then click **Control Panel.**
3. In Control Panel, open **Administrative Tools,** right-click **Manage Your Server,** and then select **Run as.**
4. In the **Run As** dialog box, select **The following user,** type a user account and password that has the appropriate permissions to complete the task, and then click **OK.**
5. In the **Manage Your Server Wizard** window, click **Add or remove a role.**
6. On the **Preliminary Steps** page, click **Next.**
7. On the **Server Role** page, select **DNS server,** and then click **Next.**

8. On the **Summary of Selections** page, click **Next**.

9. If prompted, insert the Microsoft Windows Server 2003 CD.

10. On the **Welcome to the Configure a DNS Server Wizard** page, click **Cancel**.

Note   You will configure the DNS service in a later practice.

11. On the **Configure Your Server Wizard** page, click **Finish**.

Practice: Installing the DNS Server Service

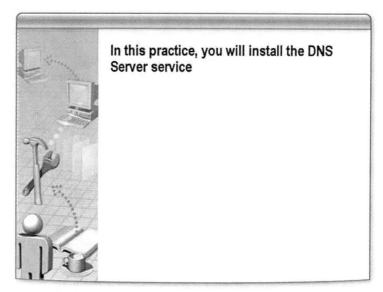

In this practice, you will install the DNS Server service

Objective

In this practice, you will install the DNS Server service.

Instructions

To complete this practice, refer to the *Implementation Plan Values* document, located in the Appendix at the end of your student workbook.

You must be logged on with an account that has non-administrative credentials and use the **Run as** command with a user account that has appropriate administrative credentials to complete the task.

Scenario

The Lab department has been designed to use a corporate DNS server for name resolution. The systems engineer has approved a new DNS server for each Lab department subnet. You will install the DNS Server service for your subnet.

Practice

▶ **Install the DNS Server service**

■ Complete this task from both student computers

■ User name: **nwtraders***ComputerName***Admin**

■ Password: **P@ssw0rd**

■ For practice purposes, do not configure the DNS server at this time.

Lesson: Configuring the Properties for the DNS Server Service

* What Are the Components of a DNS Solution?
* What Is a DNS Query?
* How Recursive Queries Work
* How a Root Hint Works
* How Iterative Queries Work
* How Forwarders Work
* How DNS Server Caching Works
* How to Configure the Properties for the DNS Server Service

Introduction

A DNS solution is made up of the DNS server, DNS clients, and the resources that are referenced by the resource records in DNS. After installing the DNS Server service, the next step is to properly configure the DNS server for your environment.

Lesson objectives

After completing this lesson, you will be able to:

■ Explain what the components of a DNS solution are.

■ Explain what a DNS query is.

■ Describe how recursive queries work.

■ Describe how root hints work.

■ Describe how iterative queries work.

■ Describe how forwarders work.

■ Describe how DNS server caching works.

■ Configure the properties for the DNS Server service.

What Are the Components of a DNS Solution?

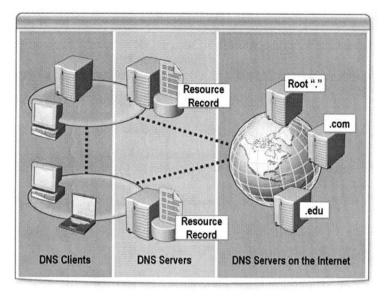

Components of DNS

The components of a DNS solution are described in the following table.

Component	Description
DNS Server	• A computer running the DNS service
	• Hosts a namespace or portion of a namespace (domain)
	• Authoritative for a namespace or domain
	• Resolves the name resolution requests that DNS clients (DNS Client=Resolver) submit
DNS Client	• A computer running the DNS Client service
DNS Resource Records	• Entries in the DNS database that map host names to resources

Note For the purposes of this course, the name server is referred to as a DNS server.

Example

The components of a DNS solution are the DNS clients, the DNS servers, and the DNS resource records. The resource records are located in the DNS server database. Alternatively, if your DNS solution is connected to the Internet, then the DNS servers on the Internet can be used.

What Is a DNS Query?

> A *query* is a request for name resolution to a DNS server. There are two types of queries: recursive and iterative
>
> * DNS clients and DNS servers both initiate queries for name resolution
> * An authoritative DNS server for the namespace of the query will either:
>   * Check the cache, check the zone, and return the requested IP address
>   * Return an authoritative, "No"
> * A non-authoritative DNS server for the namespace of the query will either:
>   * Forward the unresolvable query to a specific query server called a Forwarder
>   * Use root hints to locate an answer for the query

Definition

A *query* is a request for name resolution that is sent to a DNS server. There are two types of queries: recursive and iterative.

Note Recursive and iterative queries will be covered later in this lesson.

Purpose of a DNS query

The purpose of a DNS solution is to allow users to access resources by using alphanumeric names. A DNS query is the DNS client resolver asking the DNS server for the IP address of the supplied name. The DNS query is how the service or application obtains the IP address of the resource so that it can access it.

How DNS queries are initiated

DNS clients and DNS servers both initiate queries for name resolution.
A client-system may issue a query to a DNS server, and that DNS server may then issues queries to other DNS servers.

Authoritative and non-authoritative DNS servers

A DNS server can be either authoritative or non-authoritative for the namespace of the query. To be *authoritative* means that a DNS server hosts a primary or secondary copy of a DNS zone.

If the DNS server is authoritative for the namespace of the query, the DNS server will either:

- Check the cache, check the zone, and then return the requested address.
- Return an authoritative, "No."

If the local DNS server is *non-authoritative* for the namespace of the query, the DNS server will either:

- Forward the unresolvable query to a specific server called a forwarder.
- Use well-known addresses of multiple root servers to step up the DNS tree to locate an answer for the query. This process is also called *root hints*.

Note Forwarders are discussed later in this lesson. For more information about root hints, see the Configuring DNS Zones lesson in this module.

How Recursive Queries Work

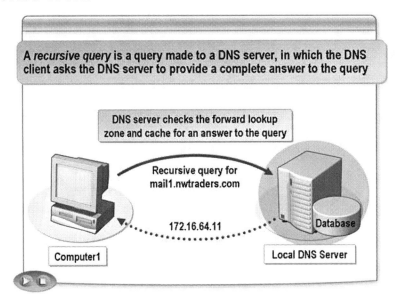

Definition	A *recursive query* is a query made to a DNS server, in which the DNS client asks the DNS server to provide a complete answer to the query. The only acceptable response to a recursive query is either the full answer or a reply that the name could not be resolved. A recursive query cannot redirect to another DNS server.
Purpose of a recursive query	By using a recursive query, the DNS client can trust the DNS server to locate the host name-to-IP address mapping. The DNS client asks the DNS server for the host-to-IP address mapping, and then accepts the response from the DNS server.
Recursive query	Recursive queries can be initiated either by a DNS client or by a DNS server that is configured for forwarders. A recursive query puts the burden of delivering a final answer on the queried server.

The answer to a recursive query will always be either a positive or negative response. In a recursive query, the queried DNS server is petitioned to respond with one of the following responses:

- The requested data.

- An error stating that data of the requested type does not exist.

- A response stating that the domain name specified does not exist.

How a recursive query works

The following steps describe how a recursive query from a client to that client's configured DNS server works:

1. The client sends a recursive query to the local DNS server.

2. The local DNS server checks the forward lookup zone and cache for an answer to the query.

3. If the answer to the query is found, then the DNS server returns the answer to the client.

4. If an answer is *not* found, then the DNS server uses a forwarder address or root hints to locate an answer.

Example

In the illustration, the DNS client is asking the DNS server for the IP address of the supplied display name. The DNS client then accepts the response from the DNS server.

The DNS client, using the DNS resolver service, sends a DNS query to the DNS server for the IP address of mail1.nwtraders.msft. The DNS server checks the cache to locate the record. If the cache does not contain the record, then the DNS server locates the authoritative DNS server for the nwtraders.msft domain. If the DNS server is authoritative for the domain, it searches the zone for the resource record. If the record exists, then the server returns the IP address for the queried record. If the record does not exist, then the DNS server informs the client that the record was not found.

How a Root Hint Works

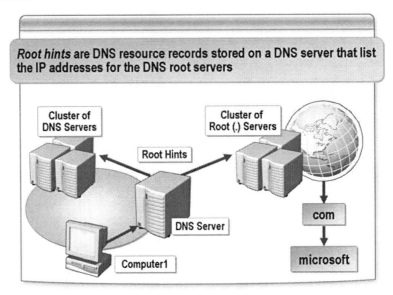

Root hints are DNS resource records stored on a DNS server that list the IP addresses for the DNS root servers

Definition

Root hints are DNS resource records, stored on a DNS server, that list the IP addresses for the DNS root servers.

Function of a root hint

When the DNS server receives a DNS query, it checks the cache. The DNS server then attempts to locate the authoritative DNS server for the queried domain. If the DNS server does not have the IP address of the authoritative DNS server for that domain, and if the DNS server is configured with the root hints IP addresses, then the DNS server will query a root server for the domain to the left of the root domain of the query.

The DNS root server then returns the IP address of the domain to the left of the root domain and the DNS server continues down the FQDN till it locates the authoritative domain.

Root hints are stored in the file Cache.dns, located in the %Systemroot%\System32\Dns folder.

Function of root hints within the organization

Under normal circumstances, root hints list the IP addresses for the DNS root servers that InterNIC maintains on the internet. Root hints can also point to a local DNS server. If the root hints point to a local server, then the only names that will be available for resolution are those to which the local DNS server can refer (normally local addresses only). This configuration can sometimes be used for security purposes, because in it only the internal domains can be resolved.

How Iterative Queries Work

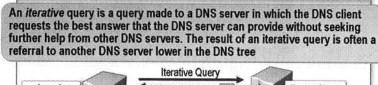

An *iterative* query is a query made to a DNS server in which the DNS client requests the best answer that the DNS server can provide without seeking further help from other DNS servers. The result of an iterative query is often a referral to another DNS server lower in the DNS tree

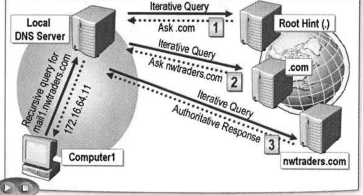

Definition

An *iterative* query is a query made to a DNS server in which the DNS client requests the best answer that the DNS server can provide without seeking further help from other DNS servers. Iterative queries are also sometimes called nonrecursive queries. The result of an iterative query is often a referral to another DNS server lower in the DNS tree. A referral would not be an acceptable response to a recursive query.

Purpose of an iterative query

The purpose of an iterative query is that the DNS server, which can now use the client's recursive query, is responsible for finding an answer to the client's question. The DNS server will search its own database for an answer, and will even query DNS servers at different levels in the domain namespace to eventually locate the authoritative DNS server for the original query.

Iterative query

A DNS server typically makes an iterative query to other DNS servers after it has received a recursive query from a client. In an iterative query, the queried name server returns the best answer it currently has to the requestor. Answers to iterative queries can be:

- Positive answers.
- Negative answers.
- Referrals to other servers.

Note One local DNS server usually issues iterative queries to another DNS server elsewhere in the namespace while trying to resolve a name query on behalf of a client. For clarification, it is the DNS Client service, on the local DNS server, that issues the iterative query.

Referral

A *referral* is a list of targets, transparent to the user, which a client receives from DNS when the user is accessing a root or a link in the DNS namespace. The referral information is cached on the client for a time period specified in the DNS configuration.

If the queried DNS server does not have an exact match for the queried name, then the best possible information it can return is a referral. A referral points to a DNS server that is authoritative for a lower level of the domain namespace.

The DNS client, on the local DNS server, can then query the DNS server for which it obtained a referral. It continues this process until it locates a DNS server that is authoritative for the queried name, or until an error or a time-out condition is met.

Recursion

Recursion is a DNS server function in which one DNS server issues a series of several iterative queries to other DNS servers while responding to a recursive query that a DNS client issues.

The queried DNS servers return referrals, which the querying server follows until it receives a definitive answer. Recursion always ends when a server that owns the namespace gives either a positive or negative reply.

How an iterative query works

In the illustration, the local DNS server has failed to resolve the requested name by using cached data and is not authoritative for the domain. So it begins the process of locating the authoritative DNS server by querying additional DNS servers. To locate the authoritative DNS server for the domain, the DNS server resolves the FQDN from the root to the host by using iterative queries. The process that this example uses is as follows.

1. The local DNS server receives a recursive query from a DNS client.

    For example: The local DNS server receives a recursive query from Computer1 for mail1.nwtraders.com.

2. The local DNS server sends an iterative query to the root server to obtain an authoritative name server.

3. The Root server responds with a referral to a DNS server closer to the submitted domain name.

    For example: The root server responds with a referral to the DNS server for .com.

4. The local DNS server then makes an iterative query to the DNS server that is closer to the submitted domain name.

    For example: The local DNS server then makes an iterative query to the DNS server for .com.

5. The process continues until the local DNS server receives an authoritative response.

    For example: The DNS server for .com responds with a referral to the DNS server for nwtraders.com. Next, the local DNS server sends an iterative query to the DNS server for nwtraders.com to obtain an authoritative name from the authoritative name server. The local DNS server then receives an authoritative response from the DNS server for nwtraders.com.

6. The response is then sent to the DNS client.

    For example: The local DNS server sends this authoritative response to Computer1, which can then connect to mail1.nwtraders.com by using the appropriate IP address.

How Forwarders Work

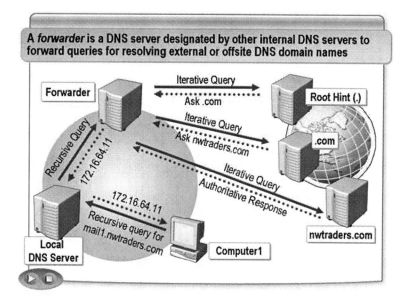

Definition

A *forwarder* is a DNS server that other internal DNS servers designate to forward queries for resolving external or offsite DNS domain names.

Purpose of forwarders

When a DNS name server receives a query, it attempts to locate the requested information within its own zone files. If this fails, either because the server is not authoritative for the domain requested or because it does not have the record cached from a previous lookup, the server must communicate with other name servers to resolve the request. On a globally connected network like the Internet, DNS queries that are outside a local zone may require interaction with DNS name servers across wide area network (WAN) links outside of the organization. Creating DNS forwarders is a way to designate specific name servers as being responsible for WAN-based DNS traffic.

Specific DNS name servers can be selected to be forwarders, which servers will resolve DNS queries on behalf of other DNS servers.

Process of DNS forwarders

In the illustration, the local DNS server has failed to resolve the requested name by using its zone files and cached data, so it forwards the request to the forwarder. The forwarder then begins the process of querying other name servers by using iterative queries.

DNS forwarders use the following process:

1. The local DNS server receives a recursive query from a DNS client.

   For example: The local DNS server receives a recursive query from Computer1.

2. The local DNS server forwards the request to the forwarder.

3. The forwarder sends an iterative query to the root server to obtain an authoritative name from an authoritative name server.

4. The root server responds with a referral to a DNS server that is closer to the submitted domain name.

   For example: The root server responds with a referral to the DNS server for .com.

5. The forwarder then makes an iterative query to the DNS server that is closer to the submitted domain name.

   For example: The forwarder then makes an iterative query to the DNS server for .com.

6. The process continues until the forwarder receives an authoritative response.

   For example: The DNS server for .com responds with a referral to the DNS server for nwtraders.com. Next, the forwarder sends an iterative query to the DNS server for nwtraders.com to obtain an authoritative name server. The forwarder then receives an authoritative response from the DNS server for nwtraders.com.

7. The forwarder sends the response to the local DNS server, which then sends the response to the DNS client.

   For example: The forwarder sends the response to the local DNS server, which then sends the response to Computer1.

Forwarder behavior

Nonforwarding name servers are configured to use forwarders. DNS servers may be configured with the address of one or more forwarders.

A name server can use a forwarder either in a nonexclusive or in an exclusive mode.

- In a *nonexclusive mode*, if the forwarder is unable to resolve the query, the name server that received the original query attempts to resolve the query on its own.

- In an *exclusive mode*, if the forwarder is unable to resolve the request, the forward-only server returns a query failure to the original requestor. Forward-only servers make no attempt to resolve the query on their own if the forwarder is unable to satisfy the request.

Conditional forwarding allows a DNS server to use a forwarder when the server resolves a selected set of domains. For example, conditional forwarding would allow a DNS server to forward IP address resolution requests for hosts in a partner organization that has a private DNS infrastructure to the DNS server in the partner organization, while all other requests could be resolved in the normal manner.

How DNS Server Caching Works

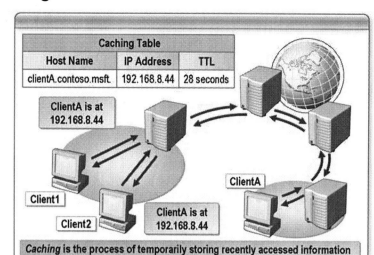

Caching is the process of temporarily storing recently accessed information in a special memory subsystem for quicker access

Definition	*Caching* is the process of temporarily storing recently accessed information in a special memory subsystem for quicker access.
Purpose of DNS server caching	Caching provides faster query responses and reduces DNS network traffic. By caching DNS responses, the DNS server can resolve future queries for that record from the cache. This greatly reduces response time, and eliminates the associated network traffic of sending the query out to another DNS server.
The process for DNS server caching	When a server is processing a recursive query, it might be required to send out several queries to find the definitive answer. In a worst-case scenario for resolving a name, the local name server starts at the top of the DNS tree with one of the root name servers and works its way down until the requested data is found.

The server caches all of the information that it receives during this process for a time period that is specified in the returned data. This amount of time is referred to as Time to Live (TTL) and is specified in seconds. The server administrator for the primary zone that contains the data decides on the TTL for the data. Smaller TTL values help ensure that information about the domain is more consistent across the network, in the event that this data changes often. However, a smaller TTL also increases the load on the name servers that contain the name, and it also increases Internet traffic. Because data is cached, changes made in resource records might not be immediately available to the entire Internet.

After a DNS server caches data, the TTL starts to count down so that the DNS server will know when to delete the data from its cache. When the DNS server answers a query by using its cached data, it includes the remaining TTL for the data. The resolver then caches this data, and uses the TTL that the server sends.

Negative caching

In addition to caching positive query responses (which contain resource record information in the reply) from DNS servers, the DNS Client service also caches negative query responses. A negative response results when a resource record for the queried name does not exist.

Negative caching prevents the repeating of additional queries for names that do not exist. Any query information that is negatively cached is kept for a shorter period of time than positive query responses; by default, no more than 5 minutes. The 5 minute value limits continued negative caching of stale information if the records later become available.

Caching-only server

Although all DNS name servers cache queries that they have resolved, caching-only servers are DNS name servers whose only job is to perform queries, cache the answers, and return the results. They are not authoritative for any domains, and they only contain information that they have cached while resolving queries. Caching-only servers do not have primary or secondary zones.

A DNS server running Windows Server 2003 in its initial installation configuration does not have any zones. With the help of root hints, it becomes a caching-only server in its initial state.

DNS client-side resolver caching

The DNS client resolver also caches resolved host-to-IP mapping data. The DNS client first checks the local cache before contacting the DNS server. DNS clients can also perform negative caching.

Note   For more information about DNS client resolver, see Module 4, "Resolving Names," in Course 2277, *Implementing, Managing, and Maintaining a Microsoft Windows Server 2003 Network Infrastructure: Network Services.*

Example

In the illustration, you can see that the first time Client1 sends a query for clientA.contoso.msft., the DNS server must use iterative queries to locate the resource. When the authoritative response is sent to the local DNS server, the DNS server caches the resource with a TTL value. (The TTL is provided by the authoritative DNS server that supplies the response.) The DNS client also caches the record in its local DNS resolver cache by using the TTL that the DNS server provides.

When Client2 queries for clientA.contoso.msft.com., the DNS server can respond from the cached response for this resource, provided that the data is still in the cache. This means that the DNS server can respond faster to the query, because the local DNS server does not have to query DNS servers outside of the organization. This eliminates the network traffic that would have to take place to resolve the query if it had not been in cache.

How to Configure Properties for the DNS Server Service

> **Your instructor will demonstrate how to:**
>
> ● Update root hints on a DNS server
>
> ● Configure a DNS server to use a forwarder
>
> ● Clear the DNS server cache by using the DNS console
>
> ● Clear the DNS server cache by using the DNSCmd command

Introduction

To configure properties for the DNS Server service, you need to update the root hints on a DNS server. Root hints determine whether your servers go to the root server on the Internet or an internal root server.

You may also want to configure a DNS server to use a forwarder in addition to updating the DNS cache.

Note   It is recommended that you log on with an account that has non-administrative credentials and use the **Run as** command with a user account that has appropriate administrative credentials to perform this task.

Procedure for updating root hints on a DNS server

To update root hints on a DNS server:

1. Open the DNS console.

2. In the DNS console, select the appropriate server.

3. On the **Action** menu, click **Properties**.

4. On the **Root Hints** tab, you can click:

   • **Add** to add a Name Server. Enter the FQDN and IP address of the Name Server.

   • **Edit** to edit a Name Server. Edit the FQDN or IP address of the Name Server.

   • **Remove** to remove a Name Server.

   • **Copy from Server** to copy the list of Name Servers from a DNS server.

5. Click **OK** to close the **Properties** dialog box, and then close the DNS console.

Procedure for configuring a DNS server to use a forwarder

To configure a DNS server to use a forwarder:

1. Open the DNS console.

2. In the DNS console, select the appropriate server.

3. On the **Action** menu, click **Properties**.

4. On the **Forwarders** tab, click **New**.

5. In the **New Forwarder** dialog box, type the name of the DNS domain that the DNS server will forward queries for, and then click **OK**.

6. On the **Forwarders** tab, in the **Selected domain's forwarder IP address list** field, type the IP address of the DNS server that will act as the forwarder for queries that are in the server's DNS domain, and then click **Add**.

7. On the **Forwarders** tab, in the **Number of seconds before forward queries time out** box, type the value in seconds.

8. If required, on the **Forwarders** tab, select the option **Do not use recursion for this domain**, and then click **OK**.

9. Close the DNS console.

Procedure for clearing the DNS server cache by using the DNS console

To clear the DNS server cache by using the DNS console:

1. Open the DNS console.

2. In the DNS console, select the server.

3. On the **Action** menu, click **Clear Cache**.

Procedure for clearing the DNS server cache by using the command line

To clear the DNS server cache by using the **dnscmd** command:

1. On the DNS server, install Support Tools from the Windows 2003 Server CD.

2. On the DNS server, at the command prompt, type **dnscmd** *Server_Name* /**clearcache** (where *Server_Name* is the name of the DNS server).

Note   The **dnscmd** command will be discussed in Module 6, "Managing and Monitoring Domain Name System (DNS)."

Practice: Configuring Properties for the DNS Server Service

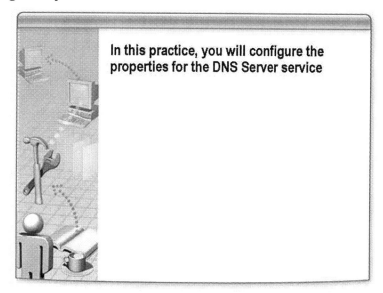

In this practice, you will configure the properties for the DNS Server service

Objective

In this practice, you will configure properties for the DNS Server service.

Instructions

To complete this practice, refer to the *Implementation Plan Values* document, located in the Appendix at the end of your student workbook.

You must be logged on with an account that has non-administrative credentials and use the **Run as** command with a user account that has appropriate administrative credentials to complete the task.

Scenario

Your company is concerned about the amount of DNS traffic that is sent across the Internet. To minimize DNS traffic you have decided to limit the number of DNS servers that can send DNS traffic out. You have configured a specific DNS server to send DNS queries out to the Internet. To allow your remaining DNS servers to resolve Internet DNS queries, you are going to configure them to use this DNS server as a forwarder. You will configure your DNS server to forward DNS queries to the DNS server that is acting as the forwarder DNS server.

Practice

▶ **Configure a DNS server to use a forwarder**

- Complete this task from both student computers
- User name: **nwtraders***ComputerName***Admin**
- Password: **P@ssw0rd**
- DNS domain: leave defaults
- Forwarder IP address: **192.168.*x*.200**
- Do not use recursion for this domain: enable

Lesson: Configuring DNS Zones

* How DNS Data Is Stored and Maintained
* What Are Resource Records and Record Types?
* What Is a DNS Zone?
* What Are DNS Zone Types?
* How to Change a DNS Zone Type
* What Are Forward and Reverse Lookup Zones?
* How to Configure Forward and Reverse Lookup Zones

Introduction

After you have created DNS zones, and when the DNS zones are populated with resource records, then the DNS service will be able to support host name resolution.

Lesson objectives

After completing this lesson, you will be able to:

- Describe how data is stored and maintained.
- Explain what resource records and record types are.
- Explain what a DNS zone is.
- Explain what DNS zone types are.
- Differentiate when to use stub zones and when to use conditional forwarders.
- Change a DNS zone type.
- Explain what forward lookup zones and reverse lookup zones are.
- Configure forward lookup zones and reverse lookup zones.

How DNS Data Is Stored and Maintained

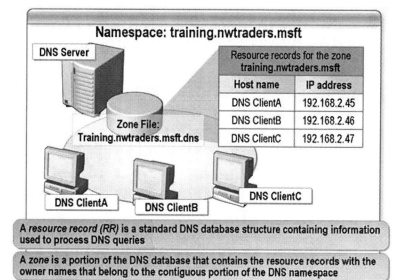

Definitions

A *resource record* is a standard DNS database structure containing information that is used to process DNS queries.

A *zone* is a portion of the DNS database that contains the resource records with the owner names that belong to the contiguous portion of the DNS namespace.

A *zone file* is the file on the DNS server's local hard drive that contains all of the configuration information for a zone and the resource records contained therein.

Process

After you have installed the DNS Server service and configured the properties of the DNS service, you are ready to complete the DNS service by adding host name-to-IP address mappings. These mappings are referred to as resource records in DNS. There are many different types of resource records. The types of resource records that you create in DNS will depend on your DNS needs.

Before you can add the resource records, you must have a structure in DNS that can hold them. These logical containers are called *zones* in DNS. When you create a zone, you create a zone file to store the zone properties and resource records. There are several different configurations of zones in DNS, and the zones that you will create are dictated by your DNS needs in your environment.

After you have created DNS zones, and when the DNS zones are populated with resource records, the DNS service will be able to support host name resolution.

What Are Resource Records and Record Types?

Record type	Description
A	Resolves a host name to an IP address
PTR	Resolves an IP address to a host name
SOA	The first record in any zone file
SRV	Resolves names of servers providing services
NS	Identifies the DNS server for each zone
MX	The mail server
CNAME	Resolves from a host name to a host name

Purpose of resource records

Users can access DNS resource records for themselves, or they can have networking components access the records for them. Examples of when DNS resource records are used include:

- A user browsing for a Web site sends a forward lookup query to a DNS server.

- When a user logs on to a computer in a domain, the logon process locates a domain controller by querying a DNS server.

Resource types

Different record types represent different types of data stored within the DNS database. The following tables list record types, along with a description and an example for each type.

Record type	Description	Example
Host (A)	• An A record represents a computer or device on the network. • A records are the most common and most frequently used DNS records. • An A record resolves from a host name to an IP address.	Computer5.microsoft.com resolves to 10.1.1.5
Pointer (PTR)	• A PTR record is used to find the DNS name that corresponds to an IP address. • The PTR record is found only in the reverse lookup zone. • PTR records resolve from an IP address to a host name.	10.1.1.101 resolves to Computer1.microsoft.com

(continued)

Record type	Description	Example
Start of Authority (SOA)	• An SOA resource record is the first record in any zone file. • An SOA resource record identifies the primary DNS name server for the zone. • An SOA resource record identifies the e-mail address for the administrator in charge of the zone. • An SOA resource record specifies the information required for replication (such as the serial number, the refresh interval, the retry interval, and the expiry values for the zone). • An SOA resource record resolves from a domain name (which is the same as the parent folder) to a host name.	microsoft.com resolves to NS1.microsoft.com
Service Record (SRV)	• An SRV resource record indicates a network service that a host offers. • An SRV resource record resolves from a service name to a host name and port.	_TCP._LDAP.microsoft.com resolves to DC01.microsoft.com
Nameserver (NS)	• An NS record facilitates delegation by identifying DNS servers for each zone. • An NS record appears in all forward and reverse lookup zones. • Whenever a DNS server needs to send a query to a delegated domain, it refers to the NS resource record for DNS servers in the target zone. • An NS record resolves from a domain name (which is the same as the parent folder) to a host name.	microsoft.com resolves to NS2.microsoft.com
Mail Exchanger (MX)	• An MX resource record indicates the presence of a Simple Mail Transfer Protocol (SMTP) e-mail server. • An MX resource record resolves to a host name.	Microsoft.com resolves to mail.microsoft.com
Alias (CNAME)	• A CNAME resource record is a host name that refers to another host name. • A CNAME resource record resolves from a host name to another host name.	www.microsoft.com resolves to webserver12.microsoft.com

Examples of resource records and record types

The slide provides a view of the DNS Manager snap-in in Microsoft Management Console (MMC), which shows the resource records and record types in the Demo.com zone.

Example of a resource record set

For example: A DNS client might query for the SMTP server at nwtraders.msft. The resource record set would provide the MX record that points to smtp.nwtraders.msft and the A record, which maps smtp.nwtraders.msft to 192.168.1.17.

What Is a DNS Zone?

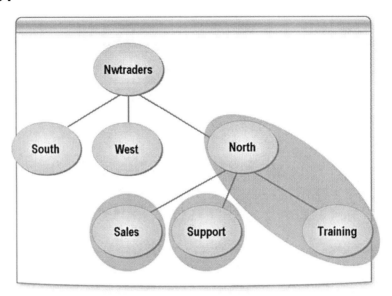

Purpose of a DNS zone

A zone can hold the resource records for one domain or it can hold the resource records for multiple domains. A zone can host more than one domain only if the domains are contiguous—that is, connected by a direct parent-child relationship.

A zone is also the physical representative of a DNS domain or domains. For example, if you have a DNS domain namespace of south.nwtraders.com, you could create a zone on a DNS server called south.nwtraders.com, and this zone could contain all resource records found in the Training domain

DNS zone

DNS allows a DNS namespace to be divided up into zones. For each DNS domain name included in a zone, the zone becomes the authoritative source for information about that domain.

Zone files are maintained on DNS servers. You can configure a single DNS server to host zero, one, or multiple zones. Each zone may be authoritative for one, or more than one, DNS domain as long as they are contiguous in the DNS tree. Zones may be stored either in flat text files or in the Active Directory database.

Characteristics of a zone include the following ones:

- A zone is a collection of host name-to- IP address mappings for hosts in a contiguous portion of the DNS namespace.

- Zone data is maintained on a DNS server and is stored in one of two ways:

    - As a flat zone file containing lists of mappings

    - In an Active Directory database

- A DNS server is authoritative for a zone if it hosts the resource records for the names and addresses that the clients request in the zone file.

A DNS zone is:

- Either a primary, secondary, or stub zone type.
- Either a forward or reverse-lookup zone.

Note Zone types and lookup zones are covered in detail later in this lesson.

Securing a DNS zone

To increase security, you can control who can administer DNS zones by modifying the discretionary access control list (DACL) on the DNS zones that are stored in Active Directory. The DACL allows you to control permissions for Active Directory users and groups that may control the DNS zones.

Note For more information about securing a DNS zone, see "Securing DNS Zones" in the Windows Server 2003 Help documentation.

Example

Referring to the illustration, there are three zones represented:

- north.nwtraders.com
- sales.north.nwtraders.com
- support.north.nwtraders.com

The first zone (north.nwtraders.com) is authoritative for two contiguous domains (north.nwtraders.com and training.north.nwtraders.com), whereas the other two zones (sales.north.nwtraders.com and support.north.nwtraders.com) each represent a single domain.

What Are DNS Zone Types?

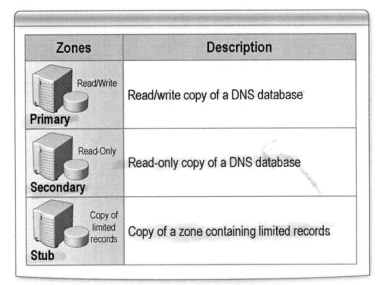

Zones	Description
Primary Read/Write	Read/write copy of a DNS database
Secondary Read-Only	Read-only copy of a DNS database
Stub Copy of limited records	Copy of a zone containing limited records

Introduction

When you configure a DNS server, you can configure it either with several zone types or with none at all, depending on the type of role that the DNS server has in the network.

There are numerous options for optimal configuration of the DNS server, based on decisions that you make about such things as the network topology and the size of the namespace. Normal DNS server operation involves three zones:

- Primary zone
- Secondary zone
- Stub zone

Purpose of DNS zone types

By using different zones, you can configure your DNS solution to best meet your needs. For example, it is recommended that you configure a primary zone and a secondary zone on separate DNS servers, to provide fault tolerance should one server fail. You can configure a stub zone if the zone is maintained on a separate DNS server.

Primary zone

A primary zone is the authoritative copy of the DNS zone, in which resource records are created and managed.

When setting up DNS servers to host the zones for a domain, the primary server is normally located where it will be accessible for administering the zone file.

Secondary zone

A secondary zone is a copy of the DNS zone that contains the read-only copy of the DNS zone. Records in the secondary zone cannot be changed; administrators can only change records in the primary DNS zone.

At least one secondary server is normally configured for fault-tolerance. However, multiple secondary servers might be configured at other locations so that the records from the zone could be resolved without the query crossing WAN links.

Stub zone

Stub zones are copies of a zone that contain only the resource records that are necessary to identify the authoritative DNS server for that zone. A stub zone contains a subset of zone data consisting of a SOA, NS, and A record, also known as a glue record. A stub zone is like a bookmark that simply points to the DNS server that is authoritative for that zone.

Stub zones can be used where root hints point to an internal DNS server rather than to the root servers on the Internet. For security purposes, the DNS server is designed only to resolve certain zones.

Note Caching-only servers do not have a zone.

How to Change a DNS Zone Type

> Your instructor will demonstrate how to change a DNS zone type

Introduction

To configure a DNS zone, you may need to change the DNS zone type.

Note It is recommended that you log on with an account that has non-administrative credentials and use the **Run as** command with a user account that has appropriate administrative credentials to perform this task.

Procedure

To change a DNS zone type:

1. Open the DNS console.

2. In the **DNS** console, select the zone that you wish to change.

3. On the **Action** menu, click **Properties**.

4. On the **General** tab, click **Change**.

5. In the **Change Zone Type** dialog box, select one of the following options, and then click **OK**.

   - **Primary zone** if this zone will contain a copy of the zone that can be updated directly.

   - **Secondary zone** if this zone stores a copy of an existing zone.

   - **Stub zone** if this zone stores a copy of a zone containing only NS (name server), SOA (start of authority), and, possibly, glue records.

6. In the zone **Properties** dialog box, click **OK**.

What Are Forward and Reverse Lookup Zones?

	Forward zone	Training	DNS Client1	192.168.2.45
			DNS Client2	192.168.2.46
			DNS Client3	192.168.2.47
	Reverse zone	1.168.192.in-addr.arpa	192.168.2.45	DNS Client1
			192.168.2.46	DNS Client2
			192.168.2.47	DNS Client3

Namespace: training.nwtraders.msft.

DNS Server Authorized for training

DNS Client2 = ?

192.168.2.46 = ?

DNS Client1

DNS Client2

DNS Client3

Introduction

After you have decided whether the zone is a primary, secondary, or stub zone type, you must decide what type of lookup zone the resource records will be stored in. Resource records can be stored either in forward lookup zones or in reverse lookup zones.

Purpose of DNS forward and reverse lookup zones

You can store a mapping as either a host name-to-IP address mapping or an IP address-to-host name mapping. You can choose the type of mapping that you need for a zone, depending upon how you want your clients and services to query resource records.

Forward lookup zone

In DNS, a *forward lookup* is a query process in which the display name for the DNS domain of a host computer is searched to find its IP address.

In DNS Manager, *forward lookup zones* are based on DNS domain names and typically hold host address (A) resource records.

Reverse lookup zone

In DNS, a *reverse lookup* is a query process by which the IP address of a host computer is searched to find its display name for the DNS domain.

In DNS Manager, *reverse lookup zones* are based on the in-addr.arpa domain name and typically hold pointer (PTR) resource records.

Example

Client1 sends a query for the IP address for client2.training.nwtraders.msft. The DNS server searches its forward-lookup zone (training.nwtraders.msft) for the IP address that is associated with the host name and returns the IP address to Client1.

Client1 sends a query for the host name for 192.168.2.46 The DNS server searches its reverse lookup zone (1.168.192.in-addr.arpa) for the host name that is associated with the IP address and returns the host name to Client1.

How to Configure Forward and Reverse Lookup Zones

> **Your instructor will demonstrate how to:**
>
> • Configure a forward lookup zone on a primary zone type
> • Configure a forward lookup stub zone
> • Configure a forward lookup zone on a secondary zone type
> • Configure a reverse lookup zone on a primary zone type
> • Configure a reverse lookup zone on a secondary zone type

Introduction

You can configure either a forward lookup zone or a reverse lookup zone on either a primary zone type or a secondary zone type. You also have the option of configuring a stub zone.

Procedure for configuring a forward lookup zone on a primary zone type

To configure a forward lookup zone on a primary zone type:

1. Open the DNS console.

2. In the DNS console, right-click the DNS server, and then click **New Zone**.

3. On the **Welcome to the New Zone Wizard** page, click **Next**.

4. On the **Zone Type** page, verify that **Primary zone** is selected, and then click **Next**.

5. On the **Forward or Reverse Lookup Zone** page, verify that **Forward lookup zone** is selected, and then click **Next**.

6. On the **Zone Name** page, type the DNS name of the zone that this server will be authoritative for, and then click **Next**.

7. On the **Zone File** page, click **Next** to accept the defaults.

8. On the **Dynamic Update** page, select one of the following options, and then click **Next**.

   a. **Allow only secure dynamic updates (recommended for Active Directory).** This option is only available for Active Directory-integrated zones.

   b. **Allow both nonsecure and secure dynamic updates.** This option is not recommended, because updates can be accepted from untrusted sources.

   c. **Do not allow dynamic updates.** This option requires you to update records manually.

9. After completing the **New Zone Wizard** page, click **Finish**.

10. Close the DNS console.

Procedure for configuring a forward lookup stub zone

To configure a forward lookup stub zone:

1. Open the DNS console.

2. In the DNS console, right-click the DNS server and then click **New Zone**.

3. On the **Welcome to the New Zone Wizard** page, click **Next**.

4. On the **Zone Type** page, select **Stub zone**, and then click **Next**.

5. On the **Forward or Reverse Lookup Zone** page, select **Forward lookup zone**, and then click **Next**.

6. On the **Zone Name** page, type the DNS name of the zone that this server will be authoritative for, and then click **Next**.

7. On the **Zone File** page, click **Next** to accept the defaults.

8. On the **Master DNS Servers** page, in the **IP address** field, type the IP address of the DNS server that this DNS server will copy the zone from. Click **Add**, and then click **Next**.

9. On the **Completing the New Zone Wizard** page, click **Finish**.

10. Close the DNS console.

Procedure for configuring a forward lookup zone on a secondary zone type

To configure a forward lookup zone on a secondary zone type:

1. Open the DNS console.

2. In the DNS console, right-click the DNS server, and then click **New Zone**.

3. On the **Welcome to the New Zone Wizard** page, click **Next**.

4. On the **Zone Type** page, select **Secondary zone**, and then click **Next**.

5. On the **Forward or Reverse Lookup Zone** page, verify that **Forward lookup zone** is selected, and then click **Next**.

6. On the **Zone Name** page, type the DNS namespace, and then click **Next**.

7. On the **Master DNS Servers** page, in the **IP address** field, type the IP address of the master DNS server, click **Add**, and then click **Next**.

8. On the **Completing the New Zone Wizard** page, click **Finish**.

9. Close the DNS console.

Procedure for configuring a reverse lookup zone on a primary zone type

To configure a reverse lookup zone on a primary zone type:

1. Open the DNS console.

2. In the DNS console, right-click the DNS server and then click **New Zone**.

3. On the **Welcome to the New Zone Wizard** page, click **Next**.

4. On the **Zone Type** page, verify that **Primary zone** is selected, and then click **Next**.

5. On the **Forward or Reverse Lookup Zone** page, select **Reverse lookup zone**, and then click **Next**.

6. On the **Reverse Lookup Zone Name** page, in the **Network ID** field, type the network ID portion of the IP address of the zone, and then click **Next**.

7. On the **Zone File** page, click **Next** to accept the defaults.

8. On the **Dynamic Update** page, select one of the following options, and then click **Next**.

   a. **Allow only secure dynamic updates (recommended for Active Directory).**

   b. **Allow both nonsecure and secure dynamic updates.**

   c. **Do not allow dynamic updates.**

9. On the **Completing the New Zone Wizard** page, click **Finish**.

10. Close the DNS console.

Procedure for configuring a reverse lookup zone on a secondary zone type

To configure a reverse lookup zone on a secondary zone type:

1. Open the DNS console.

2. In the DNS console, right-click the DNS server and then click **New Zone**.

3. On the **Welcome to the New Zone Wizard** page, click **Next**.

4. On the **Zone Type** page, select **Secondary zone**, and then click **Next**.

5. On the **Forward or Reverse Lookup Zone** page, select **Reverse lookup zone**, and then click **Next**.

6. On the **Reverse Lookup Zone Name** page, in the **Network ID** field, type the network ID portion of the IP address of the zone, and then click **Next**.

7. On the **Zone File** page, click **Next** to accept the defaults.

8. On the **Master DNS Servers** page, in the **IP address** field, type the IP address of the master DNS server, click **Add**, and then click **Next**.

9. On the **Completing the New Zone Wizard** page, click **Finish**.

10. Close the DNS console.

Practice: Configuring DNS Zones

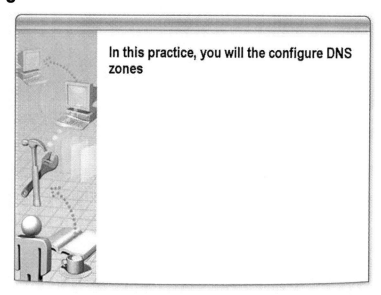

In this practice, you will the configure DNS zones

Objective

In this practice, you will configure a DNS zone.

Instructions

To complete this practice, refer to the *Implementation Plan Values* document, located in the Appendix at the end of your student workbook.

You must be logged on with an account that has non-administrative credentials and use the **Run as** command with a user account that has appropriate administrative credentials to complete the task.

Scenario

The nwtraders.msft domain namespace has grown too large. The systems engineer has planned for each DNS server in the Lab department to maintain both a forward lookup zone and a reverse lookup zone. You will create a primary forward lookup zone and a primary reverse lookup zone on your DNS computer.

Practice

▶ **Configure a forward lookup zone on a secondary zone type**

- Complete this task from both student computers

- Zone Name: **nwtraders.msft**

- Master DNS server IP address: **192.168.*x*.200**

- After you complete this task, select this DNS secondary forward lookup zone, and, in the details pane, view the DNS records to verify that the zone loaded from the master DNS server.

▶ **Configure a reverse lookup zone on a secondary zone type**

■ Complete this task from both student computers

■ Zone name: **192.168.**x

■ Master DNS server IP address: **192.168.**x**.200**

■ After you complete this task, select this DNS secondary forward lookup zone, and, in the details pane, view the DNS records to verify that the zone loaded from the master DNS server.

▶ **Configure a forward lookup zone on a primary zone type**

■ Complete this task from both student computers

■ Zone name: *srv*.**nwtraders.msft** (where *srv* is the three-letter label of the computer name)

■ Dynamic update: **Allow both nonsecure and secure dynamic updates**

Note For purposes of demonstration you are configuring Dynamic update to allow both nonsecure and secure dynamic updates. This is not ordinarily a recommended configuration.

Lesson: Configuring DNS Zone Transfers

- How DNS Zone Transfers Work
- How DNS Notify Works
- How to Configure DNS Zone Transfers

Introduction

Zone transfers are the complete or partial transfer of all data in a zone from the primary DNS server that is hosting the zone to a secondary DNS server that is hosting a copy of the zone. When changes are made to the zone on a primary DNS server, then the primary DNS server notifies the secondary DNS servers that these changes have occurred and that the changes are replicated to all the secondary DNS servers for that zone by using zone transfers.

Lesson objectives

After completing this lesson, you will be able to:

- Describe how DNS zone transfers work.
- Describe how DNS notify works.
- Configure DNS zone transfers.

How DNS Zone Transfers Work

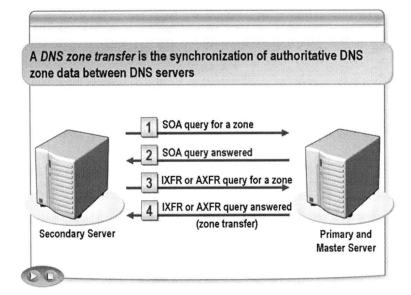

A *DNS zone transfer* is the synchronization of authoritative DNS zone data between DNS servers

1 SOA query for a zone

2 SOA query answered

3 IXFR or AXFR query for a zone

4 IXFR or AXFR query answered (zone transfer)

Secondary Server

Primary and Master Server

Introduction

There are two types of DNS zone transfers: a full zone transfer and an incremental zone transfer.

Definitions

A *primary DNS server* is both the administrative location for and the master copy of a zone. The primary DNS server both contains the read/write copy of the zone database and controls changes to the zone.

A *secondary server* is a server that maintains a copy of an existing DNS zone.

A *master server* is a DNS server that transfers zone changes to another DNS server. A master server can either be a primary DNS server or a secondary DNS server, depending on how the server obtains its zone data.

A *DNS zone transfer* is the synchronization of authoritative DNS data between DNS servers. A DNS server configured with a secondary zone periodically queries the master DNS servers to synchronize its zone data.

A *full zone transfer* is the standard query type that all DNS servers support to update and synchronize zone data when the zone has been changed. When a DNS query is made by using AXFR as the specified query type, the entire zone is transferred as the response.

An *AXFR* query is a request for a full zone transfer.

An *incremental zone transfer* is an alternate query type that some DNS servers use to update and synchronize zone data when a zone is changed since the last update. When two DNS servers support incremental zone transfer, the servers can keep track of and transfer only those incremental resource record changes between each version of the zone.

An *IXFR* query is a request for an incremental zone transfer.

Purpose of a DNS zone transfer

The purpose of zone transfer is to ensure that both DNS servers that host the same zone have the same zone information. Without zone transfers, the data on the primary server would be current, but the secondary DNS server would not have up-to-date zone information, and therefore the secondary DNS server could not support name resolution for that zone.

Zone transfer process

The following process outlines the steps for either a full or an incremental zone transfer.

1. The secondary server for the zone waits through a certain period of time (specified in the **Refresh** field of the SOA resource record that the secondary server attained from the master server). Then the secondary server queries the master server for its SOA.

2. The master server for the zone responds with the SOA resource record.

3. The secondary server for the zone compares the returned serial number to its own serial number. If the serial number that the master server sends for the zone is higher than its own serial number, then its zone database is out of date. The master server then sends an AXFR query to request a full zone transfer. If the DNS server supports incremental zone transfers (as in Windows Server 2003 and Windows 2000), then it sends an IXFR to request an incremental zone transfer, which transfers resource records that have been modified since the last transfer.

4. For a full zone transfer, the master server for the zone sends the zone database to the secondary server; for an incremental zone transfer, the master server sends only that zone data that has changed.

Note   When you create a secondary zone, the DNS server performs a full zone transfer to initially populate the database.

Important   By default, the DNS Server service only allows zone information to be transferred to servers that are listed in the name server (NS) resource records of a zone. This is a secure configuration. For increased security, however, select the option to allow zone transfers only to specified IP addresses. Allowing zone transfers to any server might expose your DNS data to an attacker attempting to footprint your network.

How DNS Notify Works

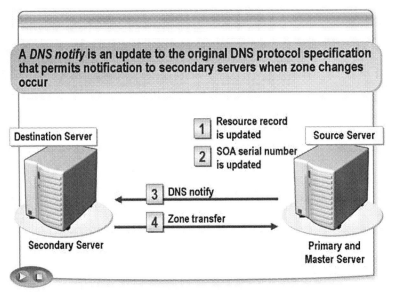

Definitions

DNS notify is an update to the original DNS protocol specification that permits notification to secondary servers when zone changes occur.

A *notify list* is a list for the zone of other DNS servers that should be notified when zone changes occur. The notify list that the master server maintains is made up of IP addresses for DNS servers that are configured as secondary servers for the zone. When the listed servers are notified of a change to the zone, they will initiate a zone transfer with another DNS server and update the zone.

Purpose of DNS notify

Servers that are notified can initiate a zone transfer to obtain zone changes from their master servers and update their local replicas of the zone.

This is an improvement over the time intervals that are set on the secondary DNS server's copy of the zone. When you use DNS notify, the copies of the DNS zone are updated when unscheduled changes occur.

DNS notify can help improve consistency of zone data among secondary servers. For example, if DNS zone transfers only occur at certain times, two situations can occur within a time period:

■ No changes may have occurred to a DNS zone.

■ Several minutes may have passed before a zone transfer is initiated. The zone may have had many zone changes occur and these changes have not yet transferred to the secondary DNS server.

With DNS notify, updates occur whenever changes occur.

Furthermore, DNS servers running Windows Server 2003 or Windows 2000 support incremental transfers, so that only the data that has been changed in the master DNS server is transferred to the secondary DNS server.

Process of DNS notify

Referring to the illustration, the following steps outline the DNS notify process:

1. The local zone on a primary DNS server is updated.

2. The **Serial Number** field in the SOA record is updated to indicate that a new version of the zone has been written to a disk.

3. The primary server then sends a notify message to all other servers that are part of its notify list.

4. All secondary servers for the zone that receive the notify message respond by initiating an SOA-type query back to the notifying primary server. This query begins the DNS zone transfer process.

How to Configure DNS Zone Transfers

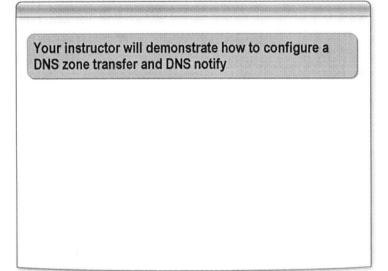

Your instructor will demonstrate how to configure a DNS zone transfer and DNS notify

Introduction

To both synchronize the authoritative DNS data between DNS servers and update DNS zone data when unscheduled changes occur, you can configure a DNS zone transfer and a DNS notify.

Note It is recommended that you log on with an account that has non-administrative credentials and use the **Run as** command with a user account that has appropriate administrative credentials to perform this task.

Procedure

To configure a DNS zone transfer and DNS notify:

1. Open the DNS console.
2. Expand the appropriate server, and then expand either **Forward Lookup Zones** or **Reverse Lookup Zones**.
3. Select the appropriate DNS zone.
4. On the **Action** menu, click **Properties**.
5. In the **Properties** dialog box for the DNS zone, on the **Zone Transfers** tab, verify that **Allow zone transfers** is selected.
6. Select **Only to the following servers**.
7. In the **IP address** field, type the IP address of the DNS server that the zone data will be transferred to, and then click **Add**.
8. In the **Properties** dialog box for the DNS zone, on the **Zone Transfers** tab, click **Notify**.
9. In the **Notify** dialog box, click the option **The following servers**.
10. In the **IP address** field, type the IP address of the DNS server that will receive the automatic notify, and then click **OK**.
11. On the **Zone Properties** tab, click **OK**.
12. Close the DNS console.

Practice: Configuring DNS Zone Transfers

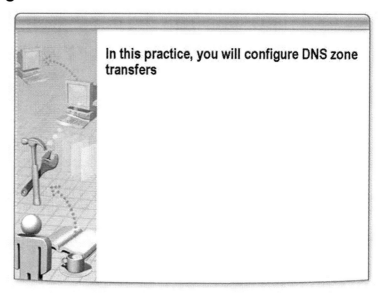

In this practice, you will configure DNS zone transfers

Objective

In this practice, you will configure DNS zone transfers.

Instructions

To complete this practice, refer to the *Implementation Plan Values* document, located in the Appendix at the end of your student workbook.

You must be logged on with an account that has non-administrative credentials and use the **Run as** command with a user account that has appropriate administrative credentials to complete the task.

Scenario

A new DNS server has been configured as the secondary server to your DNS server in the lab. You will configure zone transfer settings on the DNS zone on your DNS server. Then you will verify that zone transfer completed.

Practice

▶ **Configure DNS zone transfer and DNS notify on a primary forward lookup zone**

- Complete this task from both student computers

- Primary forward lookup zone: *srv*.**nwtraders.msft** (where *srv* is the three-letter label of your computer name)

- IP address of server requesting zone transfer: **192.168.**x**.200**

- IP address of server to notify: **192.168.**x**.200**

Lesson: Configuring DNS Dynamic Updates

* Multimedia: Overview of DNS Dynamic Updates
* What Are Dynamic Updates?
* How DNS Clients Register and Update Their Own Resource Records by Using Dynamic Updates
* How a DHCP Server Registers and Updates Resource Records by Using Dynamic Updates
* How to Configure DNS Manual and Dynamic Updates
* What Is an Active Directory-Integrated DNS Zone?
* How Active Directory-Integrated DNS Zones Use Secure Dynamic Updates
* How to Configure Active Directory-Integrated DNS Zones to Allow Secure Dynamic Updates

Introduction

Because DNS is used to access resources, it is imperative that resources in DNS are current. Errors can occur when DNS resource records are not current.

If a DNS resource record is created manually in DNS, then the DNS administrator must manually update the DNS resource record to reflect the changes to the resource when the IP address of the resource changes.

Because of the volume of resource records in DNS, manually updating the records quickly becomes overwhelming for a DNS administrator to maintain. The solution to this problem is to create a method for allowing DNS clients to update and maintain their own resource records in DNS. Dynamic updates allow DNS clients to update and maintain their own resource records in DNS.

To enable DNS updates to happen automatically, without DNS administrator interaction, the administrator must configure the DNS zone to allow dynamic updates. In addition, administrators must either configure the DNS clients to update DNS records in DNS, or configure the DHCP server supporting the DNS clients to update the DNS records on behalf of the DNS clients.

Lesson objectives

After completing this lesson, you will be able to:

- Describe how DNS dynamic updates work.
- Explain what dynamic updates are.
- Describe how DNS clients register and update their own resource records by using dynamic update.
- Describe how a DHCP server registers and updates resource records by using dynamic update.
- Configure DNS manual and dynamic updates.
- Explain what an Active Directory-integrated DNS zone is.
- Describe how Active Directory-integrated DNS zones use secure dynamic updates.
- Configure Active Directory-integrated DNS zones to use secure dynamic updates.

Multimedia: Overview of DNS Dynamic Updates

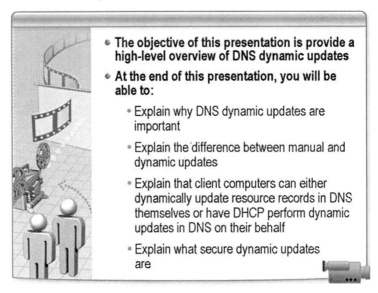

File location

To start the *Overview of DNS Dynamic Updates* presentation, open the Web page on the Student Materials compact disc, click **Multimedia**, and then click the title of the presentation.

Objectives

At the end of this presentation, you will be able to:

■ Explain why DNS dynamic updates are important.

■ Explain the difference between manual and dynamic updates.

■ Explain that client computers can either:

• Dynamically update resource records in DNS themselves.

• Have DHCP perform dynamic updates in DNS on their behalf.

■ Explain what secure dynamic updates are.

Key points

■ For users to successfully access DNS resources, it is vital that DNS resource records reflect the current TCP/IP configuration of both server computers and client computers.

■ DNS resource records can be updated either by the DNS clients themselves or by DHCP on behalf of the clients.

■ Various types of DNS resource records, such as host (A) records and pointer (PTR) records, provide DNS clients with various types of information.

■ You can use a manual update process to add and update DNS resource records, or you can enable client computers to dynamically update and maintain their own resource records in DNS.

■ A secure way of updating DNS resource records is secure dynamic update.

What Are Dynamic Updates?

A *dynamic update* is the process of a DNS client dynamically creating, registering, or updating its records in zones that are maintained by DNS servers that can accept and process messages for dynamic updates

A *manual update* is the process of an administrator manually creating, registering, or updating the resource record

- Dynamic update enables DNS client computers to interact automatically with the DNS server to register and update their own resource records
  - Organizations that have dynamic changes can benefit from the dynamic method of updating DNS resource records
- Organizations may benefit from manual update if they:
  - Are in a smaller environment that has few changes to their resource records
  - Have isolated instances, such as when a larger organization chooses to control every address on every host.

Introduction

There are two ways that DNS resource records can be created, registered, and updated in the DNS database: dynamically and manually.

When resource records are created, registered, or updated, they are stored in the DNS zone file.

Definitions

A *dynamic update* is the process of a DNS client dynamically creating, registering, or updating its records in zones which are maintained by DNS servers that can accept and process messages for dynamic updates.

A *manual update* is the process of an administrator manually creating, registering, or updating the resource record.

Purpose of dynamic updates

The process of manually updating client resource records does not scale well in a large organization that has continuous changes to DNS resource records. A large organization that has dynamic changes must rely on the dynamic method of updating DNS resource records.

Dynamic registration and update enables DNS client computers to interact automatically with the DNS server to register and update their own resource records. In a DNS implementation that uses a DNS server running Microsoft Windows NT® 4.0 and older BIND versions, the administrator has to edit the appropriate zone file manually if the authoritative information of a resource record must be changed. As the number of DNS records in a zone increases and becomes unmanageable for the administrator to maintain manually, then dynamic update becomes essential.

Circumstances for manually configuring dynamic updates

The DNS administrator may benefit from manually registering or updating the resource record if the organization has:

- A smaller environment with few changes to the resource records.

- Isolated instances, such as when a larger organization chooses to control every address on every host.

How DNS Clients Register and Update Their Own Resource Records by Using Dynamic Updates

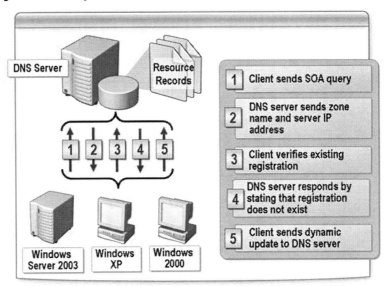

Types of DNS clients that can dynamically register and update resource records

DNS clients running Windows Server 2003, Windows 2000, and Windows XP are configured by default to dynamically register and update their host names and IP addresses in DNS.

Regardless of whether a DNS client is assigned an IP address by using DHCP or assigned an IP address statically, a DNS client can dynamically register and update its host name and IP address in DNS.

The component that registers the DNS resource record for a DNS client is the DHCP Client service. Even on clients that are configured with data for a static IP address, the DHCP Client service must be running for the static client to register its resource records in DNS.

Process

The following process outlines the steps for dynamically updating DNS clients:

1. The DNS client sends an SOA query to the DNS server that is authoritative for the resource record that the DNS client wishes to register with.

2. The DNS server returns the zone name and IP address of the DNS server that is authoritative for the zone that the DNS client wants to register on the DNS server.

3. The DNS client then sends the authoritative DNS server of the zone an Assertion Update to verify that no existing registration exists in the zone.

4. The DNS server responds to the DNS client.

5. If no registration exists in the DNS zone, then the DNS client sends a dynamic update package to register the resource record.

If the DNS client fails to update its resource record in the DNS database as described in the previous process, then the client continues to attempt updating its resource record in DNS.

1. The DNS client attempts to register the record with other primary servers in the zone. Multiple primary servers will only be an option with an Active Directory-integrated zone.

2. If all the attempts fail, the client tries to register the record again after five minutes, and then again after ten minutes.

3. Failures result in a repeated pattern of attempts 50 minutes after the last retry.

Note A remote access client works the same way as a client configured with configuration data for a static IP address. For example, no interaction occurs between the client and the DHCP server. When the remote access client connects to the network, the client is responsible for dynamically updating both A and PTR resource records in DNS. The remote access client attempts to delete both records before closing the connection, but the records are not updated (meaning that they are not current or valid) if the update failed, such as when a DNS server is not running. The records are also not updated if the connection fails unexpectedly. In these cases, a remote access server attempts deregistration (meaning that the remote access server attempts to remove the stale record) of the corresponding PTR record.

How a DHCP Server Registers and Updates Resource Records by Using Dynamic Updates

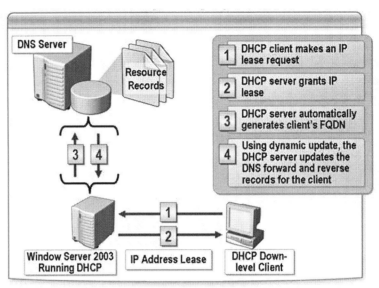

Definition

A *down-level client* is a DHCP client running Windows NT 4.0 or earlier. Down-level clients are unable to register or update their resource records in DNS on their own.

Purpose of DNS dynamic update by using a DHCP server

Because down-level clients cannot register or update their own resource records, Microsoft designed their implementation of the DHCP server with the ability to register DNS client resource records in DNS on behalf of the DHCP clients.

Types of DHCP clients that can dynamically register and update resource records

On a DHCP server running Windows Server 2003 or Windows 2000, you can configure the DHCP server to dynamically update the resource records in DNS on behalf of DHCP clients on the network. Clients that are running Windows NT 4.0 and earlier can have their resource records entered in the DNS database if DHCP is configured to dynamically update the DNS records on their behalf.

Administrators can configure DHCP servers running Windows Server 2003 and Windows 2000 to update DNS client resource records for the following client types.

- Any down-level DHCP clients that do not request dynamic updates.

- Any DHCP client, including those that are running Windows XP and Windows 2000, regardless of whether it requests a dynamic update.

Process of performing dynamic updates for a down-level client

In the illustration, the DHCP server running Windows Server 2003 performs dynamic updates for a down-level client:

1. The DHCP client makes an IP lease request.

2. The DHCP server grants an IP lease.

3. The DHCP server automatically generates the client's FQDN by appending the domain name that is defined for the DHCP scope to the client name. The client name is obtained from the DHCPREQUEST message that the client sends.

4. Using the dynamic update protocol, the DHCP server updates the:

   a. DNS forward (A) name for the client.

   b. DNS reverse (PTR) name for the client.

The ability to register both A and PTR record types allows a DHCP server running Windows Server 2003 to act as a proxy for down-level clients for the purpose of DNS registration.

Process of performing dynamic updates for a Windows XP client

The following steps reflect the process for a DHCP server running Windows Server 2003 with the default configuration to perform DNS dynamic updates for a Windows XP client:

1. The DHCP client makes an IP lease request that includes the client FQDN in option 81 of the DHCP request.

2. The DHCP server grants an IP lease.

3. The client connects to the DNS server to update the A record for itself.

4. The DHCP server updates the DNS reverse (PTR) name for the client by using the dynamic update protocol.

How to Configure DNS Manual and Dynamic Updates

Your instructor will demonstrate how to:

- Configure a DNS server running Windows Server 2003 to accept dynamic updates of DNS resource records
- Configure a Windows XP Professional client to dynamically update its DNS resource records in DNS
- Configure a DHCP server running Windows Server 2003 to dynamically update DNS resource records in DNS on behalf of DHCP clients
- Manually create a DNS resource record

Introduction

To configure dynamic updates as a solution, you need to choose and configure one or both of the following options. Dynamic updates are supported on Primary DNS zones.

To use a DNS client for dynamic updates, configure the:

1. DNS server to accept dynamic updates.
2. DNS clients to create dynamic updates for themselves.

To use a DHCP server for dynamic updates, configure the:

1. DNS server to accept dynamic updates.
2. DHCP server to create dynamic updates on behalf of the DHCP clients.

To manually create a DNS resource record, you need to add a host (A) resource record to a forward lookup zone.

Note It is recommended that you log on with an account that has non-administrative credentials and use the **Run as** command with a user account that has appropriate administrative credentials to perform this task.

Procedure for configuring a DNS server to accept dynamic updates

To configure a DNS server running Windows Server 2003 to accept dynamic updates of DNS resource records:

1. Open the DNS console.
2. In the console tree, right-click the applicable zone, and then click **Properties**.
3. On the **General** tab, in the **Dynamic updates** drop-down list, click **Nonsecure and secure**.
4. Click **OK** to close the DNS zone **Properties** dialog box, and then close the **DNS** console.

Procedure for configuring DNS clients running Windows XP Professional to dynamically update

To configure a Windows XP Professional client to dynamically update its DNS resource records in DNS:

1. In Control Panel, open the **Properties** dialog box for the appropriate network interface.

2. In the **Properties** dialog box, select **Internet Protocol (TCP/IP)**, and then click **Properties**.

3. In the **Internet Protocol (TCP/IP) Properties** dialog box, click **Advanced**.

4. On the **DNS** tab of the **Advanced TCP/IP Settings** dialog box, select **Register this connection's addresses in DNS**.

5. On the **DNS** tab of the **Advanced TCP/IP Settings** dialog box, select **Use this connection's DNS suffix in DNS registration** if required.

6. In the **Advanced TCP/IP properties** dialog box, click **OK**.

7. In the **Internet Protocol Properties** dialog box, click **OK**.

8. In the **Network Connection Properties** dialog box, click **Close**.

Procedure for configuring a DHCP server to dynamically update DNS resource records on behalf of DHCP clients

To configure a DHCP server running Windows Server 2003 to dynamically update DNS resource records in DNS on behalf of DHCP clients:

1. Open the DHCP console.

2. In the **DHCP** console, select the appropriate DHCP server.

3. On the **Action** menu, click **Properties**.

4. On the **DNS** tab, verify that **Enable DNS dynamic updates according to the settings below** is selected, and then select one of the two options:

   • **Dynamically update DNS A and PTR records only if requested by the DHCP clients**

   • **Always dynamically update DNS A and PTR records**

5. On the **DNS** tab, verify that the option **Discard A and PTR records when lease is deleted** is selected.

6. On the **DNS** tab if required, select the option **Dynamically update DNS A and PTR records for DHCP clients that do not request updates**, and then click **OK**.

7. Close the DHCP console.

Procedure for manually creating DNS resource records

To manually create a DNS resource record:

1. Open the DNS console.

2. In the console tree, right-click the applicable primary forward lookup zone, and then click **New Host (A)**.

3. In the **New Host** dialog box, in the **Name** field, type the DNS computer name for the new host.

4. In the **New Host** dialog box, in the **IP address** field, type the IP address for the new host.

5. As an option, select **Create associated pointer (PTR) record** to create an additional pointer record in a reverse zone for this host, based on the information that you entered in the **Name** and **IP address** boxes.

6. In the **New Host** dialog box, click **Add Host** to add the new host record to the zone.

7. In the **DNS** message box, click **OK**.

8. In the **New Host** dialog box, click **Done**.

9. Close the DNS console.

What Is an Active Directory-Integrated DNS Zone?

DNS zone type	Benefit
Non Active Directory-integrated zone	• Does not require Active Directory
Active Directory-integrated zone	• Stores DNS zone data in Active Directory and is thus more secure • Uses Active Directory replication instead of zone transfers • Allows only secure dynamic updates • Uses multi-master instead of single master structure

An *Active Directory-integrated DNS zone* is a DNS zone stored in Active Directory

---

Definition

An *Active Directory-integrated DNS zone* is a DNS zone stored in Active Directory.

Purpose of Active Directory-integrated DNS zones

When you configure a domain controller, Active Directory requires that DNS be installed. Zones, which are created on a DNS server that is an Active Directory domain controller, can be Active Directory-integrated DNS zones.

Active Directory-integrated DNS zones have several advantages over non-Active Directory-integrated DNS zones. Active Directory-integrated DNS zones can use Active Directory:

- To store zone configuration data in Active Directory, instead of storing zone configuration data in a zone file.

- To use Active Directory Replication instead of zone transfers.

- To allow only secure dynamic updates (instead of secure and nonsecure updates on a non-Active Directory-integrated DNS zone).

Active Directory-integrated DNS zones

In a non-Active Directory-integrated DNS zone, there is a single master copy of the DNS zone (primary) and there can be any number of additional copies of the DNS zone (secondary).

In an Active Directory-integrated DNS zone, the zone data is stored in Active Directory, so that there can be a multi-master model. Each domain controller can manage changes to the DNS zone.

Multi-master means that if a domain controller has an Active Directory-integrated zone, then any domain controller that contains that DNS zone information can act as a primary server, and can make changes to the DNS zone.

Note   Active Directory Application mode does not support hosting Active Directory-Integrated DNS.

How Active Directory-Integrated DNS Zones Use Secure Dynamic Updates

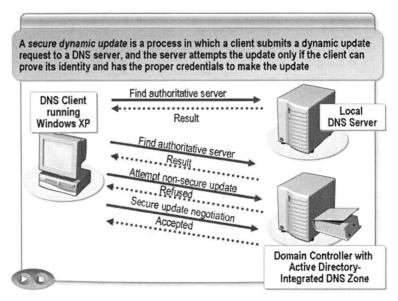

Definition	A *secure dynamic update* is a process in which a client submits a dynamic update request to a DNS server, and the server attempts the update only if the client can prove its identity and has the proper credentials to make the update. Secure dynamic updates are only available on Active Directory-integrated zones.
	The preferred method is, on a domain controller that is configured with a DNS zone, to allow only secure dynamic updates.
	The other method is to configure a zone that is on a non-Active Directory-integrated DNS server, to allow both secure and nonsecure dynamic updates.
Purpose of secure dynamic updates	DNS on Windows Server 2003 supports secure dynamic update. Secure dynamic update provides several benefits, such as:

- Protecting zones and resource records from being modified by users who do not have authorization.

- Enabling you to specify exactly which users and groups can modify zones and resource records.

By allowing dynamic updates on a DNS zone, you do not need to manually create and maintain all of the resource records. However, you cannot control what DNS clients can dynamically update. If you are using a stand-alone DNS server that is non-Active Directory-integrated, then you cannot control who dynamically updates the server. For example: If an external consultant brings a laptop into your organization that is not a part of the domain, and if the laptop dynamically updates in DNS, then you could have a security issue.

However, if a DNS server hosts the DNS zone on an Active Directory-integrated zone, then you can configure the DNS zone to allow only secure updates. This means that if the same laptop, which is not a member of the domain, attempts to dynamically update in the DNS zone, it will be denied. Using domain security, you can control dynamic updates by allowing only domain members to dynamically update their records.

Note Because the DNS zone is Active Directory-integrated, you can configure the access control list (ACL) on resource records to further secure DNS. For more information, see the Windows Server 2003 Help documentation about securing DNS by using ACLs.

Non-secure versus secure-only dynamic updates

If a zone is Active Directory-integrated, it can be configured as Secure Only. A zone configured as Secure Only authenticates the computer that is attempting to make the update, and only allows the update if the permissions on the record allow it. Zones hosted in Active Directory, in addition to those that are not, can be configured to allow nonsecure updates, which would allow DNS registrations and modifications without authenticating the client computer.

Process

Referring to the illustration, the following procedure provides the sequence of events in the secure dynamic update process:

1. The client queries the local name server to discover which server is authoritative for the name that the client is attempting to update, and the local name server responds with the reference to the authoritative server.

2. The client queries the authoritative server to verify that the DNS server is authoritative for the name that the client is attempting to update, and the server confirms the query.

3. The client attempts a nonsecure update, and the server refuses the nonsecure update. Had the server been configured for nonsecure dynamic update for the appropriate zone, rather than for secure dynamic update, the server would instead have attempted to make the update.

4. The client then attempts a secure update. If the update has the proper credentials, then the authoritative DNS server accepts the update and responds to the DNS client.

Note If a DHCP server performs the first secure dynamic update on a DNS resource record, then that DHCP server becomes the owner of that record, and only that DHCP server can update that record. This can cause problems in a few different circumstances. For example: Suppose that the DHCP server (DHCP1) created a record for the name nt4host1.nwtraders.msft and then stopped responding, and that the backup DHCP server (DHCP2) tried to update the name. DHCP2 is not able to update the name, because DHCP2 does not own the name. Therefore, if secure dynamic update is enabled, all DHCP servers should be placed in a special security group called DNSUpdateProxy. Objects created by members of the DNSUpdateProxy group have no security; therefore, any authenticated user can take ownership of the objects. For more information about DNSUpdateProxy, or about secure dynamic updates, see the Windows Server 2003 Help documentation.

How to Configure Active Directory-Integrated DNS Zones to Allow Secure Dynamic Updates

> **Your instructor will demonstrate how to:**
>
> * Configure Active Directory-integrated DNS zones to allow secure dynamic updates
> * Configure security on an Active Directory-integrated DNS zone

Introduction

You can configure both Active Directory-integrated DNS zones and non-Active Directory-integrated DNS zones to allow secure dynamic update. You can also configure security on Active Directory-integrated DNS zones.

Note It is recommended that you log on with an account that has non-administrative credentials and use the **Run as** command with a user account that has appropriate administrative credentials to perform this task.

Procedure for configuring Active Directory-integrated DNS zones to allow secure dynamic updates

To configure Active Directory-integrated DNS zones to allow secure dynamic updates:

1. Open the DNS console.
2. In the console tree, right-click the applicable zone, and then click **Properties**.
3. On the **General** tab, verify that the **Type** is **Active Directory-integrated**.
4. In the **Dynamic updates** drop-down list, select **Secure only**.
5. Click **OK** to close the DNS zone **Properties** dialog box, and then close the DNS console.

Procedure for configuring security on an Active Directory-integrated DNS zone

To configure security on an Active Directory-integrated DNS zone:

1. Open the DNS console.

2. In the console tree, right-click the applicable zone, and then click **Properties**.

3. On the **Security** tab, configure the permissions appropriately for your network.

4. Click **OK** to close the DNS zone **Properties** dialog box, and then close the DNS console.

Practice: Configuring DNS Dynamic Updates

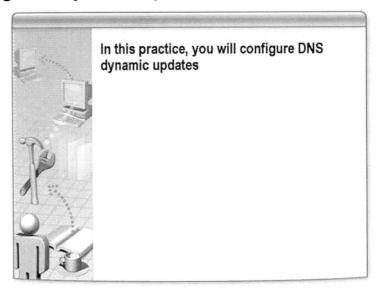

Objective

In this practice, you will configure DNS dynamic updates.

Instructions

To complete this practice, refer to the *Implementation Plan Values* document located in the Appendix at the end of your student workbook.

You must be logged on with an account that has non-administrative credentials and use the **Run as** command with a user account that has appropriate administrative credentials to complete the task.

Scenario

The number of computers in the development subnet has increased. As a result, there has been an increase in the number of DNS resource records that need to be manually created. You will configure the DHCP server to automatically create the resource records in DNS on behalf of the DHCP clients.

Practice

▶ **Configure a DNS server to accept dynamic updates for a forward lookup zone**

- Complete this task from both student computers.

- Primary forward lookup zone: *srv*.**nwtraders.msft**
  (where *srv* is the three-letter label of your computer name)

- Dynamic updates: **Nonsecure and secure**

▶ **Configure a DHCP server to dynamically update DNS resource records on behalf of DHCP clients**

- Complete this task from both student computers.

- DHCP Server: your DHCP server

- Select **Always dynamically update DNS A and PTR records**.

▶ **Manually create a DNS host resource record**

- Complete this task from both student computers.

- Primary forward lookup zone: *srv*.**nwtraders.msft**
  (where *srv* is the three-letter label of your computer name)

- Host name: *ComputerName***2**
  (where *ComputerName* is the name of your partner's computer)

- IP address: *Partner Network Connection*
  (where *Partner Network Connection* is the IP address of your partner)

Lesson: Configuring a DNS Client

- How Preferred and Alternate DNS Servers Work
- How Suffixes Are Applied
- How to Configure a DNS Client

Introduction   You have installed and configured the DNS server properties and created the appropriate zones on the DNS server. Now you need to ensure that clients can register or create their resource records in DNS and use DNS to resolve queries.

Lesson objectives   After completing this lesson, you will be able to:

- Describe how preferred and alternate DNS servers work.
- Describe how suffixes are applied.
- Configure a DNS client.

How Preferred and Alternate DNS Servers Work

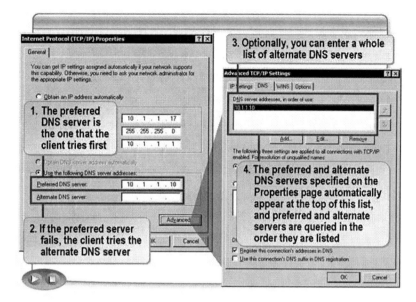

Definitions

A *preferred DNS server* is a server that is the recipient of DNS queries that the DNS client sends. It is also the server on which the DNS client updates its resource records.

An *alternate DNS server* is a server that is used if the preferred DNS server is unreachable or cannot resolve DNS queries from a particular DNS client because the DNS service has failed. The alternate server is not queried in the case of a negative name response.

Purpose of preferred and alternate DNS servers

Without a preferred DNS server, the DNS client cannot query a DNS server.

Without an alternate DNS, your queries will not be resolved if the preferred DNS server fails. You can have more than one alternate DNS server.

Process

The following steps outline the process for contacting preferred and alternate DNS servers:

1. The preferred DNS server responds first to a DNS query or a DNS update.

2. If the preferred DNS server does not respond to a DNS query or a DNS update, then the query or update is redirected to the alternate DNS server.

3. If the alternate DNS server does not respond, and if the DNS client is configured with the additional IP addresses of DNS servers, then the DNS client sends the query or update to the next DNS server in the list.

4. If any of the DNS servers (a preferred server, an alternate server, or any other server on the list), is unresponsive, then that server is temporarily removed from the list.

5. If none of the DNS servers are responsive, then the DNS client query or update fails.

How Suffixes Are Applied

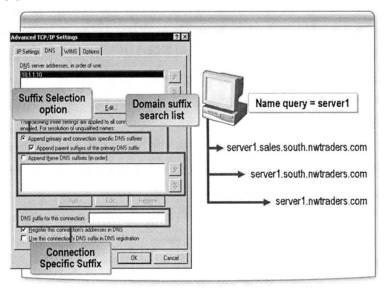

Purpose of configuring suffixes	If you do not have a DNS suffix configured on the client, then name resolution and update may not function correctly. By properly configuring DNS suffixes on the client, you ensure that name resolution is successful.
Suffix Selection option	The Suffix Selection option specifies that resolutions for unqualified names on this computer are limited to the domain suffixes of the primary DNS suffix up to the second level domain.
	For example: If your primary DNS suffix is nwtraders.msft, and if you attempt to contact Server1, then the computer queries for Server1.nwtraders.msft, in addition to any suffixes that are configured in the connection specific suffixes.
	The Append Parent Suffixes option specifies that resolutions for unqualified names on this computer are limited to the domain suffixes of the primary suffix and connection specific suffix.
	For example: If your primary DNS suffix is sales.south.nwtraders.msft, and if you attempt to contact Server1, then the computer queries server1.sales.south.nwtraders.msft. If the query is not resolved, then the computer queries server1.south.nwtraders.msft. If the query is still not resolved, then the computer then queries server1.nwtraders.msft.
Connection Specific Suffix	The Connection Specific Suffix provides a space to configure a DNS suffix for this specific connection. If a DHCP server configures this connection, and if you do not specify a DNS suffix, then the DHCP server assigns a DNS suffix if the server is configured to do so.

How suffixes are applied   When a user enters an FQDN, the DNS resolver queries DNS by using that FQDN as follows:

1. The DNS client resolver sends the query to the primary DNS server by using the primary DNS suffix.

2. If resolution is not successful, the DNS client resolver appends each connection-specfic DNS suffix.

3. If resolution is still not successful, the DNS resolver devolves the FQDN by appending the parent suffix of the primary DNS suffix name, and the parent of that suffix, and so on, until only two labels are left.

    For example, server1.sales.south.nwtraders.com devolves to server1.south.nwtraders.com, which then devolves to server1.nwtraders.com.

4. However, if the user has entered a domain suffix search list, both the primary DNS suffix and the connection-specific domain name are ignored. Neither the primary DNS suffix nor the connection-specific domain name is appended to the host name before the FQDN is submitted to DNS. Instead, the DNS resolver appends each suffix from the domain search list in order and submits it to the DNS server until it either finds a match or reaches the end of the list.

How to Configure a DNS Client

Your instructor will demonstrate how to:

- Manually configure a DNS client to use preferred and alternate DNS servers
- Configure the DNS server option and the DNS suffix option in DHCP

Introduction

You need to configure a DNS client so that the client can use DNS servers to resolve and update information for the IP address configuration.

There are two ways that a DNS client can receive IP address configuration data: manually or by using DHCP.

Important In this scenario, you must be logged on as an administrator or a member of the Administrators group to complete the first procedure. Log on as *ComputerName*Admin for the first procedure. When you have completed this procedure, log on as *ComputerName*User (where *ComputerName* is the name of your computer).

Procedure for manually configuring a DNS client to use preferred and alternate DNS servers

To manually configure a DNS client to use preferred and alternate DNS servers:

1. From Network Connections, open the **Properties** dialog box for the Network Interface that you want to configure DNS on.

2. On the **General** tab, select **Internet Protocol (TCP/IP) Protocol**, and then click **Properties**.

3. In the **Internet Protocol (TCP/IP) Properties** dialog box, select **Use the following DNS server addresses**.

4. In the **Preferred DNS server** field, type the IP address of the preferred DNS server.

5. In the **Alternate DNS server** field, type the IP address of the alternate DNS server, and then click **Advanced**.

6. In the **Advanced TCP/IP Settings** dialog box, on the **DNS** tab, in the **DNS suffix for this connection** field, type the DNS suffix to be attached to the host name of the computer, and then click **OK**.

7. In the **Internet Protocol (TCP/IP) Properties** dialog box, click **OK**.

8. Close any open windows.

Procedure for configuring the DNS server option and the DNS suffix option in DHCP

To configure the DNS server option and the DNS suffix option in DHCP:

1. Open the DHCP console.

2. Under the appropriate scope, click **Scope Options**, and then, on the **Action** menu, click **Configure Options**.

3. In the **Scope Options** dialog box, select **006 DNS Servers**.

4. In the **IP address** field, type the IP address of the DNS server, and then click **Add**.

5. In the **Scope Options** dialog box, select **015 DNS Domain Name**.

6. In the **String value** field, type the DNS domain suffix, and then click **OK**.

7. Close the DHCP console.

8. Using the **ipconfig** command, ensure that the DHCP clients renew their leases to update their IP configuration data with these new scope options.

Practice: Configuring a DNS Client

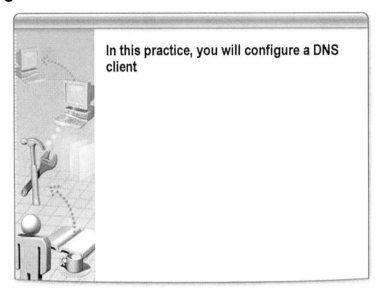

In this practice, you will configure a DNS client

Objective

In this practice, you will configure a DNS client to use a preferred DNS server, an alternate DNS server, and a DNS suffix.

Instructions

To complete this practice, refer to the *Implementation Plan Values* document located in the Appendix at the end of your student workbook.

In this practice, you must be logged on as an administrator or a member of the Administrators group to complete parts of this procedure. Log on as *ComputerName***Admin** for the entire practice. When you have completed the practice, log on as *ComputerName***User**.

Scenario

You have added two DNS servers to your *development* subnet. You need to configure the lab computers on your subnet to use a preferred and an alternate DNS server. You will configure your DNS client with the appropriate DNS settings.

Practice

► **Configure a DNS client**

■ Complete this task from both student computers

■ User name: *ComputerName***Admin**

■ Password: **P@ssw0rd**

■ Domain: **nwtraders**

■ Interface: **Classroom Network Connection**

■ Preferred DNS server IP address: *Classroom Network Connection* (where *Classroom Network Connection* is the IP address for the network connection of your computer)

■ Alternate DNS server IP address: **192.168.*x*.200**

■ DNS suffix: **nwtraders.msft**

▶ **View DNS client settings by using ipconfig**

- Complete this task from both student computers

- User name: *ComputerName***User**

- Password: **P@ssw0rd**

- Domain: **nwtraders**

- Interface: **Classroom Network Connection**

Lesson: Delegating Authority for Zones

* What Is Delegation of a DNS Zone?
* How to Delegate a Subdomain to a DNS Zone

Introduction

After you have your DNS solution working, you may find that you need to modify your DNS namespace. The process by which these DNS namespace changes are accomplished on the DNS server is called *delegation*.

Lesson objectives

After completing this lesson, you will be able to:

- Explain what delegation of a DNS zone is.
- Delegate a subdomain to a DNS zone.

What Is Delegation of a DNS Zone?

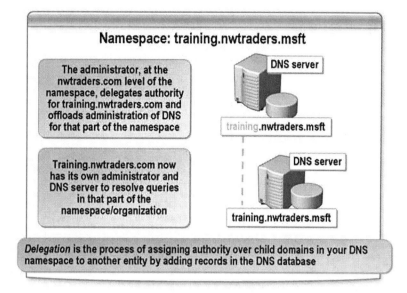

Namespace: training.nwtraders.msft

The administrator, at the nwtraders.com level of the namespace, delegates authority for training.nwtraders.com and offloads administration of DNS for that part of the namespace

DNS server

training.nwtraders.msft

Training.nwtraders.com now has its own administrator and DNS server to resolve queries in that part of the namespace/organization

DNS server

training.nwtraders.msft

Delegation is the process of assigning authority over child domains in your DNS namespace to another entity by adding records in the DNS database

Definition	In technical terms, *delegation* is the process of assigning authority over child domains in your DNS namespace to another entity by adding records in the DNS database.
Purpose of delegation	As the manager of a DNS domain, DNS provides the option of creating child domains and their respective zones, which can then be stored, distributed, and replicated to other DNS servers. These additional zones can be delegated to other administrators to manage. When deciding whether or not to divide your DNS namespace to delegate zones, consider the following potential reasons for doing so:

- A need to delegate management of part of your DNS namespace to another location or department within your organization.

- A need to divide one large zone into smaller zones for distributing traffic loads among multiple servers, improve DNS name resolution performance, or create a more fault-tolerant DNS environment.

- A need to extend the namespace by adding subdomains (for example, to accommodate the opening of a new branch or site).

Example	In the illustration, the administrator for the nwtraders.com level of the namespace delegates authority for training.nwtraders.com and offloads administration of DNS for that part of the namespace. Training.nwtraders.com now has its own administration and DNS server to resolve queries in that part of the namespace. This also reduces the workload on the administrator and DNS server for the nwtraders.com level.

How to Delegate a Subdomain to a DNS Zone

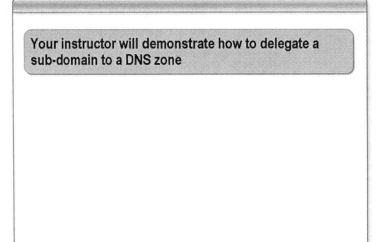

Your instructor will demonstrate how to delegate a sub-domain to a DNS zone

Introduction

To assign authority over portions of your DNS namespace to another entity, you can delegate a subdomain to a DNS zone.

Guidelines

When delegating zones within your namespace, be aware that for each new zone that you create, you will need delegation records, in other zones, that point to the authoritative DNS servers for the new zone. This is necessary both to transfer authority and to provide correct referrals to other DNS servers and clients of the new servers that are being made authoritative for the new zone.

Note It is recommended that you log on with an account that has non-administrative credentials and use the **Run as** command with a user account that has appropriate administrative credentials to perform this task.

Procedure

To delegate a subdomain to a DNS zone:

1. Open the DNS console.

2. Expand the appropriate DNS server, expand **Forward Lookup Zones** or **Reverse Lookup Zones**, and then select the appropriate zone to delegate.

3. On the **Action** menu, click **New Delegation**.

4. On the **Welcome to the New Delegation Wizard** page, click **Next**.

5. On the **Delegated Domain Name** page, in the **Delegate Domain** field, type the delegated domain name, and then click **Next**.

6. On the **Name Servers** page, click **Add**.

7. In the **New Resource Record** dialog box, in the **Server fully qualified domain name** field, type the FQDN of the DNS server to delegate the domain to, and then click **Resolve**.

8. In the **New Resource Record** dialog box, in the **IP address** field, verify that the correct IP address displays for the server that was resolved, and then click **OK**.

9. On the **Name Servers** page, click **Next**.

10. On the **Completing the New Delegation Wizard** page, click **Finish**.

11. Close the DNS console.

Lab A: Resolving Host Names by Using Domain Name System

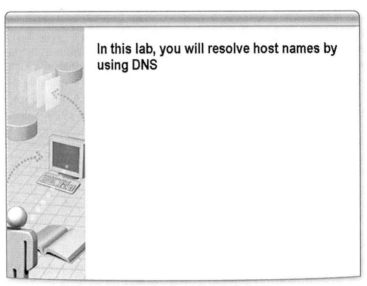

In this lab, you will resolve host names by using DNS

Objectives

In this lab, you will:

- Configure an alias resource record.
- Configure a secondary forward lookup zone.

Estimated time to complete this lab: 15 minutes

Exercise 1
Configuring an Alias Resource Record

In this exercise, you will create an alias resource record. Then you will verify the resource record configuration by using the **ping** command.

Instructions

Refer to the *Implementation Plan Values* document located in the Appendix at the end of the Student Workbook.

You must be logged on with an account that has non-administrative credentials and use the **Run as** command with a user account that has appropriate administrative credentials to complete the tasks. When completing the lab, assume that you will log on with a non-administrative account (example: *ComputerName*User), unless the Specific Instructions in the lab state otherwise.

Scenario

The systems engineer has moved the Lab department's development file shares to another server computer in the lab. The lab computers are all configured to access the original file server by using the host name FileServer2.

You will create an alias DNS record for the server to allow DNS clients in the lab to continue accessing the file server by using the old host name of FileServer2.

Tasks	Specific instructions
✋ Perform the following tasks on both student computers.	
1. Verify that you cannot connect to **FileServer2** by using the **ping** command.	▪ Use the **ping** command to contact FileServer2. ▪ Verify that the **ping** command was unsuccessful. ▪ **Question**: Why was the **ping** command unsuccessful?
2. Create an alias name for **FileServer2** by using the FQDN of *ServerName*2.*srv*.**nwtraders. msft** in the *srv*.**nwtraders.msft** forward lookup zone (where *srv* is the three-letter label of the computer name).	▪ Primary forward lookup zone: *srv*.**nwtraders.msft** zone ▪ New alias (CNAME): **FileServer2** ▪ Fully qualified domain name: *ComputerName*2.*srv*.**nwtraders.msft**. (Refer to the *Implementation Plan Values* document.) ▪ **Question**: What allows the alias record FileServer2 to be resolved to an IP address if the alias record is mapped to the FQDN for the host record *ComputerName*2.*srv*.**nwtraders.msft**?
3. Verify that you cannot connect to **FileServer2** by using the **ping** command; then view your DNS settings by using the **ipconfig** command.	▪ Use the **ping** command to locate FileServer2. ▪ Verify that the **ping** command was unsuccessful. ▪ **Question**: Why was the **ping** command unsuccessful? ▪ Use the **ipconfig** command to view your DNS suffix.

Tasks	Specific instructions
4. Verify that you can connect to **FileServer2.**_srv_**.nwtraders. msft.** (where _srv_ is the three letter label of the computer name) by using the **ping** command.	▪ Use the **ping** command to locate FileSrver2._srv_.nwtraders.msft. ▪ **Question:** Why was the **ping** command successful?
5. Configure the Classroom Network Connection interface with the DNS suffix search order of nwtraders.msft and _srv_.nwtraders.msft, and then use the **ipconfig** command to view the DNS suffix search order. Finally, use the **ping** command to locate FileServer2.	▪ Interface: **Classroom Network Connection** ▪ DNS suffix search order: **nwtraders.msft**, _srv_.**nwtraders.msft** ▪ Use the **ipconfig** command to verify DNS suffix search order. ▪ Use the **ping** command to locate FileServer2. ▪ **Question:** Why was the **ping** command successful?

Exercise 2
Configuring a Secondary Forward Lookup Zone

In this exercise, you will create a secondary forward lookup zone. Then you will verify the secondary forward lookup zone resource record configuration by using the **ping** command.

Instructions

Refer to the *Implementation Plan Values* document located in the Appendix at the end of the Student Workbook.

You must be logged on with an account that has non-administrative credentials and use the **Run as** command with a user account that has appropriate administrative credentials to complete the tasks. When completing the lab, assume that you will log on with a non-administrative account (example: *ComputerName*User), unless the Specific Instructions in the lab state otherwise.

Scenario

The subnet in the lab was affected by a power outage during the weekend. It appears that the DNS secondary forward lookup zone has been removed. You will re-create the secondary forward lookup zone.

Tasks	Specific instructions
✊ Perform the following tasks on both student computers.	
1. At a command prompt, run the C:\Moc\2277\Labfiles\Lab05\ Dns.vbs script to remove the secondary forward lookup zone nwtraders.msft from your DNS server.	▪ User name: **nwtraders***ComputerName***Admin** ▪ Password: **P@ssw0rd** ▪ In the **Run** dialog box, type **C:\moc\2277\labfiles\lab05\dns.vbs**
2. Create the secondary forward lookup zone nwtraders.msft with the master server IP address 192.168.*x*.200.	▪ Secondary forward lookup zone: **nwtraders.msft** ▪ Master DNS server IP address: **192.168.*x*.200**
3. View the resource records of nwtraders.msft to verify that the transfer occurred on the secondary forward lookup zone.	▪ Secondary forward lookup zone: **nwtraders.msft** ▪ On the details pane, verify that the records display to ensure that the zone transferred.

Microsoft®
Training &
Certification

Module 6: Managing and Monitoring Domain Name System (DNS)

Contents

Overview

- Configuring the Time-to-Live Value
- Configuring Aging and Scavenging
- Integrating DNS with WINS
- Testing the DNS Server Configuration
- Verifying that a Resource Record Exists by Using Nslookup, DNSCmd, and DNSLint
- Monitoring DNS Server Performance

Introduction

Domain Name System (DNS) servers are critical to a network; therefore, you must manage and monitor them to ensure that they are functioning properly and to optimize network performance.

Important For more information about securing DNS, see the Windows Server 2003, Enterprise Edition Help documentation.

Objectives

After completing this module, you will be able to:

- Configure the Time-to-Live value.
- Configure aging and scavenging.
- Integrate DNS with Windows Internet Name Service (WINS).
- Test the DNS server configuration.
- Verify that a resource record exists by using Nslookup, DNSCmd, and DNSLint.
- Monitor DNS server performance.

Lesson: Configuring the Time-to-Live Value

* How the Time-to-Live Value Works
* How to Configure the Time-to-Live Value

Introduction

As a part of managing DNS, you can configure the Time-to-Live (TTL) value, which is used in resource records within a zone to determine how long requesting clients should cache the records.

Lesson objectives

After completing this lesson, you will be able to:

■ Describe how the Time-to-Live value works.

■ Configure the Time-to-Live value.

How the Time-to-Live Value Works

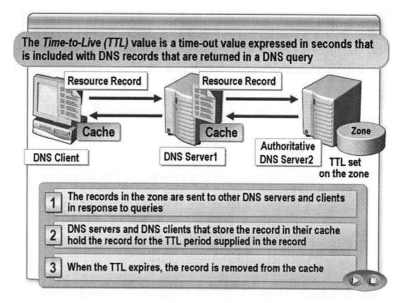

Definition

The *Time-to-Live (TTL)* value is a time-out value expressed in seconds that is included with DNS records that are returned in a DNS query. This timer value tells the recipients how long to hold or use the resource record or any of its included data before allowing the data to expire and discarding it.

How a TTL value works

The TTL value for a zone is applied to all records that are created in that zone. The TTL value for a record is applied to that record.

The TTL process functions as follows.

1. The records in the zone are sent to other DNS servers and DNS clients as responses to queries.

2. The DNS servers and DNS clients that store a record in their cache hold that record for the TTL period that is supplied in the record.

3. When the TTL expires, the record is removed from the cache on both the DNS server and the DNS client.

If the TTL is set too short, then DNS query traffic increases as the DNS clients request this information each time it expires from their cache.

If the TTL is set too long for a record, then the DNS clients may be caching outdated records.

How to Configure the Time-to-Live Value

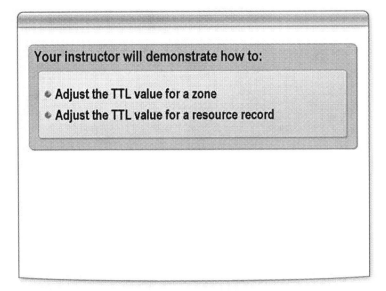

Your instructor will demonstrate how to:

* Adjust the TTL value for a zone
* Adjust the TTL value for a resource record

Introduction

To configure the TTL, you can adjust the TTL value for a zone and for a resource record.

Note It is recommended that you log on with an account that has non-administrative credentials and use the **Run as** command with a user account that has appropriate administrative credentials to perform this task.

Procedure for adjusting the TTL value for a zone

To adjust the TTL value for a zone:

1. Log on with a non-administrative user account.

2. Click **Start**, and then click **Control Panel**.

3. In Control Panel, open **Administrative Tools**, right-click **Manage Your Server**, and then select **Run as**.

4. In the **Run As** dialog box, select **The following user**, type a user account and password that have the appropriate permissions to complete the task, and then click **OK**.

5. In **Manage Your Server**, select **Manage this DNS Server**.

6. In the console tree, right-click the applicable zone, and then click **Properties**.

7. On the **General** tab, verify that the zone type is either **Primary** or **Active Directory-integrated**.

8. Click the **Start of Authority (SOA)** tab.

9. In the **Minimum (default) TTL** section, select the interval, seconds, minutes, hours, or days, and then, in the text box, type a number.

10. Click **OK** to save the adjusted interval.

Procedure for adjusting the TTL value for a record

To adjust the TTL value for a resource record:

1. Open the DNS console.

2. In the console tree, click **DNS**.

3. On the **View** menu, click **Advanced**.

4. In the console tree, expand the applicable zone, and then, in the details pane, right-click the applicable record, and then click **Properties**.

5. In the **Properties** dialog box for the record, in the **Time to live (TTL)** field, adjust the TTL.

6. Click **OK** to save the adjusted TTL.

Practice: Configuring the Time-to-Live Value

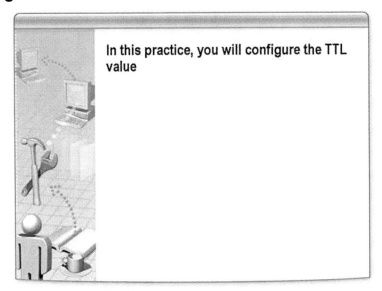

In this practice, you will configure the TTL value

Objectives

In this practice, you will configure the TTL value.

Instructions

To complete this practice, refer to the *Implementation Plan Values* document located in the Appendix at the end of your student workbook.

You must be logged on with an account that has non-administrative credentials and use the **Run as** command with a user account that has appropriate administrative credentials to complete the task.

Scenario

Query traffic to and from the DNS client has increased. To reduce the client query traffic to the DNS server, you configure a higher value for the TTL on the zone, and you also configure the TTL on your server record to 3 days.

Practice

▶ **Adjust the TTL value for a zone**

- Complete this task from both student computers

- User name: **NWTraders***ComputerName***Admin** (where *ComputerName* is the name of your computer)

- Password: **P@ssw0rd**

- Primary forward lookup zone: *srv***.nwtraders.msft**

- TTL: **2 hours**

▶ **Adjust the TTL value for a record**

- Complete this task from both student computers

- Primary forward lookup zone: *srv***.nwtraders.msft**

- DNS record: **FileServer2**

- TTL: **59 seconds**

▶ **View the TTL value for a record by using the ipconfig command**

- Complete this task from both student computers.

- Flush the DNS client resolver cache

- Use the **ping** command to locate FileServer2.*srv*.nwtraders.msft.

- Display the DNS client resolver cache to verify that the FileServer2 TTL value displays as less than 59 seconds.

Lesson: Configuring Aging and Scavenging

* What Are Aging and Scavenging Parameters?
* How Aging and Scavenging Work
* How to Configure Aging and Scavenging

Introduction

Aging and scavenging is the process that the DNS service uses to remove outdated or *stale* resource records.

Aging and scavenging are important, because outdated or stale records may:

- Not have been removed.
- Take up space in the DNS database.
- Cause unnecessarily long zone transfers.
- Be sent as responses to queries and thus cause name resolution issues for DNS clients.

Lesson objectives

After completing this lesson, you will be able to:

- Explain what aging and scavenging parameters are.
- Describe how aging and scavenging work.
- Configure aging and scavenging.

What Are Aging and Scavenging Parameters?

> *Aging* is the process that determines whether a stale DNS resource record should be removed from the DNS database
>
> *Scavenging* is the process of cleaning and removing outdated or extinct names data from the WINS database
>
> A *refresh attempt* is the process of a computer requesting a refresh on its DNS record

Parameter	Description	Example
No Refresh Interval	The time period when the DNS server *does not* accept refresh attempts	7-days (default)
Refresh Interval	The time period when the DNS server *does* accept refresh attempts	7-days (default)

Definitions

Aging is the process that determines whether a stale DNS resource record should be removed from the DNS database.

Scavenging is the process of cleaning and removing outdated or extinct names data from the DNS database.

Purpose of aging and scavenging

With dynamic update, resource records are automatically added to zones whenever a computer starts on the network. However, in some cases, resource records are not automatically removed when computers are removed from the network. For example, if a computer registers its own host (A) resource record at startup, but is later improperly disconnected from the network, its host (A) resource record might not be deleted. If your network has mobile users and computers, this situation can occur frequently.

In addition, stale resource records take up space in the DNS database and can cause unnecessarily long zone transfers. These outdated resource records may be sent as responses to queries, and may cause name resolution problems for DNS clients.

To remove outdated resource records from the DNS database, Microsoft® Windows® Server 2003 running DNS can scavenge outdated resource records by searching the database for resource records that have aged for a specified period and deleting those records from the database.

Aging and scavenging parameters for a zone

To determine when to scavenge records, DNS uses the time stamp that it gives each record, along with the parameters that you configure.

Aging and scavenging must be enabled on both the DNS server and the DNS zone. There are two configurable options for aging and scavenging,

- *No-refresh Interval.* The time period during which the DNS server does not accept refresh attempts. During a no-refresh interval, resource records cannot refresh their time stamp.
- *Refresh Interval.* The time period during which the DNS server does accept refresh attempts. During a refresh interval, resource records can refresh their time stamp.

A *refresh attempt* is the process of a computer requesting a refresh on its DNS record. A refresh attempt occurs when the client, that owns the DNS record, attempts to re-register the resource record. The refresh attempt does *not* occur when a client that owns the DNS record updates the resource record (such as when the client changes the IP address, but retains the same host name).

It is important to configure the No-refresh and Refresh intervals so that DNS will neither hold onto resource records too long nor remove resource records too soon.

Note Manually-entered DNS resource records have a time stamp of zero, which means they never age. If you want DNS resource records that are entered manually to be affected by aging and scavenging, then you must set a valid time stamp when you manually create a DNS resource record.

Purpose of the No refresh and Refresh intervals

You can configure the No refresh and Refresh intervals to reduce DNS replication in an infrastructure that uses DNS integrated with the Active Directory® directory service.

By default, a DNS client refreshes its name and IP address information every 24 hours. Other events on the system may also trigger a refresh event. Every time DNS refreshes the DNS entry in the DNS database, even if it doesn't modify the host name or the IP address, it makes a modification to an attribute on the DNS record in the Active Directory database. That modified attribute needs to be replicated to all Active Directory domain controllers that host the DNS database.

The purpose of the No refresh interval is to set a period when DNS will not accept refreshes of the time stamp on the record, so that unnecessary replication traffic is not being generated on the system. However, the DNS server will still accept updates that change the record information, such as a change to the IP address or the name. During the Refresh interval, the DNS client can refresh its record. Consequently, when a DNS client gets a new IP address, it registers the record. However, during the default No refresh interval, the DNS client will not be able to refresh the record for seven days. After the seven-day No Refresh interval passes, the record can be refreshed. When the DNS client refreshes, the No Refresh interval is set to seven days again.

How Aging and Scavenging Work

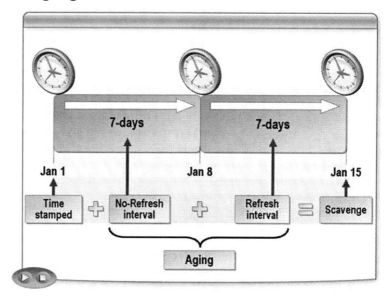

Introduction

To understand the process of aging and scavenging at the server, consider the life-span and successive stages of a single resource record.

Aging and scavenging process

The process of aging and scavenging functions as follows.

1. A sample DNS host, host-a.example.nwtraders.msft, registers its host (A) resource record at the DNS server for a zone where aging and scavenging is enabled for use.

2. When registering the resource record, the DNS server places a time stamp based on the server's current time on the record.

3. After the resource record's time stamp is written, the DNS server does not accept refreshes for this resource record for the duration of the zone's No-refresh interval. It can, however, accept updates prior to that time.

   - For example, if the IP address for server1.it.nwtraders.msft changes, the DNS server can accept the update. In this case, the server also updates (resets) the resource record time stamp.

4. Upon expiration of the No-refresh period, the server begins to accept attempts to refresh this resource record.

   - After the initial no-refresh period ends, the refresh period immediately begins for the resource record. During this time, the server does not suppress attempts to refresh the resource record for its remaining life span.

5. During the refresh period, if the server receives a refresh for the resource record, it processes it.

   - Any updates to the record will reset the time stamp for the resource record based on the method described in step 2.

6. When the server performs subsequent scavenging for the it.microsoft.com zone, the server examines the resource record and all other zone records.

    • Each resource record is compared to the current time on the server on the basis of the following sum to determine whether the resource record should be removed:

       Resource record time stamp + No-refresh interval for zone + Refresh interval for zone

7. If the value of this sum is greater than current server time, then no action is taken and the resource record continues to age in the zone.

8. If the value of this sum is less than current server time, then the resource record is deleted both from any zone data that is currently loaded in server memory and also from the applicable DnsZone object that is stored in Active Directory for the directory-integrated example.microsoft.com zone.

Example

In the illustration, a host record is registered and time-stamped in DNS on January 1st. The DNS server and the DNS zone are both configured for aging and scavenging. The No-refresh interval is set for 7-days, and the Refresh interval is set for 7-days Therefore, on January 15th the record will be scavenged from the DNS database.

How to Configure Aging and Scavenging

> **Your instructor will demonstrate how to:**
>
> * Set aging/scavenging parameters for the DNS server
> * Set aging/scavenging parameters on a DNS zone
> * Enable automatic scavenging of stale resource records on a DNS server
> * Start immediate scavenging of stale resource records
> * View when a zone can start scavenging stale resource records
> * Configure the time stamp on a DNS resource record
> * View the time stamp on a dynamic resource record

Introduction

To configure aging and scavenging on a zone, you must first enable aging and scavenging on the DNS server. When you create a zone, it inherits the aging and scavenging parameters for the no-refresh and refresh intervals that were configured on the DNS server.

When you notice a large number of outdated resource records, you can benefit from enabling automatic scavenging on the DNS server.

Note It is recommended that you log on with an account that has non-administrative credentials and use the **Run as** command with a user account that has appropriate administrative credentials to perform this task.

Procedure for setting aging/scavenging parameters for the DNS server

To set aging/scavenging parameters for the DNS server:

1. Open the DNS console.

2. In the console tree, right-click the applicable DNS server, and then click **Set Aging/Scavenging for All Zones**.

3. In the **Server Aging/Scavenging Properties** dialog box, select **Scavenge stale resource records**.

4. In the **No-refresh interval** field, select the increment, and then type a value. (For example: the increment is **days** and the value is **5**, for a No-refresh interval of 5 days.)

5. In the **Refresh** field, select the increment, and then type a value. (For example: the increment is **days** and the value is **5**, for a Refresh interval of 5 days.)

6. In the **Server Aging/Scavenging Properties** dialog box, click **OK**.

7. Close the DNS console.

Procedure for setting aging/scavenging parameters on a DNS zone

To set the aging/scavenging properties for a zone:

1. Open the DNS console.

2. In the console tree, right-click the applicable zone, and then click **Properties**.

3. On the **General** tab, click **Aging**.

4. In the **Zone Aging/Scavenging Properties** dialog box, select **Scavenge stale resource records**.

5. In the **No-refresh interval** field, select the increment, and then type a value. (For example: the increment is **days** and the value is **5**, for a No-refresh interval of 5 days.)

6. In the **Refresh** field, select the increment, and then type a value. (For example: increment is **days** and the value is **5**, for a refresh interval of 5 days.)

7. In the **Zone Aging/Scavenging Properties** dialog box, click **OK**.

8. Close the DNS console.

Procedure for enabling automatic scavenging on a DNS server

To enable automatic scavenging of stale resource records on a DNS server:

1. Open the DNS console.

2. In the console tree, right-click the applicable DNS server, and then click **Properties**.

3. Click the **Advanced** tab.

4. Select **Enable automatic scavenging of stale records**.

5. In the **Scavenging period** field, select the increment, and then type a value

6. In the *DNS server* **Properties** dialog box, click **OK**.

7. Close the DNS console.

Procedure for starting immediate scavenging of stale records

To start immediate scavenging of stale resource records:

1. Open the DNS console.

2. In the console tree, right-click the applicable DNS server, and then click **Scavenge Stale Resource Records**.

3. When asked to confirm that you want to scavenge all stale resource records on the server, click **OK**.

4. Close the DNS console.

Procedure for viewing when a zone can start scavenging stale records

To view when a zone can start scavenging stale resource records:

1. Open the DNS console.
2. On the **View** menu, verify that **Advanced** is selected. (If **Advanced** is not selected, click **Advanced** to select it.)
3. Right-click the applicable zone, and then click **Properties**.
4. On the **General** tab, click **Aging**.
5. In the **Zone Aging/Scavenging Properties** dialog box, view the value in the **Date and time** field to ascertain the date after which the zone is eligible to be scavenged for outdated resource records, and then click **OK**.
6. In the *Zone* **Properties** dialog box, click **OK**.
7. Close the DNS console.

Procedure for configuring a time stamp on a DNS resource record

To configure the time stamp on a DNS resource record:

1. Open the DNS console.
2. On the **View** menu, verify that **Advanced** is selected. (If **Advanced** is not selected, click **Advanced** to select it.)
3. Right-click the applicable resource record, and then click **Properties**.
4. In the *Resource Record* **Properties** dialog box, select **Delete this record when it becomes stale**, and then click **Apply**.
5. Verify that a date and time value displays in the **Record time stamp** field.
6. In the *Resource Record* **Properties** dialog box, click **OK**.
7. Close the DNS console.

Procedure for viewing the time stamp on a dynamic resource record

To view the time stamp on a dynamic DNS resource record:

1. Open the DNS console.
2. On the **View** menu, verify that **Advanced** is selected. (If **Advanced** is not selected, click **Advanced** to select it.)
3. Right-click the applicable resource record, and then click **Properties**.
4. In the *Resource Record* **Properties** dialog box, view the value in the **Date and time** field to ascertain when the resource record was created in DNS.
5. In the *Resource Record* **Properties** dialog box, click **OK**.
6. Close the DNS console.

Practice: Configure Aging and Scavenging

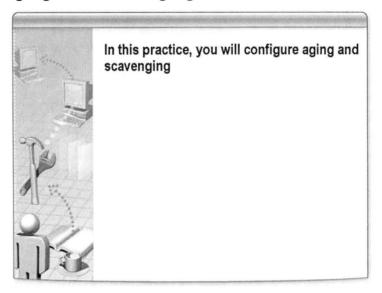

In this practice, you will configure aging and scavenging

Objectives

In this practice, you will configure aging and scavenging on a zone.

Instructions

To complete this practice, refer to the *Implementation Plan Values* document, located in the Appendix at the end of your student workbook.

You must be logged on with an account that has non-administrative credentials and use the **Run as** command with a user account that has appropriate administrative credentials to complete the task.

Scenario

Lab users are receiving a DNS name resolution error when accessing resources on the network. You try to locate a few resources by using the command prompt, and you realize that the IP addresses are no longer valid. You suspect that the resource records in DNS are outdated. You have deleted the invalid resource records in DNS, and you now implement an aging and scavenging plan to ensure that future outdated records are removed.

You will enable and configure aging and scavenging for the DNS server, and configure aging and scavenging for the DNS zone. You will also view the time on the zone when scavenging will occur, view the time stamp on a static resource record, and enable the static resource record to be deleted when it becomes outdated.

Practice

▶ **Set aging/scavenging parameters for the DNS server**

- Complete this task from both student computers
- No-refresh interval: **4 days**
- Refresh interval: **4 days**

▶ **Set aging/scavenging parameters on a DNS zone**

- Complete this task from both student computers
- Primary forward lookup zone: *srv*.**nwtraders.msft**
- No-refresh interval: **3 days**
- Refresh interval: **3 days**

▶ **View when a zone can start scavenging stale records**

- Complete this task from both student computers
- Primary forward lookup zone: *srv*.**nwtraders.msft**
- When can your zone start scavenging records? _____

▶ **Configure a time stamp on a static record**

- Complete this task from both student computers
- Primary forward lookup zone: *srv*.**nwtraders.msft**
- DNS record: **FileServer2**

▶ **View the time stamp on a resource record**

- Complete this task from both student computers
- Primary forward lookup zone: *srv*.**nwtraders.msft**
- DNS record: **FileServer2**
- Record time stamp: _____
- Record today's date: _____
- What is the difference between today's date and the record time stamp?

  _____

Lesson: Integrating DNS with WINS

* Multimedia: DNS and WINS Integration
* How to Integrate DNS with WINS

Introduction

Integrating DNS with Windows Internet Name Service (WINS) allows DNS clients to resolve resources in WINS.

Lesson objectives

After completing this lesson, you will be able to:

- Describe how DNS and WINS integration works.

- Integrate DNS with WINS.

Multimedia: DNS and WINS Integration

* The objective of this presentation is to explain how DNS and WINS can be integrated in the network infrastructure

* At the end of this presentation, you will be able to:

  * Define DNS and WINS integration

  * Explain how host names and NetBIOS names fit into DNS and WINS integration

  * Describe how DNS and WINS integration works

File location

To start the *DNS and WINS Integration* presentation, open the Web page on the Student Materials compact disc. Click **Multimedia**, and then click the title of the presentation.

Objectives

At the end of this presentation, you will be able to:

- Define DNS and WINS integration.

- Explain how host names and the network basic input/output system (NetBIOS) names fit into DNS and WINS integration.

- Describe how DNS and WINS integration works.

Key points

- DNS and WINS integration is the process in which DNS uses WINS to resolve names to IP addresses.

- DNS is used to resolve host names and services to IP addresses, and WINS is used to resolve NetBIOS names to IP addresses.

- You can manually configure NetBIOS name-to-IP address mappings on the DNS server, or you can configure the DNS server to forward the name queries to the WINS server for resolution.

- Host and NetBIOS names can be the same in Microsoft Windows 2000 or Windows Server 2003, which allow DNS and WINS to work together to resolve names.

How to Integrate DNS with WINS

Your instructor will demonstrate how to integrate DNS with WINS

Introduction

DNS is used to resolve host names and WINS is used to resolve NetBIOS names. In some circumstances, it may be advantageous for organizations to use the existing WINS database for host name lookups rather than configuring every client, which are in the WINS database, to be in the DNS database as well.

Integrating DNS with WINS allows DNS clients to use the existing NetBIOS name entries in WINS for host name lookup. The DNS service provides the ability to use WINS servers to look up names that are not found in the DNS namespace by checking the NetBIOS namespace that WINS manages.

Note   It is recommended that you log on with an account that has non-administrative credentials and use the **Run as** command with a user account that has appropriate administrative credentials to perform this task.

Procedure

To integrate DNS with WINS:

1. Open the DNS console.

2. In the console tree, right-click the applicable zone, and then click **Properties**.

3. In the *Zone* **Properties** dialog box, click the appropriate tab:

    a. The **WINS** tab, if the zone is a forward lookup zone.

    b. The **WINS-R** tab, if the zone is a reverse lookup zone.

4. On the appropriate **WINS** tab, select the applicable check box to enable the use of WINS resolution:

    a. **Use WINS forward lookup**, if the zone is a forward lookup zone.

    b. **Use WINS-R lookup**, if the zone is a reverse lookup zone.

5. On the **WINS** or the **WINS-R** tab, type the IP address of a WINS server to be used for resolution of names that are not found in DNS.

Note   For a reverse lookup zone, type a name in the **Domain to append to returned name** field, if applicable.

---

6. On either the **WINS** or the **WINS-R** tab, click **Add** to add the server IP address to the list.

Note   If additional WINS server addresses should be used for a forward lookup zone during WINS lookup referral, repeat steps 5 and 6 as needed to add those server addresses to the list.

---

7. On either the **WINS** or the **WINS-R** tab, select **Do not replicate this record** for this WINS record, if applicable.

Important   If you are replicating zone data to secondary zones on third party DNS servers that do not recognize the WINS or WINS-R records, select the **Do not replicate this record** check box. This prevents the WINS locater records from being replicated to other servers during zone transfers. If this zone will be used in performing zone transfers to Berkeley Internet Name Domain (BIND) servers, then this is a critical option because BIND will not recognize WINS locater records.

---

8. Optionally, on either the **WINS** or the **WINS-R** tab, click **Advanced** to adjust both the **Cache time-out** value and the **Lookup time-out** value.

9. Optionally, on the **WINS-R** tab, in the **Advanced** dialog box, select **Submit DNS domain as NetBIOS scope**.

10. In the *Zone* **Properties** dialog box, click **OK**.

11. Close the DNS console.

Practice: Integrating DNS with WINS

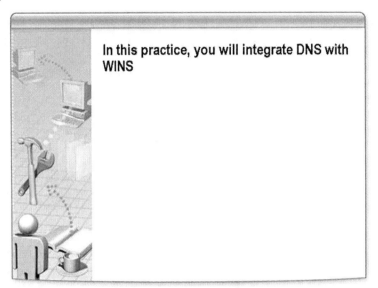

In this practice, you will integrate DNS with WINS

Objectives

In this practice, you will integrate DNS with WINS.

Instructions

To complete this practice, refer to the *Implementation Plan Values* document, located in the Appendix at the end of your student workbook.

You must be logged on with an account that has non-administrative credentials and use the **Run as** command with a user account that has appropriate administrative credentials to complete the task.

Scenario

Some computers that use only NetBIOS have been added to the Lab. To support name resolution for these clients, you have installed and configured a WINS server. The DNS client computers need to access these computers by using the NetBIOS name. Instead of configuring each DNS client to use the WINS server, you decide to integrate the lab's DNS zone with the WINS server to allow for NetBIOS name resolution for the DNS clients.

You will configure your forward lookup zone to use WINS forward lookup.

Practice

▶ **Integrate DNS with WINS**

■ Complete this task from both student computers

■ Primary forward lookup zone: *srv*.**nwtraders.msft**

■ Select **Do not replicate this record**.

■ IP address: **192.168.*x*.200**

■ Cache time-out: **25 minutes**

■ Lookup time-out: **1 minute**

Lesson: Testing the DNS Server Configuration

- • How Simple and Recursive Queries Work
- • How to Test the DNS Server Configuration

Introduction

Whenever there are changes to the DNS server configuration, it is important to test the DNS server to ensure that the configuration is still functioning properly.

Lesson objectives

After completing this lesson, you will be able to:

- ■ Describe how simple and recursive queries work.
- ■ Test the DNS server configuration.

How Simple and Recursive Queries Work

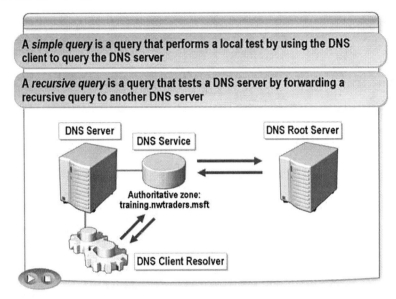

Introduction

You can test a DNS server by performing two types of queries: simple and recursive.

Purpose of simple and recursive queries

Whenever there are changes to the DNS server configuration, it is important to test the DNS server to ensure that the configuration is still functioning properly.

By using the testing query functions on the DNS server, you can verify that the DNS queries are functioning. This is useful when you are troubleshooting DNS query issues. By testing the DNS server configuration, you can narrow your search for the query issue.

Simple query

A *simple query* is a query that performs a local test by using the DNS client to query the DNS server.

This type of test specifies that the DNS server perform a simple or iterative query. This test is a localized query that uses the DNS client resolver on the DNS server to query the local DNS service, which is located on the same DNS server.

Recursive query

A *recursive query* is a query that tests a DNS server by forwarding a recursive query to another DNS server.

This type of test specifies that the DNS server perform a recursive query. This test is similar in its initial query processing to the simple query in that it uses the local DNS client resolver to query the local DNS server, which is located on the same computer.

In this test, however, the client asks the server to use recursion to resolve an NS-type query for the root of the DNS domain namespace, stated as a single period ("."). This type of query typically requires additional recursive processing, and can be helpful in verifying that server root hints or zone delegations have been properly configured.

Example

In the illustration, the DNS client resolver on the DNS server is sending a simple query to the local DNS service. The simple query either passes or fails.

The DNS client resolver on the DNS server sends a recursive query to the local DNS server, which then forwards the query to the authoritative DNS server for resolution. The recursive query either passes or fails.

How to Test the DNS Server Configuration

Your instructor will demonstrate how to:

- Manually test a simple query on the DNS server
- Manually test a recursive query on the DNS server
- Enable automatic query testing on the DNS server

Introduction

To test your DNS server configuration, you can perform simple and recursive queries. If the query passes, then your DNS server can resolve a simple query and can query a root server. If the query fails, then you must verify that DNS is configured properly.

You can perform queries either manually or automatically.

Note It is recommended that you log on with an account that has non-administrative credentials and use the **Run as** command with a user account that has appropriate administrative credentials to perform this task.

Procedure for manually testing a simple query on the DNS server

To manually test a simple query on the DNS server:

Tip You might receive incorrect results if you verify the operation of a DNS server immediately after adding or removing zones. If this occurs, either right-click the DNS server in the console tree and then click **Refresh**, or close and then reopen the DNS console.

1. Open the DNS console.
2. In the console tree, click the appropriate DNS server.
3. On the **Action** menu, click **Properties**.
4. In the *DNS Server* **Properties** dialog box, click the **Monitoring** tab.
5. On the **Monitoring** tab, select **A simple query against this DNS server**.
6. On the **Monitoring** tab, click **Test Now**.
7. In the **Test results** section, in the **Simple Query** column, verify that the word **PASS** displays.
8. In the *DNS Server* **Properties** dialog box, click **OK**.
9. Close the DNS console

Procedure for manually testing a recursive query on the DNS server

To manually test a recursive query on the DNS server:

1. Open the DNS console.

2. In the console tree, click the appropriate DNS server.

3. On the **Action** menu, click **Properties**.

4. In the *DNS Server* **Properties** dialog box, click the **Monitoring** tab.

5. On the **Monitoring** tab, select **A recursive query to other DNS servers**.

6. On the **Monitoring** tab, click **Test Now**.

7. In the **Test results** section, in the **Recursive Query** column, verify that the word **PASS** displays.

8. In the *DNS Server* **Properties** dialog box, click **OK**.

9. Close the DNS console.

Procedure for enabling automatic query testing on the DNS server

To enable automatic query testing on the DNS server:

1. Open the DNS console.

2. In the console tree, click the applicable DNS server.

3. On the **Action** menu, click **Properties**.

4. In the *DNS Server* **Properties** dialog box, click the **Monitoring** tab.

5. On the **Monitoring** tab, select the option for the type of testing to be used during automatic query testing. You can select either or both of the following options:

   - **A simple query against this DNS server**

   - **A recursive query to other DNS servers**

6. On the **Monitoring** tab, select **Perform automatic testing at the following interval**.

7. On the **Monitoring** tab, in the **Test interval** field, type a number, and then select an interval value (for example: 5 minutes).

Note   The query tests that you select are performed at the interval that you configure. The default polling interval is 1 minute.

8. On the *DNS Server* **Properties** dialog box, click **OK**.

9. Close the DNS console.

Practice: Testing the DNS Server Configuration

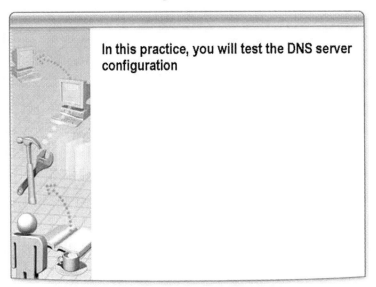

In this practice, you will test the DNS server configuration

Objectives

In this practice, you will test the DNS server configuration.

Instructions

To complete this practice, refer to the *Implementation Plan Values* document, located in the Appendix at the end of your student workbook.

Scenario

You are informed that the power was interrupted in the lab, and you want to run tests on the DNS server to ensure that it is still functioning properly. You will run both simple and recursive queries on your DNS server.

Practice

▶ **Manually test a simple query on your own DNS server**

- Complete this task from both student computers

- DNS server: *ComputerName* (where *ComputerName* is the name of your computer)

- Why did the simple query pass?

_____

_____

▶ **Manually test a recursive query on your own DNS server**

- Complete this task from both student computers

- DNS server: *ComputerName* (where *ComputerName* is the name of your computer)

- Why did the recursive query fail?

  _____

  _____

Lesson: Verifying that a Resource Record Exists by Using Nslookup, DNSCmd, and DNSLint

* Why Verify that a Resource Record Exists?
* Nslookup
* DNSCmd
* DNSLint
* How to Verify that a Resource Record Exists by Using Nslookup, DNSCmd, and DNSLint

Introduction

When monitoring DNS, you can use several command-line utilities such as Nslookup, DNSCmd, and DNSLint.

Lesson objectives

After completing this lesson, you will be able to:

- Explain the purpose of verifying that a resource record exists.
- Explain what Nslookup is.
- Explain what DNSCmd is.
- Explain what DNSLint is.
- Verify that a resource record exists by using Nslookup, DNSCmd, and DNSLint.

Why Verify that a Resource Record Exists?

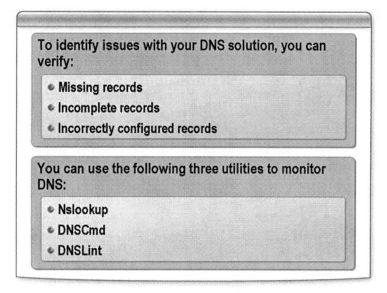

Introduction

Verifying that a resource record exists is a basic function of monitoring and troubleshooting DNS.

Purpose of verifying resource records

If the DNS server contains outdated, stale, or incorrect host name-to-IP address mappings, then the clients cannot connect to network services. With the amount of dynamic change that occurs in the DNS service, it is important to be able to verify that DNS resource records are both correct and updated.

To identify issues with your DNS solution, you can verify:

■ Missing records.

■ Incomplete records.

■ Incorrectly configured records.

Utilities

You can use the following three utilities to monitor, manage, and troubleshoot DNS.

■ Nslookup

■ DNSCmd

■ DNSLint

For purposes of this lesson, you will focus on how to verify that a resource record exists—which is only one task of many that can be accomplished with these three tools.

Nslookup

Nslookup is a command-line utility used to diagnose DNS infrastructure

Definition

Nslookup is a command-line utility that is used to diagnose the DNS infrastructure.

Purpose of Nslookup

Nslookup provides the ability to perform query testing of DNS servers and obtain detailed responses as the command output. This information is useful in troubleshooting name resolution problems, in verifying that resource records are added or updated correctly in a zone, and in debugging other server-related problems.

Nslookup syntax

Nslookup has two modes:

- *Interactive*. This mode allows you to type the commands in Nslookup and view the results at a command prompt. Use the interactive mode when you require more than one piece of data.

- *Non-interactive*. This mode allows you to execute an Nslookup command in a single step which can be either run on its own from the command line or inserted within a batch file. Non-interactive mode provides a single piece of data as output. The output can be stored in a text file for later viewing. This mode is useful when you configure a Performance Alert to run a batch file.

The following table describes the Nslookup syntax.

Syntax	Description
-option...	Specify one or more **Nslookup** commands. For a list of available commands, type a question mark (?). **Nslookup** commands include: • Exit • Help • Set type • View
computer_to_find	If you specify the IP address of a computer, then Nslookup returns the host name. If you specify the host name of a computer, then Nslookup returns the IP address. If the host name that you are querying for does not have a trailing period, then the default DNS domain name is appended to the name. To find a computer outside the current DNS domain, append a period to the name. For example, find a host record by using the following set option: **Set type=a** **London**
-server	Specify the server to use as the DNS server. If you omit the server, the currently configured default DNS server is used. For example: Server nwtraders.msft

Note For Nslookup to work properly, a PTR resource record must exist for the server on which you perform a lookup. At startup, Nslookup performs a reverse lookup on the IP address of the server that is running the DNS Server service, and reports an error if it cannot resolve the address to a name. This error does not hinder the normal performance of Nslookup for diagnostics.

Examples

The illustration provides an example of the command-line output for an Nslookup session. This session is used to verify that both the host (A) record for Lisbon and the service location (SRV) resource records, which are registered by Windows Server 2003 domain controllers, exist. In this example, the domain controller London is registered for the *nwtraders.msft* domain.

DNSCmd

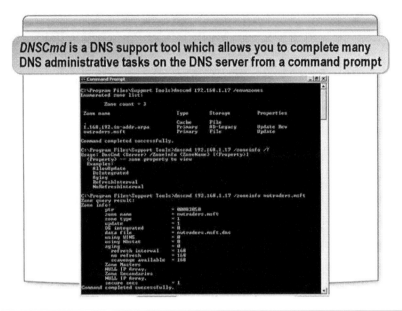

DNSCmd is a DNS support tool which allows you to complete many DNS administrative tasks on the DNS server from a command prompt

Definition

DNSCmd is a DNS support tool that is included in the support tools on the Windows Server 2003 CD. DNSCmd allows an administrator to complete many of the DNS administrative tasks on the DNS server from a command prompt.

Purpose of DNSCmd

By using DNSCmd, you can check dynamic registration of DNS resource records, including Secure DNS update, in addition to deregistration of resource records.

DNSCmd can be useful when you have to accomplish a DNS configuration task for a number of DNS servers. Instead of using the DNS administrative tool, you can use the command line.

DNSCmd is also useful when you need to modify DNS server settings remotely. By creating a batch file which includes the **DNSCmd** command, you can send the batch to a DNS server and execute it remotely.

DNSCmd parameters

The syntax of the DNSCmd is as follows:

dnscmd *<ServerName> <Command>* [*<Command Parameters>*]

The following table lists some DNSCmd parameters and their descriptions. These parameters are used to configure DNS.

Parameters	Description
ServerName	Specifies the DNS server that the administrator plans to manage, represented by local computer syntax, IP address, fully qualified domain name (FQDN), or host name. If the server name is omitted, then the local server is used.
/primary|/secondary|/stub|/cache|/auto-created	Filters the types of zones to display.
/primary	Lists all zones that are either standard primary or integrated with Active Directory.
/secondary	Lists all standard secondary zones.
/stub	Lists all stub zones.
/cache	Lists only the zones that are loaded into the cache.
/auto-created	Lists the zones that were created automatically during the DNS server installation.
/forward|/reverse	Specifies an additional filter of the types of zones to display.
/forward	Lists forward lookup zones.
/reverse	Lists reverse lookup zones.

Example

In the slide, you can view all the zones on the DNS server 192.168.1.17 from the initial **DNSCmd** command by using the DNSCmd utility.

You can use the output from the initial **DNSCmd** command to view the switches that are associated with each zone.

Furthermore, you can see that the last **DNSCmd** command displays DNS zone information on the *nwtraders.msft* zone by using the zone name that is reported in the initial **DNSCmd** command.

DNSLint

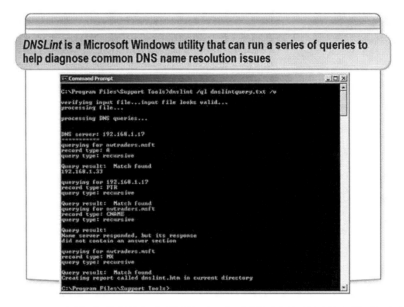

Definition

DNSLint is a DNS support tool that is included in the support tools on the Windows Server 2003 CD. DNSLint is a Microsoft Windows utility that can run a series of queries to help diagnose common DNS name resolution issues.

Purpose of DNSLint

Verifying the consistency of a particular set of DNS records on multiple DNS servers can help diagnose and fix problems that missing or incorrect DNS records can cause.

For example: If clients are experiencing problems logging on to the domain, then verifying that the SRV records (which clients use to find Lightweight Directory Access Protocol [LDAP] and Kerberos servers) are available and accurate can help ascertain whether DNS is a cause of the problem.

Another sample scenario occurs when you receive reports that customers are having problems accessing your Web site on the Internet. It would be beneficial to have a tool that quickly checks all of the DNS records that are involved with the Web farm on each of the DNS servers that are supposed to contain these records. You could then quickly determine if there are missing or incorrect DNS records that may be related to the problem.

In a third scenario, you could be experiencing problems with e-mail delivery. You can send e-mail, but are not receiving any. Name resolution could be the problem. To confirm this theory (or to eliminate it as a possibility) you want to check all of the DNS records on all of the DNS servers that are used to resolve the e-mail server's IP address.

DNSLint functions and syntax

DNSLint has three functions that verify DNS records and generate a Hypertext Markup Language (HTML) report.

- **DNSLINT /d** diagnoses potential causes of lame delegation and other related DNS problems.

  - *Lame delegation* occurs when a DNS subdomain is configured to a DNS server that either does not exist or does not act authoritatively for that subdomain.

- **DNSLINT /ql** verifies a user-defined set of DNS records on multiple DNS servers.

- **DNSLINT /ad** verifies DNS records that are specifically used for Active Directory replication.

The syntax for DNSLint is as follows:

C:\dnslint.exe /d *domain_name* | /ad [*LDAP_IP_address*] | /ql *input_file*

[/c [smtp,pop,imap]] [/no_open] [/r *report_name*]

[/t] [/s *DNS_IP_address*] [/v] [/y]

Example

The illustration provides an example of DNSLint output for a scan of Nwtraders.msft.

How to Verify that a Resource Record Exists by Using Nslookup, DNSCmd, and DNSLint

> **Your instructor will demonstrate how to:**
>
> - Verify that a resource record exists in DNS by using Nslookup
> - Install DNSCmd
> - Display a complete list of zones configured on a DNS server, by using DNSCmd
> - Display information about a specific zone that is configured on a DNS server, by using the DNSCMD
> - Create a DNSLint report

Introduction

You can use all three DNS utilities, Nslookup, DNSCmd, and DNSLint, to perform monitoring tasks, such as verifying that a resource record exists. Nslookup is available, by default, with Windows Server 2003. You must first install DNSCmd and DNSLint from the Windows Server 2003 CD support tools .

Note It is recommended that you log on with an account that has non-administrative credentials and use the **Run as** command with a user account that has appropriate administrative credentials to perform this task.

Procedure for verifying that a resource record exists in DNS by using Nslookup

Verify that a resource record exists in DNS by using Nslookup:

1. Open the command prompt.
2. At the command prompt, type **nslookup** *RootServerIPAddress*
3. At the command prompt, type **nslookup**
4. At the next prompt, type **set q=A**
5. At the next prompt, type the host name.
6. Look through the returned resource records for the fully qualified domain name (FQDN) of the host.
7. Type **exit**
8. Close the command prompt.

Procedure for installing DNSCmd

To install DNSCmd:

1. Insert the Windows Server 2003 CD into your CD-ROM drive.

2. If you are prompted to reinstall Windows, click **No**.

3. When the **Welcome** screen appears, click **Perform additional tasks**, and then click **Browse this CD**.

4. Go to the \Support\Tools folder.

5. For complete setup information, refer to the Readme.htm file that is available in this folder.

6. Double-click **suptools.msi**.

7. Follow the instructions that appear on your screen.

Procedure for displaying a complete list of zones configured on a DNS server by using DNSCmd

Display a complete list of the zones configured on a DNS server by using DNSCmd:

- At the command prompt, type:

  dnscmd [*ComputerName*] /enumzones

Procedure for displaying information on a specific zone configured on a DNS server by using DNSCmd

Display information about a specific zone that is configured on a DNS server by using the DNSCmd:

- At the command prompt, type:

  dnscmd [*ComputerName*] /zoneinfo [*zone*]

Procedure for creating the DNSLint report

To create the DNSLint report:

1. Open the command prompt for a directory in which you want to create the report.

2. At the command prompt, type **dnslint**

3. At the command prompt, type **dnslint /ql autocreate**

4. At the command prompt, type **Notepad in-dnslint.txt**

5. In Notepad, in the 6th line from the bottom of the file, change the line from **dns1.cp.msft.net** to *ComputerName*.**nwtraders.msft**.

6. In Notepad, in the last four lines of the file, change any instances of **Microsoft.com** to the name of the domain that you are querying.

7. In Notepad, in the last five lines of the file, change any instances of **207.46.197.100** to the IP address of the DNS server that you are querying.

8. In Notepad, and in the same directory where in-dnslint.txt is located, save the file as **Dnslintquery.txt**, and then close Notepad.

9. At the command prompt, type **dnslint /ql dnslintquery.txt /v**

10. When the HTML report opens, verify the contents, and then close the report.

11. Close the command prompt.

Practice: Verifying that a Resource Record Exists by Using Nslookup, DNSCmd, and DNSLint

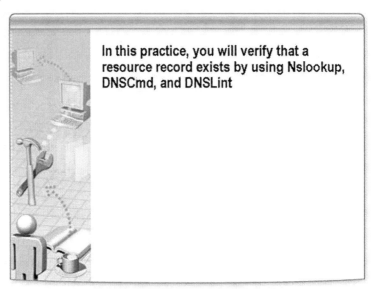

In this practice, you will verify that a resource record exists by using Nslookup, DNSCmd, and DNSLint

Objectives

In this practice, you will verify that a resource record exists by using Nslookup, DNSCmd, and DNSLint.

Instructions

To complete this practice, refer to the *Implementation Plan Values* document located in the Appendix at the end of your student workbook.

You must be logged on with an account that has non-administrative credentials and use the **Run as** command with a user account that has appropriate administrative credentials to complete the task.

Scenario

You are testing the new DNS server by using command-line utilities.

Practice

▶ **Verify that a resource record exists in DNS by using Nslookup**

■ Complete this task from both student computers

■ DNS server IP address: *IP address of Classroom Network Connection interface of your computer*

■ DNS record: **FileServer2.***srv*.**nwtraders.msft**

▶ **Display a complete list of the zones that are configured on a DNS server by using DNSCmd**

■ Complete this task from both student computers

■ DNS server: *ComputerName*
(where *ComputerName* is the name of your computer)

▶ **Display information about a zone configured on a DNS server by using DNSCmd**

■ Complete this task from both student computers

■ DNS server: *ComputerName*
(where *ComputerName* is the name of your computer)

■ DNS zone: *srv*.**nwtraders.msft**

▶ **Create a DNSLint report**

■ Complete this task from both student computers

■ DNS server: *ComputerName*
(where *ComputerName* is the name of your computer)

■ DNSLint directory: **C:\moc\2277\labfiles\lab06\dnslint**

■ DNS server name: *ComputerName*.**nwtraders.msft**

■ DNS domain name: *srv*.**nwtraders.msft**

■ DNS server IP address: *IP address of Classroom Network Connection interface of your computer*

Lesson: Monitoring DNS Server Performance

● Guidelines for Monitoring DNS Server Performance by Using the Performance Console

● What Is a DNS Event Log?

● What Is DNS Debug Logging?

● How to Monitor DNS Server Performance by Using Logging

Introduction

As an administrator, you can provide useful baseline data and troubleshoot DNS issues by using the Performance console to monitor the performance of a DNS server.

In addition, there are several tools built into a DNS server running Windows Server 2003 to help monitor DNS events and data, such as DNS Event Viewer and DNS debug logging.

Lesson objectives

After completing this lesson, you will be able to:

■ Apply guidelines for monitoring DNS server performance by using the Performance console.

■ Explain what a DNS event log is.

■ Explain what DNS debug logging is.

■ Describe how DNS debug logging works.

■ Monitor DNS server performance by using logging.

Guidelines for Monitoring DNS Server Performance by Using the Performance Console

Performance counter	What to look for after a baseline is established
Dynamic Update Rejected	Any increase over the baseline may be cause for further investigation
Recursive Queries/sec	If this counter goes dramatically up or down, then it should be further investigated
AXFR Request Sent	If this counter goes dramatically above the baseline, then it could reflect a need to review the number of changes in the zone and the configuration of zone transfers

Introduction

Because DNS servers are critically important in most environments, monitoring their performance can help by:

- Providing a useful baseline for predicting, estimating, and optimizing DNS server performance.

- Troubleshooting DNS servers where server performance has degraded— either over time, or during periods of peak activity.

As you begin your DNS server monitoring, you can review sample test results for DNS servers running Windows Server 2003 that were collected during product development and testing. You can use this information as a starting reference as you begin to monitor your DNS servers to measure and baseline performance.

Note For more information about the sample test results that were collected during product and testing for DNS servers running Windows Server 2003, see the Windows Server 2003 Help documentation for DNS performance.

Windows Server 2003 also provides a set of DNS server Performance counters that can be used with System Monitor to measure and monitor various aspects of server activity.

Guidelines

It is recommended that you monitor the critical phases of DNS activity, such as dynamic update, notify, incremental and full zone transfers, queries, and the health of the DNS server.

Performance counters	What data is collected	What the data means	What to look for after baseline is established
Dynamic Update Rejected	The total number of dynamic updates that the DNS server rejects.	A high number of rejections to a DNS server configured to allow secure updates could mean that unauthorized computers are attempting to update.	Any increase over the baseline may be cause for further investigation.
Recursive Queries/sec	Recursive Queries/sec is the average number of recursive queries received by a DNS server in each second.	This counter provides a view of the query load on the DNS server.	If this counter goes dramatically up or down, then it should be investigated further.
AXFR Request Sent	The total number of full zone transfer requests sent by the DNS Server service when operating as a secondary server for a zone.	The DNS server hosting the secondary zone is requesting incremental zone transfers. If this number is high, then there are a lot of changes happening on the primary zone.	If this counter goes dramatically above the baseline, then it could reflect a need to review the number of changes in the zone and the configuration of zone transfers.

What Is a DNS Event Log?

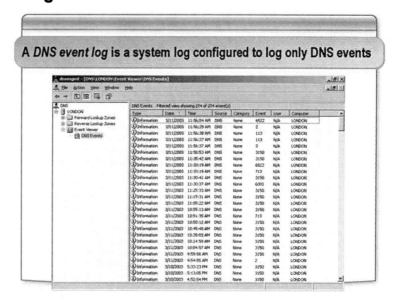

A *DNS event log* is a system log configured to log only DNS events

Definition

A *DNS event log* is a system log that is configured to log only DNS events.

Purpose of a DNS event log

You can use Event Viewer to view and monitor client-related DNS events. These appear in the System log, and they are written by the DNS Client service to any computers running Windows (all versions).

DNS event log file

For Windows Server 2003, DNS server event messages are separated and kept in their own log (the DNS server log) which can be viewed by using either the DNS console or Event Viewer.

The DNS server log file contains events that the DNS Server service logs. For example, when the DNS server starts or stops, a corresponding event message is written to this log. DNS service error events are also logged here (such as when the server starts but zone transfers fail, or when the zone information needed to start up is not available).

Type of DNS events

The following table is a partial listing of common events that are recorded in the DNS server log.

Event	Description
2	The DNS server has started.
3	The DNS server has shut down.
3150	The data in the DNS zone has updated.
6522	A change in the zone serial number prompted a zone transfer.

You can use the DNS console to change the event types that are logged by DNS servers running Windows Server 2003.

Example

In the illustration, you can see some common DNS events from the event log in Event Viewer.

What Is DNS Debug Logging?

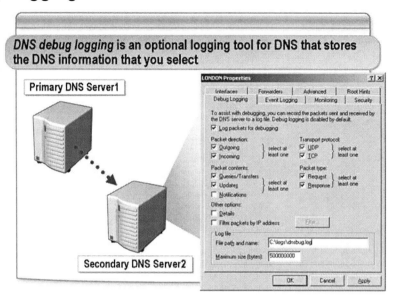

Definition

DNS debug logging is an optional logging tool for DNS that stores the DNS information that you select.

Because logging takes resources from the server, debug logging is not enabled by default. Debug logging is configured at the DNS server level, and therefore the debug logging settings affect all of the zones hosted on the DNS server.

Purpose of DNS debug logging

You can capture a great deal of DNS statistical data from the Performance tool. The Performance tool allows you to chart objects and counters. If you want to obtain even more specific information, you can enable DNS debug logging.

You can collect specific DNS data in the DNS.Log file by using DNS debug logging. For example, if you want to know what types of queries a computer was sending to the DNS server, you could configure DNS debug logging to collect just the inbound DNS queries by using User Datagram Protocol (UDP) or Transmission Control Protocol (TCP) from a certain Internet Protocol (IP) address.

DNS debug logging

Debug logging can be resource intensive, affecting overall server performance and consuming disk space. Therefore, it should only be used temporarily, when more detailed information about server performance is needed.

DNS debug logging collects information by logging any DNS traffic that fits the debug logging criteria.

Logging continues until either the log file size specified is met or the drive where the log file is stored runs out of room. After the file limit is reached, the logging process will begin to overwrite the oldest entries. Because log files can grow to be quite large, it is recommended that they be located on a separate drive.

DNS debug logging options

The following table lists and describes the options that are available when you are configuring DNS debug logging.

Options	Values	Description
Packet direction	Outgoing	Packets that the DNS server sends are logged in the DNS server log file.
	Incoming	Packets that the DNS server sends are logged in the log file.
Packet contents	Standard queries	Specifies that packets containing standard queries are logged in the DNS server log file.
	Updates	Specifies that packets containing dynamic updates are logged in the DNS server log file.
	Notifies	Specifies that packets containing notifications are logged in the DNS server log file.
Transport protocol	UDP	Specifies that packets sent and received over UDP are logged in the DNS server log file.
	TCP	Specifies that packets sent and received over TCP are logged in the DNS server log file.
Packet type	Request	Specifies that request packets are logged in the DNS server log file.
	Response	Specifies that response packets are logged in the DNS server log file.
Other options	Enable filtering based on IP address	Provides additional filtering of packets logged in the DNS server log file. This option allows logging of packets that are sent from specific IP addresses to a DNS server, or from a DNS server to specific IP addresses.
	File name	Specifies the name and location of the DNS server log file.
	Log file maximum size limit	Sets the maximum file size for the DNS server log file.

How to Monitor DNS Server Performance by Using Logging

Your instructor will demonstrate how to:

- Enable and configure debug logging options on the DNS server
- View a DNS server debug log file
- View the DNS server event log located on another computer

Introduction

To monitor DNS server performance by using logging, you can view either the DNS debug log or the event log.

To view a DNS server debug log, you must enable and configure debug logging options on the DNS server.

Note It is recommended that you log on with an account that has non-administrative credentials and use the **Run as** command with a user account that has appropriate administrative credentials to perform this task.

Procedure for enabling and configuring debug logging options on the DNS server

To enable and configure debug logging options on the DNS server:

1. Open the DNS console.

2. In the console tree, right-click the appropriate DNS server, and then click **Properties**.

3. In the *DNS Server* **Properties** dialog box, click the **Debug Logging** tab.

4. On the **Debug Logging** tab, select **Log packets for debugging**.

5. On the **Debug Logging** tab, select the options of the debug criteria that you want to store in the debug log file.

6. On the **Debug Logging** tab, in the **File path and name** field, type the path where the debug log will be stored and also type the name of the debug log. If no path and name is configured, the default path is *%Systemroot%*\System32\Dns and the default name is Dns.log.

7. On the **Debug Logging** tab, in the **Maximum size** field, type the maximum size for the Dns.log file. It is recommended that you configure a maximum log size. It is also recommended that you store the file on a separate drive from the system drive.

8. On the **Debug Logging** tab, click **OK**.

9. Close the DNS console.

Procedure for viewing a DNS server debug log file

To view a DNS server debug log file:

- Open the debug log by using NotePad.

Procedure for viewing a DNS server event log located on another computer

To view the DNS server event log located on another computer:

1. Open the DNS console, and then select **DNS**.

2. On the **Action** menu, click **Connect to DNS server**.

3. In the **Connect to DNS server** dialog box, select **The following computer**, and then specify the name or IP address of the remote computer.

4. In the console tree, expand **DNS**.

5. In the console tree, expand the **Event Viewer** folder.

6. In the details pane, click **DNS Events**.

7. To view additional details for a specific event, double-click the event.

Practice: Monitoring DNS Server Performance

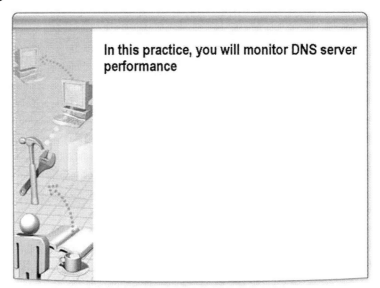

In this practice, you will monitor DNS server performance

Objectives   In this practice, you will monitor DNS server performance.

Instructions   To complete this practice, refer to the *Implementation Plan Values* document located in the Appendix at the end of your student workbook.

You must be logged on with an account that has non-administrative credentials and use the **Run as** command with a user account that has appropriate administrative credentials to complete the task.

Scenario 1   You have been asked to collect some performance data about your DNS server for a planning meeting. You will view real-time performance data prior to configuring long-term logging.

Practice 1

▶ **Monitor DNS server performance by using the Performance console**

■ Complete this task from both student computers

■ DNS server: *ComputerName*
  (where *ComputerName* is the name of your computer)

■ Performance object: **DNS**

■ DNS object counters:

  ● **AXFR Success Sent**

  ● **IXFR Success Sent**

  ● **Zone Transfer Failure**

  ● **Zone Transfer Success**

■ System Monitor Properties, Vertical scale, Maximum: **2**

▶ **Reload from the master server**

■ Complete this task from both student computers

■ DNS server: *ComputerName*
  (where *ComputerName* is the name of your computer)

■ DNS zone: **nwtraders.msft**

■ Right-click the nwtraders.msft zone, and then click **Reload from Master**.

▶ **Record the counter values for the DNS zone transfer**

■ Complete this task from both student computers

■ Record the values for the following DNS counters:

  • **AXFR Success Sent**   _____

  • **IXFR Success Sent**   _____

  • **Zone Transfer Failure**   _____

  • **Zone Transfer Success**   _____

■ Was the zone transfer successful? _____

■ Why was the zone transfer an incremental zone transfer?

  _____

  _____

Scenario 2

You have received complaints from a user who says that she is receiving errors when trying to access Web sites on the Internet. You verify that the DNS client is correctly configured. To verify that the DNS client queries are actually reaching the DNS server, you could configure DNS debug logging for the following scenarios:

■ On the DNS server, configure the DNS debug logging settings as per the following procedure.

■ Given UDP and TCP, collect DNS queries that the DNS server receives from the DNS client by using both UDP and TCP.

Practice 2

▶ **Enable and configure debug logging options on the DNS server**

- Complete this task from both student computers

- DNS server: *ComputerName*
  (where *ComputerName* is the name of your computer)

- Packet direction: **Outgoing** and **Incoming**

- Transport protocol: **UDP** and **TCP**

- Packet contents: **Queries/Transfers**

- Packet type: **Request** and **Response**

- File path and name: **C:\Moc\2277\Labfiles\Lab06\Debug.log**

- Maximum file size: **20000**

Lab A: Managing and Monitoring DNS

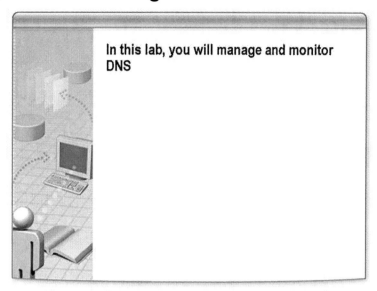

Objectives

In this lab, you will manage and monitor DNS.

Scenario

You have configured a DNS server in your lab subnet as a secondary DNS server to the primary DNS server for the lab. A new WINS server has been configured in the lab to support NetBIOS name resolution. You will configure DNS to integrate with the WINS server.

Several users have complained that they are not able to access Fileserver2 in the lab. You will use NSlookup to verify that the record exists, and also to identify the DNS server that is authoritative for the record.

You suspect that the secondary forward lookup zone on your DNS server is not receiving Notify Packets from the primary forward lookup zone on the master DNS server in the lab. You will verify that the zone transfer properties are configured correctly. You will also view the debug log file to verify that Notify Packets are sent.

Estimated time to complete this lab: 15 minutes

Exercise 1
Verifying a Record Using NSlookup

In this exercise, you will use the Nslookup utility to verify that the resource record exists and identify the DNS server that is authoritative for the record.

Instructions

To complete this practice, refer to the *Implementation Plan Values* document, located in the Appendix at the end of your student workbook.

You must be logged on with an account that has non-administrative credentials and use the **Run as** command with a user account that has appropriate administrative credentials to complete the tasks. When completing the lab, assume that you will log on with a non-administrative account (example: *ComputerName*User), unless the Specific Instructions in the lab state otherwise.

Scenario

Some DNS clients are having issues connecting to FileServer2. You will use Nslookup to verify that the record exists and that it is configured correctly. In addition, you will identify the authoritative DNS server for the record.

Tasks	Specific instructions
✊ Perform the following task on both student computers.	
1. Verify that the resource record FileServer2 exists, and verify that the alias is correctly configured by using the **Nslookup** command.	■ DNS server: *ComputerName* (where *ComputerName* is the name of your computer) ■ Query type: **CNAME**

Exercise 2
Configuring and Viewing DNS Debug Logging

In this exercise, you will enable and configure DNS debug logging on your DNS server. You will then initiate a zone transfer from the master zone. You will also view the debug log for the zone version.

Instructions

To complete this practice, refer to the *Implementation Plan Values* document, located in the Appendix at the end of your student workbook.

You must be logged on with an account that has non-administrative credentials and use the **Run as** command with a user account that has appropriate administrative credentials to complete the tasks. When completing the lab, assume that you will log on with a non-administrative account (example: *ComputerName*User), unless the Specific Instructions in the lab state otherwise.

Scenario

You need to verify that your secondary forward lookup zone is receiving zone transfer data from the primary forward lookup zone. You will configure DNS debug logging on your DNS server to collect zone transfer data. You will then view the debug log to find the last zone version that was written to the secondary server and check that against the zone version ID on the SOA record.

Tasks	Specific instructions
✋ Perform the following tasks on both student computers.	
1. Verify that debug logging is enabled and configured to: • Collect data on the zone transfer • Collect zone transfer notify data.	■ DNS server: *ComputerName* (where *ComputerName* is the name of your computer) ■ Packet direction: **Outgoing** and **Incoming** ■ Transport protocol: **UDP** and **TCP** ■ Packet contents: **Queries/Transfers** ■ Packet type: **Request** and **Response** ■ File path and name: **C:\Moc\2277\Labfiles\Lab06\Debug.log** ■ Maximum file size: **20000**
2. Initiate zone transfer from the nwtraders.msft secondary forward lookup zone.	■ On the nwtraders.msft zone, select **Reload from Master**.
3. Compare the value for the serial number on the SOA record in the nwtraders.msft zone and the value for the serial number from the Debug.log file.	■ DNS zone: **nwtraders.msft** ■ Document the serial number from the SOA _____ ■ Debug log file: **C:\Moc\2277\Labfiles\Lab06\Debug.log** ■ Document the serial number_____ ■ Are the zone serial numbers the same?_____

Microsoft®
Training &
Certification

Module 7: Resolving NetBIOS Names by Using Windows Internet Name Service (WINS)

Contents

Overview

- **Multimedia: The Role of WINS in the Network Infrastructure**
- **Installing and Configuring a WINS Server**
- **Managing Records in WINS**
- **Configuring WINS Replication**
- **Managing the WINS Database**

Introduction

In the Microsoft® Windows® Server 2003 family, the primary means for client computers to locate and communicate with other computers on an Internet Protocol (IP) network is by using Domain Name System (DNS). However, clients that use older versions of Windows, such as Microsoft Windows NT® version 4.0, use network basic input/output system (NetBIOS) names for network communication. Some applications that run on Windows Server 2003 may also use NetBIOS names for network communication. Using NetBIOS names requires a method of resolving NetBIOS names to IP addresses.

As a systems administrator, an understanding of Windows Internet Name Service (WINS) will help you to implement WINS in a Windows Server 2003 network to ensure that clients using older versions of Windows can locate and communicate with network resources as needed. This module introduces you to WINS, and explains how you can use WINS both to register NetBIOS names and to resolve those names to IP addresses.

Important For more information about securing WINS, see the Windows Server 2003, Enterprise Edition Help documentation.

Objectives

After completing this module, you will be able to:

- Describe the role of WINS in the network infrastructure.
- Install and configure a WINS server.
- Configure WINS replication.
- Manage records in WINS.
- Manage a WINS database.

Multimedia: The Role of WINS in the Network Infrastructure

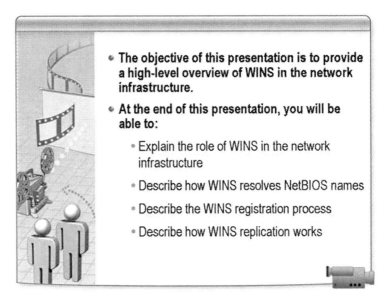

File location

To start *The Role of WINS in the Network Infrastructure* presentation, open the Web page on the Student Materials compact disc, click **Multimedia**, and then click the title of the presentation.

Objectives

At the end of this presentation, you will be able to:

- Explain the role of WINS in the network infrastructure.

- Describe how WINS resolves NetBIOS names.

- Describe the WINS registration process.

- Describe how WINS replication works.

Key Points

- WINS is a software service that dynamically maps IP addresses to NetBIOS names.

- A WINS client queries a WINS server for the IP address of a requested server. WINS sends the IP address of the requested server's NetBIOS name to the WINS client, and the WINS client then uses the IP address to attempt to connect to the server.

- For WINS to resolve NetBIOS names to IP addresses, the WINS client must register with the WINS server.

- There are two ways in which you can register WINS clients: manually or dynamically.

- In an enterprise environment with multiple WINS servers, each WINS server maintains a database of WINS client registrations.

- WINS servers share and update their records with other WINS servers in the enterprise network by using replication.

Lesson: Installing and Configuring a WINS Server

- The Components of WINS
- What Is a NetBIOS Node Type?
- How a WINS Client Registers and Releases NetBIOS Names
- How Burst Handling Works
- How a WINS Server Resolves NetBIOS Names
- How to Install the WINS Service
- How to Configure Burst Handling

Introduction

The WINS service resolves NetBIOS names, which reduces broadcast traffic and enables clients to resolve the NetBIOS names of computers that are on different network segments (subnets).

This lesson presents the skills and knowledge that are required for you to install and configure a WINS server.

Lesson objectives

After completing this lesson, you will be able to:

- Describe the components of WINS.
- Explain what a NetBIOS node type is.
- Describe how a WINS client registers and releases NetBIOS names.
- Describe how burst handling works.
- Describe how WINS clients resolve NetBIOS names.
- Install the WINS service.
- Configure burst handling.

The Components of WINS

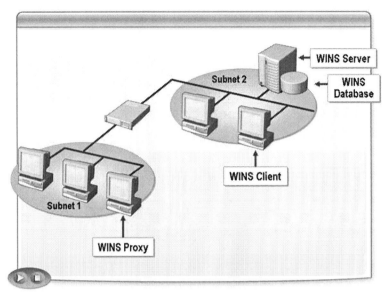

Introduction

As a systems administrator, having a thorough understanding of the components of WINS and how they function together in a network environment will help you to properly install and configure a WINS server.

Components of WINS

The complete Windows Server 2003 WINS system includes the following components:

- *WINS server.* A computer that processes name registration requests from WINS clients, registers the client's names and IP addresses, and responds to NetBIOS name queries that clients submit. The WINS server then returns the IP address of a queried name, if the name it is listed in the server database.

- *WINS database.* The WINS database stores and replicates the NetBIOS name-to-IP address mappings for a network.

- *WINS client.* Computers that you can configure to make direct use of a WINS server, which typically have more than one NetBIOS name that they must register for use with the network.

- *WINS proxy agents.* A computer that monitors name query broadcasts and responds for those names that are not on the local subnet. The proxy communicates with a WINS server to resolve names and then caches the names for a specific time period.

What Is a NetBIOS Node Type?

A *NetBIOS node type* is a method that a computer uses to resolve a NetBIOS name into an IP address

Node type	Description	Registry value
B-node	Uses broadcasts for name registration and resolution	1
P-node	Uses a NetBIOS name server such as WINS to resolve NetBIOS names	2
M-node	Combines B-node and P-node, but functions as a B-node by default	4
H-node	Combines P-node and B-node, but functions as a P-node by default	8

Definition

A *NetBIOS node type* is a method that a computer uses to resolve a NetBIOS name into an IP address.

Purpose of NetBIOS node types

NetBIOS node types allow an administrator to configure the order and method that a client uses when resolving NetBIOS names to IP addresses.

Types of nodes

Understanding how the various node types function will help you to properly configure your WINS solution. Windows Server 2003 supports the following node types:

- *B-node (broadcast)*. Uses broadcasts for name registration and resolution.

  Note In a large network, broadcasts can increase the network load. In addition, routers typically do not forward broadcasts, so only computers on the local network can respond.

- *P-node (peer-to-peer)*. Uses a NetBIOS name server (such as WINS) to resolve NetBIOS names. P-node does not use broadcasts, because it queries the name server directly, enabling computers to resolve NetBIOS names across routers. P-node requires that all computers be configured with the IP address of the NetBIOS name server. If the NetBIOS name server is not functioning, computers will not be able to communicate.

- *M-node (mixed)*. Combines B-node and P-node, but functions as a B-node by default. If M-node is unable to resolve a name by broadcast, it uses the NetBIOS name server of P-node.

- *H-node (hybrid)*. Combines P-node and B-node, but functions as a P-node by default. If H-node is unable to resolve a name by using the NetBIOS name server, it uses a broadcast to resolve a name.

Windows Server 2003 and Windows XP are configured as B-node types by default. When a computer running Windows XP, Windows Server 2003, or Windows 2000 is configured with WINS server addresses for its name resolution, it automatically changes to H-node as its node type for NetBIOS name registration. However, other operating systems may use other node types. You can use Dynamic Host Configuration Protocol (DHCP) options to assign the node type. To view the node type for a computer, type **ipconfig /all** at a command prompt.

Note   For more information about DHCP options, see Module 2, "Allocating IP Addressing by Using Dynamic Host Configuration Protocol (DHCP)" in Course 2277, *Implementing, Managing, and Maintaining a Microsoft Windows Server 2003 Network Infrastructure: Network Services*.

How a WINS Client Registers and Releases NetBIOS Names

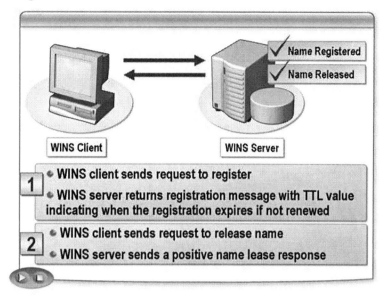

Definition

Name registration is the process of a WINS client requesting and receiving the use of a NetBIOS name for the services that the client is making available on the network. The request may be for either a unique (exclusive) name or a group (shared) name.

Name release is the process of a WINS client requesting and receiving the deletion of a NetBIOS name registration from the WINS database.

Purpose of WINS name registration

Each client component must register its name and the services that client is making available in the WINS database. The client can then perform a name query to locate and establish communication with other computers that are registered in the database.

The names registration process

A name is registered in WINS as follows:

1. At startup, or whenever a registered service is started, a WINS client computer sends a name registration request directly to the WINS server, in addition to broadcasting it on the local network.

2. The WINS server searches its database to see whether the name exists. If the name does not exist in the database, it is accepted as a new registration, and a positive response is sent back to the WINS client. If the name already exists in the database, a negative response is returned, and the client computer will report an error that a duplicate name exists on the network.

Name renewal

Because WINS name registrations are temporary, clients must periodically renew their registrations. When a client computer first registers with a WINS server, the WINS server returns a message with a Time-To-Live (TTL) value that indicates when the client registration expires or needs to be renewed.

If renewal does not occur by that time, the name registration expires on the WINS server, and the name entry is eventually removed from the WINS database. However, static WINS name entries do *not* expire, and therefore do not need to be renewed in the WINS server database.

Default renew interval

The default **Renew interval** for entries in the WINS database is six days. Renewal occurs every three days for most WINS clients, because WINS clients attempt to renew their registrations as soon as 50 percent of the TTL value has elapsed.

The name release process

Name release removes the names registered in the WINS database when the WINS client shuts down or whenever a registered service is stopped. When a name is released, it is available for registration by another computer. A name is released from WINS as follows:

1. When the client computer no longer requires a name registration, it issues a name release request. For example, when a client computer shuts down, it sends a release request to the WINS server to release its registration from the WINS database.

2. If the WINS server finds the name in the database, and if the IP address of the computer that requested the name release matches the IP address registered in the database, then the name is marked as released. The WINS server returns a release confirmation message to the WINS client.

   If the IP address of the client that requested the name release does *not* match the IP address that is registered in the database, the WINS server sends a negative name release to the client.

Note If a client computer crashes or does not shut down properly, and if as a result the name registration is not released, then the name will remain in the database until it either expires and is removed by the scavenging process or is manually deleted by an administrator.

How Burst Handling Works

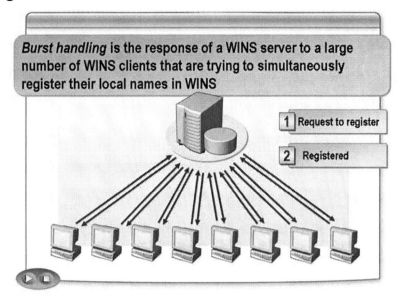

Definition	*Burst handling* is the response of a WINS server to a large number of WINS clients that are trying to simultaneously register their local names in WINS.
Purpose of burst handling	The function of burst handling is to answer requests superficially (with a positive registration response), allowing each client to begin using the registered service name. The WINS server then sets a short TTL so that the WINS client will return to reregister the name after only a few minutes. If the load continues to increase, WINS burst handling can further extend the delay interval to distribute the load over time.
How burst handling works	Burst mode uses the burst-queue size as a threshold value. This value determines how many name registration and name refresh requests sent by WINS clients can be waiting in the processing queue before burst-mode handling is started. By default, the threshold value is 500. The process of burst handling functions as follows:

1. A WINS server initiates burst handling whenever the number of WINS client registration requests in the queue exceeds the burst queue threshold.

2. After the burst queue threshold is exceeded, additional client requests are answered immediately with a positive response by the WINS server. The response also includes a very short TTL for clients (five minutes by default), which helps to regulate the client registration load and distribute processing of the requests over time. This slows the refresh and retry rate for new WINS clients, and regulates the burst of WINS client traffic.

Example of burst handling

When power is restored after a power failure, many users start and register their names simultaneously on the network, which creates high levels of WINS traffic. With burst-mode support, a WINS server can respond positively to these client requests, even before it actually processes and physically enters the updates into the WINS server database.

Note   Each single WINS client can register three unique NetBIOS names (messenger, workstation, and server). If 400 WINS clients register simultaneously after a power outage, this means that potentially 1,200 requests for NetBIOS name registration can reach a WINS server in a single burst. Therefore, it is important to configure burst handling appropriately for your network environment.

How a WINS Server Resolves NetBIOS Names

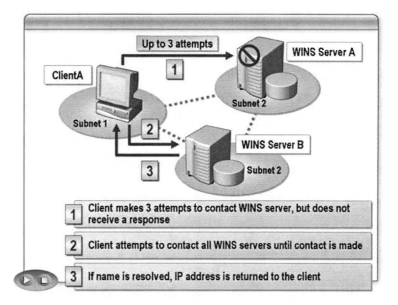

Definition of name resolution

Name resolution for WINS clients is an extension of the same name resolution process that all clients that use NetBIOS over TCP/IP (NetBT) use to resolve NetBIOS name queries on the network.

The name resolution process for WINS

For the Windows Server 2003 family, Windows XP, and Windows 2000, WINS clients use the following options for resolving a name after the NetBIOS query has been made:

1. The WINS client contacts the first WINS server three times to resolve the name by using WINS.

2. If the first WINS server does not respond, the client continues to contact other available WINS servers until it receives a response.

3. If a WINS server resolves the NetBIOS name, then the IP address is returned to the client. After the client receives the response, the client uses this address to establish a connection to the desired resource.

4. If none of the WINS servers resolve the NetBIOS name, then the resolution process continues outside of WINS. The typical H-node client attempts a broadcast. If the broadcast is unsuccessful, the client checks the Lmhosts file.

Note For more information about the name resolution process, see Module 4, "Resolving Names," in Course 2277, *Implementing, Managing, and Maintaining a Microsoft Windows Server 2003 Network Infrastructure: Network Services*

How to Install the WINS Service

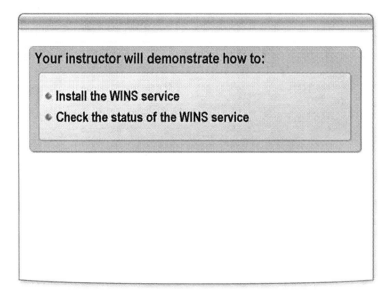

Your instructor will demonstrate how to:

- Install the WINS service
- Check the status of the WINS service

Introduction

To add the WINS service, you use the Manage Your Server tool, a new Windows Server 2003 feature. In the Windows Server 2003 family, the Manage Your Server tool is available on the **Start** menu.

Note   It is recommended that you log on with an account that has non-administrative credentials and use the **Run as** command with a user account that has appropriate administrative credentials to perform this task.

Procedure for installing the WINS service

To install the WINS service:

1. Log on by using a non-administrative user account.
2. Click **Start**, and then click **Control Panel**.
3. In Control Panel, open **Administrative Tools**, right-click **Manage Your Server**, and then click **Run as**.
4. In the **Run As** dialog box, select **The following user**, type a user account and password that have the appropriate permissions to complete the task, and then click **OK**.
5. In the Manage Your Server tool, click **Add or remove a role**.
6. On the **Preliminary Steps** page, click **Next**.
7. On the **Server Role** page, select **WINS server**, and then click **Next**.
8. On the **Summary of Selections** page, click **Next**.
9. If prompted for the Windows Server 2003 CD, insert it.
10. On the **This Server is Now a WINS Server** page, click **Finish**.

Procedure for checking the status of the WINS service

To check the status of the WINS service:

1. In the Manage Your Server tool, click **Manage this WINS server**.

2. In the WINS console, click **Server Status**.

3. In the WINS console, in the details pane, verify that **Responding** displays in the **Status column**.

How to Configure Burst Handling

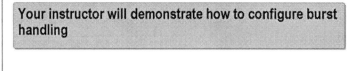

Introduction

You can choose to configure the level of burst handling that the server uses, which modifies the size of the burst queue to accommodate a low, medium, or large burst situation. By default, burst handling is enabled, and the burst queue is set to medium.

Note It is recommended that you log on with an account that has non-administrative credentials and use the **Run as** command with a user account that has appropriate administrative credentials to perform this task.

Procedure

To configure burst handling:

1. In the WINS console, click the name of the WINS server for which you want to modify burst handling properties.

2. On the **Action** menu, click **Properties**, and then click **Advanced**.

3. On the **Advanced** tab, in the **Enable burst handling** section, select one of the following options:

   - **Low** (300)

   - **Medium** (500)

   - **High** (1000)

   - **Custom** (from 50 to 5000)

4. On the **Advanced** tab, click **OK**.

5. Close the WINS console.

Practice: Installing and Configuring a WINS Server

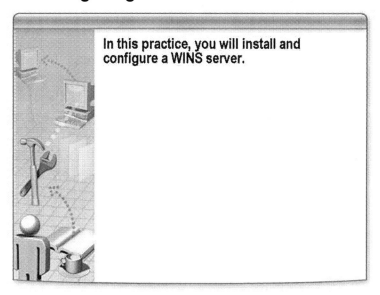

In this practice, you will install and configure a WINS server.

Objective

In this practice, you will install and configure a WINS server.

Instructions

To complete this practice, refer to the *Implementation Plan Values* document located in the Appendix at the end of your student workbook.

Scenario

The systems engineer has approved testing of an application that requires NetBIOS name support in the lab. As the number of computers that are testing this application increases, management of the Lmhosts file for each computer becomes more difficult. To support dynamic NetBIOS name registration and resolution for the client computers that are running the new application, you will install and configure a WINS server in the Lab department.

Because the lab is undergoing remodeling, it has experienced several power failures. To ensure that the WINS server can support all the computers that are registering their NetBIOS names simultaneously, you will configure burst handling on the WINS server. You have estimated that each of the 250 computers in the test lab requires the registration of eight NetBIOS name records for the applications and services running on the computer.

Practice

► **Configure your server IP configuration data for WINS**

Complete this task from both student computers.

- Interface: **Classroom Network Connection**
- WINS IP address: *IP address of your Classroom Network Connection interface*

► **Install the WINS service**

Complete this task from both student computers

- User name: **NWTraders***ComputerName***Admin**
- Password: **P@ssw0rd**

▶ **Checking the status of the WINS service**

■ Complete this task from both student computers

■ User name: **NWTraders***ComputerName***Admin**

■ Password: **P@ssw0rd**

▶ **Configure burst handling on the WINS server**

■ Complete this task from: both student computers

■ Burst handling setting: **Custom**

■ Custom value: **2000**

Lesson: Managing Records in WINS

* What Is a Client Record?
* What Is a Static Mapping?
* How to Add a Static Mapping Entry
* Methods for Filtering and Viewing Records in WINS
* How to Filter WINS Records

Introduction

WINS clients register and release NetBIOS name records. However, if a client incorrectly shut downs or is incorrectly removed from the network, the name release process does not properly complete. As a systems administrator, you will need to manually remove these records. In addition, you may need to remove WINS records that were manually added for non-WINS-enabled clients. Knowledge of how to manage WINS records will help you to keep WINS records current in your network.

Lesson objectives

After completing this lesson, you will be able to:

- Explain what client records are.
- Explain what a static mapping is.
- Add a static mapping.
- Describe various methods for filtering and viewing records in WINS.
- Filter WINS records.

What Is a Client Record?

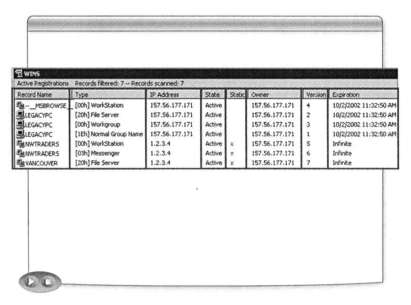

Definition

A *client record* is a database record that contains the detailed information for each NetBIOS-dependent service that runs on a client. A record indicates that these services are registered with a WINS server.

Example of a WINS record

WINS displays all records in the database and organizes WINS record information into the following columns:

- **Record Name**. The registered NetBIOS name, which can be a unique name or can represent a group, internet group, or multihomed computer.

- **Type**. The service that registered the entry, including the hexadecimal type identifier.

- **IP Address**. The IP address that corresponds to the registered NetBIOS name that is hosting the NetBIOS service.

- **State**. The state of the database entry, which can be active, released, or tombstoned. A tombstoned entry is an inactive entry that is marked for deletion from the database.

- **Static**. Indicates whether the mapping is static.

- **Owner**. The WINS server from which the entry originates. Because of replication, this is not necessarily the same server on which you view the database.

- **Version**. A unique hexadecimal number that the WINS server assigns during name registration. The server's pull partner uses the version ID number during replication to find new records.

- **Expiration**. Shows when the entry will expire. When a replica is stored in the database, it has a set expiration date. The expiration date is calculated by adding the current time on the receiving WINS server to the renewal interval that is set on the client.

What Is a Static Mapping?

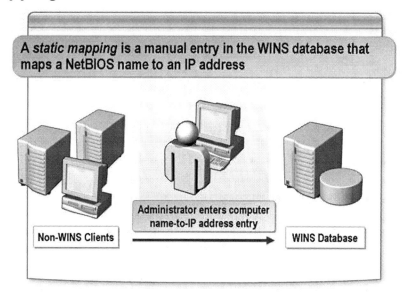

A *static mapping* is a manual entry in the WINS database that maps a NetBIOS name to an IP address

Non-WINS Clients   Administrator enters computer name-to-IP address entry   WINS Database

Definition

A *static mapping* is a manual entry in the WINS database that maps a NetBIOS name to an IP address.

Purpose of static mappings

You can configure static mappings on a WINS server to add name resolution information, about NetBIOS-based computers that are not WINS clients, to the WINS server database. When you configure static mappings, WINS clients can resolve the NetBIOS names of such computers by querying the WINS server.

Note After a static NetBIOS name-to-IP address mapping is entered in the WINS server database, it cannot be challenged or removed except by an administrator who removes the specific mapping by using the WINS management console.

Example

In some networks, client components of operating systems that use the B-node type cannot register NetBIOS names directly with a WINS server. Although these names might be added to and resolved from an Lmhosts file, or by querying a DNS server, you can also use a static WINS mapping to resolve the NetBIOS name.

Note To support non-WINS-enabled clients in NetBIOS name resolution, you can configure a WINS proxy. For more information about configuring a WINS proxy, see the Windows Server 2003 resource kit.

How to Add a Static Mapping Entry

> Your instructor will demonstrate how to add a static mapping entry

Introduction

To properly configure a static mapping, you must obtain the following elements from the client component for which you are creating the static mapping:

- *NetBIOS name.* The NetBIOS name of the computer.
- *Type of name.* Specify whether this entry is a **Unique**, **Group**, **Domain Name**, **Internet**, or **Multihomed** type.
- *IP Address.* The address of the computer.

Note It is recommended that you log on with an account that has non-administrative credentials and use the **Run as** command with a user account that has appropriate administrative credentials to perform this task.

Procedure

To add a static mapping entry:

1. In the WINS console, right-click **Active Registrations**, and then click **New Static Mapping**.
2. In the **New Static Mapping** dialog box, in the **Computer name** field, type the NetBIOS name of the computer.
3. In the **Type** drop-down menu, select the appropriate type.
4. In the **IP address** field, type the IP address of the computer that is associated with this NetBIOS name.
5. In the **New Static Mapping** dialog box, click **OK**.
6. Close the WINS console.

Methods for Filtering and Viewing Records in WINS

Search filter	Description
NetBIOS name and IP address	Based on all or part of a NetBIOS name, an IP address, or a NetBIOS name and an IP address, including or excluding the subnet mask as a parameter
Record owners	Based on the name records of one or more name record owners
Record types	Based on one or more NetBIOS name suffix record types

Introduction

The WINS console provides many methods for filtering and displaying WINS database records.

Purpose of viewing WINS records

There may be times when you want to manage WINS servers remotely. Search filters provide a way to view a subset of the data without downloading the entire WINS database to the computer running the WINS console. Search filters are also valuable for isolating name resolution issues in your network. For example, you can use the **Filter records matching name pattern** method to verify that a known NetBIOS name exists in the data that is stored at any one of your remote WINS servers. This filter typically generates minimal network traffic and can be used routinely for locating the source of Name Not Found errors that can result from NetBIOS name resolution.

Categories of search filters

When you create a search filter, you choose from three categories of filters:

- *NetBIOS name and IP address.* You can base a record query on all or part of a NetBIOS name, on an IP address, or on a NetBIOS name and an IP address together, including or excluding the subnet mask as a search parameter.

- *Record owners.* You can base a record query on the name records of one or more name record owners.

- *Record types.* You can base a record query on one or more record types for the NetBIOS name suffix.

Search filter using the record owner

You filter by record owners to obtain either a full or filtered view of the WINS database for one or more servers that own records that are registered in the database. You can use this filter to help isolate problems with local WINS databases (either on the same WINS server, or on a WINS server that is on the same local area network).

When viewing records by owner, you can also filter WINS data to be included in the view, by selecting and using NetBIOS name suffix types as criteria.

Search filter using the record type

Filtering records by record (suffix) type allows you to more precisely isolate network issues. For a search operation to successfully return one or more name records, you must select at least one record type for the NetBIOS name. You can select either any combination of record types or all record types.

Search filters using the NetBIOS name and IP address

You can use the following methods for filtering and displaying records, based on the NetBIOS name and IP address. You can use these filters in different combinations to achieve varying results. However, you must use at least one record type and one record owner for the NetBIOS name and IP address filters to function properly.

Use the **Filter records matching name pattern** method to query the WINS database and display only those NetBIOS name records that start with a specified set of one or more characters. This filter is ideal for targeting either a known name or similar names that are located on a specific WINS server.

Use the **Filter records matching name pattern** method to locate records through either a full NetBIOS name or a specified set of matching characters. For WINS to include a targeted name in the results of a find operation, the name must begin with the exact characters that are specified in **Filter records matching name pattern**. However, names that match the specified search criteria can contain additional characters after the specified string.

Use the **Filter records matching IP address** method to search for and display records that have a specific IP address.

Use the **Filter records matching name pattern** and **Filter records matching IP address** methods together to search for and display only records in which both the name and the IP address match the search criteria.

Use the **Filter records matching IP address** and **Match the IP address based on subnet mask** methods together to search for records by using the IP address and subnet mask pair. The subnet mask indicates which sections of the IP address are interpreted as a network ID and which sections of the IP address are interpreted as a host ID. The search is performed for all records with a network ID that matches the IP address search criteria.

How to Filter WINS Records

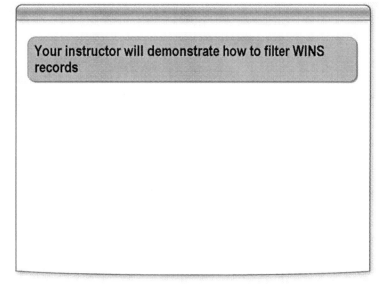

Introduction

Record searches are initiated in the WINS console **Display Records** dialog box. When WINS database records match search parameters, one or more records are displayed in the details pane of the WINS console. While a search is in progress, search statistics are dynamically displayed in the status bar above the details pane. Search statistics include the number of records scanned and filtered. When no WINS database records match search parameters, no records are displayed in the details pane.

Note It is recommended that you log on with an account that has non-administrative credentials and use the **Run as** command with a user account that has appropriate administrative credentials to perform this task.

Procedure

To filter WINS records:

1. In the WINS console, right-click **Active Registrations**, and then click **Display Records**.

2. In the **Display Records** dialog box, select the appropriate filters from one or more of the following tabs:

   • **Record Mapping**. Filter on record name and/or record IP address.

   • **Record Owners**. Filter on the WINS servers that own the records.

   • **Record Types**. Filter on the record type or service.

3. In the **Display Records** dialog box, on any of the tabs, click **Find Now**.

   If no filter settings are configured, then all of the WINS records will be displayed.

4. Close the WINS console.

Practice: Managing Records in the WINS Server

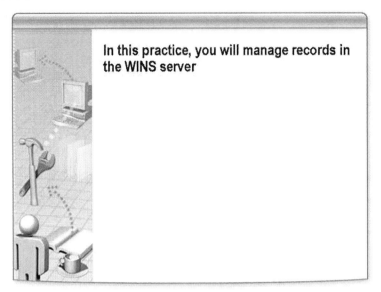

Objective

In this practice, you will manage records in the WINS server.

Instructions

You must be logged on with an account that has non-administrative credentials and use the **Run as** command with a user account that has appropriate administrative credentials to complete the task.

Scenario

The systems engineer has approved testing of an application that requires NetBIOS name support in the lab. One of the computers running this application does not support WINS. To support these client computers that are non-WINS enabled, the systems engineer has authorized you to create static mappings in WINS. After creating the static mappings, you will filter the WINS records to verify that the static mappings are correct.

Practice

▶ **Display all WINS records**

- Complete this task from both student computers

- Administrative Tool: WINS

- No filters used

▶ **Add a WINS static mapping**

- Complete this task from both student computers

- Computer name: **Glasgow**

- NetBIOS scope: *Leave this blank*

- Type: **Unique**

- IP address: **192.168.*x*.100**

▶ **Filter the WINS records to view only the new static mapping that you added**

■ Complete this task from both student computers

1. Filter records matching this name pattern: **Glasgow**

2. In the details pane, verify that only records for Glasgow are displayed. Notice that the **x** in the static column indicates that the record is a static entry.

Lesson: Configuring WINS Replication

- How WINS Replication Works
- How Push Replication Works
- How Pull Replication Works
- What Is Push/Pull Replication?
- WINS Replication Partner Properties
- How to Configure WINS Replication
- How to Configure Replication Partners Properties

Introduction

Although a single WINS server can service thousands of clients for NetBIOS name resolution requests, it is important to provide additional fault tolerance by configuring a second computer running Windows Server 2003 as a secondary (or backup) WINS server for clients. If you use only two WINS servers, you can easily set them up as replication partners of each other. This ensures that a consistent set of WINS information is maintained and distributed throughout your network.

Lesson objectives

After completing this lesson, you will be able to:

- Describe how WINS replication works.
- Describe how push replication works.
- Describe how pull replication works.
- Explain what push/pull replication is.
- Explain the purpose of specific WINS replication partner properties.
- Configure WINS replication.
- Configure replication partners properties.

How WINS Replication Works

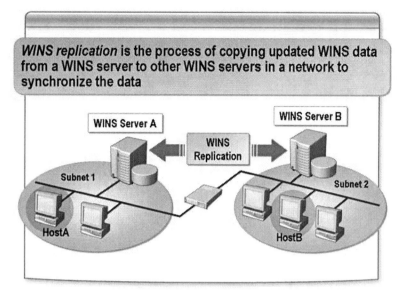

Definition

WINS replication is the process of copying updated WINS data from one WINS server to other WINS servers in a network to synchronize the data.

Purpose of WINS replication

Replication of WINS databases ensures that a name that is registered with one WINS server is replicated to all other WINS servers on the network. By using replication between WINS servers, a consistent set of WINS information is maintained and distributed throughout the network. As a result, a WINS client can resolve any NetBIOS name in the network, regardless of the WINS server on which the name was registered.

Replication partners

When a network uses multiple WINS servers, each WINS server is configured as a either a push partner, a pull partner, or a push/pull partner of at least one other WINS server. The default configuration for WINS replication partners is the push/pull replication type. However, you can modify this configuration to meet the needs of your network environment.

Example of WINS replication

The following example illustrates how WINS replicates data from one WINS server to another:

1. HostA on Subnet 1 registers with WINS Server A on Subnet 1.

2. HostB on Subnet 2 registers with WINS Server B on Subnet 2.

3. WINS replication occurs, and each WINS server updates its database with the new entry from the other server's database.

If either host later attempts to locate the other host by using WINS, replication of WINS registration information between the WINS servers makes it possible to resolve this query. For example, HostA can successfully query WINS Server A and find an IP address for HostB.

Note   Rather than replicate the entire database, WINS servers only replicate the changes that are made to their databases.

How Push Replication Works

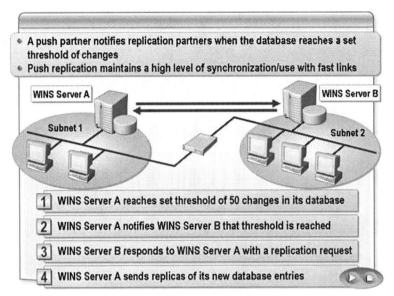

Definition

Push replication is the process of copying updated WINS data from one WINS server to other WINS servers, whenever the WINS server that contains the updated data reaches a specified threshold of changes.

The process of push replication

The process of push replication functions as follows:

1. A push partner notifies its replication partners whenever the number of changes to its WINS database passes a specific, configurable threshold. For example, you can configure a push partner to notify replication partners whenever 50 changes have occurred to the WINS database.

2. When replication partners respond to the notification with a replication request, the push partner sends replicas of its new database entries.

When to use push replication

You should configure a replication partner as a push partner if fast communication links connect the servers. This ensures that the WINS databases maintain a high level of synchronization, although the replication traffic will generally increase as a result.

How Pull Replication Works

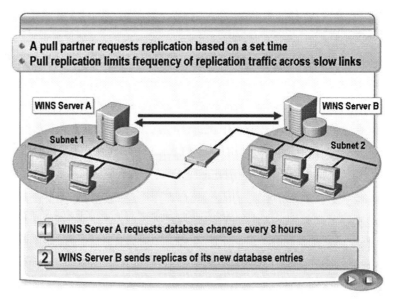

- A pull partner requests replication based on a set time
- Pull replication limits frequency of replication traffic across slow links

WINS Server A

Subnet 1

WINS Server B

Subnet 2

1 WINS Server A requests database changes every 8 hours

2 WINS Server B sends replicas of its new database entries

Definition

Pull replication is the process of copying updated WINS data from a WINS server to another WINS server at specific, configurable intervals.

The process of pull replication

The process of pull replication is as follows:

1. A pull partner requests changes in a WINS database at set intervals of time. For example, you can configure a pull partner to request database changes every eight hours.

2. Replication partners respond by sending all new database entries, which are then received by the pull partner.

When to use pull replication

You should configure a replication partner as a pull partner if slow communication links connect the WINS servers. This configuration limits the frequency of replication traffic across the link to specific times. For example, you can schedule replication to occur in off-peak hours to avoid replication during high traffic periods.

If you decide to use pull replication, remember that a slower replication frequency causes the WINS databases to become increasingly less synchronized. When a WINS server has incomplete data, some name resolution attempts may fail.

What Is Push/Pull Replication?

Push/pull replication effectively ensures that the databases on multiple WINS servers are nearly identical at any given time by:

* Notifying replication partners whenever the database reaches a set threshold of changes

AND

* Requesting replication based on a set time

Definition

Push/pull replication is the process of a WINS server updating its records with new database entries from its replication partners, based either on a replication threshold or on a replication interval, whichever occurs first.

When to use push/pull replication

You should configure a replication partner as a push/pull partner if you want to specify both a replication threshold and a replication interval for the partner. This ensures that the WINS databases remain synchronized regardless of the number of changes that occur. In effect, replication occurs either when the threshold of changes has been reached, or when a maximum period between replication notifications has been exceeded, whichever condition is satisfied first.

WINS replication partners are configured as push/pull partners by default—which is the simplest and most effective method of ensuring that the databases on these servers are nearly identical at any given time.

WINS Replication Partner Properties

Property	Description
Enable automatic partner configuration	As WINS servers are discovered joining the network, they are added as replication partners
Enable persistent connections	Increases the speed of replication so that a server can immediately send records to its partners
Enable overwrite unique static mappings at this server (migrate on)	If presented with both a static and dynamic-type entry for the same name, the static mapping is overwritten

Introduction

The successful deployment and use of WINS in your network depends on the proper configuration of the replication properties. In the **WINS Replication Partner Properties** dialog box, you can choose from several WINS service configuration options to meet the needs of your network.

Enable automatic partner configuration

You can configure a WINS server to automatically configure other WINS server computers as its replication partners. With this automatic partner configuration, other WINS servers are discovered when they join the network and are added as replication partners.

The **Automatic partner configuration** option is typically useful in small networks, such as single subnet local area network (LAN) environments.

Each WINS server announces its presence on the network by means of periodic multicasts. These announcements are sent as Internet Group Management Protocol (IGMP) messages for the multicast group address of 224.0.1.24 (the well-known multicast IP address reserved for WINS server use).

You can configure automatic partner configuration, which will enable the WINS server to monitor multicast announcements from other WINS servers and to perform the following configuration steps automatically. When you configure the **Automatic partner configuration** option, the WINS server:

- Adds the IP addresses for the discovered servers to its list of replication partner servers.

- Configures the discovered servers as both push and pull partners.

- Configures pull replication at two-hour intervals with the discovered servers.

Enable persistent connections

WINS servers typically disconnect from their replication partners each time replication is completed, In networks where WINS servers are interconnected through high-speed LAN links, it is preferable to keep connections open instead of closing them after replication is completed.

By enabling persistent connections, you can increase the speed of replication, because a server can immediately send records to its partners without incurring the cost of establishing temporary connections each time. If you set the replication threshold to 0, every record is immediately updated across the network upon registration in WINS, making replication more consistent. The bandwidth that is used by persistent connections is minimal because the connection is usually idle.

Enable overwrite unique static mappings at this server (migrate on)

Unlike dynamic mappings, which can age and which are automatically removed from WINS over time, static mappings can remain in WINS indefinitely or until administrative action is taken to remove them.

By default, if during an update process WINS is presented with both a static and a dynamic entry for the same name, it preserves the static-type entry. You can, however, use the **Overwrite unique static mappings at this server (migrate on)** setting to change this behavior.

Note You can only configure this setting from the properties dialog box of the Replication Partner object in the WINS console.

How to Configure WINS Replication

Your instructor will demonstrate how to:

- Configure WINS replication
- Modify a replication partner type
- Modify the Push Replication settings for replication partners
- Modify the Pull Replication settings for replication partners
- Replicate with all WINS partners
- Start push replication for a WINS replication partner
- Start pull replication for a WINS replication partner

Introduction

By default, WINS replication partners are configured as push/pull partners. To modify this configuration to meet the needs of your network environment, you can specify push parameters and pull parameters for each configured replication partner.

Note It is recommended that you log on with an account that has non-administrative credentials and use the **Run as** command with a user account that has appropriate administrative credentials to perform this task.

Procedure for configuring WINS replication

To configure WINS replication:

1. In the WINS console tree, select the WINS server for which you want to add a replication partner, and click **Replication Partners**.
2. On the **Action** menu, click **New Replication Partner**.
3. In the **WINS server** field, type the computer name or IP address of the WINS server that you want to add as a replication partner.
4. Click **OK**.

Procedure for modifying a replication partner type

To modify a replication partner type:

1. In the WINS console tree, expand the WINS server.
2. In the WINS console, click **Replication Partners**.
3. In the details pane, right-click the appropriate server, and then click **Properties**.

4. In the *Server* **Properties** dialog box, on the **Advanced** tab, in the **Replication partner type** field, select one of the following options:

- **Push**. Reconfigure push partner properties that this server will use when it performs replication with any of its newly added push partners.

- **Pull**. Reconfigure pull partner properties that this server will use when it performs replication with any of its newly added pull partners.

- **Push/Pull**. Reconfigure as both a push partner and a pull partner.

Note By default, WINS replication partners are configured as push/pull partners. You can reconfigure the push/pull partner properties to meet the needs of your network.

5. In the *Server* **Properties** dialog box, click **OK**.
6. Close the WINS console.

Procedure for modifying the Push Replication settings for replication partners

To modify the **Push Replication** settings for replication partners:

1. In the WINS console tree, expand the WINS server.
2. In the WINS console, click **Replication Partners**.
3. On the **Action** menu, click **Properties**.
4. In the **Replication Partners Properties** dialog box, on the **Push Replication** tab, select one or both of the following options:

- **At service startup**. Specifies whether this server informs pull partners of its database status when the WINS service is initialized.

- **When address changes**. Specifies whether this server informs pull partners of its database status when an address changes in a mapping record.

5. In the **Replication Partners Properties** dialog box, on the **Push Replication** tab, in the **Number of changes in version ID before replication** field, type a value between **1** and **32,767**. This indicates how many updates can be made before push partners are informed of changes.

6. In the **Replication Partners Properties** dialog box, on the **Push Replication** tab, select **Use persistent connections for push replication partners**. This feature is helpful because WINS servers typically disconnect from partners when replication is completed. Persistent connections increase the speed of replication, because a server can immediately send records to its partners.

7. In the **Replication Partners Properties** dialog box, click **OK**.
8. Close the WINS console.

Procedure for modifying the Pull Replication settings for replication partners

To modify the **Pull Replication** settings for replication partners:

1. In the WINS console tree, expand the WINS server.

2. In the WINS console, click **Replication Partners**.

3. On the **Action** menu, click **Properties**.

4. In the **Replication Partners Properties** dialog box, on the **Pull Replication** tab, in the **Start time** fields, configure the time from the current time that pull replication will begin.

5. In the **Replication Partners Properties** dialog box, on the **Pull Replication** tab, in the **Replication interval** fields, configure the time interval between replications.

6. In the **Replication Partners Properties** dialog box, on the **Pull Replication** tab, in the **Number of retries** field, type a value. This is the number of times the server will retry a connection to a pull partner in the event of a failed connection during replication.

7. In the **Replication Partners Properties** dialog box, on the **Pull Replication** tab, select one or both of the following options:

    - **Start pull replication at service startup**. Specifies whether this server pulls replicas from known partners whenever the WINS service is initialized.

    - **Use persistent connections for pull replication partners**. This feature is helpful because WINS servers typically disconnect from partners when replication is completed. Persistent connections increase the speed of replication, because a server can immediately send records to its partners.

8. In the **Replication Partners Properties** dialog box, click **OK**.

9. Close the WINS console.

Procedure for replicating with all WINS partners

To replicate with all WINS partners:

1. In the WINS console tree, right-click **Replication Partners**, and then click **Replicate Now**.

2. In the **WINS** warning message box, click **Yes**.

3. In the **WINS** information message box, click **OK**.

Procedure for starting push replication

To start push replication for a WINS replication partner:

1. In the WINS console tree, click **Replication Partners**, and then, in the details pane, right-click the WINS server that you wish to replicate with, and then click **Start Push Replication**.

2. In the **Start Push Replication** dialog box, click either:

    - **Start for this partner only**

    - **Propagate to all partners**

3. In the WINS information message box, click **OK**.

Procedure for starting pull replication

To start pull replication for a WINS replication partner:

1. In the WINS console tree, click **Replication Partners**, and then, in the details pane, right-click the WINS server that you wish to replicate with, and then click **Start Pull Replication**.

2. In the **Confirm Start Pull Replication** message box, click **Yes**.

3. In the WINS information message box, click **OK**.

How to Configure Replication Partners Properties

Your instructor will demonstrate how to:

- Configure the Pull properties for the replication partner
- Configure the Push properties for the replication partner

Introduction

When you first add a replication partner, it is configured with default settings. To customize WINS replication to meet the needs of your network, you can configure settings in the **Replication Partners Properties** dialog box.

Note It is recommended that you log on with an account that has non-administrative credentials and use the **Run as** command with a user account that has appropriate administrative credentials to perform this task.

Procedure for configuring Pull properties for the replication partner

To configure the **Pull** properties for the replication partner:

1. In the WINS console tree, expand the WINS server for which you want to configure replication partner properties, and then select **Replication Partners**.

2. In the details pane, right-click the appropriate server name, and then click **Properties**.

3. In the *Server* **Properties** dialog box, on the **Advanced** tab, in the **Pull replication** section, select **Use persistent connection for pull replication**.

   This feature is helpful because WINS servers typically disconnect from partners when replication is completed. Persistent connections increase the speed of replication, because a server can immediately send records to its partners.

4. In the *Server* **Properties** dialog box, click **OK**.

5. Right-click **Replication Partners**.

6. In the **Replication Partners Properties** dialog box, on the **Pull Replication** tab, in the **Start time** fields, configure the time when pull replication will begin.

7. On the **Replication Partners Properties** dialog box, on the **Pull Replication** tab, in the **Replication interval** fields, configure the time interval between replications.

8. Close the WINS console.

Procedure for configuring Push properties for the replication partner

To configure the **Push** properties for the replication partner:

1. In the WINS console tree, expand the WINS server for which you want to configure replication partner properties, and then select **Replication Partners**.

2. In the details pane, right-click the appropriate server name, and then click **Properties**.

3. In the *Server* **Properties** dialog box, on the **Advanced** tab, in the **Push replication** section, select **Use persistent connection for pull replication**.

    This feature is helpful because WINS servers typically disconnect from partners when replication is completed. Persistent connections increase the speed of replication, because a server can immediately send records to its partners.

4. In the *Server* **Properties** dialog box, on the **Advanced** tab, in the **Push replication** section, in the **Number of changes in version ID before replication** field, type a value between **1** and **32,767**. This value indicates how many updates can be made before push partners are informed of changes.

5. In the *Server* **Properties** dialog box, click **OK**.

6. Close the WINS console.

Practice: Configuring WINS Replication

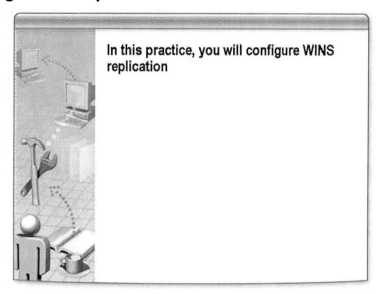

In this practice, you will configure WINS replication

Objective

In this practice, you will configure WINS replication.

Instructions

To complete this practice, refer to the *Implementation Plan Values* document located in the Appendix at the end of your student workbook.

You must be logged on with an account that has non-administrative credentials and use the **Run as** command with a user account that has appropriate administrative credentials to complete the task.

Scenario

The systems engineer has approved the testing of an application that requires NetBIOS name support. Several WINS servers have been configured to support this application on separate networks. The systems engineer wants to be able to have any computer in the lab connect to any other computer in the lab by using WINS. The systems engineer has configured a central WINS server that all other WINS servers will replicate with. You will configure your WINS server to replicate with this central WINS server.

Practice

▶ **Filter the WINS records to verify that all current WINS records are owned by your server**

- Complete this task from both student computers.

- Filter records matching this name pattern: *ComputerName* (where *ComputerName* is the name of your computer)

▶ **Configure WINS replication**

- Complete this task from both student computers

- Replication partner: **London**

- Replication type: **Push/Pull**

▶ **Modify Pull Replication settings for replication partners**

■ Complete this task from both student computers.

■ WINS Replication Partner: **London**

■ Use persistent connection for replication partners: **Selected**

■ Start time: **1 minute**

■ Replication interval: **5 minutes**

▶ **Modify Push Replication settings for replication partners**

■ Complete this task from both student computers.

■ WINS Replication Partner: **London**

■ Use persistent connection for replication: **Enabled**

■ Number of changes in version ID before replication: **1**
(This setting is based on the classroom environment, and is not
recommended outside the classroom environment)

▶ **Replicate with the London WINS server**

■ Complete this task from both student computers.

■ WINS replication partner: **London**

■ Right-click **Replication Partners**, and then click **Replicate Now**.

▶ **Restart the WINS service on your WINS server to replicate records**

■ Complete this task from both student computers.

■ To save time, restart the WINS service (to force replication) by selecting
your WINS server in the WINS console; and then, on the **Action** menu,
click **All Tasks**, and then click **Restart**.

▶ **View the WINS records to verify that WINS records from your WINS
server and London display**

■ Complete this task from both student computers.

■ Filter records matching this name pattern: **London**

■ Verify that records are displayed with the owner IP address value of
London.

Note You may have to refresh the WINS console to view the records.

Lesson: Managing the WINS Database

- Why Back Up a WINS Database?
- How to Back Up and Restore a WINS Database
- What Are Simple Deletion and Tombstoned Deletion of Records?
- How to Delete a WINS Record
- What Are Dynamic and Offline Compacting?
- How to Compact a WINS Database
- How Scavenging Works
- How to Scavenge a WINS Database
- How a WINS Database Is Checked for Consistency
- How to Check for Consistency on a WINS Database
- Guidelines for Decommissioning a WINS Server
- How to Decommission a WINS Server

Introduction

The WINS database in the Windows Server 2003 family imposes no limit on the number of records that a WINS server can replicate or store. The size of the database depends on the number of WINS clients on the network, but is not always directly proportional to the number of active client entries. It is possible for inactive and obsolete records to take up significant space in the database, and this condition can hinder performance. Knowledge about how to properly manage a WINS database will help you to maintain its integrity and performance.

This lesson includes the knowledge and skills that are required to manage a WINS database.

Lesson objectives

After completing this lesson, you will be able to:

- Explain the importance of backing up a WINS database.
- Back up and restore a WINS database.
- Explain what simple deletion and tombstoned deletion of records are.
- Manually delete a WINS record.
- Explain what dynamic and offline compacting are.
- Compact a WINS database.
- Describe the process of scavenging.
- Configure a WINS database for scavenging.
- Explain the purpose of checking consistency in the WINS database.
- Check for consistency in a WINS database.
- Explain the purpose of decommissioning a WINS server.
- Decommission a WINS server.

Why Back Up a WINS Database?

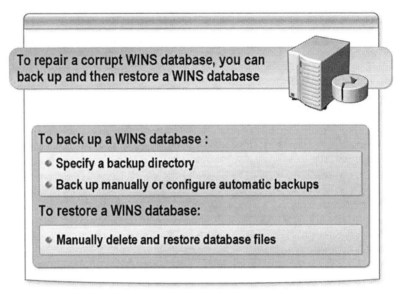

To repair a corrupt WINS database, you can back up and then restore a WINS database

To back up a WINS database :
- Specify a backup directory
- Back up manually or configure automatic backups

To restore a WINS database:
- Manually delete and restore database files

Purpose of backing up the WINS database

If you are unable to repair a corrupt database that has been caused by a system failure, a virus attack, a power failure, or a similar disaster, you can first delete the WINS database and then entirely restore it from a backup.

Default database backups

The WINS management console provides backup tools with which you can back up the WINS database. After you specify a backup directory for the database, WINS performs complete database backups every 24 hours by installation default. The WINS management console also provides a backup option which you can use to restore a server database if corruption should occur.

Restore a WINS database

Restoring a WINS database involves first stopping the WINS service. Because a server might require several minutes of processing before it can effectively stop WINS, make sure that the service is completely stopped before you begin the restore process.

Before you restore the database, delete all files in the folder path on the WINS server computer where you are restoring the database.

How to Back Up and Restore a WINS Database

> **Your instructor will demonstrate how to:**
>
> * Specify a back up directory for the WINS database
> * Manually back up a WINS database
> * Restore a WINS database from a recent backup

Introduction

To back up a WINS database, you must first specify a backup directory and initiate a manual backup.

Note   It is recommended that you log on with an account that has non-administrative credentials and use the **Run as** command with a user account that has appropriate administrative credentials to perform this task.

Procedure for specifying a backup directory and initiating a manual backup

To specify a backup directory for the WINS database:

1. In the WINS console, right-click the WINS server that you want to back up and then click **Properties**.

2. On the **General** tab in the **Default backup path** box, type the name of the path of the directory that the WINS server uses for database backups.

   Note   When WINS backs up the server database, it creates a Wins_bak\New folder in the backup folder that you specify. Actual backups of the WINS database (Wins.mdb) are stored in this folder. By default, the backup path is the root folder on your system partition. The backup folder must located be on the local computer. WINS automatically performs a full backup of its database to this directory every 24 hours. WINS uses this directory to perform an automatic restoration of the database if the database is found to be corrupted when WINS is started. Do not specify a network directory.

3. On the **General** tab, if required, select the **Back up database during server shutdown** option.

4. On the **General** tab, click **OK**.

Procedure for manually backing up a WINS database

To manually back up a WINS database:

1. In WINS, right-click the name of the server that you are configuring, and then click **Back Up Database**.

2. In the **Browse for Folder** dialog box, select the folder to which you want to back up the WINS database, and then click **OK** twice.

Important   WINS stores information about its configuration and replication partners in the registry. As part of your WINS disaster-recovery strategy, make sure that you always have a recent backup of your registry (for example, as part of a system state backup).

Procedure for restoring a WINS database

In the event that the WINS database becomes corrupt and cannot be repaired, restore it from a recent backup.

To restore a WINS database from a recent backup:

1. Stop WINS.

   Wait for WINS to stop completely before proceeding. A busy server might require several minutes before it can stop WINS and you can safely proceed with restoring the database.

2. Delete all files in the folder path on the WINS server computer to which you are restoring the database. This path is determined by the current setting of **Database path**, which is located on the **Advanced** tab in the **Properties** dialog box for the server.

3. In WINS, right-click the name of the server that you are configuring, and then click **Restore Database**.

   The **Restore Database** option is only available when you are viewing a computer on which WINS is stopped. In some cases, you might have to refresh the WINS console to activate the restore option. If necessary, right-click the server, and then click **Refresh** to refresh the server node so that WINS detects that it is stopped on the server.

4. In the **Browse for Folder** dialog box, click the folder that you used previously to back up the local WINS database, and then click **OK** twice.

5. When you restore the database, WINS requires that the backup path used for restoration match the path that was originally specified in *Server* **Properties** as the **Backup path**.

What Are Simple Deletion and Tombstoned Deletion of Records?

To recover unused space that obsolete records occupy, you can update the WINS database by:

- **Simple deletion.** Records selected by using the WINS console are removed from the current local WINS server

- **Tombstoned deletion.** Records are marked for deletion, replicated to other WINS servers, and then removed during the next scavenging operation

Purpose of deleting WINS records

By deleting obsolete records in the WINS database, you can recover unused space. The WINS management console provides improved database management by supporting the following deletion operations:

- Simple deletion of WINS database records that are stored on a single-server database.

- Tombstoned deletion, which is the removal of records that are marked for deletion (tombstoned) from the WINS database only after they have been replicated to databases on other WINS servers.

- The ability to select multiple groups of displayed database records when performing either a simple deletion or tombstoned deletion.

Simple deletion of records

When you use simple deletion, records that you select by using the WINS console are removed from the current local WINS server that you are managing.

If WINS records deleted in this way have been replicated to other WINS servers, these additional records will not be removed fully. The records on other WINS servers remain in those databases unless you specifically use the WINS console to remove them from each server, one at a time. In addition, records deleted from just one server might reappear when replication next occurs between WINS servers that are configured as replication partners. For example, the next time replication occurs, a replication partner can copy the record back to the WINS server that originally deleted the record.

Tombstoned deletion of records

When you use a tombstoned deletion to remove a record that your selected server owns, the selected records are removed from all WINS servers that replicate the records.

The WINS server owner changes the status of selected WINS records from active to tombstoned in its database. WINS then treats the records as inactive and released from use. After these records are tombstoned locally, the owning WINS server neither responds to nor resolves NetBIOS name queries for these names from other WINS clients and WINS servers unless the WINS client registers the records again. The WINS server owner replicates the selected records as "tombstoned" to other WINS servers during subsequent replication cycles.

After all WINS servers that participate in replication complete a full replication cycle and arrive at a consistent state, the tombstoned records expire and are removed from the WINS database of each server during the next database update operation. After the servers have been updated, the records no longer appear in the WINS console and are no longer physically stored in the WINS database.

How to Delete a WINS Record

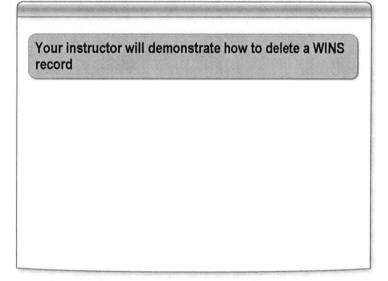

Introduction

The WINS console offers you options for deleting WINS records.

> **Note** It is recommended that you log on with an account that has non-administrative credentials and use the **Run as** command with a user account that has appropriate administrative credentials to perform this task.

Procedure

To delete or tombstone a WINS record:

1. In the WINS console, click **Active Registrations**.

2. On the **Action** menu, select **Display Records** to search for and display the names that you want to delete from the database.

3. In the details pane, click the entry that you want to delete.

4. On the **Action** menu, click **Delete**.

5. In the **Delete Record** dialog box, click one of the following options for deleting the selected records:

   - **Delete the record only from this server.** This option deletes the record immediately from this WINS server, but not from other WINS replication partners. If these records exist on other WINS replication partner servers, then it is likely that the record will reappear after subsequent replication.

   - **Replicate deletion of the record to other servers (tombstone).** The server takes ownership of the record and changes the status of the record to tombstoned, indicating that the record will not be used. Tombstoning also increments the version ID of the record to replicate to other WINS servers.

6. In the **Delete Record** dialog box, click **OK**.

What Are Dynamic and Offline Compacting?

Compacting is the process of recovering unused space in a WINS database that is occupied by obsolete records

Maintain WINS database integrity by using:

- **Dynamic compacting**. Automatically occurs while the database is in use

- **Offline compacting**. Administrator stops the WINS server and uses the **jetpak** command

---

Definition

Compacting is the process of recovering unused space that deleted records formerly occupied in a database.

Purpose of compacting a WINS database

Recovering unused space in a WINS database helps maintain performance. As WINS client entries become obsolete and are deleted, the size of the WINS database grows larger than the actual space that the database is currently using. The server does not automatically reclaim the space that is used to store obsolete records after the space is freed and no longer in use. Compacting the WINS database recovers the unused space.

Dynamic Jet compaction

In Windows Server 2003, the WINS service performs dynamic Jet compaction of the WINS database while the server is online. This arrangement reduces the need to use Jetpack.exe for offline compaction. Therefore, manually compacting the database might not be as important now as it was in the past for WINS and DHCP servers running Windows NT Server versions earlier than Windows NT 4.0. However, if necessary, you can also stop the WINS service and compact a WINS database manually.

Note   WINS uses the Jet database format for storing its data. Jet produces J<*n*>.log and other files in the *%systemroot%*\System32\Wins.

Dynamic vs. offline compaction

Although dynamic compacting greatly reduces the need for offline compaction, offline compaction reclaims the space more efficiently and should be performed periodically in all cases.

How frequently you manually compact the WINS database depends on your network. For large, busy networks with 1,000 or more WINS clients, you should compact offline each month. Smaller networks usually require less frequent manual compaction.

Why check the size of a WINS database?

Checking the file size of Wins.mdb both before and after compaction allows you to measure growth and reduction. This information helps you ascertain the actual benefits to using offline compaction. Based on this information, you can gauge how often to repeat offline compaction to secure measurable gains.

You can monitor any changes to the size of the server database file, Wins.mdb, which is located in the directory *%SystemRoot%*\System32\Wins.

How to Compact a WINS Database

Your instructor will demonstrate how to compact a WINS database offline

Introduction

By default, Windows Server 2003 compacts the WINS database automatically. However, you can manually compact the database offline by using the **jetpack** command.

Note It is recommended that you log on with an account that has non-administrative credentials and use the **Run as** command with a user account that has appropriate administrative credentials to perform this task.

Procedure

To compact the WINS database offline:

1. Stop the WINS service by using the **net** command. At a command prompt, type **net stop wins**

2. From the *%Systemroot%*\System32\ directory, run the **jetpack.exe** command-line utility by using the following command syntax at a command prompt:

   jetpack *%Systemroot%***System32\Wins\Wins.mdb** *TemporaryName*.**mdb**
   (where *TemporaryName* is any file name that you assign)

Note This procedure compacts the contents of Wins.mdb in *TemporaryName*.mdb, copies the temporary file to Wins.mdb, and deletes the temporary file.

3. Restart the WINS service by using the **net** command. At a command prompt, type **net start wins**

How Scavenging Works

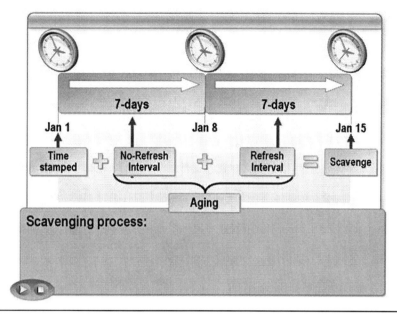

Definition

Scavenging is the process of deleting and removing expired WINS database entries. Scavenging also removes entries that were replicated from a remote WINS server and that were not removed from the local WINS database.

What is the purpose of scavenging?

Scavenging maintains the correct state information in the database by examining each record that the WINS server owns, comparing the record's time stamp to the current time, and then changing the state of those records whose state has expired. For example, scavenging changes a record's state from active to released.

Interval configurations

The scavenging process occurs automatically at intervals that are defined by the relationship between the renewal and extinction interval configurations. You configure the following properties to define this relationship.

Intervals	Description of interval
Renewal interval	The frequency at which a WINS client renews its name registration with the WINS server. The default value is six days.
Extinction interval	The interval between the time when an entry is marked as *released* (no longer registered) and the time when it is marked as *extinct*. The default value is four days.
Extinction timeout	The interval between the time when an entry is marked *extinct* and the time when the entry is scavenged (removed) from the WINS database. The default is the same as the renewal interval, and cannot be less than 24 hours.
Verification interval	The time after which the WINS server will verify that those names that it does not own—those replicated from other WINS servers—are still active. The minimum value is 24 days.

The process of scavenging

Scavenging occurs on a preset schedule as follows:

1. The scavenging timer starts when the server starts up and is equal to half the renewal interval.

> **Note**   The WINS service should not be stopped or restarted before half the renewal interval has passed, or scavenging will not occur.

2. The active names that the WINS server owns and for which the **Renew interval** has expired are marked as released.

3. Released names that the WINS server owns and for which the **Extinction interval** has expired are marked for deletion.

4. Names marked for deletion for which the **Extinction timeout** has expired are deleted and removed from the database.

5. Names marked for deletion that are replicated from other servers and for which the **Extinction timeout** has expired are deleted and removed from the database.

6. Active names that are replicated from other servers and for which the **Verification interval** has expired are revalidated.

7. Names marked for deletion that are replicated from other servers are removed from the database.

How to Scavenge the WINS Database

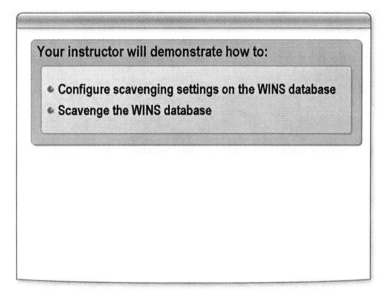

Introduction

When WINS database records are marked as released, the records remain in the database to inform replication partners of the record's status. Therefore, you must periodically remove release entries from each WINS database, in addition to removing entries that were registered at another WINS server but which were never removed. To manually delete these entries, you will initiate scavenging.

Note It is recommended that you log on with an account that has non-administrative credentials and use the **Run as** command with a user account that has appropriate administrative credentials to perform this task.

Procedure for configuring scavenging settings on the WINS database

To configure scavenging settings on the WINS database:

1. In the WINS console, right-click the server that you want to scavenge, and then click **Properties**.

2. In the **Properties** dialog box, on the **Intervals** tab, specify the intervals for each of the following options:

   - **Renewal interval**. The default value is 6 days. This option specifies how often a client renews registration of its name.

   - **Extinction interval**. The default value is 4 days. This option specifies the interval between when a record is marked as released and when it is marked as expired.

   - **Extinction timeout**. The default is the same as the renewal interval, and cannot be less than 24 hours. This option specifies the interval between the time when a record is marked extinct and when it is removed from the database.

   - **Verification interval**. The minimum value is 24 days. This option specifies the interval after which the WINS server must verify that names that are replicated from other WINS servers are still active in WINS.

3. In the **Properties** dialog box, on the **Intervals** tab, if required, click **Restore Defaults** to reset these options to the defaults.

4. In the **Properties** dialog box, click **OK**.

Procedure for scavenging the WINS database

To scavenge the WINS database:

1. In the WINS console, right-click the server that you want to scavenge, and then click **Scavenge Database**.

2. In the WINS message box, click **OK**.

How a WINS Database Is Checked for Consistency

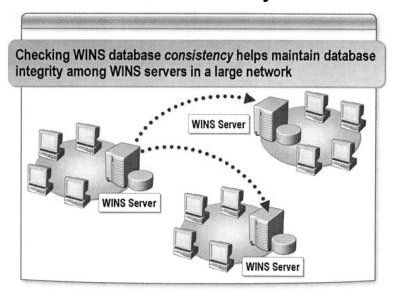

Checking WINS database *consistency* helps maintain database integrity among WINS servers in a large network

Purpose of checking WINS database consistency

Checking WINS database consistency helps maintain database integrity among WINS servers in a large network.

How it works

1. When you initiate consistency checking at the WINS console, all records are verified based on each owner listed in the current server database, including other WINS servers that are indirect (not directly configured) replication partners.

2. The WINS server compares all of its entries with entries on the other WINS servers to verify that its database contains correct entries. All records pulled from remote databases are compared to records in the local database, using the following checks for consistency:

    a. If the record in the local database is identical to the record pulled from the owner database, the record's time stamp is updated to that of the owner database.

    b. If the record in the local database has a lower version ID than the record pulled from the owner database, the pulled record is added to the local database, and the original local record is marked for deletion.

How to Check for Consistency on a WINS Database

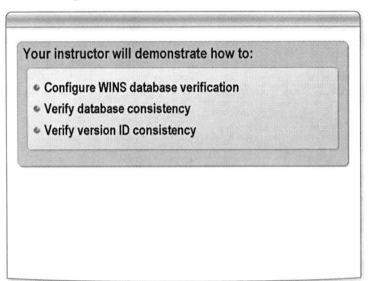

Your instructor will demonstrate how to:
- Configure WINS database verification
- Verify database consistency
- Verify version ID consistency

Introduction

You use the WINS console to periodically check the WINS database for consistency. Because consistency checking is network and resource intensive for the WINS server computer, you should run WINS consistency checks during times of low traffic, such as at night or on weekends.

Note It is recommended that you log on with an account that has non-administrative credentials and use the **Run as** command with a user account that has appropriate administrative credentials to perform this task.

Procedure for configuring WINS database verification

To configure WINS database verification:

1. In the WINS console, click the appropriate WINS server.
2. On the **Action** menu, click **Properties**.
3. On the **Database Verification** tab, select **Verify database consistency every**, and then, in the **hours** field, type a value.
4. On the **Database Verification** tab, in the **Begin verifying at** fields, configure the time that database verification will start.
5. On the **Database Verification** tab, in the **Maximum number of records verified each period** field, type a value.
6. On the **Database Verification** tab, under **Verify against**, select one of the following options:
    - **Owner servers**. This option specifies that records are checked against the server that owns each record.
    - **Randomly selected partners**. This option specifies that records are checked against randomly selected replication partners.
7. In the *Server* **Properties** dialog box, click **OK**.

Procedure for verifying database consistency

To verify database consistency:

1. In the WINS console, right-click the appropriate WINS server, and then click **Verify Database Consistency**.

2. In the WINS warning message box, click **Yes**.

3. In the WINS warning message box, click **OK**.

Procedure for verifying version ID consistency

To verify version ID consistency:

1. In the WINS console, right-click the appropriate WINS server, and then click **Verify Version ID Consistency**.

2. In the WINS warning message box, click **Yes**.

Guidelines for Decommissioning a WINS Server

> **Decommissioning** an installed WINS server is the act of removing it from a network
>
> **Guidelines for decommissioning a WINS server:**
>
> - If you reduce the number of WINS servers in your network, you can reconfigure WINS clients to point to other WINS servers in the network
> - Reconfiguration is necessary only if clients are still using WINS
> - If you eliminate WINS in your network, you can implement DNS as your primary naming service

---

Definition

Decommissioning an installed WINS server is the act of removing it from the network.

Why decommission a WINS server?

You can decommission WINS servers as you reduce or eliminate the need to use WINS in your network. For example, as you upgrade down-level clients and applications, DNS becomes the primary source for name resolution, reducing the need to use WINS.

Guidelines

Follow these guidelines when reducing WINS servers in your network:

- Before decommissioning a WINS server, make sure that any computers that were previously configured to be WINS clients of this server are reconfigured to point to other WINS servers as their primary or secondary WINS servers.

- Reconfiguration is necessary only if these clients are to continue using WINS to register and resolve network names.

Follow this guideline when eliminating WINS servers in your network:

- If you are no longer using WINS to register and resolve NetBIOS names, you should configure DNS as your primary naming service for all Windows-based computers that are active on your network.

Note   For more information about implementing DNS, see Module 5 "Resolving Host Names by Using Domain Name System (DNS)" in Course 2277, *Implementing, Managing, and Maintaining a Microsoft Windows Server 2003 Network Infrastructure: Network Services.*

How to Decommission a WINS Server

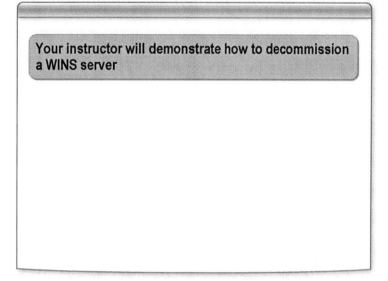

Introduction

You can use the WINS management console to mark all records as released for the owner server that you are decommissioning. This status information is then passed to other WINS servers on your network when they update their local database copies of these records during the next replication.

After the records for this server are marked for deletion on the other WINS servers in your network, they are automatically removed from other WINS server databases when the records have aged to the point of extinction.

Note It is recommended that you log on with an account that has non-administrative credentials and use the **Run as** command with a user account that has appropriate administrative credentials to perform this task.

Procedure

To decommission a WINS server:

1. In the WINS console tree, click **Active Registrations**.
2. On the **Action** menu, click **Delete Owner**.
3. In **Delete Owner**, click the IP address for the WINS server that you want to decommission.

   If the WINS server is not running locally on this computer, it might take some time to load the records for the selected server.
4. Select **Replicate deletion to other WINS servers (tombstone),** and then click **OK**. When prompted to confirm tombstoning, click **Yes**.
5. In the console tree, click **Replication Partners**.
6. On the **Action** menu, click **Replicate Now**.

7. After you have verified that records tombstoned in step 4 have been replicated to other partner servers, stop and remove WINS on the decommissioned server.

Important   Before decommissioning a WINS server, make sure that any computers previously configured to be WINS clients of this server are reconfigured to point to other servers as their primary or secondary WINS servers. Reconfiguration is necessary only if these clients are to continue using WINS to register and resolve network names.

Tombstoning ensures that the WINS servers that are replication partners with the decommissioned WINS server are updated properly so that they delete the records. If tombstone status is not properly replicated, you can manually delete the records at each WINS server on which tombstone replication failed.

Practice: Managing a WINS Database

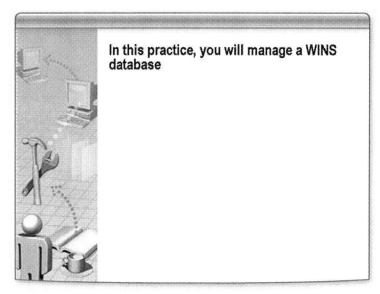

In this practice, you will manage a WINS database

Objective

In this practice, you will manage a WINS database.

Instructions

To complete this practice, refer to the *Implementation Plan Values* document located in the Appendix at the end of your student workbook.

You must be logged on with an account that has non-administrative credentials and use the **Run as** command with a user account that has appropriate administrative credentials to complete the task.

Scenario

Computers in the Lab department rely on the WINS service. You are responsible for performing several routine maintenance tasks on the WINS server.

Practice

▶ **Compact the WINS database offline**

- Complete this task from both student computers

- Temporary WINS database file name: **TEMPWINS.mdb**

▶ **Specify the backup directory for your WINS database**

- Complete this task from both student computers

- Default backup path: **C:\Moc\2277\Labfiles\Lab07**

▶ **Delete WINS records**

- Complete this task from both student computers

- WINS static records: **Glasgow (delete all records for Glasgow)**

- Delete Record: **Delete the record only from this server**

▶ **Manually back up your WINS database**

- Complete this task from both student computers
- Backup folder: **C:\Moc\2277\Labfiles\Lab07**

▶ **Restore your WINS database from the backup directory**

- Complete this task from both student computers
1. Delete all files in the *%Systemroot%*\System32\Wins folder path.
2. Backup folder: **C:\Moc\2277\Labfiles\Lab07**

Lab A: Resolving NetBIOS Names by Using Windows Internet Name Service (WINS)

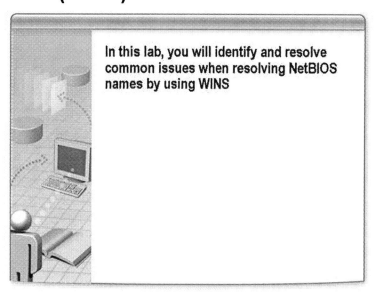

In this lab, you will identify and resolve common issues when resolving NetBIOS names by using WINS

Objectives

In this lab, you will be able to identify and resolve common issues when resolving NetBIOS names by using WINS.

Estimated time to complete this lab: 30 minutes

Exercise 1
Resolving WINS Server Configuration Issues

In this exercise, you will resolve WINS server configuration issues.

Instructions

The correct configuration data for this exercise is located in the *Implementation Plan Values* document located in the Appendix at the end of your student workbook.

You must be logged on with an account that has non-administrative credentials and use the **Run as** command with a user account that has appropriate administrative credentials to complete the tasks. When completing the lab, assume that you will log on with a non-administrative account (example: *ComputerName*User), unless the Specific Instructions in the lab state otherwise.

Scenario

While you were testing your WINS server in the lab, you identified several issues with the WINS configuration and corresponding effects on the WINS clients.

You have set up a lab for new WINS administrators so that they can both experience these configuration issues with WINS and practice resolving them.

In this lab, you will execute a script that reconfigures the WINS server to reflect configuration issues. After running the tests again, you will locate and identify the WINS server configuration errors and implement corrective actions. Finally, you will verify that the WINS server is functioning properly by running the test again both from the server and from the client computers.

Tasks	Specific instructions
Perform the following tasks on both student computers.	
1. Run **C:\MOC\2277\Labfiles \lab07\WINS.vbs** to change the settings of your WINS server to reflect configuration issues.	■ Close the WINS console and, at a command prompt, type **C:\MOC\2277\Labfiles\lab07\WINS.vbs**
2. Configure London as a WINS Push/Pull replication partner, and modify the Push/Pull replication settings.	■ Replication partner: **London** ■ Replication type: **Push/Pull** ■ Use persistent connection for Pull replication: **Enabled** ■ Start time: **1 minute** ■ Replication interval: **5 minutes** ■ Use persistent connection for Push replication: **Enabled** ■ Number of changes in version ID before replication: **25**

Tasks	Specific instructions
3. Restart the WINS service, and verify that the WINS records for London have been replicated by filtering on the record owner London.	▪ Filter records on record owner: **London**
4. Delete the incorrect static mappings for the Glasgow computer.	▪ Delete multiple records: **Delete these records only from this server**
5. Add a static mapping for the Glasgow computer.	▪ In the **New Static Mapping** dialog box, use the following values: • Computer name: **Glasgow** • NetBIOS scope: *Leave this blank* • Type of name: **Unique** • IP address: **192.168.***x***.100**
6. Verify that the WINS records for Glasgow are displayed by filtering on the record name Glasgow.	▪ Filter records matching this name pattern: **Glasgow**

Microsoft®
Training &
            Certification

Module 8: Securing Network Traffic by Using IPSec and Certificates

Contents

Overview

- Implementing IPSec
- Implementing IPSec with Certificates
- Monitoring IPSec

Introduction

As a systems administrator, an understanding of Internet Protocol security (IPSec) will help you effectively secure network traffic. This module introduces you to IPSec and how you can use it to secure traffic in your network. You will also learn how you can configure IPSec to use X..509 certificates to maximize the security of the IPSec authentication process.

Objectives

After completing this module, you will be able to:

- Implement IPSec.
- Implement IPSec with certificates.
- Monitor IPSec.

Lesson: Implementing IPSec

- ● Multimedia: The Role of IPSec in a Network Infrastructure
- ● What Is IPSec?
- ● How IPSec Secures Traffic
- ● What Is an IPSec Security Policy?
- ● How IPSec Policies Work Together
- ● Guidelines for Balancing Security and Performance
- ● How to Assign or Unassign an IPSec Policy on a Computer

Introduction

A significant amount of data that passes over a local area network (LAN) is in a form that could be easily captured and interpreted by a protocol analyzer connected to the network. If any data is captured, an attacker could potentially modify and retransmit the modified data over the network. To secure the data that is transmitted over the network from these types of attacks, you can encrypt network data by using IPSec. IPSec allows you to define the scope of your encryption. For example, you can encrypt all network communication for specific clients or for all clients in a domain.

Lesson objectives

After completing this lesson, you will be able to:

- Describe the role of IPSec in a network infrastructure.

- Explain the purpose of IPSec.

- Describe how IPSec secures traffic in Microsoft® Windows® Server 2003.

- Explain what an IPSec security policy is.

- Describe how IPSec security policies work together.

- Apply guidelines to properly balance security and performance levels.

- Assign or unassign an IPSec policy on a computer.

Multimedia: The Role of IPSec in a Network Infrastructure

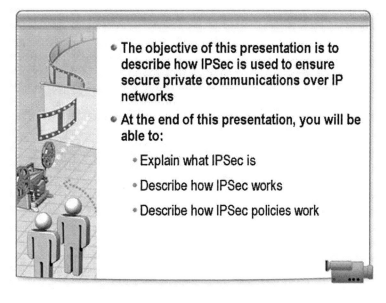

File location

To start *The Role of IPSec in the Network Infrastructure* presentation, open the Web page on the Student Materials compact disc, click **Multimedia**, and then click the title of the presentation.

Objectives

At the end of this presentation, you will be able to:

- Explain what IPSec is.
- Describe how IPSec works.
- Describe how IPSec policies work.

Key Points

- IPSec is a suite of protocols that allows secure, encrypted communication between two computers over an unsecured network.

- IPSec has two goals: to protect IP packets, and to provide a defense against network attacks.

- Configuring IPSec on sending and receiving computers enables the two computers to send secured data to each other.

- IPSec secures network traffic by using encryption, decryption, and data signing.

- You use IPSec policies to configure IPSec. A configuration policy defines the type of traffic that IPSec examines, how that traffic is secured and encrypted, and how IPSec peers are authenticated.

- There are default IPSec policies that you can use, or you can create a custom policy.

- You can configure only one IPSec policy at a time for a single computer.

What Is IPSec?

IPSec is an industry-defined set of standards that verifies, authenticates, and encrypts data at the IP packet level. IPSec is used to provide data security for network transmissions

Benefits of IPSec:

- Mutual authentication before and during communications
- Confidentiality through encryption of IP traffic
- Integrity of IP traffic by rejecting modified traffic
- Prevention against replay attacks

Definition

IPSec is an industry-defined set of standards that verifies, authenticates, and encrypts data at the IP packet level.

Encryption is the process of encoding a message or data through a mathematical key in a manner that hides its substance from anyone who does not possess the mathematical key.

Decryption is the reverse process of encryption. Decrypting data involves applying the appropriate mathematical key to decode the message or data so that it is restored to its original content.

Purpose of IPSec

IPSec is used to provide data security for network transmissions. The administrator sets a series of rules called an *IPSec policy*. These rules contain filters that specify what types of traffic require encryption, digital signing, or both. Then, every packet that the computer sends is assessed to find whether it matches the conditions of the policy. If it matches the policy conditions, it can be either encrypted or signed according to the policy. This process is transparent to the user and applications that initiate the data transmission. Because IPSec is contained inside a standard IP packet, it can travel through a network without requiring special configuration on the devices in between the two hosts. IPSec cannot encrypt some types of traffic, such as broadcasts, multicasts, and Kerberos protocol packets.

Benefits of IPSec

The major benefit of IPSec is that it provides totally transparent encryption for all protocols from Open Systems Interconnection (OSI) model layer 3 (network layer) and higher.

IPSec provides:

- Mutual authentication before and during communications.

    IPSec forces both parties to identify themselves during the communication process.

- Confidentiality through encryption of IP traffic and digital authentication of packets.

    IPSec has two modes: Encapsulating Security Payload (ESP), which provides encryption by using one of a few different algorithms, and Authentication Header (AH), which signs the traffic but does not encrypt it.

- Integrity of IP traffic by rejecting modified traffic.

    Both ESP and AH verify the integrity of all IP traffic. If a packet has been modified, the digital signature will not match, and the packet will be discarded. ESP encrypts the source and destination addresses as part of the payload.

- Prevention against replay attacks.

    Both ESP and AH use sequence numbers, so that any packets that are captured for later replay would be using numbers out of sequence. Using sequenced numbers ensures that an attacker cannot reuse or replay captured data to establish a session or gain information illegally. Using sequenced numbers also protects against attempts to intercept a message and then use the identical message to illegally gain access to resources, possibly months later.

Example

Because the capturing of confidential information can compromise an organization's success, an organization needs to have reliable network security for sensitive information, such as product data, financial reports, and marketing plans. You can use IPSec to ensure secure and private communications within a network, intranet, or extranet including workstation-to-server and server-to-server communications.

For example, you can assign IPSec policies to computers that connect to servers that hold sensitive data that could be the target of an attacker, such as financial, human resources, or strategic planning data. An IPSec policy protects your data against external attacks, keeping it secure and maintaining client integrity.

How IPSec Secures Traffic

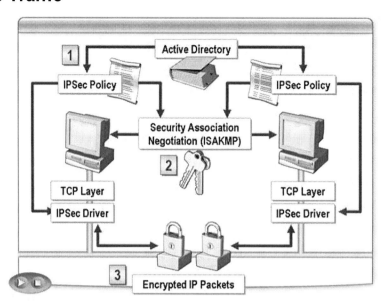

How IPSec works

IPSec configuration is set through either a local policy or a group policy in the Active Directory® directory service:

1. *IPSec policies are delivered to all targeted computers.* The policy tells the IPSec driver how to behave and defines the security associations that can be established. Security associations govern what encryption protocols are used for what types of traffic and what authentication methods are negotiated.

2. *The security association is negotiated.* The Internet Key Exchange (IKE) module negotiates the security association. IKE is a combination of two protocols: the Internet Security Association and Key Management Protocol (ISAKMP) and the Oakley Key Determination Protocol. If one client requires certificates for authentication and the other client requires the Kerberos protocol, IKE will not be able to establish a security association between these two computers. If you look at the packets in Network Monitor, you will see ISAKMP packets, but you will not see any subsequent AH or ESP packets.

3. *IP packets are encrypted.* After the security association is established, the IPSec driver monitors all IP traffic, compares traffic to the defined filters, and if directed to, either encrypts or signs the traffic.

Definition

Internet Key Exchange (IKE) is a protocol that establishes the security association and shared keys necessary for two parties to communicate by using IPSec.

What Is an IPSec Security Policy?

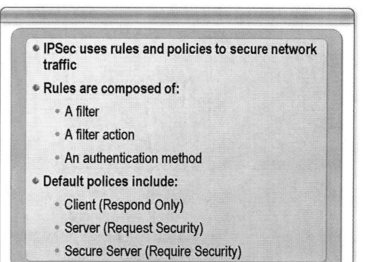

- IPSec uses rules and policies to secure network traffic
- Rules are composed of:
  - A filter
  - A filter action
  - An authentication method
- Default polices include:
  - Client (Respond Only)
  - Server (Request Security)
  - Secure Server (Require Security)

Definition

An *IPSec Security policy* consists of one or more rules that determine IPSec behavior.

IPSec Security policy rules

You implement IPSec by setting a policy. Each policy can contain several rules, but you can only assign a single policy at any one time on any computer. You must combine all desired rules into a single policy. Each rule is composed of:

- *A filter.* The filter tells the policy what type of traffic to apply the filter action to. For example, you can have a filter that identifies only Hypertext Transfer Protocol (HTTP) traffic or File Transfer Protocol (FTP) traffic.

- *A filter action.* The filter action tells the policy what to do if the traffic matches the filter. For example, you can tell IPSec to block all FTP traffic but require encryption for all HTTP traffic. The filter action can also specify which hashing and encryption algorithms the policy should use.

- *An authentication method.* There are three possible authentication methods: certificates, the Kerberos protocol, and a preshared key. Each rule can specify multiple authentication methods.

Default policies

In Windows 2000 and later, there are three policies configured by default:

- *Client (Respond only).* If a computer asks the client to use IPSec, it will respond with IPSec. The Client (Respond Only) policy will never initiate IPSec on its own. This policy has one rule, which is called the Default Response rule. This rule allows the host to respond to a request for an ESP as long as both hosts are in trusted Active Directory domains. ESP is an IPSec mode that provides confidentiality in addition to authentication, integrity, and anti-replay.

- *Server (Request Security).* You can use this policy on both servers and clients. This policy always tries to use IPSec but can go back to unsecured communications if a client is not configured with an IPSec policy. The Request Security policy has three rules; the first rule is the Default Response rule previously described. The second rule permits Internet Control Message Protocol (ICMP) traffic. ICMP is a maintenance protocol in the Transmission Control Protocol/Internet Protocol (TCP/IP) suite that reports errors and allows simple connectivity. The **ping** command uses ICMP to perform TCP/IP troubleshooting. Although ICMP is a good diagnostic utility, you may want to disable it in a highly secure network because there are several known attacks against ICMP. The third rule requests ESP for all IP traffic.

- *Secure Server (Require Security).* You can use this policy on both servers and clients. If this policy is assigned, the computer can only communicate over IPSec and will never go back to unsecured communications. This policy also has three rules. The first two, the Default Response rule and the Permit ICMP rule, are previously described. The difference in the Secure Server (Require Security) policy is that all traffic must be encrypted with ESP or else the server will not communicate. The ICMP rule overrides the rule to require security for all other IP traffic.

Note For more information about the default IPSec policies, see the Configuring Local IPSec Policies topic on the TechNet page of the Microsoft Web site at http://www.microsoft.com/technet/treeview/default.asp?url=/technet/prodtechnol/winxppro/reskit/prcc_tcp_bhzb.asp

---

How IPSec Policies Work Together

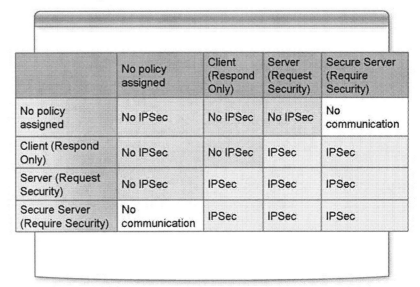

	No policy assigned	Client (Respond Only)	Server (Request Security)	Secure Server (Require Security)
No policy assigned	No IPSec	No IPSec	No IPSec	No communication
Client (Respond Only)	No IPSec	No IPSec	IPSec	IPSec
Server (Request Security)	No IPSec	IPSec	IPSec	IPSec
Secure Server (Require Security)	No communication	IPSec	IPSec	IPSec

Negotiating a security association

You should never consider policies individually. Both computers that are negotiating a security association must have complementary policies. The table in the slide shows the outcomes when default policies work with each other. If two hosts can negotiate a compatible security association, communication can occur by using IPSec. If the two hosts have incompatible policies they may return to unsecured communications or be unable to communicate.

Examples of how policies work together

The table in the slide only applies to the default policies with the default rules. If you add a rule that says computer A requests an ESP for HTTP and computer B requires an AH for HTTP, then the computers will not be able to negotiate a security association.

Kerberos authentication is the default setting for all three default policies. Kerberos protocol works for computers in the same Active Directory forest, but if a computer is not a member of the forest, the computers cannot negotiate authentication. Also, if computer B is modified to use only certificates for authentication for all IP traffic, no security association will be established. It is possible to change computer B to require either the Kerberos protocol or certificates. As long as one authentication method matches, authentication can occur.

The default policies are provided as examples. If you set the Secure Server (Require Security) policy, then that computer will not be able to communicate with any computer that does not have IPSec enabled. For example, requesting to perform a Domain Name System (DNS) lookup to a DNS server without IPSec, will fail. If the computer needs to access a server that runs Microsoft SQL Server™ without IPSec, the operation will fail. Alternatively, if you set the Server (Request Security) policy, the computer will fall back to unsecured communications with any computer that does not have a policy in place. Actual IPSec policies should be designed so that they secure the traffic that needs to be secured, while allowing basic communication to occur.

Guidelines for Balancing Security and Performance

Properly balancing minimal, standard, and high security levels requires:

- Assessing the risk and determining the appropriate level of security

- Identifying valuable information

- Determining how the policies can best be implemented

- Ensuring that management and technology requirements are in place

- Providing all users with both secure and efficient access

How to balance security and performance

IPSec protects data so that an attacker finds it extremely difficult or impossible to interpret it. The strength of the security levels that are specified in your IPSec policy structure determines the level of provided protection. However, when you implement IPSec, you need to find a balance between making information easily available to the largest number of users while protecting sensitive information from unauthorized access.

Finding the proper balance requires:

- Assessing the risk and determining the appropriate level of security for your organization.

- Identifying valuable information.

- Determining how the policies can best be implemented within the existing organization.

- Ensuring that management and technology requirements are in place.

- Providing all users with both secure and efficient access to the appropriate resources according to their needs.

Security levels

Security needs can vary widely, depending on an organization's policies and infrastructures. Consider the following security levels as a general basis for planning your IPSec deployment:

- *Minimal security.* Computers do not exchange sensitive data. IPSec is not active by default. No administrative action to disable IPSec is required.

- *Standard security.* Computers, especially file servers, are used to store valuable data. Security must be balanced so it does not become a barrier to users trying to perform their tasks. Microsoft Windows 2000, Windows XP, and the Windows Server 2003 family provide default IPSec policies that secure data but do not necessarily require the highest level of security: Client (Respond Only) and Server (Request Security). These, or similar custom policies, optimize efficiency without compromising security.

- *High security.* Computers that contain highly sensitive data are at risk for data theft, accidental or malicious disruption of the system (especially in remote dial-up scenarios), or any public network communications. Secure Server (Require Security), a default policy, requires IPSec protection for all traffic being sent or received (except initial inbound communication). The Secure Server (Require Security) policy includes stronger security methods. Unsecured communication with a non-IPSec-aware computer is not allowed.

How to Assign or Unassign an IPSec Policy on a Computer

> **Your instructor will demonstrate how to:**
>
> * Add an IP Security Management Console and then assign or unassign an IPSec policy for a local computer policy
> * Assign or unassign an IPSec policy for an Active Directory-based Group Policy

Introduction

You can create and modify IPSec policy by using the IP Security Policies snap-in that is available in Microsoft Management Console (MMC). The snap-in can manage the policy centrally for Active Directory clients, locally on the computer on which you are running the snap-in, or remotely for a computer or a domain. You can save the customized console so that it is available to use in the future.

Note It is recommended that you log on with an account that has non-administrative credentials and use the **Run as** command with a user account that has the appropriate administrative credentials to perform this task.

Procedure for assigning or unassigning an IPSec policy for a local computer policy

To add an IP Security Management Console and then assign or unassign an IPSec policy for a local computer policy:

1. Log on with a non-administrative user account.
2. Click **Start**, click **Run**, type **MMC**, and then click **OK**.
3. In MMC, click **File**, click **Add/Remove Snap-in**, and then click **Add**.
4. Click **IP Security Policy Management**, and then click **Add**.
5. On the **Select Computer or Domain** page, verify that **Local computer** is selected, and then click **Finish**.
6. In the **Add Standalone Snap-in** dialog box, click **Close**, and then click **OK**.
7. Save the console as **IPSec** to the desktop, and then close the IPSec console.
8. On the desktop, right-click **IPSec**, and then select **Run as**.
9. In the **Run As** dialog box, select the option **The following user**, and then type a user account and password that has the appropriate permissions to complete the task, and click **OK**.

10. In the console tree, click **IP Security Policies on Local Computer**.

11. In the details pane, click the IPSec policy that you want to assign or unassign, and then do one of the following:

- To assign the policy, in the details pane, right-click the appropriate policy, and then click **Assign**.

- To unassign the policy, in the details, pane right-click the appropriate policy, and then click **Un-assign**.

Procedure for assigning or unassigning an IPSec policy for Active Directory-based Group Policy

To assign or unassign an IPSec policy for an Active Directory-based Group Policy:

1. Open Active Directory Users and Computers.

2. In the console tree, right-click the domain or organizational unit for which you want to set Group Policy.

3. Click **Properties**, and then click the **Group Policy** tab.

4. Click **Edit** to open the Group Policy object that you want to edit. Or click **New** to create a new Group Policy object, and then click **Edit**.

5. In the Group Policy Object Editor console, expand **Computer Configuration**, expand **Windows Settings**, expand **Security Settings**, and then click **IP Security Policies on Active Directory**.

6. In the details pane, click the IPSec policy that you want to assign or unassign, and then do one of the following:

- To assign the policy, in the details pane, right-click the appropriate policy, and then click **Assign**.

- To unassign the policy, in the details pane, right-click the appropriate policy, and then click **Un-assign**.

Practice: Implementing IPSec

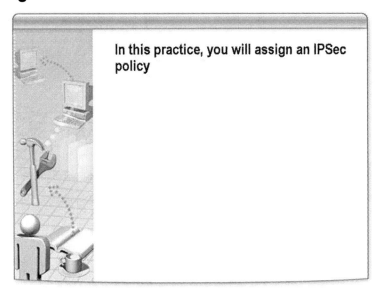

Introduction

In this practice, you will assign an IPSec policy.

Instructions

To complete this practice, refer to the *Implementation Plan Values* document, located in the Appendix at the end of your student workbook.

Scenario

Your organization is considering implementing IPSec to secure remote access clients. Before the organization implements IPSec to live clients, the architects have asked you, as the network administrator, to test how IPSec works in the test lab.

You will configure IPSec on two computers: a client and a server. Configuring IPSec twice allows you to become familiar with assigning IPSec policies to computers. You will eventually use Group Policy to assign the IPSec policy to the remote access clients. However, while practicing in the test lab, you will assign IPSec policies to individual computers.

Practice

▶ **Share the C:\Moc folder on your computer**

- Complete this task from both student computers.

- Administrative tool: **Computer Management**

- User name: **NWtraders***ComputerName***Admin** (where *ComputerName* is the name of your computer)

- Password: **P@ssw0rd**

- Folder to share: **C:\Moc**

- Access permissions: **Everyone: Read**

▶ **Verify you can connect to your partner's Moc share**

Note Wait for your partner to complete the preceding task before starting the next task. Complete the next task from both student computers.

- Complete this task from both student computers.

1. In the **Run** dialog box, type *ComputerName***Moc** (where *ComputerName* is the name of your partner's computer), and then click **OK**.

2. Verify that you can view the contents of the *ComputerName***Moc** (where *ComputerName* is the name of your partner's computer) folder.

3. Close the Moc on *ComputerName* window.

▶ **Assign an IPSec policy**

- Complete this task from the lower number student computer.

- User name: **NWtraders***ComputerName***Admin** (where *ComputerName* is the name of your computer)

- Password: **P@ssw0rd**

- IP security policy: **Secure Server (Require Security)**

▶ **Verify you cannot connect to your partner's Moc share**

- Complete this task from the higher number student computer.

1. In the **Run** dialog box, type *ComputerName***Moc** (where *ComputerName* is the name of your partner's computer), and then click **OK**.

2. Close the Windows Explorer message box.

▶ **Unassign an IPSec policy**

- Complete this task from the lower number student computer.

- User name: **NWtraders***ComputerName***Admin** (where *ComputerName* is the name of your computer)

- Password: **P@ssw0rd**

- IP security policy: **Secure Server (Require Security)**

▶ **Verify you can connect to your partner's Moc share**

- Complete this task from the higher number student computer.

1. In the **Run** dialog box, type *ComputerName***Moc** (where *ComputerName* is the name of your partner's computer), and then click **OK**.

2. Verify that you can view the contents of the *ComputerName***Moc** (where *ComputerName* is the name of your partner's computer) folder.

3. Close the Moc on *ComputerName* window.

▶ **Assign an IPSec policy**

- Complete this task from both student computers.

- User name: **NWtraders***ComputerName***Admin** (where *ComputerName* is the name of your computer)

- Password: **P@ssw0rd**

- IP security policy: **Server (Request Security)**

▶ **Verify you can connect to your partner's Moc share**

- Complete this task from both student computers.

1. In the **Run** dialog box, type *ComputerName***Moc** (where *ComputerName* is the name of your partners' computer), and then click **OK**.

2. Verify that you can view the contents of the *ComputerName***Moc** (where *ComputerName* is the name of your partner's computer) folder.

3. Close the Moc on *ComputerName* window.

Lesson: Implementing IPSec with Certificates

- What Is a Certificate?
- Common Uses of Certificates
- Why Use Certificates with IPSec to Secure Network Traffic?
- Multimedia: Certificate Enrollment
- How to Configure IPSec to Use a Certificate

Introduction

IPSec relies on mutual authentication to provide secure communications. Because IPSec is an industry standard, this authentication may need to occur between systems that do not share a centralized Kerberos protocol authentication infrastructure. X.509 certificates provide another means of authentication for IPSec that is standards-based and can be used if a trusted Public Key Infrastructure (PKI) is in place. This lesson describes how you can use public key certificates for authentication to provide trust and secure communication in your network.

Lesson objectives

After completing this lesson, you will be able to:

- Explain the purpose of a certificate.
- Define the common uses for certificates.
- Explain why you would use certificates with IPSec to secure network traffic.
- Describe the process of certificate enrollment.
- Configure IPSec to use certificates.

What Is a Certificate?

Certificates are an electronic credential that authenticates a user on the Internet and intranets

Certificates:

- Securely bind a public key to the entity that holds the corresponding private key
- Are digitally signed by the issuing certificate authority (CA)
- Verify the identity of a user, computer, or service that presents the certificate
- Contain details about the issuer and the subject

Definition

An *X.509 certificate*, also sometimes called a digital certificate, is an electronic credential that is commonly used for authentication and secure exchange of information on open networks, such as the Internet, extranets, and intranets.

A certificate securely binds a public key to the entity that holds the corresponding private key. For example, you can encrypt data for a recipient with their public key, trusting that only the recipient has the private key that is required to decrypt the data.

A *certificate issuer*, called a certification authority (CA), digitally signs certificates. The certificates can be issued for a user, a computer, or a service, such as IPSec.

Benefit of certificates

One of the main benefits of certificates is that hosts no longer have to maintain a set of passwords for individual subjects who need to be authenticated as a prerequisite to access. Instead, the host merely establishes trust in a CA that issues certificates.

Purpose of a certification authority

A CA is responsible for authenticating and validating the keys for encryption, decryption, and authentication. After a CA verifies the identity of a key holder, the CA distributes the public keys by issuing X.509 certificates. X.509 certificates contain the public key and a set of attributes. A CA can issue certificates for specific functions, such as secure e-mail or IPSec, in addition to general purpose certificates.

Certificate contents

A certificate contains the following information:

- The public cryptographic key from the certificate subject's public and private key pair.
- Information about the subject that requested the certificate.
- The user or computer's X.500 distinguished name.
- The e-mail address of the certificate's owner.
- Details about the CA.
- Expiration dates.
- A hash of the certificate contents to ensure authenticity (digital signature).

Example of using a certificate

A systems administrator can configure Group Policy to automatically install a certificate on a computer that is a member of a domain. The certificate can be used to provide authentication between two computers that are configured with IPSec. Certificates must also be installed on Web servers that will provide secure connections of Secure Sockets Layer (SSL) for users.

Common Uses of Certificates

Uses of certificates

Many organizations install their own CAs and issue certificates to internal devices, services, and employees to create a more secure computing environment. Therefore, an employee of an organization may have several certificates issued by more than one CA.

The following table describes some of the ways in which you can use certificates.

Uses for certificates	Description
Digital signatures	Use the public key in a certificate to verify that data has been signed with the corresponding private key.
Encrypting File System (EFS)	Uses the public key in a certificate to encrypt file encryption keys.
Internet authentication	Verifies the identity of a Web server for Web clients. Web servers can also use certificates to verify the identity of Web clients.
IP security (IPSec)	Verifies the identity of computers and encrypts data as it is transmitted across the network.
Secure e-mail	Verifies signed e-mail messages and decrypts e-mail messages.
Smart card log on	Verifies the identity of a user in a smart card log on.
Software code signing	Verifies the identity of a software publisher.

Why Use Certificates with IPSec to Secure Network Traffic?

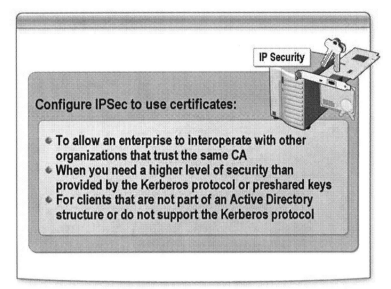

Purpose of certificates	Using certificates from a trusted CA as the method of authentication between two IPSec hosts allows an enterprise to interoperate with other organizations that trust the same CA. You can also use certificates to enable Windows Routing and Remote Access service to securely communicate over the Internet with a third-party router that supports IPSec. However, because certificates are more complex than either preshared keys or the Kerberos protocol, they require more administrative planning. Certificates are just one component of a PKI solution. Although PKI requires planning and management resources, it crosses enterprise borders to allow the bond of identity and trust to be established between organizations.
Kerberos protocol and preshared keys	The other two methods for authentication between two IPSec hosts include:

■ *Kerberos protocol*. For traffic between computers in the same forest, using the default Kerberos protocol authentication is the simplest authentication for IPSec and does not require any configuration. The Kerberos protocol is a component of Active Directory, so it is part of an enterprise domain structure. However, for clients that do not support the Kerberos protocol or for clients that are not part of the Active Directory structure, using some another means of authentication is required, such as either a preshared key or X.509 certificate.

■ *Preshared keys*. A preshared key is a large random text string that is used as a password between two IPSec hosts. Preshared keys are not considered as secure as the Kerberos protocol or certificates because they are stored in clear text in the IPSec policy. An attacker could gain administrative access to the policy and then obtain the preshared key. Preshared keys also do not scale well to multiple computer configurations.

Note For more information about using certificates, see Course 2810 *Fundamentals of Network Security*.

Multimedia: Certificate Enrollment

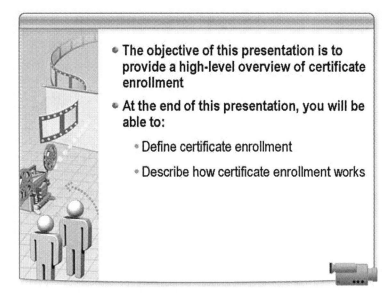

File location

To start the *Certificate Enrollment* presentation, open the Web page on the Student Materials compact disc, click **Multimedia**, and then click the title of the presentation.

Objectives

At the end of this presentation, you will be able to:

- Define certificate enrollment.
- Describe how certificate enrollment works.

Key points

- Certificate enrollment is the process of requesting and installing certificates for a user, computer, or service.
- The policies and processes of the CA define how you request and receive certificates.
- A stand-alone CA supports only Web-based enrollment, and an Enterprise CA supports both Web-based and MMC enrollment.
- A Cryptographic Service Provider (CSP) installed on the computer generates the private and public keys, also known as a key pair, for the certificate request. A CSP can be software-based or hardware-based.
- The public key is sent to the CA along with the certificate requestor information.
- The software CSP encrypts and secures the private key in a location known as the public store, or pstore.

How to Configure IPSec to Use a Certificate

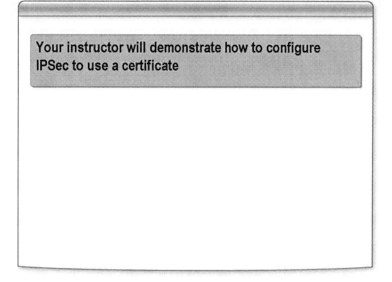

Introduction

If you choose to use a certificate for authentication, you must select a CA (most commonly the root CA for your installed computer certificate). You cannot leave this field blank.

Note It is recommended that you log on with an account that has non-administrative credentials and use the **Run as** command with a user account that has the appropriate administrative credentials to perform this task.

Procedure

To configure IPSec to use a certificate:

1. Create an IP Security Management snap-in containing IP Security policies. Or, open a saved console file containing IP Security policies.

2. Double-click the policy that you want to modify.

3. In the *Policy* **Properties** dialog box, double-click the IPSec Security rule that you want to modify.

4. In the **Edit Rule Properties** dialog box, on the **Authentication Methods** tab, click **Add**. Or, if you are reconfiguring an existing method, click the authentication method, and then click **Edit**.

5. Select **Use a certificate from this certification authority (CA)**, and then click **Browse**.

6. In the **Select Certificate** dialog box, click the appropriate certification authority, and then click **OK**.

7. On the **Authentication Method** tab, click **OK**.

8. In the **Edit Rule Properties** dialog box, click **OK**.

9. In the *Policy* **Properties** dialog box, click **OK**.

Practice: Implementing IPSec with Certificates

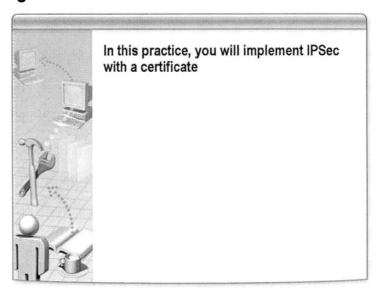

In this practice, you will implement IPSec with a certificate

Objective

In this practice, you will implement IPSec with a certificate.

Instructions

To complete this practice, refer to the *Implementation Plan Values* document, located in the Appendix at the end of your student workbook.

You must be logged on with an account that has non-administrative credentials and use the **Run as** command with a user account that has the appropriate administrative credentials to complete the task.

Scenario

Your organization is successfully using IPSec with the Kerberos protocol. The organization has purchased another company that uses certificates for authentication. To interoperate with the new company, you will need to configure IPSec to use certificates from a CA that both companies trust.

Practice

Important In this practice, the Kerberos protocol is set as the default authentication method. You will need to configure the IPSec policies on both the server and client computers to use certificates as a secondary authentication method. To use certificates as the only authentication method, you would first remove the Kerberos protocol authentication method.

▶ **Configure the Server (Request Security) IPSec policy to use the Kerberos protocol and certificates**

■ Complete this task from both student computers.

■ User name: **NWtraders***ComputerName***Admin** (where *ComputerName* is the name of your computer)

■ Password: **P@ssw0rd**

■ IP Security policy: **Server (Request Security)**

■ IP Security rule: **All IP Traffic**

■ Certificate authority: **Microsoft Root Certificate Authority**

■ Authentication method preference order:

   • The Kerberos protocol

   • Microsoft Root Certificate Authority

▶ **Verify you can connect to your partner's Moc share**

■ Complete this task from both student computers.

1. In the **Run** dialog box, type *ComputerName***Moc** (where *ComputerName* is the name of your partner's computer), and then click **OK**.

2. Verify that you can view the contents of the *ComputerName***Moc** (where *ComputerName* is the name of your partner's computer) folder.

3. Close the Moc on *ComputerName* window.

Lesson: Monitoring IPSec

- IP Security Monitor
- Guidelines for Monitoring IPSec Policies
- How to Stop and Start the IPSec Services
- How to View IPSec Policy Details

Introduction

Windows Server 2003 provides several different utilities for identifying and resolving common IPSec-related issues. This lesson introduces the IP Security Monitor and explains how you can use it to isolate errors with IPSec configuration settings.

Lesson objectives

After completing this lesson, you will be able to:

- Explain what the IP Security Monitor is.
- Apply guidelines when monitoring IPSec.
- Stop and start the IPSec services.
- View IPSec policy details.

IP Security Monitor

Use the IP Security Monitor to view details about IPSec policies such as:

- **Active IPSec policy details**
  - Name
  - Description
  - Date last modified
  - Store
  - Path
  - Organizational unit and Group Policy object (GPO) name
- **Main mode statistics**
  - Information from the Internet Key Exchange
- **Quick mode statistics**
  - Information about the IPSec driver

What is the IP Security Monitor?

The IP Security Monitor snap-in enables you to view details about active local IPSec policies and domain-assigned policies. You can monitor these details for the local computer and for remote computers. For example, you can display the following information:

- Active IPSec policy details including the name, description, date last modified, store, path, organizational unit, and Group Policy object (GPO) name.

- Main mode and quick mode generic filters, specific filters, statistics, and security associations.

Main mode statistics

Main mode statistics show information from the Internet Key Exchange (IKE).

Quick mode statistics

Quick mode statistics show information about the IPSec driver.

Note   This lesson covers how to view active IPSec policy details. For information about viewing main mode and quick mode statistics, see the Windows Server 2003 Help documentation and the Windows Server 2003 Resource Kit.

Example

You can use the IP Security Monitor to determine whether there is a pattern of authentication or security association failures; a pattern could indicate possible incompatible security policy settings.

Guidelines for Monitoring IPSec Policies

To help isolate the cause of a communication issue:

- Stop the IPSec Policy Agent on the computers and use the ping command to verify communications between them
- Restart the IPSec Policy Agent and use the IP Security Monitor to confirm that a security association is established between the computers, and the policy is in effect
- Use IP Security Policy Management to verify that the policies are assigned to both computers
- Use IP Security Policy Management to review the policies and ensure they are compatible with each other
- Restart the IP Security Monitor to ensure that all changes are applied

Guidelines

Configuration errors and other problems with an IPSec implementation most commonly manifest themselves when two or more computers are unable to communicate with each other. To help isolate the cause of a communication issue, follow these guidelines:

1. Stop the IPSec Policy Agent (IPSec services) on the computers and verify communications between them by using the **ping** command. If there is a communication issue after the policy is stopped, then general network issues are most likely the cause.

Note If there is a valid network connection, you should receive four replies to the **ping** command. Positive replies verify that you can communicate with the destination IP address.

2. Restart the IPSec Policy Agent and use the IP Security Monitor to confirm that a security association is established between the computers. Ensure that the IPSec policy is in effect.

3. Use IP Security Policy Management to verify that the policies are assigned to both computers.

4. Use IP Security Policy Management to review the policies on the computers and ensure that the policies are compatible with each other.

5. Restart the IP Security Monitor to ensure that all changes that you make are applied.

Note For more information about monitoring IPSec, see the Windows Server 2003 Help documentation.

How to Stop and Start the IPSec Services

> **Your instructor will demonstrate how to:**
>
> * Stop and start the IPSec services by using the Windows interface
>
> * Stop and start the IPSec services by using the command prompt

Introduction

You can use the Windows interface and command prompt to stop and start the IPSec services.

Note It is recommended that you log on with an account that has non-administrative credentials and use the **Run as** command with a user account that has the appropriate administrative credentials to perform this task.

Procedure for stopping and starting the IPSec services by using the Windows interface

To stop the IPSec services by using the Windows interface:

1. Open the **Services** console.

2. In the details pane, right-click **IPSec Services**, and then click **Stop**.

To start IPSec services:

1. Open the **Services** console.

2. In the details pane, right-click **IPSec Services**, and then click **Start**.

Procedure for stopping and starting the IPSec services by using the command prompt

To stop and start the IPSec services by using the command prompt:

Note If you have a server running Windows 2000 or Windows Server 2003 and the Routing and Remote Access service, you must use the command prompt to stop and start the IPSec and Routing and Remote Access services in a specific sequence.

1. Stop the Routing and Remote Access service by using the **net stop remoteaccess** command.

2. Stop the IPSec services by using the **net stop policyagent** command.

3. Start the IPSec services by using the **net start policyagent** command.

4. Start the Routing and Remote Access service by using the **net start remoteaccess** command.

How to View IPSec Policy Details

> Your instructor will demonstrate how to:
>
> * View IPSec Active Policy details by using the IPSec Security Monitor
>
> * View IPSec Active Policy Main Mode Security Associations by using the IP Security Monitor

Introduction

You can use the IP Security Monitor to view IPSec policy details.

Note It is recommended that you log on with an account that has non-administrative credentials and use the **Run as** command with a user account that has the appropriate administrative credentials to perform this task.

Procedure for viewing IPSec Active Policy details

To view IPSec Active Policy details by using the IP Security Monitor:

1. Create an MMC console containing the IP Security Monitor snap-in. Or, open a saved console file containing IP Security Monitor.

2. Expand **IP Security Monitor**, expand *ComputerName*, and then click **Active Policy**.

3. In the details pane, view the Active Policy information.

Procedure for viewing IPSec Active Policy Main Mode Security Associations

To view IPSec Active Policy Main Mode Security Associations by using the IP Security Monitor:

1. Create an MMC console containing the IP Security Monitor snap-in. Or, open a saved console file containing IP Security Monitor.

2. Expand **IP Security Monitor**, expand **Main Mode**, and then click **Security Associations**.

3. In the details pane, view the Security Associations information.

Practice: Monitoring IPSec

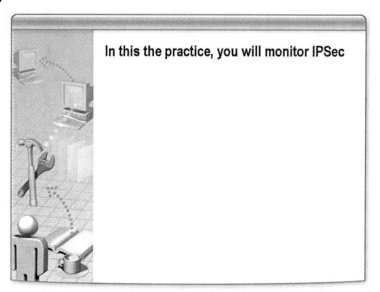

In this the practice, you will monitor IPSec

Objective

In this practice, you will monitor an IPSec policy.

Instructions

To complete this practice, refer to the *Implementation Plan Values* document, located in the Appendix at the end of your student workbook.

Scenario

You have been asked to verify the IPSec policy on the local server. You will view IPSec policy information by using the IPSec Monitor Console.

Practice

▶ **Verify you can connect to your partner's Moc share**

- Complete this task from both student computers.

1. In the **Run** dialog box, type *ComputerName***Moc** (where *ComputerName* is the name of your partner's computer), and then click **OK**.

2. Verify that you can view the contents of the *ComputerName***Moc** (where *ComputerName* is the name of your partners' computer) folder.

3. Leave the Setup folder window open.

▶ **View the IPSec Active Policy details by using IPSec Monitor Console**

- Complete this task from both student computers.

- User name: **NWtraders***ComputerName***Admin** (where *ComputerName* is the name of your computer)

- Password: **P@ssw0rd**

- MMC Snap-in: **IP Security Monitor**

- Computer: *ComputerName* (where *ComputerName* is the name of your partners computer)

▶ **View the information for IPSec Active Policy Main Mode Security Associations by using IPSec Monitor Console**

- Complete this task from both student computers.

- User name: **NWtraders***ComputerName***Admin** (where *ComputerName* is the name of your computer)

- Password: **P@ssw0rd**

- MMC snap-in: **IP Security Monitor**

- Verify that your partner's computer displays in the Security Associations information.

Lab A: Securing Network Traffic

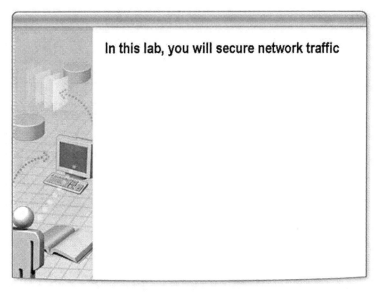

In this lab, you will secure network traffic

Objectives

In this lab, you will secure network traffic.

Estimated time to complete this lab: 30 minutes

Exercise 1
Configuring IPSec

In this exercise, you will configure a server computer and a client computer with IPSec.

Instructions

To complete this lab, refer to the *Implementation Plan Values* document, located in the Appendix at the end of your student workbook.

You must be logged on with an account that has non-administrative credentials and use the **Run as** command with a user account that has the appropriate administrative credentials to complete the tasks. When completing the lab, assume that you will log on with a non-administrative account (example: *ComputerName*User) unless the Specific Instructions in the lab state otherwise.

Scenario

You are testing sensitive data on a server computer and a client computer in your test lab and you need to secure the communication between the two computers. Refer to the following information as you configure IPSec on both computers:

- You do not have a certification authority for the lab.

- When the client computer is in the domain, you will use domain-based authentication.

- When the client computer is not in the domain, you will use shared-key authentication.

- The client computer will need to communicate with other unsecured computers outside of the test lab.

- The server computer needs to be securely accessed.

Tasks	Specific instructions
✋ Perform the following tasks on both student computers.	
Configure the Server (Request Security) IPSec policy by using the Kerberos protocol as the default authentication and preshared-key as the secondary authentication.	▪ IP Security policy: **Server (Request Security)** ▪ IP Security rule: **All IP Traffic** ▪ Preshared key: **2277course** ▪ Authentication methods: First: Kerberos protocol; Second: Preshared key
Verify that you can connect to the Moc share on your partner's computer.	▪ Use the **Run** command. ▪ Close the Moc on *ComputerName* window.

Course Evaluation

Your evaluation of this course will help Microsoft understand the quality of your learning experience.

At a convenient time before the end of the course, please complete a course evaluation, which is available at http://www.CourseSurvey.com.

Microsoft will keep your evaluation strictly confidential and will use your responses to improve your future learning experience.

Microsoft®
Training &
Certification

Module 9: Configuring Network Access

Contents

Overview

- Introduction to a Network Access Infrastructure
- Configuring a VPN Connection
- Configuring a Dial-up Connection
- Configuring a Wireless Connection
- Controlling User Access to a Network
- Centralizing Network Access Authentication and Policy Management by Using IAS

Introduction

This module introduces you to the basic knowledge and skills that are needed to allow remote users to connect to your network. The primary tasks for enabling remote access to your network include configuring a server with Routing and Remote Access service, creating appropriate remote access connections on a network access server, and configuring users' access rights.

Objectives

After completing this module, you will be able to:

- Describe a network access infrastructure.
- Configure a virtual private network (VPN) connection.
- Configure a dial-up connection.
- Configure a wireless connection.
- Control remote user access to a network.
- Centralize authentication and policy management for network access by using Internet Authentication Service (IAS).

Lesson: Introduction to a Network Access Infrastructure

- Multimedia: Introduction to the Network Access Infrastructure
- Components of a Network Access Infrastructure
- Configuration Requirements for a Network Access Server
- What Is a Network Access Client?
- What Are Network Access Authentication and Authorization?
- Available Methods of Authentication

Introduction

To maintain effective communication and connect remote locations, organizations need to set up and manage a secure network access infrastructure. This lesson introduces you to the role of a network access infrastructure, its components, and how the components work together to provide secure access to your network.

Lesson objectives

After completing this lesson, you will be able to:

- Describe how network access servers work together.
- Describe the components of a network access infrastructure.
- Explain the configuration requirements for a network access server.
- Explain what types of clients access a network.
- Explain what network access authentication and authorization are.
- Explain what types of authentication methods are used in a network access infrastructure.

Multimedia: Introduction to the Network Access Infrastructure

* The objective of this presentation is to provide a high-level overview of the network access infrastructure and how network access services work together

* After this presentation, you will be able to:

    * Explain the components of the network access infrastructure

    * Describe how the network access components work together to provide a remote access solution

    * Describe how the remote access process works

File location

To start the *Introduction to the Network Access Infrastructure* presentation, open the Web page on the Student Materials compact disc, click **Multimedia**, and then click the title of the presentation.

Objectives

At the end of this presentation, you will be able to:

■ Explain the components of the network access infrastructure.

■ Describe how the network access components work together to provide a remote access solution.

■ Describe how the remote access process works.

Key points

■ In an enterprise network, there are users that connect to the network by using local area network (LAN) topologies and users that connect by using other access methods.

■ To support users that are not using LAN topologies, you must provide a remote access infrastructure so that remote users can connect to the core network.

■ There are many components and processes involved in providing a remote access solution.

■ As a systems administrator, it is your responsibility to ensure that the network access infrastructure is working and that your remote users are able to access the network.

Components of a Network Access Infrastructure

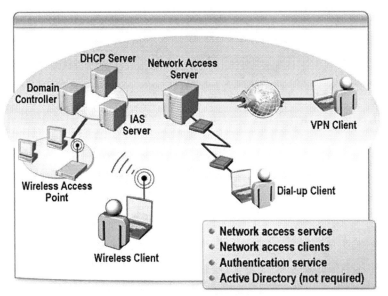

Introduction

To provide a secure network access infrastructure, an administrator needs to have an understanding of the following basic components that make up a network access infrastructure:

- Network access server
- Network access clients
- Authentication service
- Active Directory® directory service

Network access server

Microsoft's Routing and Remote Access service supports nontraditional access to a network. By configuring the Routing and Remote Access service to act as a remote access server, you can connect remote workers to an organization's networks. The network access server for these nontraditional clients authenticates sessions for users and services until the user or network administrator terminates them. Remote users can work as if their computers are physically connected to the network.

Network access clients

A network access server provides network access connectivity for VPN and dial-up clients.

These network access clients can use standard tools to access resources. For example, on a server that is configured with Routing and Remote Access service, remote clients can use Windows Explorer to make drive connections and to connect to printers. Connections are persistent so that the clients do not need to reconnect to network resources during remote sessions.

Authentication service

By providing greater network access, you need to increase the level of security in your network to safeguard against unauthorized access and usage of internal assets. You can help safeguard your network by providing strong authentication to validate identity in addition to providing strong encryption to protect data.

Authentication methods typically use an authentication protocol that is negotiated during the process of establishing a connection. The remote access server (a server configured with the Routing and Remote Access service) handles authentication between the remote access client and the domain controller.

If you have multiple network access servers, you can centralize authentication by using Remote Authentication Dial-In User Service (RADIUS) to authenticate and authorize network access clients. Using RADIUS eliminates the need for each network access server in your network to perform authentication and authorization.

Note For more information about centralizing authentication for network access, see the Centralizing Network Access Authentication and Policy Management by Using IAS lesson in this module.

Active Directory

Active Directory domains contain the user accounts, passwords, and dial-up properties that are required to authenticate user credentials and evaluate both authorization and connection constraints.

After a client is connected to your network, you can control access to resources by various administrative controls on both the client computer and the network access servers. These administrative controls include File and Printer Sharing, Local Group Policy, and Group Policy through the Active Directory service.

Configuration Requirements for a Network Access Server

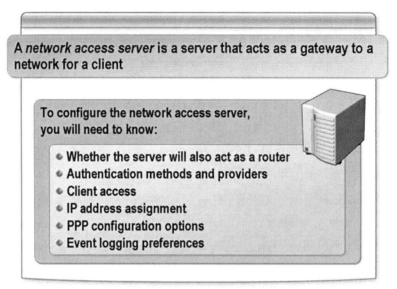

A *network access server* is a server that acts as a gateway to a network for a client

To configure the network access server, you will need to know:

- Whether the server will also act as a router
- Authentication methods and providers
- Client access
- IP address assignment
- PPP configuration options
- Event logging preferences

Definition

A *network access server* is a server that acts as a gateway to a network for a client. In this module, the network access server is a server that is configured with the Routing and Remote Access service and can also be referred to as a remote access server (for dial-up connections) or a VPN server, depending on the type of connection for which the server is configured to negotiate.

Important Only enable the Routing and Remote Access service on a server that will actively be used to provide this service. Having this service running on servers that do not require it or where it will not be used provides another possible avenue for attackers to exploit.

Configuration requirements

When the Routing and Remote Access service is initially enabled on a server, the Routing and Remote Access Wizard appears and provides onscreen instructions to help you properly configure your network access server. The configuration information that you need before you configure your network access server includes:

■ Whether the server will act as a router and/or a remote access server.

■ The authentication methods and providers that you will use.

Note   Authentication is covered in more detail later in this lesson.

■ Whether a remote client is allowed to access only this server or the entire network.

■ How Internet Protocol (IP) addresses are to be assigned to connecting clients.

■ Point-to-Point Protocol (PPP) configuration options.

■ Event logging preferences.

The wizard also requests information about how specific devices that are installed on the server are to be configured. You can configure these devices individually or as a group.

Note   After the wizard is completed, you can change the configuration for these devices by opening the **Ports Properties** dialog box for the appropriate server.

What Is a Network Access Client?

Type of Client	Description
VPN Client	• Connects to a network across a shared or public network • Emulates a point-to-point link on a private network
Dial-up Client	• Connects to a network by using a communications network • Creates a physical connection to a port on a remote access server on a private network • Uses a modem or ISDN adapter to dial in to the remote access server
Wireless Client	• Connects to a network by infrared light and radio frequency technologies • Includes many different types of devices

Introduction

Managing an IT network requires administrators to make network resources available to users who are not directly connected to the LAN. These users may be employees, contractors, partners, suppliers, or customers, and they may need network access through dial-in, the Internet, or wireless connections. As a systems administrator, it is your responsibility to configure secure access for users that have permission to connect to your network and to deny access to users who do not have permission to connect the network. Therefore, you need to know how to configure and secure your network access server for the following methods of access:

- Virtual private networking
- Dial-up remote access
- Wireless access

VPN client

A *VPN client* connects to a network across a shared or public network, such as the Internet, in a manner that emulates a point-to-point link on a private network.

Dial-up client

A *dial-up client* connects to a network by using a communications network, such as the Public Switched Telephone Network (PSTN), to create a physical connection to a port on a remote access server on a private network. This connection can be made by using several different technologies including a modem, an Integrated Services Digital Network (ISDN) adapter, or a Digital Subscriber Line (DSL) adapter to dial in to the remote access server.

Wireless client

A *wireless client* connects to a network by using infrared light or radio frequency technologies that are optimized for short-range connections. Devices that are commonly used for wireless networking include portable computers, hand-held computers, personal digital assistants (PDAs), cellular phones, pen-based computers, and pagers.

What Are Network Access Authentication and Authorization?

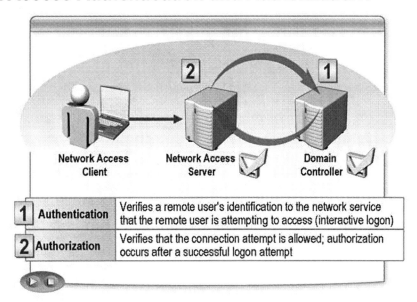

Network access authentication safeguards access to your network

By providing greater network access, organizations need to ensure that their level of security is strong enough to safeguard against unauthorized access and use of internal assets.

For VPN, dial-up, and wireless connections, Microsoft® Windows® Server 2003 implements authentication in two processes: interactive logon and network authorization. Both of these processes must be successfully completed for a user to gain access to network resources.

The difference between authentication and authorization

The distinction between authentication and authorization is important for understanding how connection attempts are either accepted or rejected.

- *Authentication* is the validation of the credentials during a connection attempt. This logon process consists of sending the credentials from the network access client (for example, a name and password) to the network access server in either a plaintext or an encrypted form by using an authentication protocol. The user's identification is then forwarded to a domain account for confirmation.

- *Authorization* is the verification that the connection attempt is allowed. After the remote client is authenticated, it is allowed or denied access based on the account credentials and remote access policies. Authorization can only occur after a successful logon attempt. If the logon fails, the user is denied access.

Acceptance or rejection of connection attempt

For a connection attempt to be accepted, the connection attempt must be both authenticated and authorized. It is possible for the connection attempt to be authenticated by using valid credentials but to not be authorized. When authentication passes but authorization fails, the connection attempt is rejected.

If the network access server is configured as the Windows authentication provider, Windows Server 2003 provides authentication of the user credentials. The dial-up properties of the user account and locally stored remote access policies provide authorization of the connection attempt. If a connection attempt is both authenticated and authorized, the connection attempt is accepted.

Available Methods of Authentication

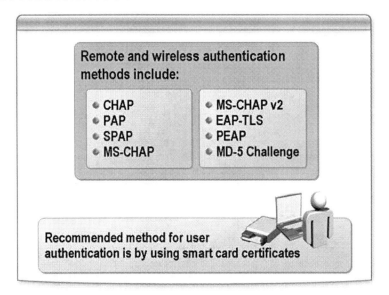

Methods of authentication

The authentication of remote access clients is an important security concern. Authentication methods typically use an authentication protocol that is negotiated during the connection establishment process. The Windows Server 2003 family supports the following authentication methods.

Authentication method	Description
Challenge Handshake Authentication Protocol (CHAP)	• Various vendors of network access servers and clients use CHAP • Routing and Remote Access service supports CHAP
Password Authentication Protocol (PAP)	• Uses plaintext passwords and is the least sophisticated authentication protocol
Shiva Password Authentication Protocol (SPAP)	• A simple encrypted password authentication protocol • Shiva remote access servers supports SPAP
Microsoft Challenge Handshake Authentication Protocol (MS-CHAP)	• Microsoft Windows 95 clients uses MS-CHAP • Supports only Microsoft clients
Microsoft Challenge Handshake Authentication Protocol version 2 (MS-CHAP v2)	• Performs mutual authentication • Microsoft Windows 2000 and later operating systems install MS-CHAP v2 by default as the remote access authentication protocol

(continued)

Authentication method	Description
Extensible Authentication Protocol-Transport Layer Security (EAP-TLS)	• Performs mutual authentication • Requires a smart card certificate infrastructure • Provides the highest level of authentication security
Protected Extensible Authentication Protocol (PEAP)	• Used with 802.1x networks to secure wired and wireless networks • Access is granted based on user identity • Increases the security of wireless network encryption
MD-5 Challenge	• Allows EAP authorization by using standard name/password combinations

EAP authentication

Extensible Authentication Protocol (EAP) provides a framework that allows customized authentication to remote access servers. The specific authentication method is negotiated between the remote access client and the remote access server. Both the remote access client and authenticator must have the same EAP authentication module installed.

Independent vendors can use the EAP application programming interfaces (API) to create new EAP types that could include technologies such as token cards or biometrics.

Recommended method of authentication

Using smart card certificates for user authentication is the strongest form of remote authentication in the Windows Server 2003 family. Smart cards are a tamper-resistant and portable way to provide security solutions for tasks, such as logging on to a Microsoft Windows Server 2003 family domain, connecting to a remote access server, and securing e-mail. Using smart card certificates for user authentication requires a public key infrastructure (PKI).

Note Support for cryptographic smart cards is a key feature of the PKI that Microsoft has integrated into Microsoft Windows XP and the Windows Server 2003 family. For more information about PKI, see Module 5, "Using a PKI to Secure Information" in Course 2810, *Fundamentals of Network Security*.

To use smart cards for remote access authentication, you must:

■ Configure remote access on the remote access server.

■ Install a computer certificate on the server computer for remote access.

■ Configure the Smart card or other certificate (TLS) EAP type in remote access policies.

■ Enable smart card authentication on the VPN or dial-up connection on the remote access client.

Lesson: Configuring a VPN Connection

- How a VPN Connection Works
- Components of a VPN Connection
- Encryption Protocols for a VPN Connection
- Configuration Requirements for a VPN Server
- How to Configure a Remote Access Server for a VPN Connection
- How to Configure a Remote Access Client for a VPN Connection
- How to Configure Smart Card Authentication on a Remote Access Server

Introduction

This lesson introduces you to the skills and knowledge that you need to properly configure a VPN connection.

Lesson objectives

After completing this lesson, you will be able to:

- Describe how a VPN connection works.
- Describe the components of a VPN connection.
- Explain what types of encryption protocols are used for a VPN connection.
- Identify configuration requirements for a VPN server.
- Configure a remote access server for a VPN connection.
- Configure a remote access client for a VPN connection.
- Configure smart card authentication for network access.
- Configure a VPN connection.

How a VPN Connection Works

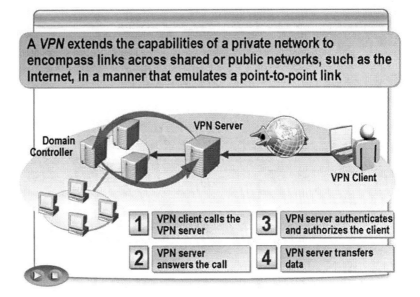

Introduction	Routing and Remote Access service provides VPN services so that users can access corporate networks in a secure manner by encrypting the transmitted data over an insecure transport network, such as the Internet.
What is a VPN?	A *VPN* extends the capabilities of a private network to encompass links across shared or public networks, such as the Internet. With a VPN, you can send encrypted data between two computers across a shared or public network in a manner that emulates a point-to-point link on a private network.

To emulate a point-to-point link, data is encapsulated, or wrapped, with a header that provides routing information, which allows the data to traverse the shared or public network to reach its endpoint. To emulate a private link, the data is encrypted for confidentiality. Packets that are intercepted on the shared or public network cannot be read without the encryption keys. The link in which the private data is encapsulated and encrypted is a VPN connection. The VPN connection is also referred to as a VPN tunnel.

VPN connection process   The process of a VPN connection is described in the following steps:

1. A VPN client makes a VPN connection to a remote access/VPN server that is connected to the Internet. (The VPN server acts as a gateway and is normally configured to provide access to the entire network to which the VPN server is attached.)

2. The VPN server answers the virtual call.

3. The VPN server authenticates the caller and verifies the caller's authorization to connect.

4. The VPN server transfers data between the VPN client and the corporate network.

Advantages of a VPN

VPNs allow users or corporations to connect to remote servers, branch offices, or to other organizations over a public network, while maintaining secure communications. In all of these cases, the secure connection appears to the user as a private network communication—despite the fact that this communication occurs over a public network. Other benefits include:

- *Cost advantages*. VPN does not use a phone line and requires less hardware (your Internet service provider (ISP) maintains the communications hardware).

- *Enhanced security*. Sensitive data is hidden from unauthorized users, but it is accessible to users authorized through the connection. The VPN server enforces authentication and encryption.

- *Network protocol support*. You can remotely run any application that depends on the most common network protocols, such as Transmission Control Protocol/Internet Protocol (TCP/IP).

- *IP address security*. Because information sent over a VPN is encrypted, the addresses that you specify are protected, and the traffic transmitted over the Internet will only have the external IP address visible. No administrative costs are incurred from having to change IP addresses for remote access over the Internet.

Components of a VPN Connection

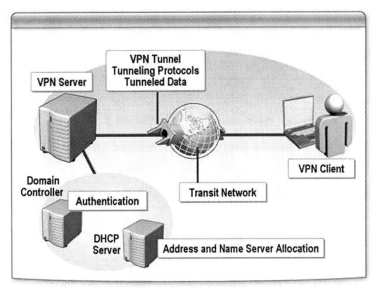

Components of a VPN connection

A VPN connection includes the following components:

- *VPN server.* A computer that accepts VPN connections from VPN clients, such as a server configured with Routing and Remote Access service.

- *VPN client.* A computer that initiates a VPN connection to a VPN server.

- *Transit network.* The shared or public network that the encapsulated data crosses.

- *VPN connection or tunnel.* The portion of the connection in which your data is encrypted and encapsulated.

- *Tunneling protocols.* Protocols that are used to manage tunnels and encapsulate private data (for example, Point-to-Point Tunneling Protocol (PPTP)).

- *Tunneled data.* Data that is usually sent across a private point-to-point link.

- *Authentication.* The identity of the client and the server in a VPN connection are authenticated. To ensure that received data originated from the other end of the connection and was not intercepted and modified, a VPN also authenticates the data that was sent.

- *Address and name server allocation.* The VPN server is responsible for assigning IP addresses, which it does either by using the default protocol, Dynamic Host Configuration Protocol (DHCP), or from a static pool that the administrator creates. The VPN server also allocates Domain Name System (DNS) and Windows Internet Name Service (WINS) server addresses to clients. The name servers allocated are those that service the intranet with which the VPN server interfaces.

Encryption Protocols for a VPN Connection

Category	Description
PPTP	Employs user-level Point-to-Point Protocol (PPP) authentication methods and Microsoft Point-to-Point Encryption (MPPE) for data encryption
L2TP/IPSec	Employs user-level PPP authentication methods over a connection that is encrypted with IPSec
	Recommended authentication method for VPN network access is L2TP/IPSec with certificates

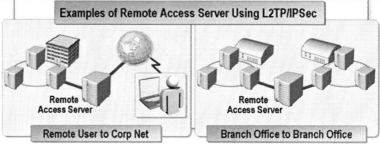

Examples of Remote Access Server Using L2TP/IPSec

Remote Access Server — Remote User to Corp Net

Remote Access Server — Branch Office to Branch Office

Tunneling protocols

There are two types of tunneling (encryption) protocols that the Windows Server 2003 family uses for secure communication:

- *Point-to-Point Tunneling Protocol (PPTP).* Employs user-level PPP authentication methods and Microsoft Point-to-Point Encryption (MPPE) for data encryption.

- *Layer Two Tunneling Protocol with Internet Protocol security (L2TP/IPSec).* Employs user-level PPP authentication methods over a connection that is encrypted with IPSec. IPSec requires host authentication using either the Kerberos protocol, shared secret, or computer-level certificates.

Recommended authentication method

It is recommended that you use L2TP/IPSec with certificates for secure VPN authentication.

By using Internet Protocol security (IPSec) authentication and encryption, data transfer through an L2TP-enabled VPN is as secure as within a single LAN at a corporate network.

The VPN client and the VPN server must support both L2TP and IPSec. Client support for L2TP is built in to the Windows XP remote access client, and the VPN server support for L2TP is built in to the Windows Server 2003 family.

L2TP server support is installed when you install the Routing and Remote Access service. Depending on your choices when running the Routing and Remote Access Server Setup Wizard, L2TP is configured for five or 128 L2TP ports.

Examples of a remote access server using L2TP/IPSec

Two common scenarios for using L2TP/IPSec are:

- Securing communications between remote access clients and the corporate network across the Internet.

- Securing communications between branch offices.

Additional reading

For a comparison between using PPTP or L2TP/IPSec and other information about VPNs, see the white paper "Virtual Private Networking in Windows 2000: An Overview" on the Student Materials compact disc.

Configuration Requirements for a VPN Server

Before adding a remote access / VPN server:

- Identify which network interface connects to the Internet and which network interface connects to your private network
- Identify whether clients receive IP addresses from a DHCP server or the VPN server
- Identify whether to authenticate connection requests by RADIUS or by the VPN server

Introduction

Before you can configure a VPN connection, you must enable Routing and Remote Access service. Enabling the Routing and Remote Access service starts the Routing and Remote Access Setup Wizard with which you will configure your VPN server. If the Routing and Remote Access service was previously enabled, you can configure the VPN network access from the remote access server properties.

Configuration requirements

The following table lists the information that you need to know before you configure a remote access/VPN server.

Before adding a VPN server role	Comments
Identify which network interface connects to the Internet and which network interface connects to your private network.	During configuration, you will be asked to choose which network interface connects to the Internet. If you specify the incorrect interface, your remote access/VPN server will not operate correctly.
Identify whether remote clients will receive IP addresses from a DHCP server on your private network or from the VPN server that you are configuring.	If you have a DHCP server on your private network, the VPN server can lease 10 addresses at a time from the DHCP server and assign those addresses to remote clients. If you do not have a DHCP server on your private network, the VPN server can automatically generate and assign IP addresses to remote clients. If you want the remote access/VPN server to assign IP addresses from a range that you specify, you must determine what that range should be.
Identify whether you want connection requests from VPN clients to be authenticated by a RADIUS server or by the VPN server that you are configuring.	Adding a RADIUS server is useful if you plan to install multiple VPN servers, wireless access points, or other RADIUS clients to your private network. Adding a RADIUS server is discussed in more detail in the following lessons in this module.

How to Configure a Remote Access Server for a VPN Connection

> **Your instructor will demonstrate how to:**
>
> * Register a remote access server in Active Directory
> * Configure a remote access server for a VPN connection
> * Configure the number of ports available on the server

Introduction

Before you can configure a VPN server, you must first add the Remote access / VPN server role. You must be a member of the Administrators group on the local computer to add a server role.

After you add the VPN server role, you use the Configure Your Server Wizard to configure the server for a VPN connection. From Manage Your Server, click **Add or remove a role**, and then select the **Remote access / VPN server** role.

Note   To perform this procedure, you must be a member of the Administrators group on the local computer. As a security best practice, consider using the **Run as** command rather than logging on with administrative credentials. If you have logged on with administrative credentials, you can also open Routing and Remote Access by clicking **Start**, clicking **Control Panel**, double-clicking **Administrative Tools**, and then double-clicking **Routing and Remote Access**.

Guidelines for registering the remote access server in Active Directory

If you are not a domain administrator, ask your domain administrator to add the computer account of the appropriate server to the RAS and IAS Servers security group in the domain of which this server is a member. The domain administrator can add the computer account to the RAS and IAS Servers security group by using Active Directory Users and Computers or with the **netsh ras add registeredserver** command.

For example, to register the Vancouver remote access server in the nwtraders domain, at a command prompt, type **netsh ras add registeredserver nwtraders Vancouver**

Procedure for registering a remote access server in Active Directory

To register a remote access server in Active Directory:

1. Log on with a user account that has permissions to register a remote access server in Active Directory.

2. At a command prompt, type the following:

   netsh ras add registeredserver *DomainName ComputerName* (where *DomainName* is the name of the domain where you are registering the remote access server, and *ComputerName* is the computer name of the remote access server)

Procedure for configuring a remote access server for a VPN connection

To configure a remote access server for a VPN connection:

1. Log on with a non-administrative user account.

2. Click **Start**, and then click **Control Panel**.

3. In Control Panel, open **Administrative Tools**, and then right-click **Manage Your Server** and select **Run as**.

4. In the **Run As** dialog box, select the option **The following user**, and then type a user account and password that has the appropriate permissions to complete the task, and then click **OK**.

5. In the Manage Your Server window, click **Add or remove a role** to access the **Configure Your Server Wizard**.

6. On the **Preliminary Steps** page, click **Next**.

7. On the **Server Role** page, click **Remote access / VPN server**, and then click **Next**.

8. On the **Summary of Selections** page, click **Next**.

9. On the **Welcome to the Routing and Remote Access Setup Wizard** page, click **Next**.

10. On the **Configuration** page, select **Remote access (dial-up or VPN)**, and then click **Next**.

11. On the **Remote Access** page, verify that the option **VPN** is selected, and then click **Next**.

12. On the **VPN Connection** page, click the network interface that connects this computer to the Internet. The network interface that you choose will be configured to receive connections from VPN clients. Any interface that you do not choose will be configured as a connection to your private network.

13. On the **IP Address Assignment** page, select either the **Automatically** or **From a specified range of addresses** option. The default selected option is **Automatically**. This selection configures your server to generate and assign IP addresses to remote clients. Click **Next**.

14. On the **Managing Multiple Remote Access Servers** page, the **No, use Routing and Remote Access to authenticate connection requests** option is selected automatically. Do not change the selection. This selection configures your server to authenticate connection requests locally by using Windows authentication, Windows accounting, and locally stored remote access policies. Click **Next**.

15. On the **Completing the Routing and Remote Access Server Setup Wizard** page, review the summary information. Verify that:

   - VPN clients connect to the correct public interface.

   - VPN clients are assigned IP addresses for the correct network interface.

   - Client connections are accepted and authenticated by using remote access policies for this VPN server.

16. If any of the summary information is incorrect, click **Back**, and then change the information. If the summary information is correct, click **Finish**.

17. A **Routing and Remote Access** message box displays stating "Windows was unable to add this computer to the list of valid remote access servers in the Active Directory. Before you can use this computer as a remote access server, the domain administrator must complete this task." Click **OK**.

18. A **Routing and Remote Access** message box displays stating "To support the relaying of DHCP messages from remote access clients, you must configure the properties of the DHCP Relay Agent with the IP address of your DHCP server." Click **OK**.

19. The Routing and Remote Access service will be started automatically, and the Configure Your Server Wizard will reappear. On the **This Server is Now a Remote Access/VPN Server** page, click **Finish**.

Note   You must ensure that there are enough ports configured to allow enough simultaneous connections to the server.

Procedure for configuring the number of ports available on the server

To configure the number of ports available on the server:

1. Open the Routing and Remote Access console.

2. In the Routing and Remote Access console, expand *ComputerrName*, click **Ports**, and then on the **Action** menu, click **Properties**.

3. In the **Ports Properties** dialog box, select the appropriate port, and then click **Configure**.

4. In the **Configure Device** – *DeviceName* dialog box, type the maximum number of ports in the **Maximum ports** field.

5. Click **OK** to close the **Configure Device** – *DeviceName* dialog box, and then click **OK** to close the **Ports Properties** dialog box.

How to Configure a Remote Access Client for a VPN Connection

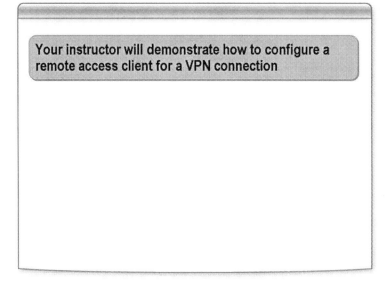

Introduction

You use Network Connections to configure a client for a VPN connection. After you create a new connection, you can copy it to the Network Connections folder and then rename the connection and modify the settings. Copying the new connection to the Network Connections folder is a quick way to create different connections to accommodate multiple modems, ISPs, dialing profiles, and so on.

Note It is recommended that you log on with an account that has non-administrative credentials and use the **Run as** command with a user account that has the appropriate administrative credentials to perform this task.

Procedure

To configure a remote access client for a VPN connection:

1. Click **Start**, and then click **Control Panel**.

2. In Control Panel, click **Network Connections**.

3. In Network Connections, double-click **New Connection Wizard**.

4. On the **Welcome to the New Network Connection Wizard** page, click **Next**.

5. On the **Network Connection Type** page, select **Connect to the network at my workplace**, and then click **Next**.

6. On the **Network Connection** page, select **Virtual Private Network connection**, and then click **Next**.

7. On the **Connection Name** page, type the appropriate name of the connection (typically the name of your organization), and then click **Next**.

8. On the **VPN Server Selection** page, type the host name (for example Microsoft.com) of the VPN server that you are connecting to or the IP address of the VPN server to which you are connecting, and then click **Next**.

9. On the **Connection Availability** page, if you have administrative permissions on the local computer, you can select **Anyone's use** or **My use only**. If you are logged on with a non-administrative account, then you can only select the option **My use only**. Click **Next**.

10. On the **Completing the New Connection Wizard** page, click **Finish**.

How to Configure Smart Card Authentication on a Remote Access Server

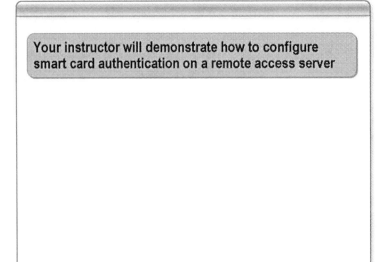

Your instructor will demonstrate how to configure smart card authentication on a remote access server

Introduction

The use of smart cards for user authentication is the strongest form of authentication in the Windows Server 2003 family. For remote access connections, you must use the EAP with the Smart card or other certificate (TLS) EAP type, also known as EAP-TLS.

Procedure

To configure smart card authentication on a remote access server:

1. Open the Routing and Remote Access console.

2. Right-click the name of the remote access server, and then click **Properties**.

3. On the **Security** tab, click **Authentication Methods**.

4. In the **Authentication Methods** dialog box, verify that the **Extensible authentication protocol (EAP)** check box is selected, and then click **OK** twice.

5. Expand your remote access server, and then click **Remote Access Policies**.

6. In the details pane, right-click the remote access policy that your remote access clients with smart cards will use, click **Properties**, and then click **Edit Profile**.

7. On the **Authentication** tab, click **EAP Methods**.

8. In the **Select EAP Providers** pane, if the EAP type you require does not display, click **Add**.

9. In the **Add EAP** dialog box, click **Smart card or other certificate** or click **Protected EAP (PEAP)**, and then click **OK**.

10. If the smart card EAP method that you added requires a certificate, select the method, click **Edit**, choose a certificate, and then click **OK**.

11. Click **OK** to save the settings of the profile, and then click **OK** again to save the settings of the policy.

Practice: Configuring a VPN Connection

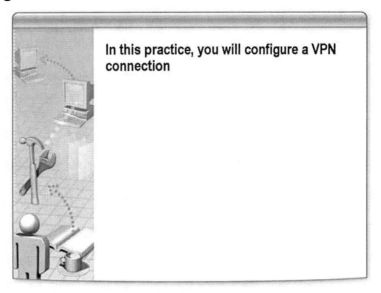

Objective

In this practice, you will configure a VPN connection.

Instructions

To complete this practice, refer to the *Implementation Plan Values* document, located in the Appendix at the end of your student workbook.

It is recommended that you log on with an account that has non-administrative credentials and use the **Run as** command with a user account that has the appropriate administrative credentials to perform this task.

Important Because your server is already configured as a Routing and Remote Access router, you will not use the Routing and Remote Access Wizard to configure it as a VPN server. You will configure the server to support VPN connections by using the previously installed Routing and Remote Access service. By configuring your server as a LAN router and a remote access server, you can enable VPN client connections in addition to routing these clients to the network.

Scenario

Some test engineers from your Lab department want to work remotely from home. The test engineers have Internet connectivity at home. The systems engineer decided to support these remote users and asked you to configure VPN support on a remote access server. You will also configure a client computer for VPN connectivity so that you can verify that there is remote access to the network.

Practice

▶ **Configure a remote access server for a VPN connection**

■ Complete this task from both student computers.

■ User name: **nwtraders*ComputerName*Admin**

■ Password: **P@ssw0rd**

■ Server Role: **Remote access/VPN server**

■ Configuration: **Remote access (dial-up VPN)**

■ Remote access: **VPN**

■ VPN connection interface: **Partner Network Connection**

■ IP address assignment: **From a specified range of addresses**

■ Address range assignment: **10.*x*.0.10** (where x is your student number)

■ Number of addresses: **5**

■ Manage multiple remote access servers: **No, use Routing Remote Access to authenticate connection requests**

▶ **Register the remote access server in Active Directory**

■ Complete this task from both student computers.

■ User name: nwtraders\Administrator

■ Password: P@ssw0rd

■ Administrative tool: netsh

▶ **Configure a remote access client for VPN connectivity**

■ Complete this task from both student computers.

■ Network connection type: Connect to the network at my workplace

■ Network connection: Virtual Private Network connection

■ Connection name: VPN *ComputerName* (where *ComputerName* is the name of your partner's computer)

■ VPN server selection: the IP address of the Partner Network Connection interface of your partner's computer

■ Shortcut on desktop: Yes

■ In the VPN *ComputerName* dialog box, click Cancel.

Note   You need to complete the remaining practices before you can connect to the VPN server.

Lesson: Configuring a Dial-up Connection

- How Dial-up Network Access Works
- Components of a Dial-up Connection
- Authentication Methods for a Dial-up Connection
- Configuration Requirements for a Remote Access Server
- How to Configure a Remote Access Server for a Dial-up Connection
- How to Configure a Remote Access Client for a Dial-up Connection

Introduction

This lesson introduces you to the skills and knowledge that you need to properly configure a dial-up connection.

Lesson objectives

After completing this lesson, you will be able to:

- Describe how dial-up network access works.
- Describe the components of a dial-up connection.
- Explain what types of authentication methods are used for a dial-up connection.
- Identify configuration requirements for a remote access server.
- Configure a remote access server for a dial-up connection.
- Configure a remote access client for a dial-up connection.

How Dial-up Network Access Works

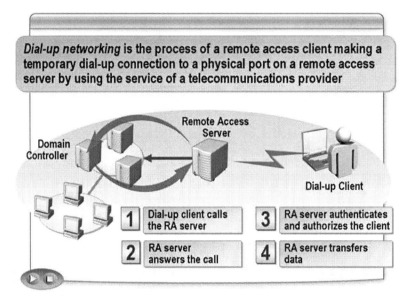

Introduction	You can use a server that is configured with Routing and Remote Access service to provide dial-up access to your corporate intranet.
What is dial-up networking?	*Dial-up networking* is the process of a remote access client making a temporary dial-up connection to a physical port on a remote access server by using the service of a telecommunications provider, such as an analog phone, Integrated Services Digital Network (ISDN), or X.25.
	Dial-up networking over an analog phone or ISDN is a direct physical connection between the dial-up networking client and the dial-up networking server. You can encrypt the data sent over the connection, but it is not required.
The dial-up access process	The process of dial-up networking is described in the following steps:

1. A client dials-up the remote access server.

2. Dial-up equipment that is installed on the remote access server answers the incoming connection requests from dial-up networking clients.

3. The remote access server authenticates and authorizes the caller.

4. The remote access server transfers data between the dial-up networking client and the organization intranet. (The remote access server acts as a gateway and provides access to the entire network to which the remote access server is attached.)

Required hardware for dial-up connections

Certain equipment is necessary for dial-up network access. For example, to allow the connection of multiple, simultaneous dial-up clients, you could have a bank of modems configured with the appropriate connections to the local telecommunications provider. You also need a multiple modem port adapter that you install on the server running Routing and Remote Access that allows connection to the modem bank.

The modem bank adapter includes drivers that are installed on the server that runs the Routing and Remote Access service so that the modem bank appears as a device with multiple modem ports.

Different vendors may also provide a single card with multiple modems. You need to verify that the hardware is on the Microsoft Windows Hardware Compatibility List at the Microsoft Web site (http://www.microsoft.com/).

Components of a Dial-up Connection

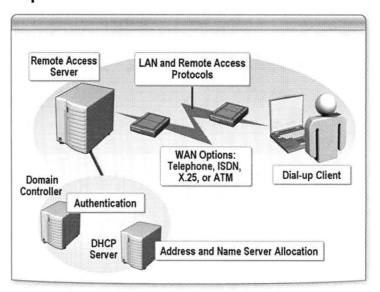

Components of a dial-up connection

A dial-up connection includes the following components:

■ *Remote access server.* A computer that accepts dial-up connections from dial-up clients, such as a server configured with Routing and Remote Access service. *Dial-up client.* A computer that initiates a dial-up connection to a dial-up server.

■ *LAN and remote access protocols.* Application programs use LAN protocols to transport information. Remote access protocols are used to negotiate connections and provide framing for LAN protocol data that is sent over wide area network (WAN) links.

■ *WAN options.* Clients can dial in to the network by using standard telephone lines and a modem or a modem pool. Faster links are possible by using ISDN. You can also connect remote access clients to remote access servers by using X.25 or asynchronous transfer mode (ATM). Direct connections are also supported through an RS-232C null modem cable, a parallel port connection, or an infrared connection.

■ *Authentication.* The identity of the client and the server in a dial-up connection are authenticated. The use of smart cards for user authentication is the strongest form of authentication in the Windows Server 2003 family.

■ *Address and name server allocation.* The remote access server is responsible for assigning IP addresses, which it does by using the default, DHCP. The remote access server also assigns DNS and WINS server addresses to clients. The name servers that allocate the addresses for remote access clients are those that service the intranet to which the remote access server interfaces.

Authentication Methods for a Dial-up Connection

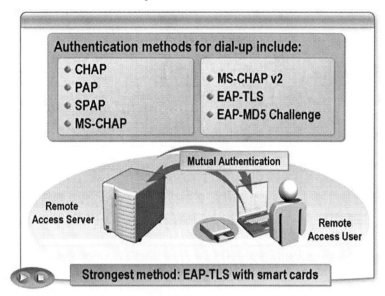

Introduction

The Windows Server 2003 family supports the following authentication methods for dial-up networking:

- CHAP

- PAP

- SPAP

- MS-CHAP

- MS-CHAP v2

- EAP-TLS

- EAP-MD5 Challenge

Note For more information about these authentication protocols, see the Network Access Authentication topic in the Introduction to a Network Access Infrastructure lesson in this module.

Recommended authentication method

The strongest form of authentication for earlier versions of Windows is EAP-TLS, a mutual authentication method that both the client and the server prove their identities to each other. During the authentication process, the remote access client sends its user certificate and the remote access server sends its computer certificate. If either certificate is not sent or is invalid, the connection is terminated.

Strongest authentication method for the Windows Server 2003 family

Using smart card certificates with EAP-TLS for user authentication is the strongest form of authentication in the Windows Server 2003 family. Using smart card certificates for user authentication requires a PKI.

Note Support for cryptographic smart cards is a key feature of the PKI that Microsoft has integrated into Microsoft Windows XP and the Windows Server 2003 family. For more information about PKI, see Module 5, "Using a PKI to Secure Information" in Course 2810: *Fundamentals of Network Security*.

Configuration Requirements for a Remote Access Server

Before adding a remote access server for dial-up access:

- Identify whether clients receive IP addresses from a DHCP server or the remote access server
- Identify whether to authenticate connection requests by RADIUS or by the remote access server
- Verify that users have user accounts configured for dial-up access

Configuration requirements

The following table lists the information that you need to know before you configure a remote access server for dial-up access.

Before adding a remote access server role	Comments
Identify whether remote clients will receive IP addresses from a DHCP server on your private network or from the remote access server that you are configuring.	If you have a DHCP server on your private network, the VPN server can lease 10 addresses at a time from the DHCP server and assign those addresses to remote clients. If you do not have a DHCP server on your private network, the dial-up server can automatically generate and assign IP addresses to remote clients. If you want the remote access server to assign IP addresses from a range that you specify, you must determine what that range should be.
Identify whether you want connection requests from dial-up clients to be authenticated by a RADIUS server or by the remote access server that you are configuring.	Adding a RADIUS server is useful if you plan to install multiple remote access servers, wireless access points, or other RADIUS clients to your private network. Adding a RADIUS server is discussed in more detail in following lessons in this module.
Verify that all users have user accounts that are configured for dial-up access.	Before users can connect to the network, they must have user accounts on the remote access server or in Active Directory. Each user account contains properties that determine whether that user can connect

How to Configure a Remote Access Server for a Dial-up Connection

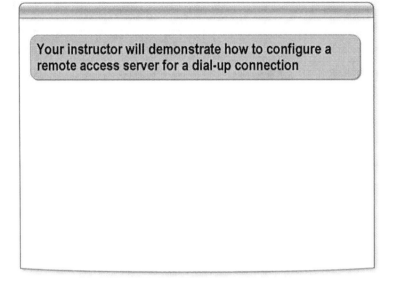

Your instructor will demonstrate how to configure a remote access server for a dial-up connection

Introduction

Before you can configure a remote access server for dial-up access, you must first add the Remote Access / VPN server role. After you add this role, the Routing and Remote Access Server Setup Wizard provides online instructions that guide you through the steps to configure your server for dial-up connections.

Note It is recommended that you log on with an account that has non-administrative credentials and use the **Run as** command with a user account that has the appropriate administrative credentials to perform this task.

Procedure

To configure the remote access server for a dial-up connection:

1. Open Manage Your Server, and then click **Add or remove a role**.

2. On the **Preliminary Steps** page, click **Next**.

3. On the **Server Role** page, select **Remote access / VPN server**, and click **Next**.

4. On the **Summary of Selections** page, click **Next**.

5. On the **Welcome to the Routing and Remote Access Server Setup Wizard**, click **Next**.

6. On the **Configuration** page, select **Remote Access (Dial-up or VPN)**, and then click **Next**.

7. On the **Remote Access** page, click **Dial-up**, and then click **Next**.

8. On the **Network Selection** page, select the network interface that is connected to the Internet, and then click **Next**.

9. On the **IP Address Assignment** page, click **Next**.

10. On the **Managing Multiple Remote Access Servers** page, click **Next**.

11. On the **Completing the Routing and Remote Access Server Setup Wizard** page, click **Finish**.

12. In the **Routing and Remote Access** dialog box, click **OK**.

13. On the **This Server is Now a Remote Access/VPN Server** page, click **Finish**.

How to Configure a Remote Access Client for a Dial-up Connection

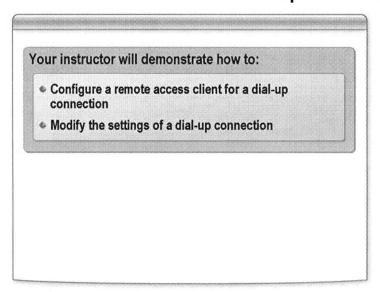

Your instructor will demonstrate how to:

- Configure a remote access client for a dial-up connection
- Modify the settings of a dial-up connection

Introduction

You use Network Connections to configure a client for a dial-up connection. You can later change this connection by modifying its settings. Dial-up settings, such as the phone number of the connection, the number of redial attempts, and so on, are defined for each connection. These pre-connection and post-connection settings do not modify or affect the settings of other connections.

Note It is recommended that you log on with an account that has non-administrative credentials and use the **Run as** command with a user account that has the appropriate administrative credentials to perform this task.

Procedure for configuring a client for a dial-up connection

To configure a remote access client for a dial-up connection:

1. Click **Start**, and then click **Control Panel**.

2. In Control Panel, click **Network Connections**.

3. In Network Connections, double-click **New Connection Wizard**.

4. On the **Welcome to the New Network Connection Wizard** page, click **Next**.

5. On the **Network Connection Type** page, select **Connect to the network at my workplace**, and then click **Next**.

6. On the **Network Connection** page, select **Dial-up connection**, and then click **Next**.

7. On the **Connection Name** page, type the name of the connection (the name of the connection is commonly the name of your organization), and then click **Next**.

8. On the **Phone Number to Dial** page, type the number of the connection, and then click **Next**.

9. On the **Connection Availability** page, select either **Anyone's use** or **My use only**, and then click **Next**.

10. On the **Completing the New Connection Wizard** page, click **Finish**.

Procedure for modifying a dial-up connection

To modify the settings for a dial-up connection:

1. Open Network Connections.

2. Right-click the dial-up connection that you want to modify, and then click **Properties**.

3. Make the appropriate modifications on any of the following tabs:

   - **General**. Change the dialing devices, phone numbers, host address, country/region codes, or dialing rules.

   - **Options**. Change the dialing and redialing options, multilink configuration, or X.25 parameters.

   - **Security**. Change the identity authentication, data encryption, or terminal window, and scripting options.

   - **Networking**. Change the configurations for the remote access server and protocols that are used for this connection.

Lesson: Configuring a Wireless Connection

* Overview of Wireless Network Access

* Components of a Wireless Connection

* Wireless Standards

* Authentication Methods for Wireless Networks

* Configuration Requirements of a Windows XP
  Professional Client for Wireless Network Access

* How to Configure the Network Access Client for a
  Wireless Connection

Introduction

Before deploying wireless LAN connectivity in your organization, it is helpful to understand the components of a secure wireless LAN and how they work together to provide wireless access to your network.

Lesson objectives

After completing this lesson, you will be able to:

■ Explain what wireless network access is.

■ Describe the components that are used for wireless network access.

■ Explain what the wireless standards are.

■ Explain what types of authentication methods are used for a wireless connection.

■ Explain the requirements that are necessary to configure a Windows XP Professional client for wireless network access.

■ Configure a network access client for a wireless connection.

Overview of Wireless Network Access

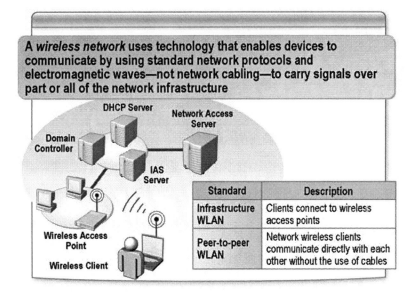

A *wireless network* uses technology that enables devices to communicate by using standard network protocols and electromagnetic waves—not network cabling—to carry signals over part or all of the network infrastructure

Standard	Description
Infrastructure WLAN	Clients connect to wireless access points
Peer-to-peer WLAN	Network wireless clients communicate directly with each other without the use of cables

Introduction

Microsoft Windows XP and Windows Server 2003 provide extensive support for wireless networking technology to extend the enterprise network to wireless devices.

What is wireless networking?

A wireless network uses technology that enables two or more devices to communicate through standard network protocols and electromagnetic waves—not network cabling—to carry signals over part or all of the network infrastructure. Devices that are commonly used for wireless networking include portable computers, hand-held computers, PDAs, cellular phones, pen-based computers, and pagers.

Benefits of a WLAN

You can use a wireless LAN (WLAN) in temporary offices or other spaces where the installation of extensive cabling would be prohibitive, or to supplement an existing LAN so that users can work at different locations within a building at different times. Mobile users can use cellular phones, PDAs, notebook computers, and other devices to access e-mail. Travelers with portable computers can connect to the Internet through base stations installed in airports, railway stations, and other public locations.

WLANs can operate two different modes

A WLAN operates in two different modes, which are defined by Institute of Electrical and Electronics Engineers (IEEE) 802.11:

- *Access Point Infrastructure WLAN.* Wireless stations (devices with radio network cards or external modems) connect to wireless access points that function as bridges between the stations and the existing network backbone. For example, wireless users within a corporate or campus building can access network resources as if they were traditionally connected to the network.

- *Peer-to-peer (ad hoc) WLAN.* In a peer-to-peer network, wireless clients communicate directly with each other without the use of cables. For example, several users within a limited area, such as a conference room, can form a temporary network to each other without using access points. Although they can communicate and share resources with each other, they cannot access network resources that are not part of this peer-to-peer network.

Components of a Wireless Connection

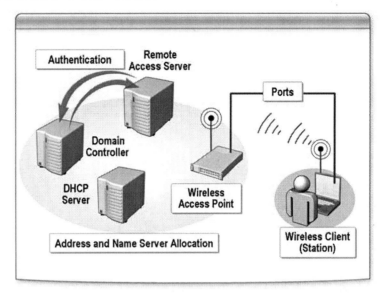

Components of a wireless connection

A wireless LAN network consists of the following components:

- *Wireless client (station).* A station is a computing device that is equipped with a wireless LAN network adapter. A personal computer equipped with a wireless LAN network adapter is known as a wireless client. Wireless clients can communicate directly with each other or through a wireless access point.

- *Wireless access point.* A wireless access point is a networking device equipped with a wireless LAN network adapter that acts as a bridge among stations and a traditional wired network. An access point contains:

  - At least one interface that connects the access point to an existing wired network (such as an Ethernet backbone).

  - Radio equipment with which it creates wireless connections to wireless clients.

  - IEEE 802.1D bridging software, so that it can act as a transparent bridge between wireless and wired networks.

- *Ports.* A port is a channel of a device that can support a single point-to-point connection. A typical wireless client with a single wireless LAN network adapter has a single port and can support only a single wireless connection. A typical wireless access point has multiple ports and can support multiple simultaneous wireless connections.

- *Authentication.* The Routing and Remote Access service provides authentication services such as Internet Authentication Service (IAS) and 802.1x authentication methods. Windows Server 2003 also provides customizable services for issuing and managing certificates that are used in software security systems that employ public key technology.

- *Address and name server allocation.* The Routing and Remote Access service supports wireless networks in the same way that other remote access clients, such as VPN or dial-up clients, are supported. The Routing and Remote Access service provides IP address allocation and remote access policies that are unique to wireless network clients.

Wireless Standards

Standard	Description
802.11	• A group of specifications for WLANs developed by IEEE • Defines the physical and MAC portion of the OSI data-link layer
802.11b	• 11 megabits per second • Good range but susceptible to radio signal interference • Popular with home and small business users
802.11a	• Transmissions speeds as high as 54 Mbps • Allows wireless LAN networking to perform better for video and conferencing applications • Works well in densely populated areas • Is not interoperable with 802.11, 802.11b, 802.11g
802.11g	• Enhancement to and compatible with 802.11b • 54 Mbps but at shorter ranges than 802.11b
802.1x	• Authenticates clients before it lets them on the network • Can be used for wireless or wired LANs • Requires greater hardware and infrastructure investment

What is 802.11?

802.11, also known as *Wi-Fi*, is a family of specifications for WLANs that a working group of IEEE developed. 802.11 defines the physical and media access control (MAC) portion of the data-link layer in the Open Systems Interconnection (OSI) model. The MAC layer is the same for all 802.11 standards, but the physical implementation varies.

Note In the IEEE 802.x specifications, MAC is the lower of two sublayers that make up the ISO (International Organization for Standardization)/OSI data-link layer. MAC manages access to the physical network, delimits frames, and handles error control.

802.11 through 802.11g

802.11b supports higher bit rates than the original 802.11 specification. 802.11b supports two additional speeds: 5.5 megabits per second (Mbps) and 11 Mbps. It has good range but is susceptible to radio signal interference. Many vendors are making reasonably priced 802.11b devices for the home and small business market.

802.11a allows for faster communication speeds, up to 54 Mbps, but usually at shorter ranges. This higher speed technology allows wireless LAN networking to perform better for video and conferencing applications. It uses 12 separate non-overlapping channels, so it works well in densely populated areas with greater resistance to interference and greater throughput. It uses a different part of the radio spectrum than 802.11, 802.11b, and 802.11g, so it is not interoperable with them.

802.11g is an enhancement to 802.11b and is compatible with that standard. Upgrading from b to g may only require a firmware update instead of all new hardware. It allows for speeds up to 54 Mbps but at shorter ranges than 802.11b. Like 802.11b, it is susceptible to interference.

802.1x

The 802.1x extension to 802.11 defines a way of authenticating access to the port before allowing access to the network. It was designed to address some of the shortcomings of 802.11 wireless security, but it can also be used for wired LANs. For authentication, 802.1x can use certificates with EAP-TLS, passwords with EAP-MS-CHAP v2, or PEAP. PEAP can be configured with TLS or MS-CHAP v2. PEAP-TLS is the recommended authentication mechanism, because it provides the strongest authentication and key determination method. A certificate is required on the network access server for MS-CHAP v2. Certificates are required for both client and network access servers for PEAP-TLS. 802.1x requires an investment in hardware and infrastructure.

Additional reading

■ For more information about how Microsoft has deployed wireless, see the white paper "Microsoft Wireless LAN Deployment and Best Practices" on the Microsoft Web site.

Authentication Methods for Wireless Networks

802.1x Authentication Methods	Description
EAP-MS-CHAP v2	• Provides mutual authentication • Uses certificates for server authentication and password-based credentials for client authentication
EAP-TLS	• Provides mutual authentication and is the strongest method of authentication and key determination • Uses certificates for both server and client authentication
PEAP	• Provides support for EAP-TLS and EAP-MS-CHAP v2 • Encrypts the negotiation process

Introduction

802.1x is an industry standard for authenticated network access to wired Ethernet networks and wireless 802.11 networks. 802.1x enhances security and deployment by providing support for centralized user identification, authentication, dynamic key management, and accounting. If you connect to an 802.11 WLAN without 802.1x authentication enabled, the data that you send is more vulnerable to attacks.

802.1x authentication methods

For authentication, the 802.11 standard defines open system and shared key authentication types. For data confidentiality, the 802.11 standard defines Wired Equivalent Privacy (WEP).

The 802.11 standard does not define or provide a WEP key management protocol that provides automatic encryption key determination and renewal. This is a limitation to IEEE 802.11 security services—especially for a wireless infrastructure mode with a large number of wireless clients.

This issue is solved by using the combination of an IEEE 802.1x port-based network access control and EAP-TLS for IEEE 802.11 networks.

802.1x uses EAP for its authentication protocol. EAP provides message exchange and open-ended conversation between the client and the server during the authentication process to allow for negotiation of authentication protocols. The support that 802.1x provides for EAP types allows you to choose from several different authentication methods for wireless clients including:

■ *EAP-MS-CHAP v2*. EAP-MS-CHAP v2 provides mutual authentication and uses certificates for server authentication and password-based credentials for client authentication.

■ *EAP-TLS*. EAP-TLS provides mutual authentication and is the strongest method of authentication and key determination. It uses certificates for both server and client authentication.

- *Protected EAP (PEAP).* PEAP further protects the authentication process by encrypting the initial EAP negotiation packets. PEAP provides support for EAP-TLS and EAP-MS-CHAP v2.

Note   If you want to use certificates or smart cards for user and client computer authentication, you must use EAP-TLS or, for enhanced security, PEAP with EAP-TLS.

Configuration Requirements of a Windows XP Professional Client for Wireless Network Access

- **Choose a network type:**
  - Access point
  - Computer-to-computer
  - Any available network
- **Configure authentication appropriately for the selected network type**
- **Balance the level of security with the deployment effort:**
  - For the highest level of security, choose PEAP with certificates (EAP-TLS)
  - For the greatest ease of deployment, choose PEAP with passwords (EAP-MS-CHAP v2)

Introduction

The Wireless Configuration service in the Windows Server 2003 family and in Windows XP supports the IEEE 802.11 standard for wireless networks and minimizes the configuration that is required to access wireless networks.

This service is enabled by default, so that you can use Windows to configure your wireless network settings.

Wireless network types

When you use Windows to configure your wireless network settings, you can create a list of preferred wireless networks, and you can specify the order in which to attempt connections to these wireless networks. You can choose from the following wireless network types:

- **Access point (infrastructure).** This setting allows users to connect to several different wireless access points as they move between different floors of a building or different buildings in a campus while still maintaining uninterrupted access to network resources.

- **Computer-to-computer (ad hoc).** If users are in a meeting with co-workers and they do not need to gain access to network resources, their wireless device can make direct connections to the wireless devices of their co-workers, and they can form a temporary network.

- **Any available network (access point preferred).** In access point preferred wireless networks, a connection to an access point wireless network is always attempted first, if there are any available. If an access point network is not available, a connection to a computer-to-computer wireless network is attempted. For example, if you use your laptop at work in an access point wireless network, and then take your laptop home to use in your computer-to-computer home network, automatic wireless network configuration will change your wireless network settings as needed, so that you can connect to your home network.

Wireless network security settings

For enhanced security over wireless networks, in the Windows Server 2003 family and in Windows XP Service Pack 1, 802.1x authentication is only available for access point (infrastructure) networks that require the use of a Wired Equivalent Privacy (WEP) network key. WEP provides data confidentiality by encrypting the data that is sent between wireless clients and wireless access points.

WEP settings

When WEP is enabled, a network key can be used to encrypt data that is sent over wireless networks. The network key can be provided for you automatically (for example, it might be provided on your wireless network adapter), or you can specify the key by typing it yourself.

801.1x authentication methods

You can choose any of the following authentication methods when configuring 802.1x for wireless network connections:

- EAP-TLS

- PEAP with EAP-MS-CHAP v2

- PEAP with EAP-TLS

Level of security vs. deployment effort

When choosing an authentication method, you should balance the level of security with the effort that is required to deploy your chosen authentication method. For the highest level of security, choose PEAP with certificates (EAP-TLS). For the greatest ease of deployment, choose PEAP with passwords (EAP-MS-CHAP v2). Consider the following options when determining your method of authentication:

- Both PEAP with EAP-TLS and EAP-TLS alone provide strong security through the use of certificates for server authentication and the use of certificates or smart cards for client computer and user authentication. But when PEAP with EAP-TLS is used, client certificate information is encrypted, whereas it is not when using only EAP-TLS.

- PEAP with EAP-MS-CHAP v2 requires the least effort to deploy. Client authentication is password-based, so certificates or smart cards do not need to be installed on client computers. Because PEAP creates an end-to-end encrypted channel before EAP-MS-CHAP v2 authentication occurs, the authentication exchange is much less vulnerable to offline dictionary attacks, where a malicious user captures the CHAP exchange and then attempts to determine the password.

- In addition, PEAP supports fast re-authentication, also known as fast roaming. PEAP allows roaming users to maintain continuous wireless network connectivity when traveling between different wireless access points on the same network, as long as each wireless access point is configured as a client of the same IAS (RADIUS) server.

Additional Reading

For more information about Windows Server 2003 support for wireless network access, see the "Windows XP Wireless Deployment Technology and Component Overview" document in the Deployment Articles section on http://www.microsoft.com/wifi.

How to Configure a Network Access Client for a Wireless Connection

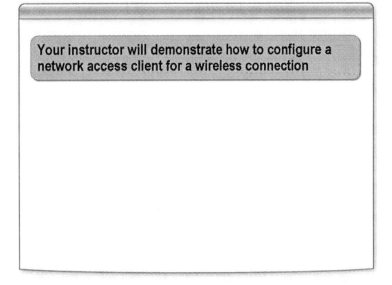

Your instructor will demonstrate how to configure a network access client for a wireless connection

Introduction

You use Network Connections to configure a client for a wireless client. This procedure assumes that the computer has the hardware already installed to support a wireless connection.

Note It is recommended that you log on with an account that has non-administrative credentials and use the **Run as** command with a user account that has the appropriate administrative credentials to perform this task.

Procedure

To configure a network access client for a wireless network connection:

1. Open Network Connections.

2. Right-click the appropriate wireless network connection, select **Properties**, and then click the **Wireless Networks** tab.

3. Determine whether to add a new wireless network connection, or modify or remove an existing one, and then select the corresponding task in the following table.

Tasks	Procedural steps
• Add a new wireless network connection	• Select the Use Windows to configure my network settings check box, and then click Add.
• Modify an existing wireless network connection	• Select the Use Windows to configure my network settings check box. Under Preferred networks, click the wireless network connection that you want to modify, and then click Properties.
• Remove a preferred wireless network connection	• Under Preferred networks, click the wireless network connection that you want to remove, and then click Remove.

4. If you are adding or modifying a wireless network connection, click the **Association** tab, and then configure settings as needed.

5. To configure 802.1x authentication for the wireless network connection, click the **Authentication** tab, and then configure the settings as needed.

6. To connect to a wireless network after configuring network settings, on the **Wireless Networks** tab, under **Available networks**, click the network name, click **Configure**, and then click **OK**.

Important If a network does not broadcast its network name, it does not appear under **Available networks**. To connect to an access point (infrastructure) network that you know is available but that does not appear under **Available networks**, click **Add**. On the **Association** tab, type the network name, and if needed, configure additional network settings.

---

7. To change the order in which connection attempts to preferred networks are made, under **Preferred networks**, click the wireless network that you want to move to a new position in the list, and then click **Move up** or **Move down** until the wireless network is at the required position.

8. To update the list of available networks that are within range of your computer, click **Refresh**.

9. To automatically connect to available networks that do not appear in the **Preferred networks** list, click **Advanced**, and then select the **Automatically connect to non-preferred networks** check box.

Lesson: Controlling User Access to a Network

- User Account Dial-in Permissions
- How to Configure User Accounts for Network Access
- What Is a Remote Access Policy?
- What Is a Remote Access Policy Profile?
- How Remote Access Policies Are Processed
- How to Configure a Remote Access Policy
- How to Configure a Remote Access Policy Profile

Introduction

This lesson presents the knowledge and skills necessary to support remote and wireless access to a Microsoft Windows Server 2003 network through the use of remote access policies and policy profiles.

Lesson objectives

After completing this lesson, you will be able to:

- Explain what user account dial-in permissions are.
- Configure user accounts for network access.
- Explain what a remote access policy is.
- Explain what a remote access policy profile is.
- Describe how remote access policies are processed.
- Configure a remote access policy.
- Edit a remote access policy profile.
- Control user access to a network.

User Account Dial-in Permissions

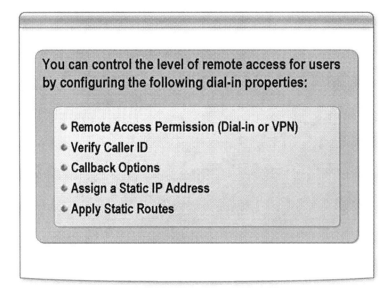

You can control the level of remote access for users
by configuring the following dial-in properties:

- Remote Access Permission (Dial-in or VPN)
- Verify Caller ID
- Callback Options
- Assign a Static IP Address
- Apply Static Routes

How you can control remote access permission and usage

In Windows Server 2003, you can define and create remote access policies to control the level of remote access that a user or group of users has to the network. Remote access policies are a set of conditions and connection settings that give network administrators more flexibility in granting remote access permissions and usage. The Windows Server 2003 Routing and Remote Access service and Windows Server 2003 IAS both use remote access policies to determine whether to accept or reject connection attempts.

Note For more information about IAS, see the Centralizing Network Access Authentication and Policy Management by Using IAS lesson in this module.

Windows Server 2003 evaluates a connection attempt based on policy conditions, user account and remote access permissions, and policy profile settings.

User account dial-in permissions

You can define dial-in permissions in the **Properties** dialog box for a user in the Active Directory or Local Users and Groups console. The dial-in properties that you can configure for a user account include:

- **Remote Access Permission (Dial-in or VPN)**. You can use this property to set remote access permission to be explicitly allowed, denied, or determined through remote access policies. In all cases, remote access policies are used to authorize the connection attempt.

- **Verify Caller ID**. By configuring this option, you are requiring that the server verifies the caller's phone number. If the caller's phone number does not match the phone number that you have configured, the connection attempt is denied.

- **Callback Options**. If this property is enabled, the server calls the caller back during the connection process. The phone number that the server uses is set by either the caller or the network administrator.

- **Assign a Static IP Address**. You can use this property to assign a specific IP address to a user when a connection is made.

- **Apply Static Routes**. This setting is designed for demand-dial routing. You can use this property to define a series of static IP routes that are added to the routing table of the server running the Routing and Remote Access service when a connection is made.

How to Configure User Accounts for Network Access

Your instructor will demonstrate how to:

• Raise the domain functional level

• Configure the dial-in properties for user accounts in a Windows 2000 native domain

Introduction

For an Active Directory-based server in a domain set at the Windows Server 2003 native domain level, the dial-in properties for a user account in Active Directory Users and Computers are configured with the **Control access through Remote Access Policy** option as the default.

For an Active Directory-based server in a domain set at the Windows 2000 native domain level, you configure the dial-in properties for a user account in Active Directory Users and Computers.

Note It is recommended that you log on with an account that has non-administrative credentials and use the **Run as** command with a user account that has the appropriate administrative credentials to perform this task.

Procedure for raising the domain functional level

To raise the domain functional level:

1. Open Active Directory Domains and Trusts.

2. Right-click the appropriate domain, and then click **Raise Domain Functional Level**.

3. In the **Raise Domain Functional Level** dialog box, select **Windows Server 2003**, and then click **Raise**.

4. In the **Raise Domain Functional Level** warning box, click **OK**.

5. In the **Raise Domain Functional Level** information box, click **OK**.

6. Close Active Directory Domains and Trusts.

Procedure for configuring the dial-in properties for user accounts in a Windows 2000 native domain

To configure the dial-in properties for user accounts in a Windows 2000 native domain:

1. Open Active Directory Users and Computers.

2. In the console tree, click **Users**.

3. In the details pane, right-click a user name, and then click **Properties**.

4. To set remote access permissions:

   • On the **Dial-in** tab, under **Remote Access Permission (Dial-in or VPN)**, click either **Allow access** or **Deny access**, and then click **OK**.

5. To enable caller ID verification:

   • On the **Dial-in** tab, select the **Verify Caller-ID** check box, and then type the number that the user is calling from.

6. To set callback options:

   • On the **Dial-in** tab, under **Callback Options**, click the callback option that you want to set for this user.

7. To assign a static IP address:

   • On the **Dial-in** tab, select the **Assign a Static IP Address** check box, and then type the static IP address for this user.

8. To configure static routes for a dial-in user:

   a. On the **Dial-in** tab, select the **Apply Static Routes** check box.

   b. In the **Static Routes** dialog box, click **Add Route**.

   c. In **Destination**, **Network Mask**, and **Metric**, type the destination network address, the network mask, and the number of hops to the destination network for this static route, and then click **OK**.

   d. Repeat steps b and c for each static route that you want to configure for this user.

What Is a Remote Access Policy?

A *remote access policy* is a named rule that
consists of the following elements:

* **Conditions.** One or more attributes that are compared to
  the settings of the connection attempt

* **Remote access permission.** If all conditions of a remote
  access policy are met, remote access permission is either
  granted or denied

* **Profile.** A set of properties that are applied to a connection
  when it is authorized (either through the user account or
  policy permission settings)

Definition

Remote access policies are an ordered set of rules that define how connections are either authorized or rejected. For each rule, there are one or more conditions, a remote access permission setting, and a set of profile settings.

Components of a remote access policy

Remote access policies are configured to specify, based on group membership or individual users, the different types of connection constraints. A remote access policy consists of the following three components that cooperate with Active Directory to provide secure access to remote access servers:

■ *Conditions*. The conditions of remote access policies are a list of parameters, such as the time of day, user groups, caller IDs, or IP addresses, that are matched to the parameters of the client that is connecting to the server. The first set of policy conditions that match the parameters of the incoming connection request are processed for access permission and configuration. If none of the condition sets are matched, the access attempt will fail.

■ *Remote access permission*. Remote access connections are permitted based on a combination of the dial-in properties of a user account and remote access policies. The permission setting on the remote access policy works with the user's dial-in permissions in Active Directory.

■ *Profile*. Each policy includes a profile of settings, such as authentication and encryption protocols, that are applied to the connection. The settings in the profile are applied to the connection immediately and may cause the connection to be denied. For example, if the profile settings for a connection specify that the user can only connect for 30 minutes at a time, the user will be disconnected from the remote access server after 30 minutes.

Example

For example, a policy can grant access to all users in Group A from 8:00 A.M. through 5:00 P.M. However, the permissions for User X in Group A can be set to deny access in Active Directory, whereas the permissions for User Y in Group A can be set to allow access in Active Directory at all times. As a result, most users in Group A are controlled by the policy setting and can gain access only from 8:00 A.M. through 5:00 P.M. However, User X is denied access completely, and User Y is granted 24-hour access.

What Is a Remote Access Policy Profile?

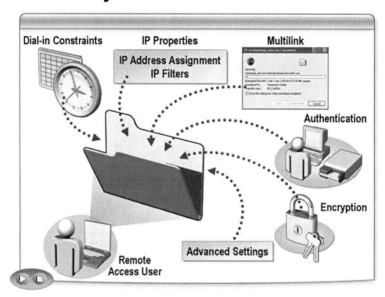

Definition

A *remote access policy profile* is a set of properties that are applied to a connection when it is authorized—either through the user account or policy permission settings.

After a connection is authorized, the profile for the remote access policy specifies a set of connection restrictions. The dial-in properties of the user account also provide a set of restrictions. Where applicable, connection restrictions for a user account override the connection restrictions for the for the remote access policy profile.

Elements of a profile for a remote access policy

The remote access policy profile specifies what kind of access the user is given if the conditions match. Access is granted only if the connection attempt does not conflict with the settings of the user account or the profile. You can configure a profile in the **Edit Dial-in Profile** dialog box by clicking **Edit Profile** in the **Properties** dialog box for a policy. You can configure the following settings in the dialog box:

- **Dial-in constraints**. You can use these settings to determine the amount of idle time before disconnection; the maximum session time; and the days, times, telephone numbers, and media types (ISDN, VPN, and so on) that are allowed.

- **IP Properties**. You can configure a client's IP address assignment and Transmission Control Protocol/Internet Protocol (TCP/IP) packet filtering on this tab. You can define separate filters for inbound or outbound packets.

- **Multilink**. With Multilink, multiple physical links appear as a single logical link over which data is sent and received. You can set Multilink properties that both enable Multilink and determine the maximum number of ports that a Multilink connection can use. Additionally, you can set BAP policies that both determine BAP usage and specify when extra BAP lines are dropped.

- **Authentication**. You can set authentication properties to both enable the authentication types that are allowed for a connection and specify the EAP type that must be used. You can also configure the EAP type. By default, MS-CHAP and MS-CHAP v2 are enabled.

- **Encryption**. You can use this tab to specify the types of encryption that are prohibited, allowed, or required.

- **Advanced**. You can set advanced properties to specify the series of RADIUS attributes that the IAS server sends back to be evaluated by the RADIUS client. RADIUS attributes are specific to performing RADIUS authentication and are ignored by a server that is running the Routing and Remote Access service and is configured for Windows authentication.

How Remote Access Policies Are Processed

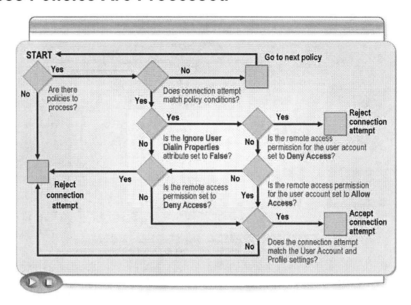

Process for applying remote access

Windows Server 2003 evaluates a connection attempt that is based on policy conditions, user and remote access permissions, and profile settings. The flow of the process consists of three basic parts that include first checking conditions, then permissions, and then the profile. The first policy that meets all of the conditions is the policy that is used for the connection.

Remote access policies are processed as follows:

1. Routing and Remote Access matches the conditions of the remote access policy to the conditions of the attempted connection:

   • If there is no policy defined, access is denied.

   • If there is no policy that matches, access is denied.

   • If there is a match, the policy is used to determine access.

2. Routing and Remote Access checks the user account's dial-in permissions:

   • If the permission on the user account is set to **Deny access**, the user is denied access.

   • If the permission on the user account is set to **Allow access**, the user is granted access and the profile for the policy is applied.

   • If the permission is set to **Control access through Remote Access Policy**, the policy's permission setting determines user access.

3. Routing and Remote Access applies the settings in the policy's profile to the incoming connection.

   • The connection may not be allowed if a critical setting in the profile does not match a setting on the remote access server. For example, the profile for an incoming connection may specify that a group can only connect at night. If a user in that group tries to connect during the day, the connection attempt will be denied.

   • The connection may be disconnected at a later stage due to a setting in the profile, such as a time restriction for connecting.

How to Configure a Remote Access Policy

> **Your instructor will demonstrate how to:**
>
> - Configure a remote access policy
> - Configure a new policy condition for a remote access policy

Introduction

You can configure a remote access policy and an associated profile under **Remote Access Policies** in the console tree of the Routing and Remote Access console.

For an Active Directory-based server in a domain set at the Windows Server 2003 native domain level, the dial-in properties for a user account in Active Directory Users and Computers are configured with the **Control access through Remote Access Policy** option as the default.

Note   It is recommended that you log on with an account that has non-administrative credentials and use the **Run as** command with a user account that has the appropriate administrative credentials to perform this task.

Procedure for configuring a remote access policy

To configure a remote access policy:

1. Open the Routing and Remote Access console.
2. Expand the console tree, right-click **Remote Access Policies**, and then click **New Remote Access Policy**.
3. On the **Welcome to the New Remote Access Policy Wizard** page, click **Next**.
4. On the **Policy Configuration Method** page, type the Policy name, and then click **Next**.
5. On the **Access Method** page, select one of the following methods of access:

   - **VPN**. Use for all VPN connections.
   - **Dial-up**. Use for dial-up connections that use a traditional phone line or ISDN line.
   - **Wireless**. Use for wireless LAN connections only.
   - **Ethernet**. Use for Ethernet connections, such as connections that use a switch.

6. On the **User or Group Access** page, select either:

- **User** – User access permissions are specified in the user account.

- **Group** – Individual user permissions override group permissions.

7. On the **Authentication Methods** page, select one or more of the following options (by default EAP and MS-CHAPv2 are selected), and then click **Next**:

- **Extensible Authentication Protocol (EAP)**

  - **Protected EAP (PEAP)**. Configure the appropriate certificate.

  - **Smart Card or other certificate**. Configure the appropriate certificate.

- **Microsoft Encrypted Authentication version 2 (MS-CHAPv2)**. Select this option if your users must supply a password for authentication.

- **Microsoft Encrypted Authentication (MS-CHAP)**. Select this option if your network runs operating systems that do not support MS-CHAPv2.

8. On the **Policy Encryption Level** page, select one or more of the following options, and then click **Next**.

- **Basic encryption (IPSec 56-bit DES or MPPE 40-bit)**

- **Strong encryption (IPSec 56-bit DES or MPPE 56-bit)**

- **Strongest encryption (IPSec Triple DES or MPPE 128-bit)**

9. On the **Completing the New Remote Access Policy Wizard** page, click **Finish**.

Procedure for configuring a new policy condition for a remote access policy

To configure a new policy condition for a remote access policy:

1. Open the Routing and Remote Access console.

2. In the console tree, click **Remote Access Policies**.

3. In the details pane, double-click the remote access policy that you want to configure.

4. In the *Policy* **Properties** dialog box, click **Add**.

5. In the **Select Attribute** dialog box, select the attribute to add, and then click **Add**.

6. In the *Attribute* dialog box, configure the attribute, and then click **OK**.

7. To grant access to callers matching the policy conditions, click **Grant remote access permission**, or to deny access, click **Deny remote access permission**.

8. In the *Policy* **Properties** dialog box, click **OK**.

How to Configure a Remote Access Policy Profile

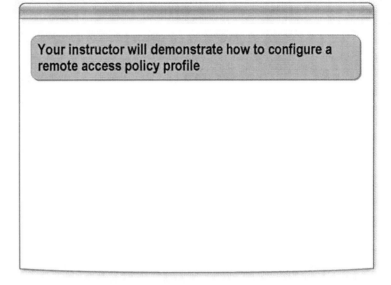

Introduction

The remote access profile specifies what kind of access the user will be given if the conditions match. Access will be granted only if the connection attempt does not conflict with the settings of the user account or the profile.

Procedure

To configure a remote access policy profile:

1. Open the Routing and Remote Access console.

2. In the console tree, click **Remote Access Policies**.

3. In the details pane, double-click the remote access policy that you want to configure.

4. Click **Edit Profile**.

5. In the **Edit Dial-in Profile** dialog box, specify any required settings for the following areas of a remote access policy profile:

   - **Dial-in Constraints**. You can use these settings to determine the amount of idle time before disconnection; the maximum session time; and the days, times, telephone numbers, and media types (ISDN, VPN, and so on) that are allowed.

   - **IP**. You can configure a client's IP address assignment and TCP/IP packet filtering on this tab. You can define separate filters for inbound or outbound packets.

   - **Multilink**. You can configure Multilink and Bandwidth Allocation Protocol (BAP) on this tab. Use these settings to disconnect a line if the bandwidth falls below a certain level for a given length of time. Multilink can also be set to require the use of BAP.

- **Authentication**. You can use these settings to define the authentication protocols that are allowed for connections that use this policy. Make sure that any protocols that you select here are also enabled in the **Properties** dialog box for the server.

- **Encryption**. You can use this tab to specify the types of encryption that are prohibited, allowed, or required.

- **Advanced**. You can use this tab to configure additional network parameters that can be sent from RADIUS servers running non-Microsoft operating systems.

Practice: Controlling User Access to a Network

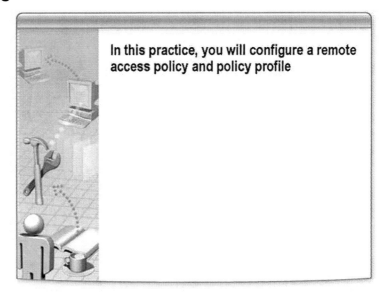

In this practice, you will configure a remote access policy and policy profile

Objective

In this practice, you will configure a remote access policy and policy profile.

Instructions

To complete this practice, refer to the *Implementation Plan Values* document, located in the Appendix at the end of your student workbook.

The instructor-led demonstration, Configuring a Remote Access Policy, must be completed before starting this practice.

It is recommended that you log on with an account that has non-administrative credentials and use the **Run as** command with a user account that has the appropriate administrative credentials to perform this task.

Scenario

Because you have configured a remote access server to support VPN connections for the lab test engineers, you now need to configure user access. Some lab test engineers will need greater access to the lab computers from remote connections than others. You will control user access by configuring a remote access policy and policy profile.

Practice

▶ **Configure a remote access policy named VPN Policy**

- Complete this task from both student computers.

- User name: **nwtraders***ComputerName***Admin**

- Password: **P@ssw0rd**

- Administrative tool: **Routing and Remote Access**

- Policy name: **VPN Policy**

- Access method: **VPN**

- User or Group Access:

    • Domain name: **nwtraders.msft**:

    • Group: **G** *ComputerName***Admins** (where *ComputerName* is the name of your computer)

- Authentication Methods: Accept defaults

- Policy Encryption Level: Accept defaults

▶ **Verify that the VPN policy is the first on the list of policies**

- Complete this task from both student computers.

- Administrative tool: **Routing and Remote Access**

- In the details pane, verify that VPN Policy is displayed at the top of the list.

▶ **Configure a remote access policy profile for the VPN Policy**

- Complete this task from both student computers.

- Dial-in constraints: **Allow access only through these media**

    • Media type: **Virtual (VPN)**

▶ **Connect to your partner's computer by using the VPN connection**

- Complete this task from the higher number student computer.

1. On the desktop, double-click **VPN** *ComputerName* (where *ComputerName* is your partner's computer).

2. In the **Connect VPN** *ComputerName* dialog box, type in the following:

    • User name: *ComputerName***Admin** (where *ComputerName* is the name of your computer)

    • Password: **P@ssw0rd**

3. Verify that a pop-up balloon is displayed in the notification area that states the VPN *ComputerName* (where *ComputerName* is the name of your partner's computer) is now connected.

4. On the desktop, right-click **VPN** *ComputerName* and then click **Status**.

5. In the **VPN** *ComputerName* **Status** dialog box, verify that **Status** is displayed as **Connected**, and then note the **Duration** time.

▶ **Verify the connection duration for the remote access client**

- Complete this task from the lower number student computer.

1. In Routing and Remote Access, expand *ComputerName* and then click **Remote Access Clients**.

2. Verify in the details pane the duration that the client has been connected. (You must press F5 to refresh the console; it will not update automatically.)

▶ **On the client computer, disconnect from your partner's computer**

- Complete this task from the higher number student computer.

- On the desktop, right-click **VPN** *ComputerName* and click **Disconnect**.

Lesson: Centralizing Network Access Authentication and Policy Management by Using IAS

* What Is RADIUS?
* What Is IAS?
* How Centralized Authentication Works
* How to Configure an IAS Server for Network Access Authentication
* How to Configure the Remote Access Server to Use IAS for Authentication

Introduction

This lesson introduces you to the knowledge and skills that are needed to use Internet Authentication Service (IAS) to centralize network authentication and policy management.

Lesson objectives

After completing this lesson, you will be able to:

- Explain what RADIUS is.
- Explain what IAS is.
- Describe how centralized authentication and policy management works.
- Configure an IAS server for network access authentication.
- Configure the remote access server to use IAS for authentication.
- Centralize network access authentication and policy management by using IAS.

What Is RADIUS?

RADIUS is a widely deployed protocol, based on a client/server model, that enables centralized authentication, authorization, and accounting for network access

- RADIUS is the standard for managing network access for VPN, dial-up, and wireless networks
- Use RADIUS to manage network access centrally across many types of network access
- RADIUS servers receive and process connection requests or accounting messages from RADIUS clients or proxies

Why centralize network access authentication and policy management?

Today network access security must be comprehensive to securely grant appropriate access to business partners, consultants, and employees. Organizations need to grant different levels of network access based on who the user is, what credentials they are using, how they are connecting, what level of encryption is used in the connection, time of day, and more. This requires a centralized network access authentication and policy management system that can support the demands of large networks.

Remote Authentication Dial-In User Service (RADIUS) has become a standard for performing authentication and management of network access policy.

What is RADIUS?

RADIUS is a widely deployed protocol, based on a client/server model, that enables centralized authentication, authorization, and accounting for network access.

Purpose of RADIUS

Originally developed for dial-in solutions, the RADIUS protocol has evolved to become the standard for managing network access for VPN, dial-up, and wireless networks. By carefully integrating this management service for network access policy with the operating system's identity services, and by implementing comprehensive support for RADIUS rule processing, you can manage network access centrally across many types of network access.

What is a RADIUS server?

A *RADIUS server* receives and processes connection requests or accounting messages that RADIUS clients or RADIUS proxies send. In the case of connection requests, the RADIUS server processes the list of RADIUS attributes in the connection request. Based on a set of rules and the information in the user account database, the RADIUS server either authenticates and authorizes the connection and sends back an **Access-Accept** message or sends back an **Access-Reject** message.

What is a RADIUS client?

A *RADIUS client* can be a RADIUS proxy or an access server, such as a dial-up server, a VPN server, or a wireless access point . The RADIUS client receives authorization requests from the remote access client for network access and passes them to the RADIUS server for verification.

What is a RADIUS proxy?

A *RADIUS proxy* can be configured in an infrastructure that has multiple RADIUS servers available to authorize access requests. A RADIUS proxy receives an authorization request from a RADIUS client, determines the appropriate RADIUS server, and forwards the authorization request to that RADIUS server.

For example, several organizations may outsource their dial-up access to an ISP. When a client dials in to the ISP, the client connects to a RADIUS client that passes the authorization request to the RADIUS proxy. The RADIUS proxy determines to which organization the user belongs and then forwards the request to that organization for authentication of the user's dial-up access.

What Is IAS?

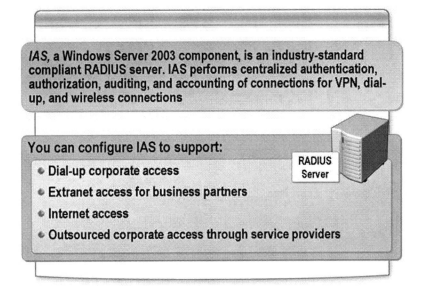

IAS, a Windows Server 2003 component, is an industry-standard compliant RADIUS server. IAS performs centralized authentication, authorization, auditing, and accounting of connections for VPN, dial-up, and wireless connections

You can configure IAS to support:

- Dial-up corporate access
- Extranet access for business partners
- Internet access
- Outsourced corporate access through service providers

RADIUS Server

Definition

The *Internet Authentication Service* (IAS) component of Windows Server 2003 is an industry-standard compliant RADIUS server. IAS performs centralized authentication, authorization, auditing, and accounting of connections for VPN, dial-up, and wireless connections.

Why use IAS?

By using IAS, you can centrally manage and control remote and wireless access to your network and track usage statistics. You can also centrally manage remote access permissions and connection properties.

If you have more than one remote or wireless access server, rather than administer the access policies of all the access servers separately, you can configure a single server with IAS as a RADIUS server and configure the remote access servers as RADIUS clients.

When an IAS server is a member of an Active Directory domain, IAS uses the directory service as its user account database and is part of a single sign-on solution. The same set of credentials is used for network access control (authenticating and authorizing access to a network) and to log on to an Active Directory domain.

Note   After you configure a server that runs Routing and Remote Access service to use RADIUS authentication, the remote access policies stored on the remote access server are no longer used. Instead, the remote access policies stored on the IAS server are used. You can copy the current set of remote access policies to the IAS server.

IAS interoperates with network access devices from a multitude of vendors. Organizations that want to build an integrated authentication system that securely authenticates users against a single directory, regardless of the access method or the device that they are using, can take advantage of IAS.

Examples

You can configure IAS to support several business scenarios, including:

- *Dial-up corporate access.* You can configure IAS to support remote employees with authenticated dial-up connections so that the IAS server can give access to employees based on the group to which they belong.

- *Extranet access for business partners.* You can set up IAS to allow your business partners limited access to specific resources on your network while protecting other resources from unauthorized access.

- *Internet access.* You can configure IAS to support customer-authenticated dial-up connections to an ISP so that the IAS server grants access to customers based on the service plan for which they sign up.

- *Outsourced corporate access through service providers.* You can use IAS to support an organization that uses ISPs to provide the remote access infrastructure, but the organization retains control over user authentication, authorization, and accounting. When an employee connects to the remote access server at the ISP, the authentication and usage records are forwarded to the organization's IAS server. The IAS server enables the organization to control user authentication, track usage, and control which employees are allowed to gain access to the network.

How Centralized Authentication Works

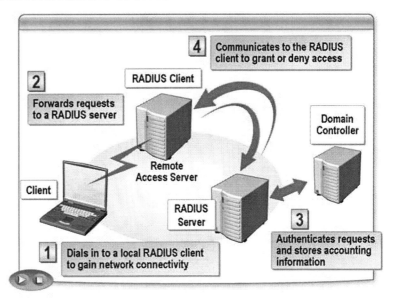

The process of centralized authentication and authorization

The following steps describe the basic process that network access servers, a RADIUS server, and RADIUS clients use to perform authentication and authorization:

1. A user connects to a network access server (a Windows-based computer that is configured with the Routing and Remote Access service) by using a VPN, dial-up, or wireless connection.

2. The network access server forwards authentication requests to a RADIUS (IAS) server. (The network access server acts as a RADIUS client.) If the verification of the digital signature is successful, the IAS server queries the domain controller.

3. The RADIUS (IAS) server accesses the user account information on a domain controller and checks the remote access authentication credentials. (The IAS server performs the functions of a RADIUS server.)

4. If the user's credentials are authenticated, the IAS server evaluates the connection attempt against the configured remote access policies and the dial-in properties of the user's account to decide whether to authorize the request. If the connection attempt matches the conditions of at least one policy and the user account dial-in properties, IAS sends a RADIUS **Access-Accept** message back to the network access server that sent the authentication request.

    If the connection attempt is either not authenticated or not authorized, IAS sends a RADIUS **Access-Reject** message back to the network access server and the connection attempt is rejected.

How to Configure an IAS Server for Network Access Authentication

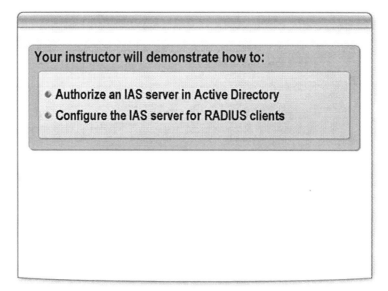

Your instructor will demonstrate how to:

- Authorize an IAS server in Active Directory
- Configure the IAS server for RADIUS clients

Introduction

If an IAS server must access Active Directory to authenticate users, you must authorize the IAS server to ensure that IAS has the correct permission to access account information from Active Directory.

You must also add the RADIUS clients to the IAS server. The RADIUS clients are the remote access servers that will use the IAS server for authentication and authorization.

Note It is recommended that you log on with an account that has non-administrative credentials and use the **Run as** command with a user account that has the appropriate administrative credentials to perform this task.

Procedure for authorizing an IAS server in Active Directory

To authorize an IAS server in Active Directory:

1. Open the Internet Authentication Service console.
2. Right-click **Internet Authentication Service (Local)**, and then click **Register Server in Active Directory**.
3. In the **Register Internet Authentication Server in Active Directory** dialog box, click **OK**.

Note When you authorize an IAS server, Windows Server 2003 adds the server's computer account to the RAS and IAS Servers' security group, which has the required Active Directory permissions to access user data in Active Directory.

Procedure for configuring the IAS server for RADIUS clients

To configure the IAS server for RADIUS clients:

1. Open the Internet Authentication Service console.

2. In the console tree, right-click **RADIUS Clients**, and then click **New RADIUS Client** to start the **Add Client Wizard**.

3. On the **New RADIUS Client** page, specify the following information, and then click **Next**:

   • **Friendly name**. Type a name for the RADIUS client that you are adding.

   • **Client address (IP or DNS)**. Type IP address or DNS name for the RADIUS client. Typically, it is more efficient to specify an IP address so that IAS does not have to resolve all host names at startup. If you only know a client's DNS name, click **Verify** to resolve the name to an IP address.

4. On the **Client Information** page, specify the following:

   • **Client-Vendor**. Select **Microsoft** if you are adding a Routing and Remote Access server. If you are adding a RADIUS client from a vendor that is not listed, select **RADIUS Standard**.

Note   The **Client-Vendor** setting is only required if you are using remote access policies that are based on a client-vendor attribute.

   • **Request must contain the Message Authenticator attribute**. Select this check box if the RADIUS client must send a signature attribute in the Access-Request packet. You must specify a signature attribute if you use EAP for authentication.

   • **Shared secret**. Type the secret, and then retype the secret in the **Confirm shared secret** box.

   A shared secret is a text string that serves as a password among an IAS server and the remote access servers that forward requests to it. Shared secrets:

   • Must be exactly the same on both servers.

   • Are case sensitive.

   • Can use any standard alphanumeric and special characters. Using combinations of uppercase and lowercase letters, numbers, and special characters makes the shared secret more secure.

   • Can be up to 255 characters long. Long shared secrets are more secure than shorter ones.

5. Click **Finish**.

How to Configure a Remote Access Server to Use IAS for Authentication

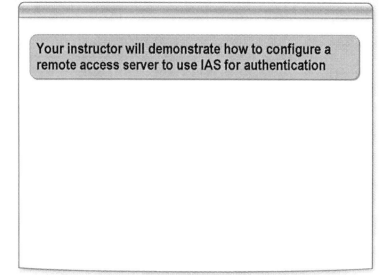

Your instructor will demonstrate how to configure a remote access server to use IAS for authentication

Introduction

To configure a remote access server as a RADIUS client, you must configure the remote access server to forward authentication requests to an IAS server.

Note It is recommended that you log on with an account that has non-administrative credentials and use the **Run as** command with a user account that has the appropriate administrative credentials to perform this task.

Procedure

To configure a remote access server to use IAS for authentication:

1. From the **Administrative Tools** menu, open Routing and Remote Access.

2. In the console tree, right-click *ComputerName* (where *ComputerName* is the name of your computer), and then click **Properties**.

3. On the **Security** tab of the *ComputerName* **(local) Properties** dialog box, in the **Authentication provider** box, select **RADIUS Authentication**, and then click **Configure**.

Note To use **Windows Authentication**, in the *ComputerName* (local) Properties dialog box, in the **Authentication provider** box, select **Windows Authentication**, and then click **OK**.

4. In the **RADIUS Authentication** dialog box, click **Add**.

5. In the **Add RADIUS Server** dialog box, in the **Server name** box, type the name of the IAS server that you are using for RADIUS authentication.

6. If you have a shared secret configured on the IAS server, click **Change** to set the shared secret on the remote access server, and then click **OK**.

7. In the *ComputerName* **(local) Properties** dialog box, click **OK**.

8. In the **Routing and Remote Access** warning box, click **No** to configure RADIUS Accounting.

9. In the **Routing and Remote Access** warning box, click **OK**.

10. In the second **Routing and Remote Access** warning box, click **OK**.

11. In the Routing and Remote Access console, right-click *ComputerName*, click **All Tasks**, and then click **Restart**.

Practice: Centralizing Network Access Authentication by Using IAS

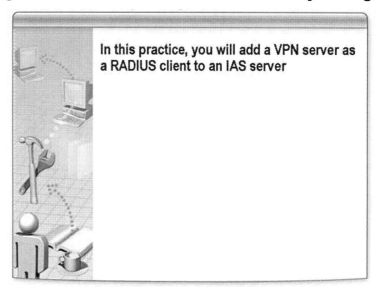

In this practice, you will add a VPN server as a RADIUS client to an IAS server

Objective

In this practice, you will add a VPN server as a RADIUS client to an IAS server.

Instructions

To complete this practice, refer to the *Implementation Plan Values* document, located in the Appendix at the end of your student workbook.

You must be logged on with an account that has non-administrative credentials and use the **Run as** command with a user account that has the appropriate administrative credentials to complete the task.

Scenario

Because the number of remote access servers has grown in your organization, the systems engineer installed an IAS server and configured it with remote access policies. The systems engineer asked you to add your remote access / VPN server to the IAS server as a RADIUS client and then configure your VPN server to use RADIUS authentication.

Practice

▶ **Configure a remote access server to use IAS for authentication**

- Complete this task from both student computers.

- User name: **nwtraders***ComputerName***Admin**

- Password: **P@ssw0rd**

- Administrative tool: **Routing and Remote Access**

- RADIUS Authentication provider: **RADIUS Authentication**

- RADIUS Authentication server: **London**

- Shared Secret: **2277**

- Restart Routing and Remote Access.

▶ **Connect to your partner's computer by using the VPN connection**

- Complete this task from the higher number student computer.

- User name: *ComputerName***Admin** (where *ComputerName* is the name of your computer)

- Password: **P@ssw0rd**

- Verify that a pop-up balloon is displayed in the notification area that states the VPN *ComputerName* (where *ComputerName* is the name of your partner's computer) is now connected.

- On the desktop, right-click **VPN** *ComputerName* and then click **Status**.

- In the **VPN** *ComputerName* **Status** dialog box, verify that **Status** is displayed as **Connected**, and then note the **Duration** time.

▶ **Verify the connection duration of remote access client**

- Complete this task from the lower number student computer.

- User name: **nwtraders***ComputerName***Admin**

- Password: **P@ssw0rd**

- Administrative tool: **Routing and Remote Access**

- Remote access clients: **nwtraders***ComputerName***Admin** (where *ComputerName* is the name of your partner's computer)

▶ **Disconnect from your partner's computer by using the VPN connection**

- Complete this task from the higher number student computer.

- On the desktop, right-click **VPN** *ComputerName* (where *ComputerName* is the name of your partner's computer), and then click **Disconnect**.

▶ **Configure your VPN server to use Windows authentication**

- Complete this task from both student computers.

- User name: **nwtraders***ComputerName***Admin**

- Password: **P@ssw0rd**

- Administrative tool: **Routing and Remote Access**

- RADIUS Authentication provider: **Windows Authentication**

- Restart Routing and Remote Access.

Lab A: Configuring Network Access

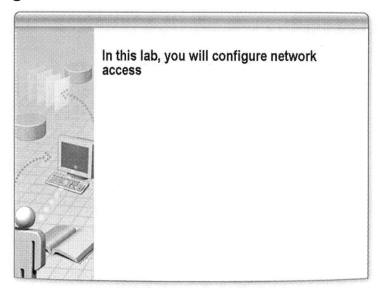

In this lab, you will configure network access

Objectives

In this lab, you will configure network access.

Estimated time to complete this lab: 30 minutes

Exercise 1
Configuring Network Access

In this exercise, you will you will configure network access.

Instructions

To complete this lab, refer to the *Implementation Plan Values* document, located in the Appendix at the end of your student workbook.

All practices and the demonstration must be completed before starting the lab.

You must be logged on with an account that has non-administrative credentials and use the **Run as** command with a user account that has the appropriate administrative credentials to complete the tasks. When completing the lab, assume that you will log on with a non-administrative account (example: *ComputerName*User), unless the Specific Instructions in the lab state otherwise.

Scenario

In your lab, you have configured a VPN server and a VPN connection on a client computer for testing purposes. The systems engineer has provided you with a design plan to allow for the future deployment of wireless clients and the use of certificates. You will configure your remote access server according to the following details that are outlined in the plan:

■ The remote access server needs to support 150 clients that will use PPTP connections.

■ The remote access server needs to support 150 clients that will use L2TP connections.

■ The remote access server needs a second policy to authenticate administrators that will connect remotely by using wireless. This policy should:

  • Limit the administrators' access to Monday through Friday, 7 A.M. to 7 P.M.

  • Limit access only through a wireless 802.11 connection.

  • Support authentication only by using a Smart Card or other certificate.

  • Allow for only MPPE 128-bit encryption.

After configuring your remote access server according to the plan details, you will verify connectivity by using the VPN connection on the client computer. A VPN connection to the client computer confirms that the existing Routing and Remote Access service was not disrupted.

Tasks	Specific instructions
Perform the following task on both student computers.	
1. Configure a total of 150 PPTP ports and 150 L2TP ports.	■ On the remote access server, configure PPTP ports to equal 150. ■ On the remote access server, configure L2TP ports to equal 150.
Perform the following task on both student computers.	
2. Create a new remote access policy for wireless clients.	■ On the remote access server, create a new Remote Access policy titled Wireless. ■ The Wireless policy conditions are for wireless connections and apply to the *ComputerName* administrator's group (where *ComputerName* is the name of your partner's computer). ■ The Wireless policy will be configured to allow access only during Monday through Friday from 7 A.M. to 7 P.M. ■ The Wireless policy will allow access only through Wireless 802.11 media. ■ The Wireless policy will support the Extensible Authentication Protocol method Smart Card or other certificate. ■ The Wireless policy will only support a MPPE 128-bit encryption.
Perform the following task on the higher number student computer.	
3. Verify the connectivity to the remote access server by using the VPN connection.	■ Use the VPN connection to connect to the remote access server as nwtraders*ComputerName*Admin (where *ComputerName* is the name of your computer). ■ Note the duration time of the connection.
Perform the following task on the lower number student computer.	
4. Verify the duration of the remote access client connection.	■ Verify the connection by confirming that nwtraders*ComputerName*Admin (where *ComputerName* is the name of your partner's computer) is displayed as a remote access client. ■ Note the duration time of the client connection.
Perform the following task on the higher number student computer.	
5. Disconnect from your partner's computer.	■ The VPN connection shortcut is located on the desktop.

Microsoft®
Training &
Certification

Module 10: Managing and Monitoring Network Access

Contents

Microsoft®

Overview

* Managing the Network Access Services
* Configuring Logging on a Network Access Server
* Collecting and Monitoring Network Access Data

Introduction

This module introduces the skills and knowledge that are necessary to manage and monitor the network access of dial-up, virtual private network (VPN), and wireless clients.

Objective

After completing this module, you will be able to:

* Manage the network access services.
* Configure logging on the network access server.
* Collect and monitor network access data.

Lesson: Managing the Network Access Services

- Guidelines for Managing Network Access Services
- How to Manage Remote Access Clients

Introduction

This lesson presents the skills and knowledge that are necessary to enable you to perform basic management functions on the network access services provided by the Routing and Remote Access service.

Objectives

After completing this lesson, you will be able to:

- Apply guidelines for managing a remote access server.
- Manage remote access clients.

Guidelines for Managing Network Access Services

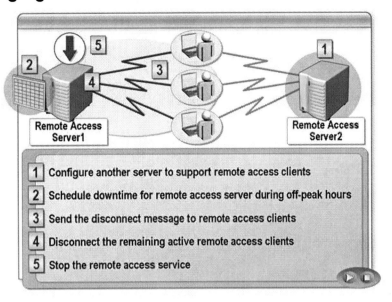

Guidelines for stopping and starting the Routing and Remote Access service

Periodically, it is necessary to shut down the Routing and Remote Access service. For example, you may need to change the location of a remote access server that is in your organization's building. Or, you may need to shut down the service to repair or upgrade hardware. You can follow a few simple guidelines to help ensure that your clients are minimally affected during the scheduled service shut down.

When you need to shut down the Routing and Remote Access service, you should:

1. Configure a replacement remote access server.

2. Schedule the downtime during the least busy time of business.

3. Send a message to your clients to alert them of the time and length of the scheduled downtime.

4. Use the Routing and Remote Access console to disconnect any clients that did not disconnect from the remote access servers.

5. Stop the Routing and Remote Access service.

How to Manage Remote Access Clients

Your instructor will demonstrate how to:

- Send a message to a single remote access client
- Send a message to all remote access clients
- Disconnect a remote access client
- Start and stop the Routing and Remote Access service

Introduction

You use the Routing and Remote Access console to:

- Send a message to clients to notify them that they need to switch to a different remote access server.

- Disconnect any clients that did not switch to remote access servers.

Note It is recommended that you log on with an account that has non-administrative credentials and use the **Run as** command with a user account that has the appropriate administrative credentials to perform this task.

Procedure for sending a message to a single remote access client

To send a message to a single remote access client:

1. Log on with a non-administrative user account.

2. Click **Start**, and then click **Control Panel**.

3. In Control Panel, open **Administrative Tools**, right-click **Routing and Remote Access**, and then select **Run as**.

4. In the **Run As** dialog box, select **The following user**, and then type a user account and password that has the appropriate permissions to complete the task. Click **OK**.

5. Open Routing and Remote Access, and click **Remote Access Clients**.

6. Right-click the appropriate user name, click **Send message**, and then click **OK**.

Procedure for sending a message to all remote access clients

To send a message to all remote access clients:

1. Open the Routing and Remote Access console, and right-click **Remote Access Clients**.

2. Select **Send to All**, and then click **OK**.

Procedure for disconnecting a remote access client

To disconnect a remote access client:

1. Open the Routing and Remote Access console, and right-click **Remote Access Clients**.

2. Select the appropriate user name, and then click **Disconnect**.

Procedure for starting and stopping the Routing and Remote Access service

After you disconnect all clients from a remote access server, you can properly shut down the service for that server.

To start and stop the Routing and Remote Access service:

1. In the Routing and Remote Access console, in the console tree, click **Server Status**.

2. In the details pane, right-click a server name, point to **All Tasks**, and perform one of the following steps:

   • To start the service, click **Start**.

   • To stop the service, click **Stop**.

Note You can also start and stop the Routing and Remote Access Service by using the **net start remoteaccess** and **net stop remoteaccess** commands.

Practice: Managing the Remote Access Service

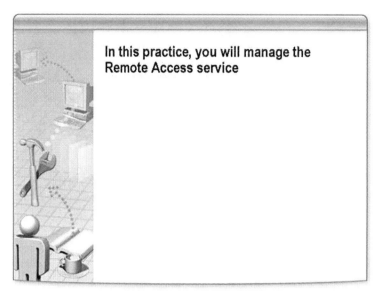

In this practice, you will manage the
Remote Access service

Objective

In this practice, you will manage the Remote Access service.

Instructions

To complete this practice, refer to the *Implementation Plan Values* document, located in the Appendix at the end of your student workbook.

You must be logged on with an account that has non-administrative credentials and use the **Run as** command with a user account that has the appropriate administrative credentials to complete the task.

Scenario

The remote access server in your Lab department is scheduled to be shut down for a hardware upgrade. The systems engineer has created a replacement remote access server to support remote access clients during the scheduled outage. You will properly shut down the remote access server.

Practice

▶ **Connect to your partner's computer by using the VPN connection**

■ Complete this task from the higher number student computer.

1. On the desktop, double-click **VPN** *ComputerName* (where *ComputerName* is your partner's computer).

2. In the **Connect VPN** *ComputerName* dialog box, type the following information and then click **Connect**.

   a. User name: *ComputerName***Admin** (where *ComputerName* is the name of your computer)

   b. Password: **P@ssw0rd**

3. Verify that a pop-up balloon is displayed in the notification area that states the **VPN** *ComputerName* **is now connected**.

4. On the desktop, right-click **VPN** *ComputerName* and then click **Status**.

5. In the **VPN** *ComputerName* **Status** dialog box, verify that **Status** is displayed as **Connected**, and note the **Duration** time.

▶ **Verify the connection duration for the remote access client**

■ Complete this task from the lower number student computer.

1. Open the Routing and Remote Access console.

2. In the Routing and Remote Access console, in the console tree, select **Remote Access Clients**.

3. In the Remote Access Clients details pane, under **User Name**, verify that **nwtraders***ComputerName***Admin** is displayed, and note the duration time.

▶ **Send a message to all remote access clients**

■ Complete this task from the lower number student computer.

■ Audience: **Send to All**

■ Message text: **This remote access server will be shutting down in 10 minutes**

▶ **Verify that the message is displayed and then disconnect from your partner's computer**

■ Complete this task from the higher number student computer.

■ Read the text of the **Messenger Service** message box.

■ Disconnect from **VPN** *ComputerName* (where *ComputerName* is your partner's computer).

▶ **Verify the connection duration of the remote access client**

■ Complete this task from the lower number student computer.

1. Open the Routing and Remote Access console.

2. In the Routing and Remote Access console, in the console tree, select **Remote Access Clients**.

3. On the **Action** menu, click **Refresh**.

4. In the Remote Access Clients details pane, verify that no items are displayed.

▶ **Stop the Routing and Remote Access service**

■ Complete this task from the lower number student computer.

■ Administrative tool: **Routing and Remote Access**

▶ **Start the Routing and Remote Access service**

■ Complete this task from the lower number student computer.

■ Administrative tool: **Routing and Remote Access**

Lesson: Configuring Logging on a Network Access Server

* Routing and Remote Access Logging
* Authentication and Accounting Logging
* How to Configure Authentication and Accounting Logging
* Log Files for Specific Connections
* How to Configure Logging for Specific Connection Types

Introduction

This lesson introduces the knowledge and skills that are necessary to be able to use certain types of logging to help isolate common issues with network access.

Lesson objectives

After completing this lesson, you will be able to:

■ Describe the types of logging that are supported by the Routing and Remote Access service.

■ Explain what authentication and accounting logging is.

■ Configure authentication and accounting logging.

■ Identify log files that are used for specific connections.

■ Configure logging for specific connection types.

Routing and Remote Access Logging

Type of logging	Description
Event logging	Records remote access server errors, warnings, and other detailed information in the system event log
Local authentication and account logging	Tracks usage and authentication attempts on the local remote access server
RADIUS-based authentication and account logging	Tracks remote access usage and authentication attempts

Introduction

A server that runs Routing and Remote Access supports three types of logging:

- Event logging
- Local authentication and account logging
- RADIUS-based (Remote Authentication Dial-In User Service) authentication and account logging

Event logging

You can use event logging to record remote access server errors, warnings, and other detailed information in the system event log. You can enable event logging and configure the levels of events logged on the **Event Logging** tab in the **Properties** dialog box of the remote access server.

For example, the event log can record the stopping and starting of the remote access service in addition to recording the users who have been denied access and the reasons why.

In the **Properties** dialog box for the remote access server, you can also enable the logging of additional Routing and Remote Access information. When you enable logging, the computer creates numerous detailed log files in the *%Systemroot%\Tracing* directory, which contains a more detailed record of Routing and Remote Access functions.

Note   Tracing consumes system resources and should only be used sparingly to help identify network problems.

Local authentication and account logging

The Routing and Remote Access service supports the logging of authentication and accounting information for connection attempts when Microsoft® Windows® authentication or the accounting provider is configured. This logging is separate from the events that are recorded in the system event log.

Authentication and account logging is especially useful in isolating remote access policy issues. For each authentication attempt, the name of the remote access policy that either accepted or rejected the connection is logged.

RADIUS-based authentication and account logging

A server that runs Routing and Remote Access supports the logging of authentication and accounting information for remote access connections at a RADIUS server when RADIUS authentication and accounting are enabled. RADIUS authentication and accounting logging is separate from the events that are recorded in the system event log. You can use the information that is logged on your RADIUS server to track remote access usage and authentication attempts.

For example, the RADIUS accounting log records connection information, including how long you were connected to the remote access server.

Authentication and Accounting Logging

Authentication and accounting logging is a process that records detailed information about remote access connection requests

Use authentication and accounting information to:

- Track remote access usage and authentication attempts
- Maintain records for billing purposes
- Isolate remote access policy issues

Refine your logging methods after you determine which data best matches your needs by specifying:

- The log file properties
- The types of request logging

Definition

Authentication and accounting logging is a process that records detailed information about remote access connection requests.

Benefits of using authentication and accounting logging

You can use the logged information to track remote access usage and authentication attempts. By setting up and using log files to track authentication information, you can simplify the administration of your remote access service. You can set up and use logs to track accounting information (such as logon and logoff records) to maintain records for billing purposes. Authentication and accounting logging is especially useful for isolating remote access policy issues. For each authentication attempt, the name of the remote access policy that either accepted or rejected the connection attempt is recorded.

The authentication and accounting information is stored in a configurable log file or in files stored in the *%Systemroot%*\System32\LogFiles folder. The log files are saved in Internet Authentication Service (IAS) or in a database-compatible format so that any database program can read the log file directly for analysis. You can configure both the Routing and Remote Access service and IAS to send the authentication and accounting information directly to a database server that allows multiple servers to input data into the same database.

Log file properties

When you set up logging, you can specify:

- The requests to be logged.
- The log-file format.
- How often new logs are started.
- Automatic deletion of the oldest log file when the disk is full.
- Where log files are recorded.
- What information the log file records contain.

Types of request logging

All types of request logging are disabled by default. Initially, it is recommended that you enable the logging of authentication and accounting requests. You can refine your logging methods after you determine the data that best matches your needs. As shown in the following table, you can select the types of requests to log. The origin and destination of the log file items depend on whether they are being submitted by a RADIUS client to a RADIUS server or whether they are being logged locally in a Routing and Remote Access log file using Windows Authentication and Accounting.

Types of requests	Description of log entries
Accounting requests	• **Accounting-on** indicates that the server is online and is ready to accept connections. • **Accounting-off** indicates that the server is going offline. • **Accounting-start** indicates the start of a user session. • **Accounting-stop** indicates the end of a user session.
Authentication requests	• **Authentication requests** logs incoming attributes that a connecting user sends. These entries in the log file contain only incoming attributes. • **Authentication accepts and rejects** logs entries that indicate whether the user is accepted or rejected.
Periodic status	• **Periodic status** logs entries for interim accounting requests that are provided by some remote access servers during sessions. • **Accounting-interim requests** logs entries that are provided periodically by the remote access server during a user session.

Note   You can log accounting, authentication, and periodic status on a Microsoft SQL Server™ database. For more information, see "SQL Server database logging" in the Windows Server 2003 Help documentation.

How to Configure Authentication and Accounting Logging

Your instructor will demonstrate how to:

- Enable Windows accounting
- Configure local authentication and accounting logging
- Configure RADIUS-based authentication and accounting logging

Introduction

To configure authentication and accounting logging, you must first enable either Windows authentication or Windows accounting. Then, you can configure the type of activity that you want to log (an authentication or accounting activity) and the log file settings.

If the computer running the Routing and Remote Access service is configured for RADIUS authentication or the accounting provider, and the RADIUS server is a computer running Windows Server 2003 and IAS, the logging information is recorded on the IAS server computer.

Note It is recommended that you log on with an account that has non-administrative credentials and use the **Run as** command with a user account that has the appropriate administrative credentials to perform this task.

Procedure for enabling Windows accounting

To enable Windows accounting:

1. Open the Routing and Remote Access console, right-click the server name for which you want to configure Windows accounting, and then click **Properties**.

2. On the **Security** tab, in **Accounting provider**, click **Windows Accounting**, and then click **OK**.

Procedure for configuring local authentication and accounting logging

To configure local authentication and account logging:

1. Open the Routing and Remote Access console.

2. In the console tree, click **Remote Access Logging**.

3. In the details pane, right-click **Local File**, and then click **Properties**.

4. In the **Local File Properties** dialog box, on the **Settings** tab, select one or more of the three options:

   - **Accounting requests**. This option logs information such as the start of a user session and the end of a user session.

   - **Authentication requests**. This option logs information such as whether a user access request is accepted or rejected.

   - **Periodic status**. This option logs information such as accounting interim requests. To log these requests the **Acct-Interim-Interval RADIUS** attribute must be configured in the remote access profile on the IAS server.

5. In the **Local File Properties** dialog box, on the **Log File** tab, select the following appropriate logging options:

   a. **Directory**: Path to the folder where the log files are stored

   b. **Format**: **IAS** or **Database-compatible**

   c. **Create a new log file**: **Daily, weekly, monthly, Never (unlimited size), When the log file reaches this size**

6. In the **Local File Properties** dialog box, on the **Log File** tab, if applicable, select **When disk is full delete older log files**, and then click **OK**.

Note   Whenever you change the Authentication provider or Accounting provider on the **Security** tab, you must stop and start the Routing and Remote Access service for these changes to be applied.

Procedure for configuring RADIUS-based accounting `

To configure RADIUS-based accounting:

1. Open the Routing and Remote Access console.

2. Right-click the server name for which you want to configure RADIUS-based accounting, and then click **Properties**.

3. On the **Security** tab, in the **Accounting provider** field, select **RADIUS accounting**, and then click **Configure**.

4. In the **RADIUS Accounting** dialog box, click **Add**.

5. In the **Add RADIUS Server** dialog box, in the **Server name** field, type the host name of the RADIUS server.

6. In the **Add RADIUS Server** dialog box, click **Change**.

7. In the **Change Secret** dialog box, in the New secret field and the Confirm new secret field, type the secret, and then click **OK**.

8. In the **RADIUS Accounting** dialog box, click **OK**.

9. In the *ServerName* **Properties** dialog box, click **OK**.

Log Files for Specific Connections

Connection type	Log file name	Description of log file
PPP	PPP log	Records the series of programming functions and PPP control messages during a PPP connection
L2TP/IPSec	Audit log	Records information about IPSec-related events
L2TP/IPSec	Oakley log	Records information about all Internet Key Exchange main-mode or quick-mode negotiations

Introduction

To help gather detailed information and to isolate problems with the remote access server, you can configure additional logging functions. You should be cautious when enabling this type of logging because it can add substantial overhead to the remote access server.

PPP Log

You can use Point-to-Point Protocol (PPP) logging to record the series of programming functions and PPP control messages during a PPP connection. PPP logging is a valuable source of information when you are trying to resolve the failure of a PPP connection.

Audit log

You can use the Event Viewer snap-in to view the following IPSec-related events:

- Internet Protocol security (IPSec) Policy Agent events in the audit log.

- Internet Key Exchange (IKE) events (security association details) in the security log. To view these events, enable success or failure auditing for the **Audit logon events** audit policy for your domain or local computer.

- IPSec policy change events in the security log. To view these events, enable success or failure auditing for the **Audit policy change** audit policy for your domain or local computer.

- IPSec driver per-packet drop events in the system log. In the Windows Server 2003 family, you can enable packet event logging for the IPSec driver by using the Netsh **ipsec** command-line tool.

  To enable logging of dropped inbound and outbound packets, specify a value of 7. At the command prompt, type **netsh ipsec dynamic set config ipsecdiagnostics 7**, and then restart the computer.

Enabling audit logging for Internet Security Association and Key Management Protocol (ISAKMP) events and viewing the events in Event Viewer is the fastest and simplest way to isolate failed main-mode or quick-mode negotiations.

When you enable success or failure auditing for the Audit logon events audit policy, IPSec records the success or failure of each main-mode and quick-mode negotiation and the establishment and termination of each negotiation as separate events. However, enabling this type of auditing can cause the security log to fill up with IKE events. For example, for servers that are connected to the Internet, attacks on the IKE protocol can cause the security log to fill up with IKE events. IKE events can also fill up the security log for servers that use IPSec to secure traffic to many clients. To avoid filling up the log with IKE events, you can disable auditing for IKE events in the security log by modifying the registry.

Oakley log

You can use the Oakley log to view details about the security association establishment process. The Oakley log is enabled in the registry; however, it is not enabled by default.

After you enable the Oakley log, which is stored in the %*Systemroot*%\Debug folder, it records all ISAKMP main-mode or quick-mode negotiations. A new Oakley.log file is created each time the IPSec Policy Agent is started, and the previous version of the Oakley.log file is saved as Oakley.log.sav.

How to Configure Logging for Specific Connection Types

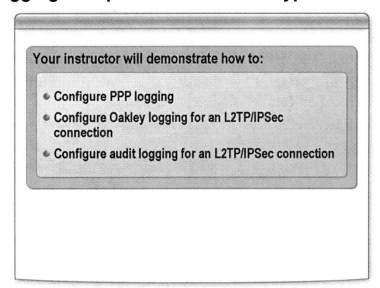

Your instructor will demonstrate how to:

- Configure PPP logging
- Configure Oakley logging for an L2TP/IPSec connection
- Configure audit logging for an L2TP/IPSec connection

Introduction

You can use the remote access diagnostic functions that are available in the Windows Server 2003 family to collect detailed logs and information about a remote access connection.

After you are finished troubleshooting, you should disable logging.

Note It is recommended that you log on with an account that has non-administrative credentials and use the **Run as** command with a user account that has the appropriate administrative credentials to perform this task.

Procedure for configuring PPP logging

To configure PPP logging:

1. In the Routing and Remote Access console, right-click the server name, and then click **Properties**.

2. In *ServerName* **Properties** dialog box, on the **Logging** tab, select one of the following:

   - **Log errors only**
   - **Log errors and warnings**
   - **Log all events**
   - **Do not log any events**

3. On the **Logging** tab, if applicable, select **Log additional Routing and Remote Access information**, and then click **OK**. This option logs events in the PPP connection establishment process.

Procedure for configuring Oakley logging for an L2TP/IPSec connection

To configure Oakley logging for a L2TP/IPSec connection:

1. To enable the Oakley log, set the **HKEY_LOCAL_MACHINE\System\CurrentControlSet\Services\PolicyAgent\Oakley\EnableLogging** DWORD registry setting to a value of **1**. (The Oakley key does not exist by default and, therefore, it must be created.)

Note   For more information about adding values to registry keys, see the Windows Server 2003 Help documentation.

---

2. To activate the new **EnableLogging** registry setting after modifying its value:

   a. Stop the Routing and Remote Access service by typing **net stop remoteaccess** at the command prompt.

   b. Stop the IPSec services by typing **net stop policyagent** at the command prompt.

   c. Start the IPSec services by typing **net start policyagent** at the command prompt.

   d. Start the Routing and Remote Access service by typing **net start remoteaccess** at the command prompt.

Procedure for configuring audit logging for an L2TP/IPSec connection

To configure audit logging for an L2TP/IPSec connection:

1. Set the **KEY_LOCAL_MACHINE\System\CurrentControlSet\Services\IPSec\DiagnosticMode** registry setting to **1**.

2. To activate the new **DiagnosticMode** registry setting after modifying its value:

   a. Stop the Routing and Remote Access service by typing **net stop remoteaccess** at the command prompt

   b. Stop the IPSec services by typing **net stop policyagent** at the command prompt.

   c. Start the IPSec services by typing **net start policyagent** at the command prompt.

   d. Start the Routing and Remote Access service by typing **net start remoteaccess** at the command prompt.

Note   The IPSec driver only writes events to the system log once an hour. For additional information about IPSec driver event logging, see the Windows Resource Kits.

Practice: Configuring Logging on a Remote Access Server

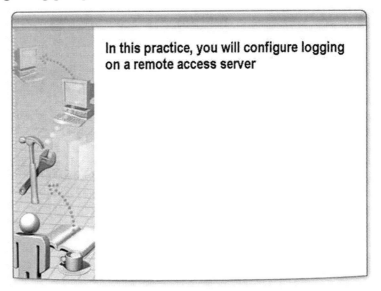

In this practice, you will configure logging on a remote access server

Introduction

In this practice, you will configure logging on a remote access server.

Instructions

You must be logged on with an account that has non-administrative credentials and use the **Run as** command with a user account that has the appropriate administrative credentials to complete the task.

Scenario

The systems engineer has created a logging plan for the remote access server in the lab. You will configure the remote access server to log authentication and accounting data.

Practice

▶ **Configure local authentication logging on your remote access server**

■ Complete this task from both student computers.

■ Administrative tool: **Routing and Remote Access**

■ Log the following information:

- **Accounting requests**

- **Authentication requests**

- **Periodic status**

■ Log file directory: C:\moc\2277\labfiles\lab10

■ Create a new log file: Daily

▶ **Verify that the log file does not exist**

■ Complete this task from both student computers.

■ Using Windows Explorer, open: **C:\moc\2277\labfiles\lab10**

■ Verify that no log file exists and leave the folder open

▶ **Stop and start the Routing and Remote Access service**

- Complete this task from both student computers.

- Administrative tool: **Routing and Remote Access**

▶ **Verify that the log file does exist**

- Complete this task from both student computers.

- Verify that the log file exists and close the folder.

Lesson: Collecting and Monitoring Network Access Data

- Why Collect Performance Data?
- Tools for Collecting Network Access Data
- How to Monitor Wireless Network Activity

Introduction

The information in this lesson presents the skills and knowledge that are necessary to enable you to collect and monitor network access data for the Routing and Remote Access service or IAS.

Lesson objectives

After completing this lesson, you will be able to:

- Explain the reasons for collecting performance data for network access.
- Identify and describe the different tools that are used for collecting network access data.
- Monitor wireless network activity.

Why Collect Performance Data?

> **Collect performance data to:**
>
> - Evaluate the workload of your server and the effect on resources
> - Observe changes and trends in workloads
> - Track resource usage
> - Test configuration changes or other tuning efforts
> - Isolate problems
> - Target components or processes

Reasons to collect performance data

Monitoring system performance is an important part of maintaining and administering your network access services. You can use performance data to:

- Evaluate the workload of your server and the corresponding effect on your system's resources.

- Observe changes and trends in workloads.

- Track resource usage so that you can plan for future upgrades.

- Test configuration changes or other tuning efforts by monitoring the results.

- Isolate problems such as a connection failure, the dropping of active connections, and the overall performance.

- Target components or processes for optimization.

Tools for Collecting Network Access Data

Tool	Description
System Monitor	Provides a way to view real-time performance data that is targeted toward specific components and services
Performance Logs and Alerts	Enables you to capture specific performance data for components and services
Wireless Monitor	Provides details about wireless network access points and clients

Tools for gathering data

Windows Server 2003 includes the following tools that you can use to gather data to help identify and predict network access issues:

System Monitor. This tool provides a way to view real-time performance data that is targeted toward specific components and services. You can also use the System Monitor tool to view previously captured or archived performance data.

Performance Logs and Alerts. This tool enables you to capture specific performance data for components and services over a configurable period of time in a log file. You can also set alerts that take action when certain events occur, such as:

- Sending a message.
- Running a program.
- Making an entry to the application event log.
- Starting a log when a selected counter's value exceeds or falls below a specified stetting.

Wireless Monitor. The Wireless Configuration service logs information in Wireless Monitor that allows you to:

- Identify service configuration changes.
- Check the events logged in the Wireless Configuration service log that are generated from outside of your wireless network, such as media event notifications, 802.1x events, and timer expiration events.
- View details about wireless network access points and clients.

You can use log information to isolate issues with your wireless service.

Examples of common objects

Commonly used objects for monitoring network access servers include:

- **Memory, Processor, Network, and Disk**. These objects contain standard network service counters that you can use for all types of servers. With the Routing and Remote Access service, the most common place that a bottleneck can occur is the network. The Routing and Remote Access service and IAS do not normally place a significant demand on the processor, memory, and disk if the server is dedicated to dial-in functions. However, if a remote access server or IAS server also hosts other applications or services, they could compete for resources. You should then monitor the four primary counters globally for the server to make sure one application or service is not over using resources that could compromise the other functions on the server.

> **Note**   For more information about standard performance objects, see Course 2275: *Maintaining a Microsoft Windows Server 2003 Environment*.

- **IAS Authentication Server**. This object contains counters that you can use to monitor incoming and outgoing requests and errors that the authentication server encounters.

- **IAS Authentication Clients**. This object contains counters that you can use to monitor incoming and outgoing requests and errors that the authentication client encounters.

- **IPv4**. This object contains counters that you can use to isolate Transmission Control Protocol/Internet Protocol (TCP/IP) performance data, errors, failures, and potential network attacks.

- **IPv6**. This object contains the same counters and capabilities as IPv4, but the IPv6 object counters are focused on IPv6.

- **RAS Port**. This object contains counters that provide information about the performance and throughput of individual remote access ports.

- **RA Total**. This object contains counters that provide information about the performance and throughput of all of the remote access ports together.

Examples of counters

You can create a Performance Log to keep track of the errors in IAS. Examples of counters that you can use to isolate and resolve common network access issues include:

- **Datagrams Received Discarded**. Amount of input IP datagrams that were discarded when a problem prevented their continued processing, such as the lack of buffer space.

- **Datagram Received Address Errors**. Amount of IP datagrams that were discarded because of address errors, such as invalid (0.0.0.0) and unsupported classes (Class E).

- **Access-Request**. Amount of access requests received.

- **Access-Rejects**. Amount of access requests rejected.

- **Bad Authenticators**. Amount of packets that contain an invalid message authenticator attribute (RADIUS).

- **Unknown Type**. Amount of unknown type (non-RADIUS packets received).

How to Monitor Wireless Network Activity

> **Your instructor will demonstrate how to:**
>
> ● Enable or disable wireless client information logging
> ● View details about wireless network access points
> ● View details about wireless network clients

Introduction

You use the Wireless Monitor snap-in to monitor wireless network activity.

Note It is recommended that you log on with an account that has non-administrative credentials and use the **Run as** command with a user account that has the appropriate administrative credentials to perform this task.

Procedure for enabling or disabling wireless client information logging

To enable or disable wireless client information logging:

1. Create a console containing Wireless Monitor. Or, open a saved console file containing Wireless Monitor.

2. Expand the name of the server that you want to configure.

3. Right-click **Wireless Client Information**, and then configure one of the following:

   • To enable logging for wireless network clients, click **Enable Logging**.

   • To disable logging for wireless network clients, click **Disable Logging**.

Procedure for viewing details about wireless network access points

You can view the name of the network on which the access point exists, the network type, the network address, and the current activity in addition to the signal strength.

To view the details about wireless network access points:

1. Create a console containing Wireless Monitor. Or, open a saved console file containing Wireless Monitor.

2. Double-click **Access Point Information**.

Procedure for viewing details about wireless network clients

You can view the network source from where the wireless client is communicating, the type of communication, when the communication occurred, and the name of the network.

To view the details about wireless network clients:

1. Create a console containing Wireless Monitor. Or, open a saved console file containing Wireless Monitor.

2. Double-click **Wireless Client Information**.

Practice: Collecting and Monitoring Network Access Data

In this practice, you will:

* Determine the best tools to use for monitoring and identifying certain network access issues

* Configure Performance Logs

Objective

In this practice, you will

- Determine the best tools to use for monitoring and identifying certain network access issues.

- Configure Performance Logs.

Instructions

To complete this practice, refer to the *Implementation Plan Values* document, located in the Appendix at the end of your student workbook.

You must be logged on with an account that has non-administrative credentials and use the **Run as** command with a user account that has the appropriate administrative credentials to complete the task.

Scenario

Network access clients in the Lab department have been experiencing difficulties connecting to and staying connected to the network access server. There are multiple remote access policies that are configured.

Other network access users have complained that their connections were dropped after being validated. These users have not documented the error messages that they received when they were disconnected. You suspect that the remote access servers are being overworked.

Practice

▶ **Determine the tools to use**

■ Both students in a pair are to answer the following questions:

1. What tool would you configure to verify that the appropriate policy is being applied?

   _____

   _____

2. What tool would you use to identify why users are being disconnected?

   _____

   _____

▶ **Configure Performance Logs**

■ Complete this task from both student computers

1. From **Administrative Tools**, open the Performance console.

2. Create a new **Counter Log**.

3. In the **New Log Settings** box, in the **Name** field, type **RAS Counter Log**

4. Add the objects and counters that are displayed in the following table.

Objects	Counters
Memory	Available KBytes
Network Interface	Bytes Total/Sec
Processor	% Processor Time

5. On the **Schedule** tab, verify that **Start log** is configured for **Manually (using the shortcut menu)**.

6. On the **Log Files** tab, configure the log file location as **C:\Moc\2277\LabFiles\Lab10** with the file name of *ComputerName***Stress.log**

7. Save the Performance console as **Remote Access Logging** to the desktop.

Lab A: Managing and Monitoring Remote Access

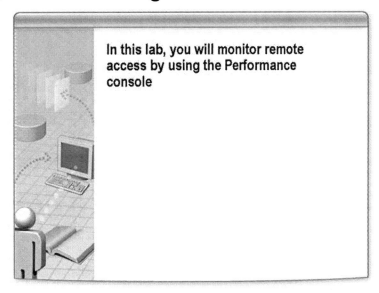

In this lab, you will monitor remote
access by using the Performance
console

Objectives

In this lab, you will monitor remote access server performance by using the
Performance console.

**Estimated time to
complete this lab: 30
minutes**

Exercise 1
Monitoring a Remote Access Server

Objective

In this exercise, you will monitor remote access errors and correct them.

Instructions

To complete the lab, refer to the Implementation Plan Values document, located in the Appendix at the end of your student workbook.

You must be logged on with an account that has non-administrative credentials and use the **Run as** command with a user account that has the appropriate administrative credentials to complete the tasks. When completing the lab, you should assume that you will log on with a non-administrative account, for example: *ComputerName*User, unless the Specific Instructions in the lab state otherwise.

Scenario

Your remote access clients are experiencing issues with connecting to a test remote access server in the lab. Your clients are using VPN connections. You will make changes to the lab VPN server and then monitor the effects of those changes on the VPN clients.

Tasks	Specific instructions
✋ Perform the following task only on the computer with the higher student number.	
1. Connect to the remote access server by using the VPN connection, verify your connection, and then disconnect.	▪ User name: *ComputerName***Admin** (where *ComputerName* is the name of your computer) ▪ Password: **P@ssw0rd** ▪ Verify that **Status** is displayed as **Connected**, and note the **Duration** time. ▪ Disconnect.
✋ Perform the following task only on the computer with the lower student number.	
2. Configure the Point-to-Point Tunneling Protocol (PPTP) and L2TP ports for the remote access server to allow only demand-dial routing connections.	▪ PPTP Ports: Disable the remote access connections. ▪ L2TP Ports: Disable the remote access connections.

Tasks	Specific instructions
✋ Perform the following task only on the computer with the higher student number.	
3. Attempt to connect to the remote access server by using the VPN connection and record the error information that is displayed in the message box.	■ User name: *ComputerName***Admin** (where *ComputerName* is the name of your computer) ■ Password: **P@ssw0rd** ■ In the **Error connecting to VPN Server** message box, verify the error ID is **913**. ■ Record the text information that is displayed in the message box. ■ Document the text in the error box:_____ ■ Leave the **Error connecting to VPN Server** message open.
✋ Perform the following task only on the computer with the lower student number.	
4. Configure the **VPN Policy** remote access policy to deny access.	■ VPN policy: Deny remote access permission.
✋ Perform the following task only on the computer with the higher student number.	
5. Attempt to connect to the remote access server by using the VPN connection and record the error information that is displayed in the message box.	■ In the **Error connecting to VPN Server** message box, click **Redial**. ■ In the **Error connecting to VPN Server** message box, verify that the error ID is **649**. ■ Record the text information that is displayed in the message box, and then click **Cancel** to close the message box. ■ Document the text in the message box:_____ ■ Leave the **Error connecting to VPN Server** message open.
✋ Perform the following task only on the computer with the lower student number.	
6. Configure the remote access policy profile for **VPN Policy** to allow access only on Sunday from 8 A.M. to 8 P.M., and then configure the policy to grant access.	■ VPN policy: **Allow access only during these days and at these times** ■ Dial-in hours: **Sunday 8am to 8pm** ■ VPN policy: **Grant remote access permission**

Tasks	Specific instructions
✋ Perform the following task only on the computer with the higher student number.	
7. Attempt to connect to the remote access server by using the VPN connection and record the error information that is displayed in the message box.	■ In the **Error connecting to VPN Server** message box, click **Redial**. ■ In the **Error connecting to VPN Server** message box, verify that the error ID is **649**. ■ Record the text information that is displayed in the message box, and then click **Cancel** to close the message box. ■ Document the text in the message box:_____ ■ Leave the **Error connecting to VPN Server** message open. ■ Is this error the same error that you received when you configured the VPN policy to deny access permissions? ■ Using the **More Info** button on the **649** message box, list the possible causes of this message message. ■ In the **649 more information** message box, read the third bullet.
✋ Perform the following tasks only on the computer with the lower student number.	
8. For the VPN Policy profile, clear **Allow access only on these days and at these times**.	■ VPN policy: Clear **Allow access only during these days and at these times**.
9. Configure the PPTP and L2TP ports on the remote access server to allow both remote access and demand-dial routing connections.	■ PPTP Ports: Enable the remote access connections. ■ L2TP Ports: Enable the remote access connections.
✋ Perform the following task only on the computer with the higher student number.	
10. Connect to the remote access server by using the VPN connection.	a. In the Error connecting to VPN Server message box, click Redial. b. In the **Status** dialog box, verify that the Status displays as **Connected**, and note the duration time. c. Disconnect.

Course Evaluation

To complete a course evaluation, go to http://www.CourseSurvey.com.

Microsoft will keep your evaluation strictly confidential and will use your responses to improve your future learning experience.

Appendix B: Implementation Plan Values

Directions: Refer to the values in this document when completing practices and labs for Course 2277: *Implementing, Managing, and Maintaining a Microsoft® Windows® Server 2003 Network Infrastructure: Network Services*. The shaded and non-shaded columns in the following tables represent computer partners for the purposes of the practices and labs. The *x* in the third octet represents the classroom number. Ask your instructor to provide the classroom number.

	London	Glasgow	Vancouver	Denver	Perth	Brisbane
ComputerName	London	Glasgow	Vancouver	Denver	Perth	Brisbane
srv	LON	GLA	VAN	DEN	PER	BRI
Partner	Lower	Higher	Lower	Higher	Lower	Higher
Classroom Network Connection	192.168.x.200	192.168.x.100	192.168.x.101	192.168.x.102	192.168.x.103	192.168.x.104
Partner Network Connection	192.168.100.1	192.168.100.2	192.168.101.1	192.168.101.2	192.168.102.1	192.168.102.2
ComputerNameAdmin	LondonAdmin	GlasgowAdmin	VancouverAdmin	DenverAdmin	PerthAdmin	BrisbaneAdmin
ComputerNameUser	LondonUser	GlasgowUser	VancouverUser	DenverUser	PerthUser	BrisbaneUser

	Lisbon	Bonn	Lima	Santiago	Bangalore	Singapore
ComputerName	Lisbon	Bonn	Lima	Santiago	Bangalore	Singapore
srv	LIS	BON	LIM	SAN	BAN	SIN
Partner	Lower	Higher	Lower	Higher	Lower	Higher
Classroom Network Connection	192.168.x.105	192.168.x.106	192.168.x.107	192.168.x.108	192.168.x.109	192.168.x.110
Partner Network Connection	192.168.103.1	192.168.103.2	192.168.104.1	192.168.104.2	192.168.105.1	192.168.105.2
ComputerNameAdmin	LisbonAdmin	BonnAdmin	LimaAdmin	SantiagoAdmin	BangaloreAdmin	SingaporeAdmin
ComputerNameUser	LisbonUser	BonnUser	LimaUser	SantiagoUser	BangaloreUser	SingaporeUser

	Casablanca	Tunis	Acapulco	Miami	Auckland	Suva
ComputerName	Casablanca	Tunis	Acapulco	Miami	Auckland	Suva
srv	CAS	TUN	ACA	MIA	AUK	SUV
Partner	Lower	Higher	Lower	Higher	Lower	Higher
Classroom Network Connection	192.168.x.111	192.168.x.112	192.168.x.113	192.168.x.114	192.168.x.115	192.168.x.116
Partner Network Connection	192.168.106.1	192.168.106.2	192.168.107.1	192.168.107.2	192.168.108.1	192.168.108.2
ComputerNameAdmin	CasablancaAdmin	TunisAdmin	AcapulcoAdmin	MiamiAdmin	AucklandAdmin	SuvaAdmin
ComputerNameUser	CasablancaUser	TunisUser	AcapulcoUser	MiamiUser	AucklandUser	SuvaUser

	Stockholm	Moscow	Caracas	Montevideo	Manila	Tokyo
ComputerName	Stockholm	Moscow	Caracas	Montevideo	Manila	Tokyo
srv	STO	MOS	CAR	MON	MAN	TOK
Partner	Lower	Higher	Lower	Higher	Lower	Higher
Classroom Network Connection	192.168.*x*.117	192.168.*x*.118	192.168.*x*.119	192.168.*x*.120	192.168.*x*.121	192.168.*x*.122
Partner Network Connection	192.168.109.1	192.168.109.2	192.168.110.1	192.168.110.2	192.168.111.1	192.168.111.2
*ComputerName*Admin	StockholmAdmin	MoscowAdmin	CaracasAdmin	MontevideoAdmin	ManilaAdmin	TokyoAdmin
*ComputerName*User	StockholmUser	MoscowUser	CaracasUser	MontevideoUser	ManilaUser	TokyoUser

	Khartoum	Nairobi
ComputerName	Khartoum	Nairobi
srv	KHA	NAI
Partner	Lower	Higher
Classroom Network Connection	192.168.*x*.123	192.168.*x*.124
Partner Network Connection	192.168.112.1	192.168.112.2
*ComputerName*Admin	KhartoumAdmin	NairobiAdmin
*ComputerName*User	KhartoumUser	NairobiUser

Microsoft® Windows® Server 2003
Enterprise Edition 180-Day Evaluation

The software included in this kit is intended for evaluation and deployment planning purposes only. If you plan to install the software on your primary machine, it is recommended that you back up your existing data prior to installation.

System requirements

To use Microsoft Windows Server 2003 Enterprise Edition, you need:

- Computer with 550 MHz or higher processor clock speed recommended; 133 MHz minimum required; Intel Pentium/Celeron family, or AMD K6/Athlon/Duron family, or compatible processor (Windows Server 2003 Enterprise Edition supports up to eight CPUs on one server)

- 256 MB of RAM or higher recommended; 128 MB minimum required (maximum 32 GB of RAM)

- 1.25 to 2 GB of available hard-disk space*

- CD-ROM or DVD-ROM drive

- Super VGA (800 · 600) or higher-resolution monitor recommended; VGA or hardware that supports console redirection required

- Keyboard and Microsoft Mouse or compatible pointing device, or hardware that supports console redirection

Additional items or services required to use certain Windows Server 2003 Enterprise Edition features:

- For Internet access:
  - Some Internet functionality may require Internet access, a Microsoft Passport account, and payment of a separate fee to a service provider; local and/or long-distance telephone toll charges may apply
  - High-speed modem or broadband Internet connection

- For networking:
  - Network adapter appropriate for the type of local-area, wide-area, wireless, or home network to which you wish to connect, and access to an appropriate network infrastructure; access to third-party networks may require additional charges

Note: To ensure that your applications and hardware are Windows Server 2003—ready, be sure to visit **www.microsoft.com/windowsserver2003**.

* Actual requirements will vary based on your system configuration and the applications and features you choose to install. Additional available hard-disk space may be required if you are installing over a network. For more information, please see **www.microsoft.com/windowsserver2003**.

Uninstall instructions

This time-limited release of Microsoft Windows Server 2003 Enterprise Edition will expire 180 days after installation. If you decide to discontinue the use of this software, you will need to reinstall your original operating system. You may need to reformat your drive.

Notes

Notes

Notes

Notes

Microsoft® Windows® Server 2003 Enterprise Edition 180-Day Evaluation

The software included in this kit is intended for evaluation and deployment planning purposes only. If you plan to install the software on your primary machine, it is recommended that you back up your existing data prior to installation.

System requirements

To use Microsoft Windows Server 2003 Enterprise Edition, you need:
- Computer with 550 MHz or higher processor clock speed recommended; 133 MHz minimum required; Intel Pentium/Celeron family, or AMD K6/Athlon/Duron family, or compatible processor (Windows Server 2003 Enterprise Edition supports up to eight CPUs on one server)
- 256 MB of RAM or higher recommended; 128 MB minimum required (maximum 32 GB of RAM)
- 1.25 to 2 GB of available hard-disk space*
- CD-ROM or DVD-ROM drive
- Super VGA (800 × 600) or higher-resolution monitor recommended; VGA or hardware that supports console redirection required
- Keyboard and Microsoft Mouse or compatible pointing device, or hardware that supports console redirection

Additional items or services required to use certain Windows Server 2003 Enterprise Edition features:
- For Internet access:
  - Some Internet functionality may require Internet access, a Microsoft Passport account, and payment of a separate fee to a service provider; local and/or long-distance telephone toll charges may apply
  - High-speed modem or broadband Internet connection
- For networking:
  - Network adapter appropriate for the type of local-area, wide-area, wireless, or home network to which you wish to connect, and access to an appropriate network infrastructure; access to third-party networks may require additional charges

Note: To ensure that your applications and hardware are Windows Server 2003–ready, be sure to visit **www.microsoft.com/windowsserver2003**.

* Actual requirements will vary based on your system configuration and the applications and features you choose to install. Additional available hard-disk space may be required if you are installing over a network. For more information, please see **www.microsoft.com/windowsserver2003**.

Uninstall instructions

This time-limited release of Microsoft Windows Server 2003 Enterprise Edition will expire 180 days after installation. If you decide to discontinue the use of this software, you will need to reinstall your original operating system. You may need to reformat your drive.